Studies in the Philosophy
of the
Scottish Enlightenment

Studies in the Philosophy
of the
Scottish Enlightenment

Edited by
M. A. STEWART

CLARENDON PRESS · OXFORD

Oxford University Press, Walton Street, Oxford OX2 6DP
Oxford New York Toronto
Delhi Bombay Calcutta Madras Karachi
Petaling Jaya Singapore Hong Kong Tokyo
Nairobi Dar es Salaam Cape Town
Melbourne Auckland
and associated companies in
Berlin Ibadan

Oxford is a trade mark of Oxford University Press

Published in the United States
by Oxford University Press, New York

First published 1990
First issued in paperback 1991

British Library Cataloguing in Publication Data
Studies in the philosophy of the Scottish
Enlightenment.—(Oxford studies in the history of philosophy; v 1.)
1. Scottish philosophy
I. Stewart, M. A.
192
ISBN 0-19-824966-7

Library of Congress Cataloging in Publication Data
Studies in the philosophy of the Scottish enlightenment
edited by M. A. Stewart.
(Oxford studies in the history of philosophy; v. 1).
Includes index.
1. Philosophy, Scottish—18th century. 2. Enlightenment—
Scotland. 3. Scotland—Intellectual life—18th century.
I. Stewart, M. A. (Michael Alexander), 1937- . II. Series.
B1402.E55S88 1989 192—dc20 89—33656
ISBN 0-19-824966-7

Printed and bound in
Great Britain by Courier International Ltd.,
East Kilbride, Scotland

OXFORD STUDIES IN THE HISTORY OF PHILOSOPHY

The editor wishes to acknowledge the particular assistance of Professor David Norton in planning this collection, and to thank the contributors for their close co-operation both in the preparation of their papers and in helping to determine the final constitution of the volume. Others who supplied readers' reports were David Berman, Alexander Broadie, Phillip Cummins, John Dunn, Roland Hall, Peter Jones, Manfred Kuehn, Thomas Mautner, and Christine Shepherd. Angela Blackburn of Oxford University Press has given the editor much appreciated advice, encouragement, and practical help.

CONTENTS

ABBREVIATIONS

AUL	Aberdeen University Library
EUL	Edinburgh University Library
GUA	Glasgow University Archives
GUL	Glasgow University Library
NLS	National Library of Scotland
RCPE	Royal College of Physicians of Edinburgh Library
SRO	Scottish Record Office
E. (+page no.)	*Enquiries concerning human understanding and concerning the principles of morals,* by David Hume, edited by L. A. Selby-Bigge, revised by P. H. Nidditch (Oxford 1975)
HL (+vol., page no.)	*The letters of David Hume,* edited by J. Y. T. Greig, 2 vols. (Oxford 1932)
NHL (+page no.)	*New letters of David Hume,* edited by Raymond Klibansky and Ernest C. Mossner (Oxford 1954)
T. (+page no.)	*A treatise of human nature,* by David Hume, edited by L. A. Selby-Bigge, revised by P. H. Nidditch (Oxford 1978). This volume contains also Hume's *Abstract.*

INTRODUCTION

M. A. STEWART

After the successful launching in 1983 of *Oxford studies in ancient philosophy* under the editorship of Julia Annas, I was invited to prepare plans for a companion project to be called *Oxford studies in the history of philosophy*. This would avoid poaching on Professor Annas's territory unless it was plain to both parties that ancient philosophy was in need of further outlets, but it would not discourage work which deliberately linked developments in classical and post-classical philosophy. We were also advised from several quarters that there are sufficient channels at present for such quality work as exists on exclusively medieval philosophy, although this is certainly an area of research which we would hope to open up to a wider public at some future date. The field of post-medieval philosophy is still a vast one, and the diversity of study generated by it is immense. As consultations proceeded and plans progressed, it became clear to the editor and the publishers that the issue of an annual yearbook of unrestricted coverage would spread the interest too thinly to appeal to any but compulsive subscribers. To give the volumes a clear focus and a clear market, we have created instead a series which will consist of individual collections, each dedicated to a pre-announced theme, even if necessary at the cost of a less rigid publication schedule.

An early decision was taken to launch the project with a volume on the philosophy of the Scottish Enlightenment, since this was a field in which substantial research was known to be developing; it would therefore provide a good test of the new product's ability to attract and deliver something new and unhackneyed in history of philosophy. At the same time we advertised an intention of devoting the second volume to philosophy in the seventeenth century, and that volume is now being prepared for publication. We have provisional plans for a volume on the history of philosophical thought in the Netherlands, and another on the relation of the history of philosophy to the development of deism and the critical study of religion. I would be happy to receive further enquiries and submissions from potential contributors on these later themes, as well as suggestions for further themes of comparable scholarly appeal.

The term 'history of philosophy' means different things to different practitioners. At its weakest, and in many English-speaking university departments where the content of the study is laid down by those who do not teach it, it refers to vicarious and unmemorable philosophical exercises of an entirely modern kind, fought out round a narrow, generally derivative, and frequently fanciful picture of at least one dead philosopher. Some journals still see a worth in this kind of academic shadow-boxing and there is one which actively invites it: we are not competing with them. The philosophical dividends to be derived from a serious study of the history of philosophy vary considerably with the authors and problems studied: they depend upon the talents and interests of the individual reader as much as the expertise of the commentator. Philosophy has not always had its present boundaries. In its more fruitful periods it has always impinged upon other concerns and they on it. Its history is therefore of as much legitimate interest to scholars working outside the modern discipline as to those within it, and one purpose of this new project is to improve the quality of the dialogue between those with different disciplinary perspectives and to extend the mutual benefits that can be derived from it. This is not from any mistaken belief that if only some ideal cross-disciplinary mix can be found, or the right neutral ground located, then the true reading of a past thinker or a past philosophical movement will be revealed. In no other branch of history is there an expectation that there is only one fitting perspective on a subject, and there is no such expectation here. What there is is an assumption that at least some perspectives are patently unhistorical and counter-historical, and that whatever interpretation of past thinkers is put forward in the name of *history* of philosophy must be an interpretation that is first and foremost historically credible. It should be based upon a thorough and accurate knowledge of primary sources whether published or unpublished, of the circumstances both philosophical and extra-philosophical in which those sources were created, and the way in which such circumstances may have materially determined the intended meaning of the text. Our paramount aim is to penetrate the minds of the past, not the mind of some impressionistic mimic.[1]

The term 'Scottish Enlightenment' in the title of this volume is used as an established term of convenience. There are some to whom this will

[1] Those who deny the possibility or value of an objective study of the past nevertheless give short shrift to any contemporary opponent who typecasts or criticizes *them* for views they have never held. The general thrust of my remarks here is not intended to be original: it is explicit or implicit in several recent collections of papers, and there is no space in a brief introduction to break further new ground or prove that because the old ground was barren the new ground must be fertile. That is the task of our contributors. My own viewpoint coincides most closely with that of J. M. Dunn's Preface to *The political thought of John Locke* (Cambridge 1969).

give no satisfaction: in trying to serve one polemical purpose we may have to do less than justice to another. The term was brought into currency by W. R. Scott at the end of the last century,[2] and is also used here, to identify a shift (for good or ill) in the traditions of Scottish philosophy and the disciplines directly related to it, which began in the early part of the eighteenth century and continued for the rest of the century—a shift which is re-examined and redefined in the papers by Roger Emerson and James Moore in this collection. The term has since been extended to less narrowly philosophical developments in the science and culture of the period: this is perfectly reasonable in itself, but it has led to an unhelpful redrawing of the chronological boundaries, a narrowing of the topographical boundaries, and a preoccupation with change at the expense of tradition, by some whose primary interests lie outside philosophy. Was Hume a part of this enlightenment or in competition with it? His philosophy has seemed to stand some way apart from the mainstream of Scottish thinking except in so far as that adapted itself to try to counter his impact; but there is something odd in excluding the premier thinker of his age from a central place in his own national culture. Scotland is however unusual, though not unique, in that much of its philosophical development in the eighteenth century occurred within the universities, so that the history of philosophy is more closely bound up with the history of academic institutions than was often the case elsewhere before the present century. It is also unusual in the particular extent to which relatively new philosophical ideas were a part of the currency of thought of most educated Scots and were assimilated into legal, historical, medical, theological, and other studies.

These several features are explored by the contributors to this volume. Our first five contributors bring complementary skills and perspectives to bear on the distinctive development of institutional moral philosophy in eighteenth-century Scotland, and in doing so necessarily touch on the law, politics, and religion of the period. Roger Emerson provides a very useful historian's overview of the whole period, and with Paul Wood reopens our eyes to the significance of Aberdeen as a centre of philosophical activity from an early stage, where the effects of tradition and innovation appear instructively side by side. James Moore, Knud Haakonssen, and Richard Sher in different ways continue the important work of dismantling the old stereotype of Hutcheson as the forerunner of

[2] W. R. Scott, *Francis Hutcheson* (Cambridge 1900), p. 2, etc. The term has come into wider circulation in the debate sparked off by H. R. Trevor-Roper [Lord Dacre], 'The Scottish Enlightenment', *Studies on Voltaire and the 18th century* 58 (1967), 1635–58; for an extended bibliography see R. B. Sher, *Church and university in the Scottish Enlightenment* (Edinburgh 1985), pp. 329–76. Older historians when dealing specifically with philosophy referred to a "Scottish philosophy" or "Scottish school", associated more often than not with the rise of Reid and therefore falling a little late in the period covered by this volume.

Hume, Professor Sher seeing in him more the model for Adam Ferguson. Our three contributors on Hume himself have all opened up new terrain. Michael Barfoot offers a remarkable documented reconstruction of Hume's actual scientific training from the age of 13 (he had entered university at 10) and traces its impact on his early philosophical writing. David Wootton and David Raynor address more familiar topics in the Hume corpus, but they also show the considerable benefits in understanding that are to be gained from a close analysis of the text in relation to Hume's sources. John Wright, who has previously argued controversially for the influence of scientific and medical debate on the metaphysics and epistemology of the eighteenth century, now looks at the reverse relationship in tracing the influence of metaphysic upon physic in the teaching of the foremost Scottish physicians of the day.

In assembling this collection it has been necessary to strike a balance between major and minor thinkers: the progress of philosophy cannot be understood without some regard for both and for interactions between them, but in a volume of this size it is not possible to offer more than a sample. The partisans of Smith and Reid may regret the greater space afforded to less known figures. I would myself have welcomed further submissions on Ferguson as a social thinker and on the work of Lord Monboddo, but they were not forthcoming. There is still too little information on philosophical activity in St Andrews in the eighteenth century, but the philosophical theology of Archibald Campbell would merit reappraisal.

Given the intended appeal of this volume, it may be useful if I briefly draw attention to several matters affecting Scottish philosophy scholarship which have come to our notice during its preparation.

The first is the relocation of the world's principal deposit of Hume manuscripts, which lay in the Royal Society of Edinburgh from 1838 to 1987. Provision for the security and conservation of these priceless documents was not wholly adequate, and on 25 May 1987 they were moved and placed on permanent deposit with the National Library of Scotland. The volume numbers which figured in *RSE Proceedings* 52 (1931/2) and in many generations of commentaries are now obsolete; they have been replaced as follows:

RSE vol. no.	NLS ms. no.	Contents
I	23151	Letters by Hume, A–Mi
II	23152	Letters by Hume, Mu–Z
III	23153	Letters to Hume, A–Bouf
IV	23154	Letters to Hume, Boul–D
V	23155	Letters to Hume, E–K
VI	23156	Letters to Hume, L–Ram
VII	23157	Letters to Hume, Ray–Z

The ownership of the volumes remains with the Society, who must be consulted on matters relating to publication, or reproduction for publication. Individuals who require microfilm or photographs for personal use only may write direct to the National Library. At the transfer ceremony, David Norton gave an address on the history of the manuscripts and on the nervousness with which the Society had first received them. This has been published in an informative pamphlet, available for £1 from the Royal Society of Edinburgh, entitled *Baron Hume's bequest: the Hume manuscripts and their first use.*

Although the Society never extended its Hume collection, other archives in Edinburgh and other Scottish centres have over the years recovered by gift or purchase many other documents of seminal importance for the history of the national heritage. Unfortunately commercial interests moved in on this scene a few decades ago—as they have done also elsewhere, for example in Locke studies, and in studies pertaining to the intellectual history of Ireland. Owners with more concern for profit than for the maintenance of either national assets or international scholarship have been persuaded by adventuresome tradesmen to treat manuscripts like potsherds and to seek purchasers in all corners of the world. Whatever pride of possession these acquisitions may bring to their new owners, it is at great cost to the impecunious majority of those for whom the documents would have real practical value; and they can rarely have a fraction of the use holed up in their new corners which they might have had if they had been made available to institutions whose established holdings put them on the flight-path of any serious scholar who could benefit from them. It is difficult to see the moral justification for this new dispersal of cultural treasures.

These thoughts have been prompted by the appearance in the auction room of at least two remarkable documents during the past year, which now appear to be heading back to the obscurity from which they came. The first was withdrawn after no purchaser could be found to satisfy the cupidity of the vendor, and is possibly still somewhere in this country. The second was assuredly undervalued by the saleroom, but it was sold and the new whereabouts are unknown.

The first item was a copy of the twin issues of the short-lived 1755–56 *Edinburgh review*, the second issue being heavily annotated in the margins in the hand of Hume. This constituted lot 296 in Sotheby's sale of English Literature and History on 15 December 1987.[3] The auction house claimed that the *Edinburgh review* "is a noted rarity", and that "virtually all" Hume's marginalia can be reconstructed in spite of the severe cropping of the edges which has often lost up to an inch or more of writing. Both claims can be disputed.

It was this eighteenth-century journal which established the tradition which has dominated subsequent scholarship until very recently, that the union of the crowns plunged Scotland into an intellectual dark age— "Letters could not be cultivated where humanity was neglected; the precepts of philosophy suited ill with the rage of party" (p. i)—and that while the 1688 revolution helped turn the tide, it was the eventual parliamentary union which consolidated the improvement in political stability, civil order, and progress in knowledge and learning; but enlightened Scots were still held back by a generally inadequate command of the means of expression and the primitiveness of their printing trade. This assessment is implicit throughout the *Review*, but explicit in the contributions of Wedderburn and Smith. The journal was to contribute to the cause as it perceived it, by promoting improving literature and castigating the crudeness of traditional preaching. Its demise after two issues is often attributed to the great offence created by the latter policy, but this surely exaggerates the number of clerical contributions and underestimates the volatile character and impulsive temperament of the original editor. Whatever its historical view of Scottish culture, however, the *Review* is a significant indicator of educated taste in mid-century Edinburgh. Readers of Hutcheson's *System of moral philosophy* were equally expected to take in their stride von Haller's *Dissertation on the sensible and irritable parts of animals*—a work whose Edinburgh reception is also discussed by Professor Wright in the course of the present volume—even if they were encouraged to be sceptical of Tissot's claim that Haller's researches into the interaction of mind and matter were an antidote to deism or could provide a scientific foundation for morals.

Although the standard identification of the original reviewers published with the 1818 reprint was based on hearsay collected long after the event, there has never been any suspicion that Hume was a contributor. But the first number carried an open invitation to interested parties to contribute, and the appearance of Hume's extensive scribblings on a copy of the second number may have led the recent vendor to

---

[3] Page 6 of the original is reproduced on p. 158 of the catalogue. There were also two minor Adam Smith items in this sale (lots 311–12): the original of Smith's letter of 21 Jan. 1790 from Edinburgh, to Henry Herbert at Glasgow College (Mossner and Ross, 2nd edn., p. 433); and a copy of the 1761 second edition of *The theory of moral sentiments* with some egregious printing errors corrected in Smith's hand on pp. 17, 131, 188, and 201.

imagine that this cast new light on the authorship. Having examined all the marginalia I have to conclude it does not; in this I concur with Professor Norton, who also examined the greater part of them. Hume annotated half of the pieces in the second issue—nos. I, V, VI, and VII very slightly; nos. II and IV and the concluding 'Letter to the authors' in some detail. With few exceptions the changes appear to be stylistic, and a good deal of the phrasing which he amended is phrasing which no-one familiar with Hume's style would suppose was Hume's original. On page 21, for example, the reviewer (believed to have been William Robertson) wrote:

The piratical states upon the coast of Affrica, are not considerable enough to be dangerous to great cities, or formidable to states, but they are often the cause of infinite distress to particulars.

—where the anglicizing Hume understandably scored out the last word, amending it to 'individuals'.

The following passage from page 12 illustrates the problems posed by the loss of the margins:

But to invent types at pleasure, or at best to squeeze them from some allusions and metaphors found in Scripture; and from such types to form conclusions concerning the antitype, or thing supposed to be typified, is a most dangerous and unjustifiable method of reasoning, if it deserves the name of reasoning at all.

Hume deleted the phrase 'at best' and what survives by way of correction is a nonsensical 'early the': I conjecture that the complete—and slightly mischievous—revision was '⟨what is n⟩early the ⟨same thing,⟩'. He also deleted 'from such types to form' and appears to have replaced it with '⟨upon these⟩ Types to build'. With cropping on this scale it is difficult to be sure that every emendation is stylistic. One indeed is plainly an aside prompted by the writer's ambiguous phrasing: where the reviewer looked forward to "a better opportunity to entertain [our readers] on Quick-lime" (p. 22), Hume quipped that this was a "bad diet".

The most tantalizing fragments which stand a chance of being substantive changes—or if they are still stylistic, at least they could not have been set down without a greater understanding of the subject-matter than is conveyed in the bare wording of the review—are in the comparison of the Hutchinsonian and Newtonian systems in review no. II. Their fragmentary state is particularly vexing in view of Michael Barfoot's revelations in this volume about Hume's scientific reading. Hume also proposed a few substantive corrections to the concluding 'Letter' which has been traditionally ascribed to Adam Smith; and while it is an engaging thought that the survey of European science and philosophy in that letter could have been Hume's own, the non-Humean mannerisms which Hume also eliminated must count against this. On page 64 he rejected Smith's inclusion of mathematics among the "sciences which require only plain judgment joined to labour and assiduity, without demanding a great deal of what is called either taste or genius", and replaced it with anatomy; on page 65 he deleted Spenser from a list of the more imaginative English poets; and on page 79 he added to Smith's complaint against Voltaire's "great number of very gross misrepresentations with regard to the share which Great Britain had in the last war" a particular mention of the injustice to "General S'clar⟨es⟩ Expedition"—in which of course Hume himself had been professionally employed.

Scholars can puzzle at leisure over why Hume methodically corrected these pieces if he did not write them. It is difficult to see him doing it for his own benefit—both because he did not need to and because we would then have expected other examples from his surviving library. The presumption is therefore that he did it for the benefit of the reviewers, with their ambitions to emulate and promote southern literary English, at one of those gatherings with his scholarly friends which have come down to us in the garbled anecdotes of Henry Mackenzie.

There has been a second sale item, of somewhat more significance—I would think the most significant Hume document since the discovery of *A letter from a gentleman to his friend in Edinburgh*. This was lot 473 in Sotheby's sale of English Literature and History on 21–22 July 1988, illustrated on page 240 of the saleroom catalogue. It is now the earliest known manuscript in Hume's hand, antedating by a year the earliest autograph letter to Ramsay in the National Library of Scotland; so it belongs to Hume's post-university period when biographers have believed that he was pretending to study law while secretly devouring Cicero and Virgil. It is a 1726 transcription, either directly from dictation or indirectly from some other dictated copy, of the narrative of lectures on the theory of fluxions delivered by George Campbell, but without the diagrams to which the lectures relate. Campbell, subsequently a Fellow of the Royal Society, was an extramural teacher of mathematics who had been defeated in the contest for the Edinburgh chair by Colin MacLaurin the previous year and later quarrelled with him.[4] The National Library has a student's notebook from Campbell's algebra class (MS. 2821). The new manuscript is understood to have come from the family library of a titled household to which Hume was distantly related and with whom he tried unsuccessfully to obtain his first employment in 1739, and its full significance for Hume studies will remain problematic so long as we do not know how or why or when it

---

[4] I owe this information to M. Barfoot. For further detail see the MacLaurin–Stirling correspondence in C. Tweedie, *James Stirling* (Oxford 1922).

came to be in that household—for example, if we do not know for certain whether Hume had copied it for himself or, just possibly, for another. The first half of the transcription is complete and continuously paginated, but there are two lacunae in the later part where the pagination is abandoned, so either he missed two attendances or his archetype was defective. Hume appears never to have read through the manuscript again after copying it; he had occasional problems with the technical terminology (as what fifteen-year-old might not?) and periodic solecisms in spelling and expression go unamended. But that he was exposed to the content of these lectures at all is a further turn in the extraordinary revolution in our understanding of his early studies which was already contained in the original draft of Dr Barfoot's paper before this additional discovery. It puts a radically new gloss on the remark that "I found an unsurmountable Aversion to every thing but the pursuits of Philosophy and general Learning", and on Hume's claim to have been almost equally inclined after leaving college "to Books of Reasoning & Philosophy" alongside his "Poetry & the polite Authors" (HL i. 1, 13).

Certain editorial standardizations, for example in forms of bibliographical reference, have been introduced throughout this collection, over and above the normal copy editing conventions of the Clarendon Press. These will remain standard in other volumes in this series and should be adopted by future contributors. The most distinctive convention, for those unfamiliar with the philosophical practice, is the retention of single quotation marks to distinguish the *mention* of linguistic forms (words or phrases) from other, non-self-mentioning, uses of them. Single quotation marks are also used to distinguish the *titles* of articles or chapters from the *subject-matter* which may be referred to if the same expressions occur within ordinary (double) quotation marks. In quotations themselves, angle brackets '⟨. . .⟩' are used to reconstruct lost or omitted words or characters which we assume it was the author's actual intention to write; square brackets '[. . .]' are to mark unavoidable glosses, paraphrases, or annotations by the commentator.

SCIENCE AND MORAL PHILOSOPHY IN THE SCOTTISH ENLIGHTENMENT

ROGER L. EMERSON

Any educated Scot at the end of the seventeenth century would have come to a consideration of moral philosophy from a prior understanding of his duties as they were taught by the ministers of the Kirk. As a child, he would have learned from *The shorter catechism*, Answer 41, that "The moral law is summarily comprehended in the ten commandments", which the Lord spoke to Moses from burning Mount Sinai, where He also wrote them on two stone tablets. At a later age, students in grammar schools and colleges would have read *The larger catechism* and have learned that "The duty which God requireth of man is obedience to his revealed will", a will "revealed to Adam in the estate of innocence, and to all mankind in him" (Ans. 91, 92). "The moral law is the declaration of the will of God to mankind, directing and binding every one to personal, perfect, and perpetual conformity and obedience thereunto, in the frame and disposition of the whole man, soul and body, and in performance of all these duties of holiness and righteousness which he oweth to God and man: promising life upon the fulfilling, and threatening death upon the breach of it." (Ans. 93)

The moral law was held to be unmistakably revealed and certainly known even to unregenerate gentiles (Ans. 96). For all who have fallen with and through Adam's sin, the revealed law awakens consciences, convicts of sin, and shows the regenerate their obligations to Christ, who both fulfilled the law and vicariously suffered for our sins. While the justified are not bound to and by the law, they conform to it from their love of God, who has engendered within them saving faith. Sinners are made "humble . . . in the sense of their sin and misery" (Ans. 95), and so turned in repentance to the comforting gospel of Christ, outside whose covenant of grace there is no salvation. Morality has, then, a religious origin in God's will, ends in the eternal happiness of men and the glory of God, and concerns salvation more than any temporal interest. These doctrines were propagated in the schools, both within the episcopalian Calvinist tradition and among the presbyterians.

The greatest episcopalian scholar of the period *c.*1650–75 was Robert

Leighton (1611–84), principal of Edinburgh University from 1653 to
1662, later bishop of Dunblane and archbishop of Glasgow. Sweet-
tempered and gentle in a violent age, Leighton accepted the Calvinism of
the catechisms, but glossed it as might a more mystical Pascal, with
whom he shared a kind of Christian fideism. He was interested in the
current epistemology, believed that we must be critical in outlook, but
despaired of attaining certain and true useful natural knowledge.[1]
Typical of Leighton's views is his caution against hoping to derive a
proof of immortality from rational demonstration instead of revelation.

There are indeed very few demonstrations in philosophy, if you except the
mathematical sciences, that can be truly and strictly so called; and, if we inquire
narrowly into the matter, perhaps we shall find none at all; nay, if even the
mathematical demonstrations are examined by the strict rules and ideas of
Aristotle, the greatest part of them will be found imperfect and defective. . . .
But, if we were well acquainted with the nature and essence of the soul, or even
its precise method of operation on the body, it is highly probable we could draw
from hence evident and undeniable demonstrations of that immortality which
we are now asserting: whereas, so long as the mind of man is so little acquainted
with its own nature, we must not expect any such. (*Works*, pp. 563–4)

Natural knowledge is not certain and perhaps never can be made so.
However, if it is to improve we need to attend to the facts of experience,
particularly those concerning the nature of our minds.

While we must be diligent in our inquiries to understand aright both
ourselves and the world, we must recognize that "Every man walks in a
vain show" (Psalm xxxix. 6). If we would know God and our moral
obligations, if we would defend Christianity, we must begin with the
Bible and with faith (pp. 311–23, 511–13, 594). True knowledge of the
end of man and of all things originates in faith, which is the gift of God.
Conscience and reason are the means to its elaboration, but both are
good only when guided by the certain word of God. The true dignity of
man is found in his ability to know God, to pursue His ends and glory,
and to strive in this world for the true happiness which can be found only
in heaven. The love of Christ must lead to good works which in the saints
engenders "one spirit" and "a living sympathy amongst them, as making
up one body, animated with one spirit; for that is the reason why the
members of the body have that mutual feeling, even the most remote and
distant, and the most excellent, with the meanest" (p. 156). Such
feelings supplement the natural principles of union among men whose
bodies are "made of the same earth, and their souls breathed from the
same God" (p. 158). Even so, the pessimism of Solomon and the

---

[1] *The whole works of Robert Leighton, D.D.*, ed. J. Aikman (Edinburgh 1832), pp. 27–8,
316–18.

Psalmist is all too just. A renunciation of this carnal show and its delusions is the way to piety, freedom, and the content preached by the great mystics. The happiness of man, which our appetites and desires frustrate here, is to be found in "the life to come", adumbrations of which were and are known even to the heathen (pp. 555–67).

Unfilled desires for this happiness and "a sense of religion" (p. 567) Leighton took as implying the existence of a provident and just God. These and a variety of other arguments proving His existence, unity, goodness, and providence, he sketched in some of his Edinburgh lectures (pp. 553–617). He quoted Iamblicus and Plato on innate ideas before setting out an argument to show "that there should be some eternal Being, otherwise nothing could ever have been" (p. 569). That argument is supported by others from the design in nature, from the intelligence of men, and from effects resembling in some way their cause. The being of God can be known and from it follow His attributes and the requirement that men do what is right. What Leighton says of providence, however, applies to all these doctrines: "all these maxims we have mentioned, are more clearly taught and more firmly believed in the Christian religion, which is of undoubted truth" (p. 574). Like Calvin's, his rational theology gives the believer only an uncertain glimpse of "the glory and brightness of the Divine Majesty", which is "so great, that the strongest human eye cannot bear the direct rays of it", but must view it "in the glass of those works which he created at first, and by his unwearied hand, continually supports and governs" (p. 575). For the rational theologian more mysteries remain than for the Christian, who also finds many beyond his ken.

In Leighton's world, then, the only certainties come from God. Morality is subordinated to religion and faith, which are based neither on reason nor sense, but on revelation and grace. Such views also marked the work of Henry Scougal (1650–78), an episcopalian regent and professor at King's College, Aberdeen, in the 1670s, and the most influential Scottish episcopalian writer of the period. His most notable work, *The life of God in the soul of man* (1677), was recommended to Scottish undergraduates well into the following century and probably always found many readers who did not share its author's views on ecclesiastical polity. This classic of the "mystics of the North-East"[2] was written by a man who knew well the works of the Cambridge Platonists, Leighton, and an earlier Aberdeen episcopalian with mystical tendencies, John Forbes of Corse. Scougal's succinct call to believers to accept the full meaning and promise of their faith is a fine work of mystical

---

[2] Scougal and his successors are the subject of G. D. Henderson's Spalding Club volume, *Mystics of the North-East* (Aberdeen 1934).

piety. He called Christians to experience in this world "a divine life",[3]
presaging the splendours of heaven. It is "an union of the soul with God,
a real participation of the divine nature, the very image of God drawn
upon the soul, or in the apostle's phrase, *it is Christ formed within us*". It
comes and endures with our efforts to obtain a grace freely given to us,
which "all our natural endeavours" cannot produce, nor can they "merit
those supernatural aids by which it must be wrought" (p. 62). The gift of
grace transforms men's lives. They no longer vainly attempt to obey
harsh laws which are the despair of the conscientious. Now they act from
a love of God and live confidently in this world guided by His holy spirit
dwelling in them. Moral men are religious and the truly religious will be
moral. Reason can never produce a good will, fully suppress self-love, or
produce more than the similitude of virtue (pp. 13–16). At most it can
lead people to want to become true Christians. Once they are, they must
be active in ways appropriate to their age, learning, and sex. These ways
may change over time but the virtues displayed do not. Neither does the
need to make them habitual (p. 79). A change of "our inward
disposition", or at least a regulation of "our outward deportment",
should be followed by a greater knowledge of God and His requirements, a knowledge sustained by study, prayer, and the sacraments.
Pascal and Jansenism probably had some influence in Aberdeen.

The beliefs and attitudes about moral philosophy which Leighton and
Scougal expressed persisted longer than did episcopacy, which was
abolished in 1690. In Aberdeen they were taught by some masters
probably until *c.*1715.[4] At Edinburgh too, moral philosophy tended to
begin with the nature of man, whose desire for happiness was stressed;
this was then shown to be found only by the religious and only in heaven.
As late as 1739 Scougal's little book was reprinted for the booksellers to
the university. Their edition came with a "Recommendatory Preface"
by Principal Wishart; a "new light" minister, Wishart still thought the
book peculiarly fit for "the poor of our flocks" and for "our young
Students who have their views toward the sacred Function" (pp. v–vi).[5]
Elsewhere, teaching is unlikely to have been very different, but students
at Glasgow and Edinburgh were more likely to have read texts by Henry
More and Pufendorf, whose ideas would have somewhat qualified those
of Scougal. The views of Leighton and Scougal persisted, because they

---

[3] Henry Scougal, *The life of God in the soul of man . . . with a recommendatory preface by
William Wishart* (Edinburgh 1739), p. 4.

[4] C. M. Shepherd, 'The arts curriculum at Aberdeen at the beginning of the eighteenth
century', in *Aberdeen and the Enlightenment*, ed. J. J. Carter and J. H. Pittock (Aberdeen 1987),
at pp. 148–9. The men whom Dr Shepherd cites (several of whom repeated Scougal's dictates)
taught for some years after the dates of the evidence she provides.

[5] It is sometimes assumed that cheap tracts subsidized for free distribution and for the poor
came to Britain only after *c.*1770. This book was advertised on its title page as "Price bound
Sixpence, and to those that give them away, five Shillings the Dozen".

were shared by presbyterian divines and regents who gave them a somewhat harsher expression. Among these one could cite Samuel Rutherford (1600–1661), James Wodrow (1637–1705), and Thomas Halyburton (1674–1712). All had some influence in the colleges and divinity schools where they taught.

Rutherford became professor of Divinity at St Andrews in 1639 and was one of the divines who wrote the Westminster Confession of Faith in 1645–47, but he is probably best known for his letters and for *Lex, rex : or The law and the prince* (1644). That work begins with an assertion which eliminated a morality independent of revealed religion: "What is warranted by the direction of nature's light is warranted by the law of nature, and consequently by a divine law; for who can deny the law of nature to be a divine law?" (Question 1). Rutherford argued from both laws, but it is clear that those on the two tablets clinched all his arguments. Wodrow's somewhat similar attitudes can be glimpsed in correspondence with his son Robert. They were carried into the eighteenth century by seven hundred students he is said to have taught at Glasgow between 1690 and his death. Halyburton of St Andrews taught divinity for a short time—from 1710 to 1712—but his autobiography and doctrinal works kept this view of morality current among "high-flying" presbyterians well into the nineteenth century.[6]

All of these, but particularly Leighton, Scougal, and Halyburton, had clear interests in the challenges presented to Christian theology by the philosophical and scientific novelties of the seventeenth century. Leighton had attacked the Epicureans and Lucretian atomism, doctrines of fate and the naturalism which led to an identification of God with nature (*Works*, pp. 568, 578, 587). In these concerns he was close to the Cambridge Platonists, as in his belief that we can "contemplate God" by looking "to the heavens, sometimes to the sea, and the earth, with the animals and plants that are therein, and very often to ourselves" (p. 580). That Leighton may have stressed these topics in his Edinburgh lectures is also suggested by unpublished papers of Sir Robert Sibbald (1641–1723), his student and admirer.[7] Scougal was the first person in Aberdeen "who taught the youth that philosophy which has now the preference by all the knowing world", according to his obituarist in 1678.[8] This was the study of nature in both macrocosm and microcosm.

[6] J. Macleod, *Scottish theology* [1946], 2nd edn. (Edinburgh 1974), has extensive discussions of Rutherford (pp. 68–78) and Halyburton (pp. 117–30). Wodrow's views are to be found in *Early letters of Robert Wodrow, 1698–1709*, ed. L. W. Sharp (Edinburgh 1937), pp. xviii–xxii. See also Robert Wodrow, *The life of James Wodrow, A.M.* (London 1828).

[7] R. L. Emerson, 'Sir Robert Sibbald, Kt., the Royal Society of Scotland and the origins of the Scottish Enlightenment', *Annals of science* 45 (1988), 41–72.

[8] [George Gairden], 'A sermon preached at the funeral of the Rev. Henry Scougal' (many editions). Gairden was a close ally and himself contributed to the *Philosophical transactions* of the Royal Society, so he was in a position to assess Scougal's innovations.

Scougal's support for the new philosophy suggests that he saw the pursuit of a Baconian programme of co-operative empirical investigations of nature as appropriate for natural philosophers. Unlike the moral philosophers, they followed a discipline with more autonomy, although it too was bound to the Bible and served Christian ends. Halyburton was exercised by the problem of certainty and the status of our beliefs about Christ, revelation, and the Christian mysteries; his doubts are recorded in his autobiography and works, as is the regimen of prayer and study by which he overcame them. Halyburton's unbelief and qualms on bad days must have been as great as those of Thomas Aikenhead, the Edinburgh student hanged in 1697 for retailing in the taverns the heresies of the English deist Charles Blount.[9] These academic Calvinist moralists had been responding to an epistemological upheaval whose origins can be traced to the revival of scepticism in the sixteenth century. That they were not isolated cases is clear from dictates and theses of other late seventeenth-century regents.

The arts course was everywhere a systematic and structured one which surveyed logic, metaphysics, moral and natural philosophy, and included both natural and some revealed religion. Every science was given its place in an ordered hierarchy, and the corresponding arts or practical employments of the theories were noted. Most projections of the map of the intellectual world also found a place for the great chain of being. Everything ultimately led to God, flowed from Him, and was grounded in His will. Nothing could be secular or even agnostic in most such systems. Because natural knowledge was systematically elaborated, and because it generally led to religious conclusions, anything which upset part of the system was likely to reverberate throughout it. Methodological changes, discoveries, or new ideas sent ripples through the fabric, as did both limited and systematic doubts. The systems might be seen or presented as deductive structures, but the increasing experimentalism would loosen the links between propositions or portions of the structure. In the seventeenth century the greatest methodological and conceptual shocks came from logicians, natural philosophers, historians, and theologians themselves, pursuing enquiries which raised epistemological issues.[10] By *c*.1700 philosophers had replaced divines as the chief inquirers into the grounds of certainty and acceptable belief. As that happened, a sharper distinction was made between revealed and natural knowledge, and more assurance was placed in the adequacy of the latter. Naturally grounded beliefs might not be certain, but probabilities were or could be guides to life, and even

[9] See Michael Hunter's discussion of Aikenhead in *Atheism from the Reformation to the Enlightenment*, ed. M. Hunter and D. Wootton (Oxford, forthcoming).

[10] B. J. Shapiro, *Probability and certainty in seventeenth-century England* (Princeton 1983).

to the acceptance of the sources of Christianity (now less likely to be held to be self-warranting). Because Scottish regents taught all areas of philosophy to their charges over a three- or four-year period, any novelty which interested them was likely to be reflected in more than one field of inquiry. This has been amply demonstrated in the work of Christine Shepherd and others who have recently written on the universities,[11] and their scholarship discredits Lord Dacre's [Professor Trevor-Roper's] repeated contention that seventeenth-century Scots were isolated from the main currents of European thought.[12] As Shepherd, Russell, and Forbes have shown, Scottish regents cited, discussed, used, or refuted most of the leading thinkers of seventeenth-century Europe.

Towards the end of the century, they also began to make assertions which were not generally compatible with the moral stance of Leighton, Scougal, or Halyburton. Herbert Kennedy of Edinburgh believed that the methods of Descartes and Gassendi would restore man's fallen intellect. That implied a belief in the certainty of natural knowledge which Leighton would have found unacceptable. But by *c.*1700 most regents, including Kennedy, had ceased to praise Descartes as "that supreme glory of France", and were bestowing their plaudits on Boyle, Newton, and Locke.[13] The methods of the philosophers of the new science, as well as their discoveries and ideas, were starting to be accepted by regents teaching in all the arts colleges. Empirical methods, with their Baconian emphasis on the nature of the human mind and on natural and civil histories, brought in tow antiquarian and historical studies which vindicated the new methods that had produced progress. That there was a history of the advancement of learning was made clear in historical prefaces which by the early eighteenth century increasingly appeared as preliminaries to university courses. But the regents were not consistently on the side of the moderns: Aristotelian, scholastic, and more recent elements co-existed, in tensions which were ultimately to get more secular resolution.

[11] C. M. Shepherd, *Philosophy and science in the arts curriculum of the Scottish universities in the seventeenth century* (Ph.D., University of Edinburgh 1975); ead., 'Newtonianism in Scottish universities in the seventeenth century', in *The origins and nature of the Scottish Enlightenment*, ed. R. H. Campbell and A. S. Skinner (Edinburgh 1982), 65–85; ead., 'University life in the seventeenth century', in *Four centuries: Edinburgh university life 1583–1983*, ed. G. Donaldson (Edinburgh 1983), 1–15; ead., 'The arts curriculum at Aberdeen' (above, n. 4); E. G. Forbes, 'Philosophy and science teaching in the seventeenth century', in Donaldson, 28–37; R. G. Cant, 'Origins of the Enlightenment in Scotland: the universities', in Campbell and Skinner, 42–64; J. L. Russell, 'Cosmological teaching in the seventeenth-century Scottish universities', *Journal of the history of astronomy* 5 (1974), 122–32, 145–54.

[12] H. Trevor-Roper, 'The Scottish Enlightenment', *Studies on Voltaire and the 18th century* 58 (1967), 1635–58; id., 'The Scottish Enlightenment', *Blackwood's magazine* 322 (1977), 371–88.

[13] Shepherd (1975), p. 68.

Out of this *pot-pourri* of new methods and ideas emerged several things relevant to the discussion of moral philosophy. The denial of natural human sociability, associated with Hobbes, could be rebutted from Grotius, Pufendorf, and Cumberland, generating an interest in these thinkers at just the time that Scottish lawyers such as Sir George Mackenzie and James Dalrymple, first Viscount Stair, were using natural-law principles to structure a Scottish legal system which had previously lacked systematic expositions and printed teaching texts. In Grotius, and to a lesser extent in other natural lawyers, Scots found philosophers eager to reduce law to a system which rested on self-evident principles and on the practice of ancient and modern times. They also found here rudimentary but secular conjectural histories, and systems which paid more attention to social, political, and economic matters than had been given to these topics in the ethics courses prior to *c.*1680. After 1688, even more attention would be paid to the bases of government and the nature of political obligation by whig and presbyterian masters at the colleges outside Aberdeen. Accompanying these developments were others which had been given importance by Descartes in particular, but also Hobbes, and later Locke, all of whom had reworked rational psychology or philosophy of mind. Scougal and most regents had touched upon the nature of simple apprehension, the passions, will, reason, and the other faculties of the mind, whose analysis was essential both for logic, moral philosophy, and even natural religion and its attendant metaphysics. Indeed, given the interest in epistemology and Cartesian physics, this interest in the mind was essential for natural philosophy. The two most discussed problems of the ethics dictates, the nature of happiness and the freedom of the will, also clearly required an analysis of the human psyche. Grotius, Hobbes, Descartes, More, the Port-Royal authors, and many others, provided ideas which fed debate until the 1690s, when Locke's *Essay* began to colour the discussions. Most of these had found their own epistemic concerns rooted in the religious, scientific, and political perplexities of their times and places. This was no less true in Scotland. But only after 1690, and the solution of some of the political and religious difficulties besetting the Scots, was there a systematic attempt to synthesize and integrate diverse moral conceptions.

The pioneer of this change was Gershom Carmichael (1672–1729), whose academic career had been made possible by the whig revolution which brought to power his relatives and friends, and which purged of Jacobites the universities in which he taught. His moral philosophy took shape in the late 1690s and early 1700s, during which he was also shifting from Cartesianism to a more empirical position which included

Newtonian elements.[14] That shift is apparent in his 1713 view of natural law, which for him included all of ethics: "it is clear that knowledge of natural law is not innate to men's minds . . . nor is it inscribed there by nature, as some believe; nor is it to be learnt from the mere consensus of opinion of various races and ages, whether speculative or practical, as others contend; but rather it is to be derived from the nature of things and their uninterrupted course, and a proper use of reason."[15] Carmichael's moral philosophy rested upon a rational and natural foundation, not upon revelation. While morality still required a religious base, his proofs for the existence of God were drawn from Ray, Pelling, Cheyne, Derham, and Nieuwentijt, four of whom were fellows of the Royal Society and used the new science for apologetic purposes.[16] Their proofs were adequate for those who believed that matter by its nature was incapable of movement or thought, a belief Carmichael shared. Where seventeenth-century thinkers had tended to find in the Decalogue a compend of all human duties, Carmichael found it in the rationally known laws of nature which revelation now confirmed. Ethics had not been secularized, but it had been de-Christianized. That also implied a greater ability in men both to understand and to act than had been conceded by most seventeenth-century Scots. Carmichael's view of the motives for acting morally was also different. Obedience to God now rested not upon biblical denunciations of sinners, but upon the love of God which follows from our recognition of His goodness, and from our desire for happiness which only He can make complete and lasting. While Carmichael's description of our passions, desires, and reason were as derivative as his natural theology, they represented a coherent attempt by a former Cartesian to incorporate Grotian and other elements into a system of morals which he equated with natural jurisprudence.

Even if the ideas were not themselves original, Carmichael was no doubt an innovator in 1690s Scotland, when he was complained of to the Visitation Commission sitting during those years.[17] By 1699 an Edinburgh regent, William Scott, had used natural-law principles to defend the Darien Company and had taught these principles. He wanted

---

[14] J. McCosh, *The Scottish philosophy* (London 1875), p. 37; J. Moore and M. Silverthorne, 'Gershom Carmichael and the natural jurisprudence tradition in eighteenth-century Scotland', in *Wealth and virtue*, ed. I. Hont and M. Ignatieff (Cambridge 1983), at p. 75.

[15] Quoted in Forbes (above, n. 11), p. 33. We now know that this had been Locke's position too: *Essays on the law of nature*, ed. W. von Leyden (Oxford 1954), pp. 96–7.

[16] I am indebted to J. Moore and M. Silverthorne who have allowed me to use the unpublished typescript of their English translation of Carmichael's Latin notes and commentary to Pufendorf's *De officio hominis et civis*.

[17] J. Moore and M. Silverthorne, 'Natural sociability and natural rights in the moral philosophy of Gerschom Carmichael', in *Philosophers of the Scottish Enlightenment*, ed. V. M. Hope (Edinburgh 1984), at p. 2.

the Regius chair of Public Law which was established for his friend Charles Erskine in 1707.[18] Similar interests in the promotion of the discipline may be evident in the 1698 creation by the Scottish Parliament of a professorship of Civil Law in Scotland for Alexander Cunningham of Block, a man who like Carmichael was beholden to the newly created Earl of Hyndford. By 1718, when Carmichael's annotated edition of Pufendorf became available as a text, there were others in Scotland ready to adopt it and to make it standard reading in moral philosophy courses into the middle of the century.

Interesting as the class-rooms were, there was beyond them a wider intellectual community which was equally stirred by new ideas, and one whose leading figures could and did institutionalize novelties in a variety of contexts.[19] Its dominant figures were lawyers like Mackenzie and Stair, and physicians such as Sibbald and Pitcairne, both of whom are important for the understanding of the interplay between the new philosophy and moral theory c.1680–1720.

Sibbald was a Baconian who shared the Pansophist vision of using new methods and newly found knowledge for the improvement of the human condition, and particularly for the amelioration of conditions in Scotland. Unimportant as a philosopher, he was more than a competent chorographer, antiquary, and naturalist. He helped establish in Scotland the methods of the modern critical civil and natural historians. Archibald Pitcairne's role was similar, but in his case a general interest in iatro-mechanism became a specific concern for the promotion of Newtonianism. By 1700, both had friends and followers who helped to bring the new science and medicine and their attendant conceptions of method, as well as the basic distinctions of philosophy, into the universities. Sibbald's protégés at Edinburgh included James Suther-land, Charles Preston, and his brother George (the three professors of Botany from 1676 to 1736), James Paterson (keeper of the University Museum given by Sibbald and Sir Andrew Balfour in 1696), and probably the regent who became the first professor of Natural Philosophy in 1708, Robert Steuart. At Glasgow, Sibbald found a virtuoso correspondent in Robert Wodrow, the university librarian. He wrote also to men in Aberdeen, and almost certainly would have had

---

[18] William Scott, *Hugonis Grotii De jure belli ac pacis . . . in usum studiosae juventutis academiae Edinensis* (1707); C. P. Finlayson, 'Edinburgh University and the Darien scheme', *Scottish historical review* 34 (1955), 97–102. (I owe this reference to R. B. Sher.) Scott's account of his appointment as professor of Greek and his failure to obtain the Law chair is given in letters to James Anderson, W.S., 2 and 7 Dec. 1714: NLS, Adv. MS. 29.1.2, ff. 178–83.

[19] H. Ouston, 'York in Edinburgh: James VII and the patronage of learning in Scotland 1679–1688', in *New perspectives on the politics and culture of early modern Scotland*, ed. J. Dwyer and others (Edinburgh [1982]), 133–55; R. L. Emerson, 'Natural philosophy and the problem of the Scottish Enlightenment', *Studies on Voltaire and the 18th century* 242 (1986), 243–91.

similar contacts at St Andrews. Sir Robert was at the centre of a number of clubs which collectively pursued antiquarian, natural historical, and medical inquiries. His surviving correspondence shows him to have been an important link between Scots, particularly young MDs and surgeons, and English and foreign virtuosi.[20] Most of these things can also be said of Pitcairne, who, like Sibbald, had been made a professor of Medicine at Edinburgh in 1685, when an attempt was made to establish a medical school within the university. The project failed at that time, but Pitcairne did teach at Leiden for a brief period in the early 1690s.

Pitcairne was a competent mathematician who mastered Newton's contributions to both mathematics and natural philosophy. Among his friends and protégés were David, James, and Charles Gregory, professors of Mathematics at Edinburgh and St Andrews, and Thomas Bower, the first professor of Mathematics at King's College, Aberdeen. They were probably also experimenters and certainly innovative teachers. Among Pitcairne's extra-mural students in Edinburgh or those who attended his Leiden lectures were James and John Keill, George Cheyne, Richard Mead, and several who went on to teach medicine and anatomy in Edinburgh. Pitcairne had ties to doctors, savants, and virtuosi in England and Europe, where his work was known and admired. He and his circle were active in promoting the Newtonian philosophy which they helped to make acceptable in Scottish colleges.[21] By 1713, when Pitcairne died, the ideas and methods of these new scientists also had been institutionalized in several contexts. Newton's work, like Locke's, figured in the regents' teaching; he was also expounded by professors of mathematics, even by one professor of natural philosophy. More important was the presence of one or more such men at each of the arts colleges. Newtonian iatro-mechanism was surely debated at the Surgeons' Hall and at the Royal College of Physicians of Edinburgh, since Pitcairne and his friends were active in both bodies. That was also likely to have been true of the clubs and tavern societies to which they belonged, societies which included laymen with scientific interests such as Sir John Clerk, second baronet, of Penicuik, or Thomas Kincaid the younger.[22] Students in the early years of the century would have known, then, of a flourishing and prestigious, although small, set of Scottish natural historians and philosophers outside their colleges. What would they have found in the natural philosophy classroom itself which could have been carried over to the

[20] For more on Sibbald, see Emerson (above, n. 7).

[21] A. Guerrini, 'The tory Newtonians: Gregory, Pitcairne and their circle', *Journal of British studies* 25 (1986), 288–311.

[22] On Clerk, see I. G. Brown, *Sir John Clerk of Penicuik, 1676–1755: aspects of a virtuous life* (Ph.D., University of Cambridge 1980); a biography of Clerk is forthcoming.

moral philosophy classes, classes still taught in many cases by the same regents who lectured on logic, metaphysics, and natural philosophy?

The most important things would have been methodological statements such as Newton's 'Rules of reasoning in philosophy'—not natural philosophy, but philosophy. There sense experience and experiments are presented as the surest ways to useful, natural knowledge. Many teachers were doubtless more familiar with Boyle's similar views and with his repetitious denunciations of systems, hypotheses, and speculations. Similar statements and equal praise for Bacon could be found in many works by fellows of the Royal Society and some of their continental contemporaries. The similar ideas of Dutch professors such as Senguerdius would probably have been familiar to many Scots who studied abroad. By *c.*1710 the experimentalist position was well known, summarized impressively in the works of Boyle, Locke, Newton, and Le Clerc. It was available in texts and was seemingly vindicated by the discoveries which had accumulated so rapidly since the beginning of the previous century.

The impact of these ideas can be discerned at each of the colleges as they adapted their teaching to fit the new philosophy. Between *c.*1708 and 1720 Glasgow, Edinburgh, the St Andrews colleges, and King's and Marischal, all acquired or extended existing collections of teaching instruments, aids, and toys. All gave or announced the intention of giving courses in experimental philosophy, courses which exemplified the new methods and which vindicated their demonstrations. At King's the spirit which informed this teaching can be seen in Bower's subscription paper for the instrument collection. He wanted "Mathematical Instruments" because of the "publick advantage" which would come from "the many usefull observations and experiments which may be dayly made by the Professors themselves for improvement of Learning, as for the instruction of the Youth under their care, by shewing them to the eye the Truths that are abstractly demonstrated in Mathematicks, and their great usefulness in all Arts and Sciences, which conduce to the happiness of human life and societies".[23] At Edinburgh much the same outlook is manifested by Robert Steuart's catalogue of the Physiological Library which he began for his students.[24] This lists books in a collection formed in 1724 for the natural philosophy students. Steuart, a devout Calvinist who had originally been made professor of Natural Philosophy and Ethics, idolized Boyle, whose works were held with near completeness in the Library. His catalogue confirms what Carmichael's Glasgow lectures had made clear: natural religion was

---

[23] Thomas Bower to James Erskine, Lord Grange, n. d.: SRO, GD124/15/966/2.
[24] 'The Physiological Library begun by Mr. Steuart, and Some of the Students of *Natural Philosophy*': EUL, De 10.127. For fuller discussion, see M. Barfoot's paper in this volume.

shifting its base to arguments founded upon the observed order in the creation, which also revealed the power and glory of the Calvinist God. What was less orthodox was the claim that moral principles could be deduced from the nature of this naturally and rationally known deity. In Steuart's case it is clear that natural philosophy had both religious and moral philosophical uses and that he taught it in this fashion. That others were doing so is suggested by library purchases as well as surviving dictates and theses. Finally, there was a clear parallel between the critical methods of the scientists and those of the historians and antiquaries who were also coming into the universities in the first quarter of the century.

Between *c*.1690 and 1720 the universities began to teach history and to teach it using critically examined sources. "Blind [William] Jameson", the first lecturer appointed at Glasgow in 1692, was physically unable to pursue such tasks, but he approved of them and encouraged the collection of Scottish manuscripts and artefacts by Wodrow the librarian. Their interests were shared at Edinburgh by Principal Carstares and the first two professors of Ecclesiastical History, John Cuming and William Dunlop. In 1720 Charles Mackie was installed as the first professor of Universal History, Roman Antiquities and the History of Scotland. Mackie regaled his classes with the debunking of old myths, and recommended books by scholars who had read and followed the advice of Père Mabillon and other critical historians. King's College found a historian in John Ker, who probably also gave a historical background to the Greek courses which he offered after 1717. At Glasgow, the Humanist was providing some historical coverage by the late 1690s. If this practice did not antedate the younger Thomas Blackwell's appointment at Marischal College in 1723, he began to teach in this manner shortly thereafter. Probably only St Andrews by the mid-1720s had not accepted these changes. By the 1720s historical prefaces were appearing in some lectures on anatomy and medicine and no doubt in other subjects.

The new interest in history and in the reconstruction of the Scottish past in particular benefited from the revival of teaching in law which was contemporary with it. This reflected Scottish anxieties over the status of their independent kingdom, after 1707 a kingdom whose laws had been guaranteed by the Act of Union which had ended the independence of the state. Legal scholarship, which helped to trace the development of Scottish law, was historical, and revealed much about the nature of feudal and barbarous [Highland] societies. Most of the prominent antiquaries of this period were medical men or lawyers, who would have been familiar with the methodological works of Sydenham or with the practices of those who were compiling the historical records of other nations. They were also accustomed to see law as the application of moral principles in particular times and places, the circumstances of which determined the real limits on human thought and action. What was morally and legally possible depended on the state or conditions in which people lived, and the experiences which shaped their minds and characters as they impinged upon a *tabula rasa*. Such views would interest not only students preparing for the legal profession, but others destined for the Kirk. They would have considered the decay and revival of the primitive church just as philosophers were beginning to consider the apparent cyclical flourishing of the arts and sciences in cultures as different, yet alike, as fifth-century BC Athens and sixteenth-century Italy. Only a renewed attention to the recoverable facts of the past could untangle the problems inherent in such discussions.[25]

Method was important, but so were the philosophic concepts which came in the wake of the new science. The absolute passivity of matter was generally accepted. So too by the 1710s was its description in Newtonian terms and the belief that the forces governing its behaviour were to be presented in the language of mathematics. Precise and definite though that might be, the system was no more certain than its axioms. These were seen to depend upon the analysis of experiences which might include experiments. Contingent and probable truths recognized as such—and most philosophical statements were now only that—could lead only to "moral" certainties. Sceptical doubts could not be eradicated and had to be tolerated. Tolerance as an enlightened virtue found its origins and the reasons for its acceptance in logic and science as much as in religious deviations and the practical problems of civil control. If matter was passive and inert, spirit was not. The new science set off consciousness and the mind or soul, which it revealed as a topic for study through introspection and the observation of others taken to be like ourselves. The obligation to make a new study of the mind was very great, for, as Bacon had shown, all that was known related to the mind of man. To produce a new science of the mind had been Locke's enterprise in the *Essay*, but he had left it incomplete and lacking a moral theory or even the clear basis for an empirical one. If minds were to be understood as well as matter, that deficiency had to be made good.

The first steps toward a phenomenology of moral experience had already been taken by Hobbes, and by those who sought to refute him by questioning the facts from which he argued. The Cambridge Platonists and their admirer the third Earl of Shaftesbury had tried to show that people were not wholly selfish and unsociable. Shaftesbury in particular was eagerly read by some young Scots excited by the prospects and promises made by the new science and philosophy as these were

[25] R. L. Emerson, 'Conjectural history and Scottish philosophers', *Historical papers/Communications historiques* (1984), 63–90.

expounded in their class-rooms. Their excitement continued from c.1700 to the 1730s as other issues and controversies became entwined with the novel claims of moralists and scientists. If moralists wished to keep their philosophical outlook unified and to understand man and his duties, they would have to emulate the natural philosophers. It was equally clear that they would have to be careful that their work did not come into conflict with their religious commitments.

The Scottish intellectuals who came to maturity during the 1710s and 1720s were fascinated not only by Newtonianism and natural-law theory, but also by the empiricism of Berkeley, the moral and aesthetic writings of Shaftesbury and his followers, and the manifold controversies set off by the deists and by the political fireworks of the turbulent first third of the century. Among these Scots were the members of Edinburgh's Rankenian Club, which included such later professors as William Wishart the younger, George Turnbull, Charles Mackie, Colin MacLaurin, John Stevenson, and John Pringle.[26] Overlapping this age group were other prominent Scottish intellectuals—Andrew Baxter, Andrew Michael Ramsay, Francis Hutcheson, Thomas Reid, David Fordyce, David Hume. Each in different ways introduced into their works the methods of the scientists or the critical historians. They did so wittingly and generally with the intention of founding what since Hobbes had been called a science and what Beattie was to call "moral science". Going with their efforts in the cases of Hume and Reid was a clear attempt to relate a new empirical rational psychology to the current wisdom in physiology; for several others the slant was more towards the feelings discerned by the connoisseur or sensed by the highly cultivated moral individual living in a polite age.[27]

It is instructive to look at the first edition of the *Encyclopaedia Britannica*, published in Edinburgh in 1771, to see how thoroughly the great generation of Scottish thinkers had made science and its methods part of the intellectual culture of their time. Of about one hundred writers mentioned in the "list of the principal authors made use of in the compilation", about eighty were naturalists, natural philosophers, medical men, or authors of some technical or technological work. Of the books cited, over three-fourths fell into those categories. No doubt this

---

[26] M. A. Stewart, 'Berkeley and the Rankenian club', in *George Berkeley: essays and replies*, ed. D. Berman (Dublin 1986), 25–45; id., 'William Wishart, an early critic of *Alciphron*', *Berkeley newsletter* 6 (1982/3), 5–9; id., 'George Turnbull and educational reform', in Carter and Pittock (above, n. 4), 95–110. Robert Wodrow identified Patrick Cuming as an early member or closely associated with the early members; James Boswell included, and Ramsay of Ochtertyre excluded, Henry Home. At least five others at some time either sought university posts or taught extra-murally or as professors' deputies.

[27] See, selectively, J. P. Wright, *The sceptical realism of David Hume* (Manchester 1983); D. F. Norton, *David Hume: common-sense moralist, sceptical metaphysician* (Princeton 1982); and several of the papers in this collection.

reflects a perceived need for this kind of information among readers, just as it probably shows us the interests and bias of William Smellie, the editor and chief compiler. But this emphasis is also to be found where philosophy is considered. *Philosophy* is defined as "the knowledge or study of nature and morality, founded on reason and experience" (vol. 3, p. 477). The reader is then referred to "MECHANICS, OPTICS, ASTRONOMY, LOGIC, MORALS, &c.". The article on *Moral philosophy, or Morals* (pp. 270–309) defines its subject as "the science of MANNERS or DUTY; which it traces from man's nature and condition and shews to terminate in his happiness". Morals is the "knowledge of our DUTY and FELICITY" which gives rise to "the art of being VIRTUOUS and HAPPY". This was hardly the vocabulary of Leighton or Scougal. "It is likewise called a science, as it deduces those rules from the principles and connexions of our nature, and proves that the observance of them is productive of our happiness." After commenting on the "dignity, importance, and use" of this science and art, the author went on to relate morals to sciences of another sort:[28]

Moral Philosophy has this in common with Natural Philosophy, that it appeals to nature or fact; depends on observations; and builds its reasonings on plain uncontroverted experiments, or upon the fullest induction of particulars of which the subject will admit. We must observe, in both these sciences, how nature is affected, and what her conduct is in such and such circumstances. Or, in other words, we must collect the appearances of nature in any given instance; trace these to some general principles, or laws of operation; and then apply these principles or laws to the explaining of other phaenomena. (p. 270)

Here the methods of analysis and synthesis (which had been explained in the article on *Logic*, vol. 2, pp. 1002–3) are applied to morals with an optimism based upon the accomplishments of the natural sciences. The writer, with a fine disregard for the naturalistic fallacy, goes on to confuse normative ethics with rational psychology and with what we might call sociology:

Therefore Moral Philosophy inquires, not how man might have been, but how he is, constituted: not into what principles or dispositions his actions may be artfully resolved; but from what principles and dispositions they actually flow: not what he may, by education, habit, or foreign influence, come to be, or do; but what, by his nature, or original constituent principles, he is formed to be and do.

---

[28] Smellie took this article from David Fordyce's 'On ethics, or morality', Part 9 of Robert Dodsley's popular educational work *The preceptor* (London 1748). Fordyce's work was printed posthumously as *Elements of moral philosophy* (London 1754). I am grateful to R. B. Sher for identifying the source and authorship of the article. In its three forms it was a widely read and popular account of moral philosophy. The *Encyclopaedia* version is only slightly abridged from that which appeared in the third edition of *The preceptor* (1758); the deletions are mainly short passages of moral preaching (including the two concluding paragraphs), comments on divorce, and encomia to the British constitution. Smellie added little in the way of bridging sentences and changed almost nothing else, although he did delete references to Fordyce's sources.

We discover the office, use, or destination of any work, whether natural or artificial, by observing its structure, the parts of which it consists, their connection or joint action. It is thus we understand the office and use of a watch, a plant, an eye, or hand. It is the same with a living creature, of the rational, or brute kind. Therefore, to determine the office, duty, or destination of man; or, in other words, what his business is, or what conduct he is obliged to pursue; we must inspect his constitution, take every part to pieces, examine their mutual relations one to the other, and the common effort or tendency of the whole. (vol. 3, p. 270)

This is followed by thirty-nine pages which draw upon the Stoics, Shaftesbury, Hutcheson, and Butler. Instincts, passions, a moral sense, and reason are found from their analyses to be the principles necessary to the understanding of morals. These same traits and abilities also explain social development and change in the rude and refined societies in which men had and still lived. They need only to attend to their experience to find the source of, and to understand, the idea of moral obligation, or to discover the obligations that are required of them (p. 276). These can be set out in a systematic "scheme of duty" (p. 277), "which seems to be confirmed by experience, consonant to reason, and approved by [man's] most sacred senses". The scheme is the familiar one which runs from the self to others and to God. The virtues and the good in this life still lead to God,

the supreme and inexhausted source of good, on whom the happiness of the whole creation depends; as he is the highest object in nature, and the only object who is fully proportioned to the intellectual and moral powers of the mind, in whom they ultimately rest and find their most perfect exercise and completion; he is therefore termed the *chief good* of man *objectively* considered: And virtue, or the proportioned and vigorous exercise of the several powers and affections on their respective objects, as above described, is, in the schools, termed the *chief good formally* considered, or its *formal* idea, being the inward temper and native constitution of human happiness. (p. 288)

Integral to both Fordyce's and Smellie's views of the "history of man" is a sense of change. From childish helplessness and unreason to peevish old age and beyond, from the simplest societies to the most complex, from early times to the present, the duties and happiness of "such a progressive creature as man can never be at a stand, or continue a fixed invariable thing" (p. 288). There is always room for improvements and active men will make them as they do their duties.

The same had been true of Fordyce's teaching as a university moralist. In a fragment which survives from his 1743–44 course,[29] Fordyce told

---

[29] 'A brief Account of the Nature, Progress and Origins of Philosophy delivered by the late Mr. David Fordyce P.P. Marish. Col. Abdn. to his Scholars, before they began their Philosophical course. Anno 1743/4': AUL, MS. M 184. The MS. is unpaginated, but the paragraphs are numbered and cited here.

his students, as Dugald Stewart would later tell his, that "The reformation & the gradual progress of liberty especially in Great Britain, tended considerably to the improvement of the Arts & Sciences; & the great plan of Science which Ld. Bacon had projected put men upon a more genuine & successful method of enquiry" (para. 33). This "natural & proper Method of attaining to true knowledge" (36) had to be used in every inquiry; not even "Rules or Precepts of life Can be given, or any Scheme of Conduct prescribed, but what must suppose a settled Course of things conducted in a regular uniform manner" (36). Moreover, "in order to denominate those Rules just, & to render those Schemes successful the Course of things must be understood & observed" and "all Philosophy even the most didactic & practical parts of it must be drawn from the Observation of things or at least resolved into it" (36). That is what the moralist does in pneumatology, ethics, and politics; and it is what he must do if he is to progress in the understanding of the "one great & universal source, the System or Whole of things originally made & subjected to the government of the most simple most perfect & most glorious of all beings the God & Father of all" (37).

In the mid-1770s all but two of the moral philosophy teachers in Scotland are known to have had extensive training and interest in both natural and moral philosophy. The Glasgow professor was Thomas Reid, whose first love had been mathematics, whose avocation was the sciences, and who had ended up as a professor of moral philosophy somewhat by accident.[30] As a former King's College regent he had lectured on logic, metaphysics, science, mathematics, and morals. He is known for having tried to base his philosophy on empirical foundations which would not lead to the scepticism which he found in Berkeley and Hume. Edinburgh's Adam Ferguson had not only taught natural philosophy between 1759 and 1764, but he was also much interested in the attempts of Montesquieu to work out an account of human manners, morals, and law founded upon both introspection and the facts of history and experience. Indeed, Ferguson says, "When I recollect what the President Montesquieu has written, I am at a loss to tell, why I should treat of human affairs." He concluded that he should, because he might "utter them more to the comprehension of ordinary capacities".[31] Ferguson saw both of them as natural historians, "obliged to collect facts, not to offer conjectures" (*Essay*, p. 2). From an analysis of these facts would come the various moral sciences in which politics or political economy found a place. Like Reid's, Ferguson's moral philosophy

[30] P. B. Wood, *Thomas Reid, natural philosopher: a study of science and philosophy in the Scottish Enlightenment* (Ph.D., University of Leeds 1984).

[31] Adam Ferguson, *An essay on the history of civil society*, ed. D. Forbes (Edinburgh 1966), p. 65. Perhaps Hume disliked this work because it deviated so much from *The spirit of the laws*.

sought to show how the metaphysics of inert nature differed from that of the vital kingdoms and from the moral realm in which man lived and acted.[32] Both philosophers showed that the same methods worked in all areas of analysis. Ferguson's "moral science" proceeds upon those assumptions (*Principles*, vol. 1, pp. 114–19, 157–62).

So too did that of the professor of Logic, Rhetoric, and Moral Philosophy at Marischal College, James Beattie. His *Elements of moral science* (1790–93) contains the substance of his lectures since c.1760. These are less explicitly scientific, but Beattie was an active member of the Aberdeen Philosophical Society and a competent if undistinguished anatomist of the mind. He had almost certainly chosen to teach logic and rhetoric in 1760 because of his literary interest, not because he was unknowing about science. At neighbouring King's College, Thomas Gordon, Roderick McLeod, and James Dunbar all taught moral philosophy in these years. Dunbar, like Ferguson, consciously worked in a tradition set by Montesquieu and Reid. His impressive *Essays on the history of mankind in rude and cultivated ages* (1780) also seems to derive from his class-room and from the papers which he read to the Wise Club.[33] Less is known of the work of Gordon and McLeod, but manuscripts surviving at King's College suggest that they adhered to the same general approaches. This may also therefore have been true of the St Andrews professors, John Young and John Cook, who published nothing. From Reid derived the more psychologically oriented philosophers of the next generation, while from Ferguson, Dunbar, and Adam Smith (who resigned the Glasgow chair in 1764) came men whose concerns were more political and sociological. Of these two types James Gregory and Dugald Stewart were, perhaps, the most interesting. It is also worth noting that Gregory was a physician, while Stewart had taught mathematics at Edinburgh; both were scientists, though of different sorts.

Stewart and Gregory defended versions of the philosophy of common sense worked out by Reid, but it is in Gregory's work that one sees the closest relationship between science and morals, or, rather, the metaphysical basis of morals. Gregory wanted to use "the common way of physical observation and experiment"[34] to study ordinary languages and the metaphysical distinctions that they made. These he believed expressed thought or the activity of knowing and willing minds which he

---

[32] Adam Ferguson, *Principles of moral and political science* (Edinburgh 1792), vol. 1, pp. 1–35; vol. 2, pp. 2–21.

[33] C. J. Berry has written a thesis and a number of articles on Dunbar which can be found listed in the latest, 'James Dunbar and the Enlightenment debate on language', in Carter and Pittock (above, n. 5), 241–50.

[34] M. Barfoot, *James Gregory (1753–1821) and Scottish scientific metaphysics 1750–1800* (Ph.D., University of Edinburgh 1983), p. 19.

took to be universally the same. His study would produce a universal grammar and a dictionary of the "simple, natural, uniform notions or conceptions" which all men have formed with respect to the most basic truths of metaphysics and hence of natural philosophy and morals (Barfoot, p. 19). Doing philosophy became in his work a kind of philological study ideally pursued by the description of every natural language and the production of inductive generalizations about their most basic terms and syntax. In each and every normal man speaking a developed language, there would be the same identity of linguistic form and thought. Without that, communication, complex socializing, and all else which we regard as distinctively good and human, would be impossible. Essential to that humanity was the notion of *power* from which Gregory derived concepts of *action, responsibility*, and *obligation*. Power and thought separated men from both vital and inert realms in nature, but the methods which philosophy required for the study of these were equally scientific. What these methods had in common was a sentient reasoning mind working in similar ways on the data of experience.

In Stewart's case the relation between science and moral philosophy is set out in both his philosophical and historical works, but is more interesting in the latter. It is particularly so in the *Dissertation* which originally appeared as a supplement to the third edition of the *Encyclopaedia Britannica*. There Stewart occasionally wrote about the "philosophical spirit" (p. 432)[35] which had affected every area of thought and which had marked the revival of letters and what he called "the literary history of Scotland during the latter half of the eighteenth century". The "philosophical spirit" was the product of the humanism of men such as Erasmus, Vives, and Thomas More (pp. 27–30), of the discoveries of explorers and the polemics of reformers. It also owed much to "the gradual effects of time and experience in correcting the errors and prejudices which had misled philosophers during so long a succession of ages". Indeed, "To this cause, chiefly, must be ascribed the ardor with which we find various ingenious men, soon after the period in question, employed in prosecuting *experimental* inquiries; a species of study to which nothing analogous occurs in the history of ancient science" (p. 33). All of this was furthered by printing and the consequent "diffusion of knowledge" which Stewart related both to "the shock and collision of different and opposite prejudices" and to "the rise of the lower orders" (p. 32). These causes combined to "necessarily contribute to the improvement of useful science, not merely in proportion to the arithmetical number of cultivated minds now

[35] Cited from *The works of Dugald Stewart*, vol. 6 (Cambridge 1829).

combined in the pursuit of truth, but in a proportion tending to accelerate that important effect with a far greater rapidity" (p. 32). The "Genius of the human race" (pp. 35–6) awoke to produce Copernicus, Tycho Brahe, Kepler, Galileo, and Bacon, to cite only those to whom Stewart gave a special place in the production of "an atmosphere of floating knowledge, where every mind may imbibe somewhat congenial to its own conceptions" (p. 59: he is quoting Sir Joshua Reynolds's 'Discourse' for 1769). The sceptical, logical, practical, and improving views of such men threw down the idols described by Bacon. Increasing political stability and freedom allowed the philosophic spirit to enlarge and take root in institutions such as academies which again expanded "the field of scientific curiosity, and the corresponding grasp of the emancipated mind" (p. 89). Descartes carried out the first steps of "the great instauration" which Bacon had sought to further. Both prepared the way for Locke, Berkeley, Hume, and Reid, whose philosophies progressively worked out what was valuable in the Cartesian legacy (p. 117). As they did so, they also clarified the empirical bases of ethics which are rooted in the consciousness of the free, active, sensing, and reasoning being we call man. Stewart thought that seventeenth-century moral philosophers had failed to put their doctrines of conscience or the natural law on an explicitly empirical footing. That had been done by Shaftesbury, Butler, Hutcheson, and their Scottish followers (pp. 386–428), who had transformed moral and metaphysical thought by giving it a secure basis. In politics the transformation was effected by Montesquieu, seen by Stewart as a descriptive writer who sought to show not "what laws *ought* to be,—but how the diversities in the physical and moral circumstances of the human race have contributed to produce diversities in their political establishments, and in their municipal regulations" (p. 177). By connecting "Jurisprudence with History and Philosophy", Montesquieu had made politics and political economy scientific subjects. This allied to the extension of the philosophic spirit to other areas of thought had also given rise to *theoretical* or *conjectural* history, of which Stewart approved because of its instructive value (pp. 350–51).

Stewart began Part II of the *Dissertation* by noting that his subjects could not be kept separate: "They all run into each other by insensible gradations; and they have all been happily united in the comprehensive speculations of some of the most distinguished writers of the eighteenth century" (p. 192). This was notably true of Locke. The empirical methods he had learned to adopt in medical studies were suited to the investigation of logic (rational psychology), metaphysics, ethics, politics, education, and religion. They were similar to those employed by Newton, since whose time "the ontology and pneumatology of the dark ages have been abandoned for inquiries resting on the solid basis of experience and analogy. . . . So completely has the prediction been verified which he himself hazarded in the form of a query, at the end of the *Optics*, that 'if natural philosophy should continue to be improved in its various branches,.the bounds of moral philosophy would be enlarged also' " (p. 266). It was that improvement to metaphysics and morals which Stewart saw as the essential task of eighteenth-century Scottish philosophy. Newtonian methods and science had buttressed Baxter's arguments on the nature of the soul and its active powers. Hume and others had consciously set out to become emulators of Newton as they constructed their "Science of Man". Common sense philosophy shared the same outlook, as did "the best historical compositions of the last century" (p. 432). In all this there was something preternatural. The newly-generated "spontaneous order"[36] of the intellectual world could still be seen as providential and as verifying not only Baconian prophecies of progress but also that of Daniel: "Many shall go to and fro, and knowledge shall be increased" (p. 35; Daniel xii. 4). Moral philosophy still maintained its ties to religion, but the providence of God had become general and was expressed through secondary causes.

All that has been said above has long been accepted by some students of the Scottish Enlightenment. Why then is it worth repeating?

First, some popular accounts of the Scottish Enlightenment, such as Lord Dacre's, tend to reduce it to the moral-social-political-economic thinking of a handful of people who seem to have had little connexion to the scientific or "philosophical spirit" of their times. Lord Dacre emphasizes the novelty of a very few Scots, but his position can only convince those who ignore the relationships between these Scots and their British and continental predecessors and contemporaries. His distinction between "the Enlightenment in Scotland" and "the Scottish Enlightenment" takes the members of the latter out of a common European philosophical movement, and concentrates upon their achievements while largely ignoring the methods by which they were realized. Stewart, who was part of that movement, moved in his historical account from England to France to Scotland, and everywhere found men pursuing a common quest and, by the eighteenth century, committed to common methods. That kinship with thinkers abroad led Scots to translate not only Montesquieu and Rousseau, but more obscure writers such as Antoine Yves Gouget, who is listed as a principal

---

[36] R. Hamowy, *The Scottish Enlightenment and the theory of spontaneous order* (Carbondale 1987). Hamowy's monograph deals almost exclusively with "social arrangements" (p. 18) but there was also an ideological dimension which deserves notice. The "spirit of an age" or a "philosophical spirit" also assume the characteristics of a spontaneous order in the works of the Scots.

source for the first edition of the *Britannica*. The Scottish Enlightenment may have been at its best in moral philosophy, but that ought not to be considered without reference to its proper philosophical context or to its roots in late seventeenth-century Scottish scientism. That others besides Lord Dacre have made this mistake can be seen in Gladys Bryson's *Man and society* (1945) and anthologies such as Jane Rendall's *The origins of the Scottish Enlightenment* (1978).

Another group of commentators also tend to see the Scottish Enlightenment particularly in terms of its moral philosophy and related disciplines, but they relate these to a republican tradition, classical in origin, but coming to the Scots through Machiavelli, Harrington, and Andrew Fletcher of Saltoun. This viewpoint takes its rise in the work of John Pocock,[37] but it has been put forth in greatest detail in the articles of Nicholas Phillipson, in John Robertson's *The Scottish Enlightenment and the militia issue* (1985), and in some of the papers in the collection *Wealth and virtue*. The Pocockian view of the Scottish Enlightenment is one squinted at from a political angle, and in Pocock's own work pretends to be nothing else. He is interested in the language or discourse of civic virtue and of republicanism. He also admits that Scots used other languages and drew upon other traditions including that of natural jurisprudence.[38] Pocock is not interested in other aspects of the Scottish Enlightenment, or much concerned with the methods used by Scots to solve the substantive problems which fascinate him as a historian of political theory. Among the *epigoni*, however, these oversights become more important. Dr Robertson unduly magnifies the significance of Fletcher, who had few followers in his own time and who actually complained about the attention which Scots were paying to science and metaphysics around 1700. Dr Phillipson's understanding of the Scottish Enlightenment is one which seeks to explain how this phenomenon arose out of the social and political disorders of the same period, as these were discussed by men seeking to preserve their traditional statuses and powers. The crisis of the Union threw up Fletcher, who found in Machiavelli and Harrington a republican ideology which well served minor aristocrats like himself. When the Union with England scuppered their plans, the search for power and prestige was channelled into the improvement movement which served them as a substitute for, or as a supplement to, decaying civic virtue of a political sort. Addisonian politeness served a similar function. The thought of the Scottish Enlightenment then becomes a rationalization of interest, an ideology which ought to be uniquely Scottish but is not. Phillipson's references to

[37] J. G. A. Pocock, *The Machiavellian moment* (Princeton 1975), pp. 423–505.
[38] Pocock, 'Cambridge paradigms and Scotch philosophers', in Hont and Ignatieff (above, n. 14), 235–52.

philosophy do not always take either the philosophers' arguments or their methods seriously. Even less often does he look at the Scots' own accounts of the origins of their ideas or the stated purposes of their works. Also ignored very often by him and others are native sources for enlightened activities and concerns. Scotland before Fletcher and Allan Ramsay, Sr. may have lacked politeness, but not learning. Without recourse to the philosophy and the spirit which set the atmosphere of the time described by Stewart, no one can understand either the Scottish concern with men and societies or the Scottish Enlightenment.

Similar problems arise with respect to Richard Sher's otherwise splendid account of the moderate literati of Edinburgh, in his *Church and university in the Scottish Enlightenment* (1985). Dr Sher does not claim to have given a full account of the Scottish Enlightenment, but only a cultural history of one, central, group within it (p. 14). However, there are times when it does seem as if these clerics are being made typical of many other men. It is particularly easy to think that, when many of the enlightened either backed this party in the Kirk or shared most of its political and intellectual aspirations. But from the book one would not guess that science and its methods had a large part in the culture in which these same persons moved. Sher sees Ferguson's interest in science as somewhat faddish (p. 308) and, before 1759, as trivial enough to make the subjects of his new natural philosophy chair "unfamiliar" (pp. 106–8). He believes that "with the institutionalization of the common sense school [at Edinburgh, 1785–1820] Scottish moral philosophy came to speak a technical language that physical scientists could utilize in formulating their own methodologies" (p. 314). This surely understates the very long interplay between moral and natural philosophy, and misconceives the importance of logic and pneumatics to both fields. In Sher's cultural history, his personalities hardly created or gave decisive turns to many institutions: they defined precious few roles. But a culture is usually seen as a complex of institutions, defining roles and embodying distinctive values; the place of science and experiment and the application of empirical methods in that world deserve a bigger place.

The second reason why one should attend to the relationship between science and moral theory in this period is that scientists thinking about *substances, causality, purpose, life, power,* or *agency,* were also thinking about the metaphysical bases of morals. Natural philosophy shaped moral philosophy, and tended to shape it in a way which emphasized human choice and freedom. If men were unlike stones, they were in some sense or other likely to make meaningful choices. For thinkers like Reid, this led away from Calvinist determination, although the same was not true of the systems of Hume or Kames. But it was Reid's system, not either of theirs, which was institutionalized at four of the colleges by the 1780s; and it was a version of his common-sense philosophy which most affected teaching in America after 1800 just as it interested thinkers in France and elsewhere in Europe. The Scottish Enlightenment produced an analytic and metaphysical moral science as well as political economy and related disciplines. Without this tie to natural philosophy and metaphysics, Scottish moralists who went to Calvinist churches were likely to have been more deterministic in outlook and very likely would have produced moral sciences less secular in tone.

A third reason to attend to the relations between morals and science is that the characteristics of science became more apparent in ethics. Science could claim only probabilities which reached no further than one's experience and inductions. Uncertainty bred toleration and a willingness to believe that one might be wrong. By *c.*1750 there were few like Leighton to argue that there were alternative sources of certainty with respect to moral truths. The progressiveness of science also seemed to assure moralists that human beings could become better in time. If they were to gain in civility and refinement, they had to cultivate their tastes and their abilities to think clearly and to act on what seemed true and proper. The methods of the scientists defined what clear thinking was while attention to the prompting of sociability and the moral sense sharpened one's ethical consciousness. Reflective thinkers like Hume, Smith, or Millar could easily imagine that the progressive search for happiness would now end in this world. What counted was the ability to understand one's position and the forces which limited change. Spontaneously generated systems of order were not easily or quickly changed but they could be modified over time. Control of human destiny, like control over nature, was not easy to achieve. Burke but not Priestley found friends in Scotland, and it was assumed by Scots that they had learned the lessons of empiricism better than had the English chemist who upheld phlogiston and the aims of French revolutionaries.

Finally, the moralists' concerns with method provided them with a dynamic and secularizing principle which was ultimately to divorce morals from religion and to break the systematic patterns of thought widely accepted in the Enlightenment. Empirical methods allowed for the autonomous and discrete study of societies, man, and his mind, or of physics, chemistry, and any number of other specialities. As those developed and became independent, their connexions to metaphysics, religion, and normative modes of thinking became weaker. The progress of moral science which Stewart praised was leading in directions he could not foresee. The "philosophical spirit" which permeated the work of enlightened thinkers everywhere changed the relations between intellectual disciplines and made possible a historical ordering of ideas.

The nineteenth century tended to find its grand principles of order not in the analytic and synthetic methods associated with empirical science and the structures they produced, but in historicisms of one sort or another. British moralists tended, however, to become increasingly empirical in outlook. Utilitarianism even in Scotland provided an alternative to common-sense philosophy. In both, science had gone a long way towards breaking the ties between morals and religion; it also stripped from moral philosophy such subjects as politics, economics, sociology, and anthropology, which the empirical moral philosophers of the Enlightenment had done so much to found.

Department of History
University of Western Ontario

THE TWO SYSTEMS OF FRANCIS HUTCHESON: ON THE ORIGINS OF THE SCOTTISH ENLIGHTENMENT

JAMES MOORE

It has become common practice among historians, in the past thirty years, to describe the collective achievement of philosophers, scientists, builders, and educators in eighteenth-century Scotland as the "Scottish enlightenment". The remarkable changes in thought and behaviour that occurred in Scotland at this time, in the church and in the universities, in agriculture and in commerce, in the arts and sciences, have been documented and described from various points of view.

For Marxist scholars, like Roy Pascal and Ronald Meek, the defining characteristics of the Scottish school, as they chose to characterize the thinkers of eighteenth-century Scotland, was their common consciousness of fundamental changes in the modes of production and subsistence that had occurred in Scotland in this period and their representation of these changes in the four-stages theory of society.[1] For others, notably Duncan Forbes, writing in the 1950s, it was the emergence of a sceptical understanding of the forces of social change, an appreciation of the unintended consequences of the acts of individuals, institutions, and governments, which distinguished the Scottish enlightenment from the rationalist ideals of the enlightenment in France.[2] In the historiography of Hugh Trevor-Roper, it was a new awareness of Europe and of the humanist learning of Italian historians and political writers, brought back to Scotland in the early part of the century by returning Jacobite refugees and cosmopolitan men of letters like Andrew Fletcher of Saltoun, which inspired new ideals of citizenship and fulfilment.[3] Nicholas Phillipson has elaborated the humanist theme to call attention to the diffusion of polite learning in coffee houses, salons, and polite

[1] R. Pascal, 'Property and society', *Modern quarterly* 1 (1938), 167–79; R. Meek, 'The Scottish contribution to Marxist sociology', in *Democracy and the labour movement*, ed. J. Saville (London 1954), 84–103.

[2] D. Forbes, 'Scientific whiggism', *Cambridge journal* 7 (1954), 643–70.

[3] H. Trevor-Roper, 'The Scottish Enlightenment', *Studies on Voltaire and the 18th century* 58 (1967), 1635–58.

society, following the Act of Union in 1707.[4] The humanist thesis has
been juxtaposed by Istvan Hont and Michael Ignatieff with an interest
on the part of other scholars—Peter Stein, Duncan Forbes again—with
the use made in universities in Scotland, in the early eighteenth century,
of the European traditions of natural law.[5] All of these constructions are
under fire from Scottish nationalist historians who believe that, in their
different ways, the Marxist, sceptical, humanist, and jurisprudential
constructions all impose foreign points of view on the Scottish national
identity. These critics deplore even the use of the term 'Scottish
enlightenment', on the grounds that it periodizes the Scottish past, while
obscuring the achievements of the Scottish middle ages and the culture
of the Scottish highlands.[6]

One of the problems, perhaps, with the term is that it may suggest a
more uniform pattern of change in eighteenth-century Scotland than the
evidence will permit. It is of the first importance, no doubt, to
distinguish the different problems and questions to which the successive
figures of the period were replying. The questions to which Hutcheson
was responding in Dublin and Glasgow were not, it would appear, the
problems which engaged Hume in Edinburgh, Rheims, La Flèche,
London, and Edinburgh again. Adam Smith may have been obliged to
teach a syllabus already in place in Glasgow, but the perspective he
brought to this assignment was his own. The same must be said of the
moderate theological and social ideas of William Robertson, Adam
Ferguson, and Hugh Blair; each provides an understanding of natural
and revealed religion and of the history of society which is different from
that of his contemporaries and associates in construction and inspiration.
But for all their diversity and individuality, one may recognize in the
writings of these distinct and admirable intelligences a common concern.
They were all engaged in argument with a cast of mind that may be
recognized to belong to the age that preceded the period we call the
"enlightenment". It is not surprising that a dialectic of this kind should
be discoverable in their writings. For in so far as we are entitled to speak
of their collective achievement as an enlightenment, it can only be in
relation to some understanding on our part of the kind of thought and

---

[4] N. T. Phillipson, 'Culture and society in the 18th century province', in *The university in
society*, ed. L. Stone, vol. 2 (Princeton 1975), 407–48; id., 'The Scottish Enlightenment', in *The
Enlightenment in national context*, ed. R. Porter and M. Teich (Cambridge 1981), 19–40.

[5] *Wealth and virtue*, ed. I. Hont and M. Ignatieff (Cambridge 1983); P. G. Stein, *Legal
evolution* (Cambridge 1980); D. Forbes, *Hume's philosophical politics* (Cambridge 1975); id.,
'Natural law and the Scottish Enlightenment', in *The origins and nature of the Scottish
Enlightenment*, ed. R. H. Campbell and A. S. Skinner (Edinburgh 1982), 186–204.

[6] See the Spring 1987 issue of *Cencrastus*; and D. J. Withrington, 'What was distinctive
about the Scottish Enlightenment?', in *Aberdeen and the Enlightenment*, ed. J. J. Carter and
J. H. Pittock (Aberdeen 1987), 9–19.

behaviour that we (and perhaps, though certainly not uniformly, they) recognize to have been in need of enlightening. There are no doubt various ways of characterizing the mentality of Scotsmen in the seventeenth and early eighteenth centuries. I propose to describe it, very schematically and discursively, under the rubric provided by theologians and historians of the Reformed church, and call it *Reformed scholasticism*.

From about 1580 until the early eighteenth century, the several nations of Reformed Europe—the Swiss confederation, Geneva, the United Provinces of the Netherlands, and Scotland—were dominated by the dogmatic and disputatious cast of mind that has been called "Reformed dogmatism" or "Reformed scholasticism".[7] It emerged late in the period of the Reformation, and was expounded by theologians whose names are not now familiar to us: Lambertus Danaeus, Hieronymus Zanchius, Marcus Friedrich Wendelin, Gisbertus Voetius, Francis Turretin, and Benedict Pictet. It was elaborated in scholastic and didactic language in response to the revival of Thomistic theology and philosophy on the part of Jesuit controversialists of the sixteenth century, and in distinction from the Protestant Aristotelianism expounded by Lutherans like Johann Gerhard. The Reformed went back to an earlier Augustinian scholasticism which they found in the treatises of Anselm, Abelard, Hugh of St Victor, and the *Sentences* of Peter Lombard. They held (1) that the natural state or condition of human affairs was a condition of sinfulness; (2) that all men long for or aspire to a condition of beatitude or lasting happiness; (3) that some, but not all, are predestined for eternal felicity; (4) that the marks or signs of divine favour or election are signalled in the regular observance by such persons of the divine and natural law; (5) that societies are formed to enable all men to live in accordance with the law of God and nature, even those, the lapsed and unregenerate, who lack the motivation to live in accordance with that law; (6) that the natural rulers of such societies are persons whose conduct testifies that they enjoy divine favour and whose characters exhibit the attributes of divinity (or at least those attributes which are *communicable* or capable of being shared between God and man)—wisdom, power, majesty (but not omniscience, omnipotence, aseity, etc.). These doctrines, expounded in treatises of natural or systematic theology and in courses of moral philosophy derived from this theology, were circulated in universities across Reformed Europe. They were debated and codified with much else, at the Synod of Dort, in the Westminster Confession, and in the Formula Consensus Helveticae.

---

[7] For an exposition of protestant scholastic theology, see Heinrich Heppe, *Reformed dogmatics* [1860], trans. G. T. Thomson (Grand Rapids 1978).

Their establishment in the Scottish universities occurred somewhat later than in mainland Europe. It happened only in or after the 1690s as the universities came to be purged of episcopalian and Jacobite regents. The establishment of the Reformed scholastic curriculum in theology appears to have been the work of James Wodrow in Glasgow and George Campbell in Edinburgh.[8] In the philosophy curriculum, its main promoters seem to have been Gershom Carmichael and John Loudon at Glasgow and William Law in Edinburgh. All of these changes were made possible through the political influence of the king's chaplain in Scotland, William Carstares, who sought to bring the Scottish universities closer to their counterparts in the Netherlands, a project he had reason to believe that the king would not find disagreeable.

Now, ironically, at the moment that Reformed scholasticism was being established in the Church of Scotland and in the Scottish universities, it was losing ground in Europe. The main forces for change and moderation of the dogmatism of Reformed theology and philosophy came from Geneva and surrounding cities within and without the Helvetic confederation. Jean-Alphonse Turretin, the son of the author of the Formula Consensus, Francis Turretin, was determined to use his authority in the ministry and in the University of Geneva to bring about a moderation of the Reformed dogmas and a relaxation of the requirement that ministers and professors subscribe the Formula. He was joined by Samuel Werenfels in Basel and J. F. Ostervald in Neuchâtel.[9] This initiative was welcomed, of course, by Jean Le Clerc and the Remonstrant or Arminian community in the Netherlands. In the case of Arminians, themselves Augustinians of a sort, there were outstanding doctrinal differences with the Reformed which they had maintained throughout the century. The moderate movement in Geneva and the Swiss confederation was conducted more subtly and bears strong marks of the style of the English latitudinarians, many of whom— John Tillotson, William Wake, Gilbert Burnet—considered themselves friends and admirers of the younger Turretin. Here the tendency was to ignore the most controversial dogmas and to assert a few articles of natural and revealed religion which were taken as fundamentals. It was a style which would later commend itself to leaders of the moderate clergy in Edinburgh.[10]

One of the earliest and most direct challenges to the Augustinian mentality of Reformed scholasticism occurred in Glasgow. It was

---

[8] Robert Wodrow, *The life of James Wodrow, A.M.* (Edinburgh 1828); H. M. B. Reid, *The divinity professors in the University of Glasgow* (Glasgow 1923), p. 187.

[9] J. W. Beardslee, *Theological development at Geneva under Francis and Jean Alphonse Turretin* (Ph.D., Yale University 1956); E. Budé, *Vie de J.-A. Turretin* (Lausanne 1880).

[10] See R. B. Sher, *Church and university in the Scottish Enlightenment* (Princeton 1985).

triggered in part by a controversy conducted among ministers and their congregations in Belfast, concerning the duty of subscription to the Westminster Confession, which was similar in inspiration to the non-subscription movement in Geneva. The Belfast ministers who insisted on their right of conscience to decline subscription received encouragement from presbyterian ministers in Dublin. But in Scotland itself, this challenge focused on the University of Glasgow; on its procedures, its staffing arrangements, and, above all, on the philosophical and theological instruction available to students, many of whom (including the most radical of their number) were Irish. A leading figure in this initiative was Francis Hutcheson, once a student at the University of Glasgow, then master of a dissenting academy in Dublin, then professor of Moral Philosophy at Glasgow.

Hutcheson has always been considered a figure of primary importance in the Scottish enlightenment. The influence of his thinking, exercised through writings published during and after his lifetime, and still more, perhaps, through his teaching, was readily and cheerfully acknowledged by most who knew him. He remains none the less a difficult thinker to interpret. It has been recognized by many scholars[11] that his various writings do not cohere together. Hutcheson himself, who was renowned for his candour (at least in communications to his friends; the greatest of his contemporaries, David Hume, should not, perhaps, be included in their number), regretted the lack of order, regularity, and method in what was to have been his last and greatest work.[12] W. R. Scott's explanation of this incoherence was that Hutcheson's thinking had changed fundamentally in the course of his career. His work had passed through four stages (a characteristically Scottish progression): from the moral sense theory (the *Inquiries*, 1725), to naturalism (*An essay on the nature and conduct of the passions and affections*, 1728), to teleology (*A system of moral philosophy*, largely written 1734–37), to stoicism (*Philosophiae moralis institutio compendiaria*, 1742). He never succeeded in integrating these phases of this thought into a synthetic and coherent system.

In the following discussion I will propose a different interpretation of Hutcheson's writings. I will suggest that there are not four phases of Hutcheson's thinking, but only two: a coherent public philosophy, expounded in the four philosophical treatises written in Dublin in the

[11] Notably by the finest of Hutcheson scholars, W. R. Scott, in his *Francis Hutcheson* (Cambridge 1900), chaps. 9–12.

[12] "In running over my papers, I am quite dissatisfied with Method Style Matter & some Reasonings . . . [A]s to composing in order I am quite bewildered, and am Adding confusedly to a confused Book all valuable Remarks in a Farrago to refresh my Memory in my class Lectures on the several Subjects." (Hutcheson to Thomas Drennan, 15 June 1741: GUL, MS. Gen. 1018, item 8).

1720s (the two parts of *An inquiry concerning the original of our ideas of beauty and virtue*, together with the *Essay*, and *Illustrations upon the moral sense*);[13] and a parallel academic philosophy conceived in accordance with the pedagogic demands of the College of Glasgow (which includes his *Logicae compendium*, *Synopsis metaphysicae*, and *Philosophiae moralis institutio compendiaria*). These two philosophies were each of them systematic statements of his thinking. The four philosophical treatises of the 1720s are mutually supportive in their reasoning; they are complementary treatises in aesthetics, ethics, and psychology, reinforced by polemical and illustrative discussion. The Latin writings also comprehend a system of a sort, of logic, metaphysics, and moral philosophy. But the arguments they advance, and the philosophical writers celebrated in the texts and notes, are in many cases the theoretical positions and authors which are denounced in the writings of the 1720s.

The incoherence of these two clusters of works derives, I believe, not from the progress or development of Hutcheson's thinking, but from the circumstance that the two sets of texts were addressed to different groups of readers. The intended readers of the philosophical treatises of the 1720s were the mature and adult readers of *The London journal* and the *Dublin weekly journal*, and his fellow teachers and ministers in Scotland and Ireland. There is no reason to suppose that he ever abandoned the positions taken in these treatises: they were reissued in successive editions through the course of his life with merely minor revisions and alterations. In contrast, Hutcheson spoke of his Latin writings with diffidence and even some contempt. He also revised his Latin texts on metaphysics and morals extensively, but remained unsatisfied with them; his logic was published only after his death. But these later works in Latin (and, in one case, in English translation, but not by Hutcheson) were read and studied with great care in the colleges of Scotland and America, and in the dissenting academies in England and Wales, and were extensively reprinted through the century.[14]

What was Hutcheson attempting to achieve in his philosophical treatises? What were the problems he was attempting to answer? And why did he consider his arguments inappropriate when he composed his

---

[13] The warrant for regarding these as four separate treatises is provided by the Contents pages of the two volumes which contain them, and by the Preface to the second of the volumes. In this paper I shall frequently refer to the dual contents of the first volume collectively as "the *Inquiries*". Subsequent page references are to the first editions.

[14] On the printing history, see P. Gaskell, *Bibliography of the Foulis press*, 2nd edn. (London 1986); and on the academies, H. McLachlan, *English education under the Test acts* (Manchester 1931). R. B. Sher, in his paper later in this volume, records that William Cleghorn at Edinburgh—who was clearly critical of the moral philosophy expressed in Hutcheson's English works—nevertheless prescribed the Latin compend in his classes.

Latin works? In order to address these questions, it will be necessary to examine the sources and the inspiration of Hutcheson's philosophical enterprise. That inspiration can be best discovered in the pedantic and rebellious environment of the College of Glasgow when Hutcheson was a student.

Irish presbyterian youths were ineligible for admission to Trinity College, Dublin, or to Oxford or Cambridge Universities; like English presbyterians they were obliged to pursue their university studies in Scotland. Many Irish (and English) students were carefully prepared for their university careers in Scotland in dissenting academies. Many were so well prepared that they entered directly into the final year of study; as did Hutcheson, when he arrived in Glasgow in 1710 and matriculated in the class of John Loudon.[15] Loudon taught at Glasgow for fifty-three years all told; he was hired in 1698, became professor of Logic in 1727, and held the post until his death in 1751. He was one of four philosophy regents in Hutcheson's student days; Gershom Carmichael was another: they both taught (which is to say dictated) much the same texts to their students. The activity of dictation was less mechanical, at least for the professor, than the term and the activity might suggest. For both Loudon and Carmichael were thoughtful men and their expositions of the texts they dictated are subtle, closely reasoned, and not devoid of creativity in the way they combined the various texts in the syllabus to make them cohere with their own theological and philosophical commitments.

In their first year under the regents, Glasgow students in the early eighteenth century learned logic through study of *The art of thinking* by Arnauld and Nicole; the arguments were often revised by Carmichael and Loudon by reference to Locke's *Essay concerning human understanding*.[16] In their second year, students were instructed in metaphysics, through dictation structured around De Vries's *Determinationes pneumatologicae et ontologicae*,[17] revised by reference to Malebranche's *De la Recherche de la vérité* and again to Locke's *Essay*. The

---

[15] Hutcheson's recognizable signature appears three times in the registers of Glasgow University: he was one of thirteen Irish students who signed the class register as members of Loudon's class in natural philosophy on 5 March 1711 (i.e. he entered in session 1710–11); he signed the graduation register on 14 Nov. 1712, and the divinity class register on 10 Feb. 1713.

[16] Carmichael's syllabus from some time in the 1690s is preserved in GUA, MS. 43170, but has been updated in the lectures which survive in a student's notebook of 1697 (NLS, MS. 2741). For additional detail, see C. M. Shepherd, *Philosophy and science in the arts curriculum of the Scottish universities in the seventeenth century* (Ph.D., University of Edinburgh 1975). One set of Carmichael's logic dictates which was not included in her survey is explicitly headed 'Annotationes . . . dictatae in artem cogitandi' (Mitchell Library, MS. 90).

[17] Gerard de Vries, *De natura dei et humanae mentis determinationes pneumatologicae. Accedunt de catholicis rerum attributis ejusdem determinationes ontologicae* (Utrecht 1687: several Scottish editions).

more acceptable Protestant scholasticism of the Geneva theologians, Francis Turretin and Benedict Pictet, replaced the third part of De Vries's pneumatology, entitled 'De deo', which neglected the distinction crucial for Protestant dogmatics, of the dual attributes of the deity, perhaps because of De Vries's preoccupation with the Cartesian distinction between the understanding and the will. The third year was devoted to moral philosophy through the exposition of a substantially altered text of Pufendorf's shorter work, *De officio hominis et civis*. The revisions were designed to cultivate greater reverence for the deity than Pufendorf (or his annotator, Barbeyrac) had demonstrated, and also to promote respect for the rights of individuals, again as taught by the celebrated Locke, in his *Second treatise of government*. The final year offered the student an introduction to natural philosophy, through the Cartesian physics of Le Clerc, supplemented with additional experimental and mathematical studies. There is some evidence that 'sGravesande's work eventually replaced Le Clerc's.

One can discern in this cluster of texts, or at least in the presentation of them at Glasgow, a coherence which derives as much from the theological orientation of the authors and their expositors, as from the philosophical tradition to which they belonged. For all of these authors—Arnauld, Nicole, Malebranche, De Vries, Pufendorf—were Augustinian in their theology, convinced of the sinfulness of fallen man and of the gulf which separates his sensations, imagination, passions, morals, and politics from the ideal or heavenly world available through divine grace. The language used to express this conviction was, to be sure, frequently the secular philosophical idiom of Descartes. But it was the Augustinian inspiration of this body of philosophical writing—Jansenist, Oratorian, Dutch Reformed, Pietistic—which made it so eminently adaptable and teachable by orthodox Calvinist instructors like Loudon and Carmichael. It was this Augustinian mentality which Hutcheson would soon confront in his philosophical and pedagogic initiatives.

Following graduation in 1712, Hutcheson remained at Glasgow for six years as a theology student and family tutor. The professor of Sacred Theology was John Simson, a man of controversial talents, who was deeply opposed to the Protestant scholasticism favoured by the Church of Scotland, and by colleagues like Loudon and Carmichael. Simson was particularly opposed to the dogma of the Incarnation: that God became man in Jesus Christ while remaining God. The scholastic formulation of this dual nature of the deity was unfolded in the doctrine of the two kinds of divine attributes. Some attributes of God, such as omniscience, omnipotence, infinity, were described as "incommunicable", i.e. were possessed by God alone. Other attributes, such as knowledge, volition, majesty, were described as "communicable", or common to God and men; provided these men were redeemed from their sinful condition through the mediation of Jesus Christ.[18] Simson found no place for this doctrine in his theology: he was doubtful of the assumption of man's sinful condition; he thought it possible that any man might be saved, even those who have no knowledge of Christ. He is reported to have told his students that when they read in Pictet that *Christus est summus deus*, they must always understand it *cum grano salis*.[19] Not surprisingly, his colleagues and fellow ministers exhibited concern about the quality and the orientation of his theological instruction. He enjoyed an entrenched position at Glasgow, however: he was the principal's brother-in-law; and he was ready to support the principal, John Stirling, in his autocratic style of university government. In order to strengthen their hand in their dealing with the principal, Carmichael and Loudon tried to revive in 1717 the natural and historic right of the students to elect their rector.[20] The initiative failed; but the campaign would be revived five years later, under different auspices.

Hutcheson had returned to Ireland in 1718, and within a year or two had established an academy of his own, in Dublin, which prepared students for university study. The students from Ireland, north and south, who arrived at Glasgow during this period exhibited a flair for student politics, for clubs, student societies, and for the theatre. One of their number, James Arbuckle, organized a production of *Tamerlane*, with a prologue which was widely construed as deploring tyranny in university as well as civil government.[21] Carmichael and Loudon, now worried by the possibilities of immorality in the theatre, where men might have to perform women's roles, proposed that all female roles be excised and love scenes turned into scenes of male friendship, as Carmichael remembered had been done "very judiciously" by his schoolmaster with one of Terence's comedies. "But whatever was done by that great Man, his School-Master, it was to be feared there could no such skilful Hand be found about the University of *Glasgow*, and therefore the Gentlemen persisted in their Resolution to act the Play."[22]

Arbuckle was in correspondence at this time with Viscount Moles-

---

[18] Gershom Carmichael, *Synopsis theologiae naturalis* (Edinburgh 1729); Franciscus Turretinus, *Institutio theologiae elencticae* (Geneva 1680); Benedictus Pictet, *Theologia Christiana* (Geneva 1696).

[19] Robert Wodrow, *Analecta*, vol. 3 (Edinburgh 1843), p. 276.

[20] 'Memorial for the Scholars and other Matriculated Members of the University of Glasgow', 21 Dec. 1717: NLS, Pamph. 1. 10 (142).

[21] *A short account of the late treatment of the students of the University of G——w* (Dublin 1722). M. A. Stewart, in 'John Smith and the Molesworth circle', *Eighteenth-century Ireland* 2 (1987), 89–102, identifies the future bookseller John Smith as the primary author of this pamphlet. But there may have been a co-author, and this could have been Arbuckle.

[22] *A short account*, pp. 17–18.

worth, who had retired to Dublin in 1722, and found in some of the Scots and Irish students a most receptive audience for his obsession with liberty and virtue. Arbuckle reported to Molesworth in 1723 that he and his fellows now despaired of support from any parliamentarians against the "tyranny" of the university administration and faculty: "This New Disappointment has confirmed us in the Apprehension, that we need never hope for the Redress of our Grievances, till the Generality of Politicians be of another Complexion than we have yet seen them. The Love of Virtue for Virtue's Sake is almost worn out of the World. We are debauched in the very first Principles of our Morality."[23]

Molesworth had let it be known that he would himself introduce a bill for the reform of the Scottish universities in the House of Commons if he should be re-elected to that body. The misinformation that he had been elected in 1722 had prompted another Irish student, John Smith, to light a bonfire. Carmichael took the initiative to appear before the students to stamp it out. But the students defended themselves, citing Carmichael's own arguments for the right of self-defence, in his notes to Pufendorf's *De officio*. Mr Smith, it is unpleasant to report, was expelled from the university for his trouble. He moved to Dublin, soon to become a successful bookseller. In partnership first with William Smith, he commissioned the publication of Hutcheson's *Inquiries*; and then, in partnership with Hutcheson's cousin, William Bruce, he published Hutcheson's *Essay on the nature and conduct of the passions and affections*. Arbuckle had meanwhile followed Smith to Dublin and become literary editor of the *Dublin weekly journal*, which published Hutcheson's letters of 1725, and he collected these with other documents of his own in *A collection of letters and essays on several subjects* in 1729.

Other Scots were encouraged by Molesworth's concern for the apparent absence of virtue and liberty in the Scottish universities. William Wishart, later principal of the University of Edinburgh, and George Turnbull, a regent at Aberdeen, wrote eloquent, if at times obsequious, letters to Molesworth in which they fulsomely expressed their gratitude for his interest in the plight of Scottish higher education. Molesworth responded with recommended readings for students of moral philosophy: Machiavelli's *Discourses*, Harrington's *Oceana*, Tillotson's *Sermons*, the writings of Molesworth himself and, above all, of his friend, the third Earl of Shaftesbury, whose exchange of private letters with Molesworth had been published by John Toland in 1721. It is sometimes asserted, notably by Caroline Robbins, that Locke was an important author in the Molesworth canon.[24] But Locke's name is not

[23] Quoted by Stewart, p. 101. The further information on the Molesworth correspondence, below, is derived from unpublished material by the same scholar.
[24] C. Robbins, *The eighteenth-century commonwealthman* (Cambridge, Mass. 1959), chap. 4.

mentioned by Arbuckle, Wishart, or Turnbull, in their reports back to Molesworth on the progress of their reading. And there is at least one excellent reason why he should not have been cited in this list of writers. Locke had been identified by Shaftesbury, in letters published in 1716, as the philosopher who had done most to undermine the cause of virtue:

'Twas Mr. LOCKE that struck at all Fundamentals, threw all *Order* and *Virtue* out of the World, and made the very *Ideas* of these (which are the same as those of GOD) *unnatural*, and without Foundation in our Minds.[25]

This was the context of Hutcheson's early letters to *The London journal* (1724) and *Dublin weekly journal* (1725) and of his four philosophical treatises of the 1720s. They were written as part of a campaign waged by the friends of Molesworth to put higher education in Scotland and Ireland on a new foundation. Even as he wrote, one of Hutcheson's Dublin students, William Robertson, was being expelled from the University of Glasgow.[26] This may account for the shrillness of tone one finds in the *London journal* articles: in particular, in Hutcheson's characterization of contemporary moralists as "*sour* and *morose* in their Deportment; they shall be *easily put out of Humour* by every trifling Accident; soon *dejected* with common Calamities, and *insolent* upon any prosperous Change of Fortune". Are these characteristics best explained, he asks, "by a natural *Corruption* in us, . . . or should we suspect some *Mistakes* in the Premises of our moral Science, some *wrong Steps* in the Instruction we derive from them"?[27]

In the tenth number of the *Dublin weekly journal*, he tells us that "the grand Instructor in Morals to all who have of late given themselves to that Study" is Samuel Pufendorf. He had no doubt that Pufendorf's writing was "much preferable to the generality of the *School-men* in distinct intelligible Reasoning"; but much had also been lost. Pufendorf had strongly imbibed Hobbes's first principles, although he had drawn better consequences from them. Hobbes had attempted to deduce human actions from self-love; he had overlooked everything which is generous or kind in mankind; friendship, love, and social affection were for him the product of hypocrisy or selfish calculation or fear. Pufendorf had retained Hobbes's emphasis on fear and self-love but had deduced from them the obligation of all men to be sociable; and he had reminded Hobbists that the laws of nature which followed from this duty to be sociable were sanctioned by a divine lawmaker and were violated at our

[25] Shaftesbury to Michael Ainsworth, 3 June 1709, in *Several letters written by a noble lord to a young man at the university* (London 1716), letter VIII, p. 39.
[26] Stewart, pp. 96 (n. 21), 98–9 (n. 29). On the subsequent career of William Robertson (1705–83), see *DNB*; this is a different individual from the Edinburgh cleric and historian of the same name.
[27] *London journal*, no. 277 (14 Nov. 1724).

peril. Hutcheson rejected Pufendorf's moral philosophy on two grounds.

His first objection was to Pufendorf's conception of natural law, which rested, he thought, on an unsatisfactory idea of God, as a tyrant who alternately bribes and threatens us to secure obedience to his laws. It is an objection which appears to resemble a similar criticism made by Carmichael. But Hutcheson's critical position was quite different from Carmichael's, as his subsequent dismissal of scholastic moralists makes clear:

they flew so high, immediately to the Beatific Vision and Fruition and so lightly passed over, with some trite common-place Remarks, all ordinary human Affairs, that one must be well advanced in a *visionary Temper* to be profited by them. (*London journal*, no. 278)

A better understanding of the deity is of a being of boundless goodness:

Could we enlarge Men's views beyond themselves, and make 'em consider the whole Families of Heaven and Earth, which is supported by the indulgent Care of this Universal Parent, we should find little need of other sorts of Arguments to engage an unprejudiced Mind to love a Being of such extensive Goodness. (No. 277)

But how, a Pufendorfian jurist might still ask, would the rights and obligations, secured by the law of nature that sociability be maintained, be enforced? Hutcheson's answer was that *human nature itself*, by virtue of its natural affection and predispositions, could not fail to bring about and secure this sociable condition:

Were Men once possess'd with just Notions of Humane Nature; had they lively Sentiments of the *natural Affections* and *kind Passions* . . . did Men understand the Distress, the Dejection of Spirit, the Diffidence in all kind Attempts, and the Uncertainty of every Possession under a Tyrant; these Thoughts wou'd soon rouse Men into another kind of Love to their *Country* and Resolution in its *Defence*, than the mere Considerations of Terror either in this World or in the next. (No. 278)

It was not only Pufendorf's idea of *God* that was unsatisfactory; he had also (like Hobbes) left out of his understanding of human nature the qualities cherished by classical moralists.

[T]he old Notions of *natural Affections*, and kind *Instincts*, the *Sensus communis*, the *Decorum* and *Honestum*, are almost banish'd out of our Books of Morals; we must never hear of them in any of our Lectures for fear of *innate Ideas*: all must be *Interest* and some selfish View. (*Dublin weekly journal*, no. 10)

The reference to innate ideas and the supposed importance of avoiding them reminds us of the influential position enjoyed by Locke's

Essay at this time. That Locke should be connected with Pufendorf on this subject was certainly appropriate: for Pufendorf also rejected innate ideas in his polemical and selected academic writings; and Locke's writings on the understanding, on toleration, and on government were linked with Pufendorf's by academic commentators in Europe like Barbeyrac, as well as in Scotland.[28] This circumstance would seem to reinforce recent arguments that Hutcheson's moral epistemology was a species of realism that was developed quite independently of Locke's theory of the understanding.[29] Certainly, the direct allusions to Locke's writings in the *Inquiries* and the *Essay* identify him much as Shaftesbury did, as one of the great contributors to the misunderstanding of beauty, virtue, the passions and affections.

Nothing is more ordinary among those who, after Mr. LOCKE have shaken off the groundless Opinion about *innate Ideas,* than to alledge, "That all our Relish for *Beauty,* and *Order* is either from *Advantage* or *Custom,* or *Education,*" for no other Reason but the Variety of Fancys in the World. (*Inquiry,* pp. 73–4)

Hutcheson was at pains to distance his theory from the ideas of those philosophers who "deduce all Ideas of *Good* and *Evil* . . . from Relation to a *Law* and its *Sanctions*" (p. 247). Whereas Locke had contended at *Essay* II. xxviii. 5 that "*Morally Good and Evil* . . . is only the Conformity or Disagreement of our voluntary Actions to some Law, whereby Good or Evil is drawn on us from the Will and Power of the Lawmaker", Hutcheson was determined to show "that we have Ideas of *Virtue* and *Vice,* abstractly from any *Law, Human* or *Divine*" (p. 249). His project in his philosophical treatises of the 1720s was to prove that our ideas of beauty and virtue and our kind affections and desires were real ideas, perceived by internal senses whose sensibilia were quite distinct from the dependent and contingent sensations of the external senses. When we perceive a beautiful object, a natural object or a work of art, we apprehend its beauty by a distinctive sensibility: our recognition of beauty in the object is an idea which attends the peculiar pleasures of this internal sense. Similarly, our approval of a virtuous character, one in whom the kind affections, compassion, desire for the good of others, is manifest, is not a relational judgement that this character is in accordance with a law or rule imposed upon him and others; it is rather an immediate apprehension of the qualities of his character attended by an idea of virtue. Thus the ideas of beauty and virtue were real ideas: but

---

[28] Samuel von Pufendorf, 'Apologia', sec. xxiv, and 'Specimen controversiarum', chap. IV, sec. xxiii, in *Eris Scandica* [1686] (Frankfurt 1706, pp. 33–5, 224–7; Jean Barbeyrac, in Pufendorf, *Of the law of nature and nations* [1672], trans. B. Kennett, 4th edn. (London 1729), p. 133, n. 1.

[29] See K. Haakonssen's contribution to this volume, and references cited there.

not ideas of sensation or reflection, or modes compounded of simple ideas, as Pufendorf and Locke would have had us understand.

What other ways of conceiving ideas were available to Hutcheson? One was provided by the Augustinian Cartesianism which had dominated the curriculum in the early eighteenth century. In *The art of thinking* and in the works of Malebranche, ideas were thought to be real existences. They were not to be confused with the impressions of the senses or the whimsies of the imagination; these were variable, fleeting, and inevitably misleading. Ideas were thoughts, generated by the understanding, aided perhaps by divine grace. It is noteworthy, perhaps, that Hutcheson's ideas of beauty and virtue were thought by Jean Le Clerc to be much indebted to this tradition. In his review of the *Inquiries* in 1725,[30] Le Clerc observed that Hutcheson's idea of beauty was remarkably similar in conception and in illustration to the idea of beauty presented in Crousaz's *Traité du beau*.

Crousaz's work is sometimes considered the first work in aesthetics in the French language.[31] He understood beauty, as Hutcheson did, as uniformity in variety; and he was at pains to demonstrate that this was a real idea, distinct from mere feeling or sensation. Le Clerc's remarks, sharpened by the accusation that Hutcheson had largely plagiarized his first *Inquiry* from the work of Crousaz, drew from Hutcheson a lengthy rejoinder. It was written to Samuel Card, who communicated the letter to Le Clerc, who passed it on to Armand de la Chapelle, who translated it and published it in his *Bibliothèque angloise*. The letter is revealing, not so much for its exhibition of what Hutcheson may have learned from Crousaz, which he contended was nothing (although this may have been disingenuous), but for its indication of what Hutcheson thought he was arguing against in this first *Inquiry*.

I remember nothing more of Mr Crousaz's *Treatise* than his general idea of beauty, which consists in unity in variety, in which he is as unoriginal as I. And the distinction he makes between beauty as idea and beauty as sentiment (feeling) is one I have never favoured, and which I have even formally attacked in my book.[32]

What Hutcheson was countering in Crousaz's work was the dualism inherent in Crousaz's treatment of the subject. In an ideal world (i.e. before the fall of man), our sentiments or feelings about what is beautiful

---

[30] *Bibliothèque ancienne et moderne* 24:2 (1725), 421–37.

[31] T. M. Mustoxidi, *Histoire de l'esthétique française, 1700–1900* (Paris 1920), p. 12.

[32] *Bibliothèque angloise* 13:2 (1726), p. 515 (my re-translation). An Irish student named Samuel Card, age 18, registered in the Faculty of Law at the University of Leiden on 15 Sept. 1725; it seems likely that he had previously been a student of Hutcheson's in Dublin. For another discussion of Hutcheson's alleged plagiarism, see D. R. Raynor, 'Hutcheson's defence against a charge of plagiarism', *Eighteenth-century Ireland* 2 (1987), 177–81.

and virtuous (for the terms were correlatives in Crousaz's thought) were merely confirmed by our thoughts or ideas. But this correspondence between feeling and idea no longer holds for sinful man, Crousaz maintained. The fall of man, the necessity of work, illnesses, annoyances, all contribute to disharmony between our feeling and our ideas. Now when the sentiments are in conflict, or when they are corrupted, as they frequently are in this mortal life, they must be corrected and regulated by our ideas.[33] Hutcheson's "formal attack", as he described it, on this dualism was to remind his readers that the senses of beauty and virtue were natural powers of perception; that our normal experience cannot fail to excite the distinctive prompting of these internal senses; that when we are in error in our moral and aesthetic judgements it is never due to the sinfulness of our natural or native disposition: we are misled instead by artifice, by treachery, by bad education, by custom, and by misleading associations of ideas (*Inquiry*, pp. 79–87). Once we cease to be imposed upon by philosophers and educators who would convince us of the sinfulness of man, we cannot fail to apprehend beauty and virtue by the natural faculties of internal sensation.

The second of Hutcheson's philosophical treatises, *An inquiry concerning the original of our ideas of moral good*, was also directed against a form of Augustinian dualism, perhaps the most notorious dualism of his age: the private vices, public benefits, dichotomy enunciated in Mandeville's *The fable of the bees*. There was little that was devout about Mandeville's Augustinianism: it was a celebration of the earthly city, where every vice is perceived to contribute to the prosperity and civility of the state and its subjects. Hutcheson's best arguments against Mandeville's dualism are to be found in his letters to the *Dublin weekly journal* in February 1726, where he directly challenges Mandeville's arguments that drunkenness is conducive to the public good through increased revenue in excise taxes; that robbers provide work for locksmiths, and arsonists work for carpenters and builders. Hutcheson solemnly reasons that as much revenue would be raised from consumption of wine and spirits if they were distributed more widely among moderate imbibers; that money spent on locks might be diverted to purchase other household items which in turn could provide work for silversmiths and others; that making adequate provision for oneself and others will only be considered vice by cynics and popish hermits— identifying Mandeville, not imperceptively, as an able satirical representative of both these schools of thought. In the *Inquiry*, his only remarks on Mandeville defend the reality of our ideas of virtue and vice from

---

[33] Jean-Pierre de Crousaz, *Traité du beau* (Amsterdam 1715), pp. 7–8, 63–82.

Mandeville's theory that moral ideas are fabrications, cunningly devised by artful politicians, employers, and parents to enhance their power over their subjects, servants, and children. Unless some notions of good and evil were already present in the minds of the latter, Hutcheson argues, they could never be persuaded by the ruses, bribes, and threats too often employed by the former. One might suspect that one of Hutcheson's reasons for advertising his second *Inquiry* as an attack on Mandeville was that, like Filmer's *Patriarcha* in the eyes of Tyrrell, Locke, and Sidney, the *Fable* was such an egregiously outrageous representation of the position he was arguing against that it presented an irresistible target or object of criticism. The *Fable* continued to appear an extraordinarily persuasive document, however, to Calvinist readers in Scotland, and also in other nations with a strong Augustinian tradition and mentality: Holland, Geneva, etc.[34]

The third and last instalment of Hutcheson's critique of Augustinian moralism from the standpoint of moral realism was his *Essay on the nature and conduct of the passions*. His fourth treatise, *Illustrations upon the moral sense*, consisted of a series of replies to his critics. In the *Essay*, Hutcheson set out to rewrite the subtle Augustinian psychology of Malebranche. In Book V, chapters 3 and 4, of *De la Recherche de la vérité* Malebranche had presented a sharp dichotomy between the natural inclinations of the soul when it is assisted by divine grace, and the violent and confused passions of the body. Hutcheson thought it strange

that the thoughtful MALEBRANCHE did not consider, that "*Desire* and *Aversion* are obviously different from the Modifications called *Passions*; that these two directly lead to Action, or the Volition of Motion, and are wholly distinct from all sort of Sensation." (*Essay*, p. 59)

But the thoughtful Malebranche did not think that any passion was ever wholly distinct from sensation. He did think that the inclinations of a soul inspired by divine grace might be attended by feelings of joy or delight capable of overwhelming the desire of sensible pleasure. But such joy was available only to souls that were redeemed:

what I have just been saying in behalf of joy of the mind against sensuous joy is true only among Christians, and it would be absolutely false coming from the mouth of Seneca, or even Epicurus, or any of the seemingly most reasonable philosophers, because the word of Jesus Christ is sweet only to those who belong to Jesus Christ, and His burden seems light to us only when His grace helps us to carry it.[35]

---

[34] E. J. Hundert, 'The thread of language and the web of dominion', *Eighteenth-century studies* 21 (1987/8), 169–91.

[35] Nicolas Malebranche, *The search after truth*, trans. T. M. Lennon and P. J. Olscamp (Columbus 1980), p. 356.

Hutcheson's challenge was to show that affection for others and desire for the good of the public at large might prevail over the promptings of particular selfish passions; and that such kind and public affection could prevail over the sensuous passions without the assistance of divine grace.

We obtain *Command* over the *particular Passions*, principally by strengthening the *general Desires* thro' frequent Reflection, and making them *habitual* so as to obtain Strength superior to the *particular Passions*. (*Essay*, p. 30)

He agreed that

these Affections, *viz., Desire, Aversion, Joy and Sorrow*, we may, after MALEBRANCHE, call *spiritual* or *pure Affections* . . . But beside these Affections, which seem to arise necessarily from a rational Apprehension of Good and Evil, there are in our Nature violent *confused Sensations* connected with *bodily Motions*, from which our *Affections* are denominated *Passions*. (p. 62)

He will leave it to others more knowledgeable of the vital spirits and motions of body and soul to explain the division. Hutcheson's concern is to persuade the reader that his happiness must depend neither on divine grace nor on the gratification of particular selfish passions. Everyone must acknowledge, he suggests, that "even the most immediate and lively *Sensations of Delight*, of which his Nature is susceptible, immediately flow from a *Publick Spirit*, a *generous, human⟨e⟩, compassionate Temper*, and a suitable *Deportment*" (p. 202).

Hutcheson's early philosophical treatises and his letters to *The London journal* and *Dublin weekly journal* exhibit, then, an underlying coherence. These writings comprehended an aesthetics, an ethics, and a psychology, which postulated the natural abilities or powers to perceive and to act in a manner consistent with a sense of beauty and virtue. Together they comprised a stoic exercise in the experience and cultivation of civic life for its own sake. Secondly, the treatises manifest a coherence in their critical posture, in their agreements on the character of the writings to which they stand opposed: they were opposed to the selfish and legalistic theories of Pufendorf and Locke; and they were opposed to various forms of Augustinian dualism in aesthetics, ethics, and psychology. In both respects, in terms of what they advocated (the cultivation of beauty, virtue, and the kind affections) and in terms of what they opposed (the selfish systems of natural jurisprudence and the dualistic aesthetics, ethics, and psychology of the Augustinians), Hutcheson's early treatises and letters mounted a systematic and a powerful attack on the ideas and the materials used for the instruction of youth in the presbyterian academies and Scottish universities.

His intensive literary activity, the efforts and the protests of the students who found their way from Ireland to Glasgow, the initiatives of his friends in the ministry (William Wishart), in visiting commissions (Lord Ilay), and in the faculty (the professor of Greek, Alexander Dunlop), finally came to fruition in 1730, in Hutcheson's appointment as professor of Moral Philosophy at the University of Glasgow, in a closely contested competition with Frederick Carmichael, the otherwise not well-qualified son of the previous occupant of the chair.

In his on-going account of Scottish life in the early eighteenth century, particularly as it related to the Church of Scotland, Robert Wodrow regretfully recorded that on the death of Carmichael "all the English Students have left the University; and, indeed, it's very thin this winter, and his name and reputation brought many to it" (*Analecta*, vol. 4, p. 98). The succession of Hutcheson is reported in November 1730:

Upon the 30th of this moneth Mr. Francis Hutcheson was publickly admitted, and had his inaugurall discourse. It's in print, and I need say no more of it. He had not time, I knou, to form it, and it's upon a very safe generall subject.... He delivered it very fast and lou, being a modest man, and it was not well understood. His character and carriage seems prudent and cautious, and that will be the best vidimus of him. (pp. 186–7)

The "very safe generall subject" of Hutcheson's inaugural lecture was "the natural sociability of man". It was indeed prudent of him to have "delivered it very fast and lou", since much of the lecture was in fact an extended criticism of Pufendorf (and, by implication, a comment on the less than satisfactory manner in which Pufendorf's work had been amended and revised by others). After some perfunctory ceremonial remarks concerning the usefulness of moral science and the contributions to it of many worthy men, he warms to his theme, which is human nature and the many virtues found in our nature. This had been the theme of the best moral philosophers of antiquity, who had never tired of observing those qualities that make a man cherished by his companions, his family, his country. None of this, he observes, is to be credited to good health, a strong body, or riches; for many who have those advantages in abundance are none the less vile, odious, and morose, a shame to their companions and to themselves. He will not attempt, he says, to review all aspects of human nature, but only those qualities which incline us to a sociable life.

Many recent writers have determined that sociability is the source of nearly all duties, but they have not distinguished with sufficient care whether those sociable qualities are natural to man; what those sociable qualities are; and whether they dispose us to live in society with or without civil government. As long as these questions remain unanswered it is possible for writers of another persuasion (e.g. the cynics, sceptics, and Augustinians) to portray human nature in the most disagreeable and unsociable light.

Hutcheson embarks on an extended discussion of the term 'natural' which is designed to show that we judge the nature of all things by the ends for which they are contrived: eyes for seeing, teeth for chewing, etc. The skilled spectator will always be able to judge the end for which these are designed. One may infer, if a home collapses, that it was the weakness of the material or the incompetence of the builder, but one would not infer that it was the intent or aim of the architect that his house would collapse.

He emphatically rejects the abuse of words which has allowed Hobbes and Pufendorf to distinguish not only the natural from the civil state but also the natural condition of mankind from everything that requires strength, industry, and sagacity. Not only has Hobbes been refuted in this matter, but also Pufendorf himself, by distinguished authors like Titius, Barbeyrac, Cumberland, Carmichael, and above all the most elegant Earl of Shaftesbury. The most natural state of men, properly understood, is that state or condition which encourages them to exercise their strength and aptitudes. 'The natural state of mankind' may signify either the common condition of mankind or the most perfect condition men can attain by the realization of their capacities.

He concludes with an apostrophe to youth to put aside monastic struggle, gloominess, and despondency, and live instead a joyous, pleasant life, taking nature and providence as their guides. He hopes that he has shown that human beings are sociable creatures in the absence of civil government. He will offer an account of the origin of civil government on another occasion.[36]

But he does not do so. His next public pronouncement on the subject of government and the first new work published by him in moral philosophy appeared twelve years later in 1742. It was his *Philosophiae moralis institutio compendiaria*. It appeared together with a complementary treatise, *Metaphysicae synopsis*, substantially revised for the second edition in 1744 as *Synopsis metaphysicae*. The *Philosophia moralis* or moral compend was also revised and annotated for publication in 1745. Combined with the *Logicae compendium* published posthumously in 1756, the three works appear to constitute another system: one which was very different, however, from the philosophical treatises of the 1720s. The *Philosophia moralis* is an exposition of the law of nature, natural rights and obligations, the origins of the family, the household, and civil society. It does not neglect to include passing comments on the virtues and vices and the kind affections; but these are incidental to the

---

[36] Francis Hutcheson, *De naturali hominum socialitate oratio inauguralis* (Glasgow 1730). I am drawing on a translation of this lecture by Michael Silverthorne.

discussion. The introduction speaks glowingly of Carmichael's edition of Pufendorf; and the argument with respect to the law of nature, natural rights, and all the other topics reviewed in the book, is strongly indebted to Carmichael.[37] The *Synopsis metaphysicae* was divided into three parts: an ontology and a pneumatology (or science of the soul) and a natural theology, all of it ordered and expounded in the manner of Gerard de Vries, qualified by insights derived from Locke's *Essay*, and occasional, but again merely incidental, discussions (e.g. of the internal senses) which are discernibly Hutcheson's.[38] The *Logicae compendium* with its four-part structure—apprehension, judgement, discursive reasoning, and method—was again nothing but the *Art of thinking* of the Port-Royal logicians, which was to be supplemented with the reading of Locke.[39] Most remarkably, perhaps, the part of the *Synopsis metaphysicae* which discoursed upon the attributes of God substituted the Protestant scholastic formulation of the division of attributes into incommunicable and communicable, the dichotomy required by the emphasis on the Incarnation in opposition to various forms of Arminianism and Socinianism.[40]

There are, I believe, two errors to be avoided in interpreting these Latin texts: one is to regard these texts as a distinct phase in Hutcheson's thinking; the other is to consider them an integral part of his philosophical writings. First, the compends were not an exercise in stoicism in the manner of Cicero's *De finibus* or the writings of Epictetus or the *Meditations* of Marcus Aurelius (which Hutcheson was translating at the time in collaboration with a colleague).[41] They form a system of natural jurisprudence, and partake of the stoic philosophy only in the fundamental and residual sense in which all studies of the law of nature are stoical. Moreover, Hutcheson had always been a stoic, in his admiration of a life lived for the sake of liberty and public virtue. It is merely confusing, however, if one attempts to reconcile the argument and orientation of all three works with his philosophical treatises, still regarded by him as authentic expressions of his mature thinking as late as

---

[37] See the posthumous English translation, *A short introduction to moral philosophy* (Glasgow 1747), dedication 'To the students in universities', p. i.

[38] Hutcheson, *Synopsis metaphysicae*, 2nd edn. (Glasgow 1744), part II, secs. 4–5.

[39] Prefixed to the *Logicae compendium* is a dissertation on the origins of philosophy, to which is added an inventory of the principal authors. Hutcheson celebrates the "new road" which philosophers have "not without glory pointed to or entered upon", in physics, ethics, and logic and metaphysics, naming Locke as the prime innovator in logic and metaphysics (p. 11).

[40] *Synopsis metaphysicae*, part III ('De deo'), chap. ii, sec. 1. Hutcheson's Sunday lectures, by contrast, which were open to the public, followed the Arminian theology of Hugo Grotius's work, *The truth of the Christian religion* (Scott, p. 63).

[41] *The meditations of the emperor Marcus Aurelius Antoninus. Newly translated from the Greek: with notes, and an account of his life* (Glasgow 1742). Hutcheson was responsible for books III–XII, and his former pupil James Moor, soon to be professor of Greek, for books I–II (Scott, p. 144).

1742, when the third edition of the *Essay on the nature and conduct of the passions* was published.

How then should one interpret the Latin works? They are parallel texts, I would suggest, which together constitute a pedagogical system suitable for the instruction of youth. It was possible for Hutcheson to remain a civic moralist in his compositions for mature audiences, such as his *Considerations on patronages*,[42] while believing that youth was best served by the catalogue of rights and obligations found in Pufendorf's work on the duty of men and citizens.[43] There seems little doubt that he perceived the Latin works as teaching manuals and not much more. He expressed this reservation about his Latin writings in the preface to the moral compend,[44] and he was at pains to remind his correspondents of their limitations. He asked Drennan to "send by first safe Hand the copy [of *Synopsis metaphysicae*] directed to Bishop Syng. . . . [H]e is wanting such Elementary books for his Son."[45] But he describes the same book, in the same letter, as "a trifle which I don't own as it was first most imperfectly & foolishly printed without my knowledge, from some loose hastily wrote papers". I believe that these Latin works were composed early in Hutcheson's teaching career at Glasgow;[46] and that they were published when they were—so far as Hutcheson had control

[42] [Francis Hutcheson], *Considerations on patronages, addressed to the gentlemen of Scotland* (London 1735). This was a thoroughly classical republican document, advocating the removal of the power to make ecclesiastical appointments from the corrupt influence or patronage of remote civic officials, while avoiding the injudicious preferments which would follow from allowing entire congregations to vote on the choice of minister: Hutcheson's solution was to invest the selection in landed gentlemen. The context in which this pamphlet should be read is provided by R. B. Sher and A. Murdoch, 'Patronage and party in the Church of Scotland', in *Church, politics and society: Scotland 1408–1929*, ed. N. Macdougall (Edinburgh 1983), 197–220.

[43] Pufendorf himself considered his *De officio hominis et civis* (1673) to be a work suitable for students at universities. See the author's preface, 'To the benevolent reader—greetings'. The book was widely known in Britain in the early eighteenth century as *The whole duty of man according to the law of nature*, the title given it by Andrew Tooke, in a translation published in 1691, reissued in 1698, 1705, 1716, and 1735. It may therefore have been this work that Hume had in mind when he told Hutcheson, in 1739, "I desire to take my Catalogue of Virtues, from *Cicero's Offices*, not from the *Whole Duty of Man*" (HL i. 34). Hutcheson later defended his adaptation of Pufendorf's shorter work, in the preface to the second edition of his compend, as a work better designed for young persons than Cicero's *Offices*, which have been "mistaken inconsiderately by some very ingenious men, who speak of these books as intended for a compleat system of morals and ethics" ('To the students in universities', p. ii).

[44] "These elementary books are for your use who study at Universities, and not for the learned. When you have considered them well, go on to greater and more important works." (*Short introduction*, p. iv.)

[45] Hutcheson to Drennan, 29 Oct. 1743: GUL, MS. Gen. 1018, item 14.

[46] It has, however, been suggested to me by Dr Stewart that they may date from still earlier, and that we may be looking at the curriculum of Hutcheson's Dublin academy. Hutcheson had no responsibilities for logic or metaphysics as professor of Moral Philosophy at Glasgow, whereas he did in Dublin; and at Dublin he was preparing students to go on to further studies in disciplines in which their principal reading would be still in Latin.

over their publication—so that he and others could put into the hands of students, compends in logic, metaphysics, and morals, more elegant and accessible than the treatises of Port-Royal, De Vries, and Pufendorf, while remaining within the formal requirements of the curriculum as it was then conceived.

In the second editions of his metaphysics and morals, Hutcheson did attempt to introduce more of his public philosophy, his civic moralism, into these texts. Many of the additions and revisions appear to have been his responses to a provocative and generally misleading set of questions posed to him by his young contemporary, David Hume (HL i. 45–8). Hutcheson's warning to his youthful readers not to take Cicero's *De officiis* as a complete guide to moral life, but only as a book which may be of use to already established men of the world, was added to the preface to the second edition of the moral compend in 1745, at a time when he was strenuously opposing Hume's candidacy for the chair of Pneumatic and Ethical Philosophy at the University of Edinburgh.

Hume expressed his disappointment and surprise at this dénouement in their relationship (HL i. 58). The surprise may well have been genuine. But the differences between Hutcheson and Hume on moral and political questions were always profound, and their contributions to the Scottish enlightenment were entirely different in inspiration. They were both reacting against "our scholastic headpieces", as Hume called them (T. 175), who had still controlled the Scottish universities in the 1720s. But Hume's use of the experimental method of reasoning to respond to the Pyrrhonian scepticism of Bayle has no counterpart in Hutcheson's work. Hutcheson perceived Bayle, in the way he regarded Mandeville, as an enemy of the cause of civic virtue, more dangerous, if anything, than more orthodox Augustinians. It is not surprising, in this light, that he should have recognized that Hume's morals and politics had little in common with the cause of civic virtue.[47]

The circumstance that Hume never held a university chair may have had the fortunate, if unintended, consequence that he was never obliged to compromise his treatment of philosophical themes by having to adjust them to a syllabus drawn up by others. Hutcheson, on the other hand, struggled through the last years of his short life to integrate the argument of the various treatises published in the 1720s, with the exposition of his scholastic textbooks published in the 1740s, into a single systematic *magnum opus*. He never succeeded in setting out the argument to his satisfaction in any orderly, methodical, and systematic way. The result

[47] Bayle was perceived in the early eighteenth century to be a Pyrrhonian not only in his metaphysics but also in his morals and politics. See my 'Natural law and the Pyrrhonian controversy', in *Philosophy and science in the Scottish Enlightenment*, ed. P. H. Jones (Edinburgh 1989), 20–38.

was as he described it, "a confused Book . . . a Farrago". *A system of moral philosophy* never exercised the influence that Hutcheson's early treatises or his later textbooks had on his contemporaries and successors; while the continuing popularity of the latter—the despised textbooks— may have been due as much to the creative adaptation of those texts by his immediate successors in the chair at Glasgow as it was to their intrinsic merit.

Hutcheson, Hume, Smith, and Reid each made their own distinctive contributions to what we have come to call the Scottish enlightenment. My purpose in this paper has been to call attention to the mentality that may be said to have pre-dated this age of enlightenment, and the different ways in which one very influential philosopher endeavoured to combat it.[48]

Department of Political Science
Concordia University, Montreal

[48] It is a pleasure to acknowledge the assistance I have received from David Weston of the Special Collections department, Glasgow University Library, and Arnott Wilson, formerly of Glasgow University Archives. The Institute for Advanced Studies in the Humanities, University of Edinburgh, and the History of Ideas Unit, Australian National University, provided stimulating and congenial working conditions.

NATURAL LAW AND MORAL REALISM: THE SCOTTISH SYNTHESIS

KNUD HAAKONSSEN

I. INTERPRETING SCOTTISH MORAL PHILOSOPHY

English-language scholarship has recently made a number of salutary efforts to draw connecting lines between Scottish moral thought in the eighteenth century and the history of European natural law theory. The latter is, however, a less than uniform tradition. Even Protestant natural law theory in the century after Hugo Grotius was sufficiently multifarious, that any attempt to use it without differentiation as a key, let alone *the* key, to the moral thought of the Scottish Enlightenment must lead to ungainly trimming.[1] Furthermore, it is only when we attend to the differences and the fundamental debates within modern natural jurisprudence that we shall be able to appreciate how different kinds of natural law could be combined with ideas apparently foreign to the jurisprudential tradition, such as the notions of virtue, character, or quality of personality, which were central to the humanism of neo-republicanism and the evolving culture of politeness.

In some earlier essays I have sketched the way in which the division between a theory of subjective natural rights which must be traced partially to Grotius, and a Pufendorfian theory of natural law and natural duties, finds a kind of extension in Scottish moral thought in the eighteenth century.[2] David Hume's and Adam Smith's theories of justice as a negative virtue, sharply different from and holding cognitive, moral, and political priority over the rest of morality, distance them from the mainstream of moral philosophy among their contemporaries.[3] This division is certainly not in all cases and all respects a simple and neat one,

© Knud Haakonssen 1989

[1] The latest example of this is R. F. Teichgraeber III's stimulating *"Free trade" and moral philosophy* (Durham, NC 1986). See my review in *Albion* 19 (1987), 441–3.

[2] K. Haakonssen, 'Hugo Grotius and the history of political thought', *Political theory* 13 (1985), 239–65; id., 'Natural law and the Scottish Enlightenment', in *Man and nature* 4 (Edmonton 1985), 47–80.

[3] K. Haakonssen, *The science of a legislator* (Cambridge 1981); id., 'John Millar and the science of a legislator', *Juridical review* (June 1985), 41–68.

nor by any means the only one, but it is nevertheless a basic feature of the moral thought of the Scottish Enlightenment.

The mainstream of Scottish moral philosophy in the eighteenth century I take to be a basically cognitivist and realist tradition. It stretches from Francis Hutcheson via Lord Kames, Adam Ferguson, Thomas Reid and the Common Sense philosophers, to Dugald Stewart and his circle; and it forms the philosophical backbone of more popular moralizing by enlightened clergymen and others, such as the group of "moderate literati" recently so well explored.[4] While exhibiting variations in moral psychology, epistemology, and ontology, as well as theology, these thinkers generally claimed that mankind's potential for moral knowledge has an extent and a certainty quite beyond that allowed by Hume and Smith, and they took this to have important political implications. These range from Hutcheson's more or less Harringtonian republicanism, via Reid's eventual resignation in the face of the Utopian implications of his moral thought, to Stewart's historicization of this Utopianism. Just beyond, but with clear connections, lies James Mill's replacement of the march of history with social engineering.[5] In other words, this tradition subscribed to a view of morals which did not set the sorts of limits to the scope of politics which we find at the heart of Hume's and Smith's thinking.

This general line of interpretation labours under two obvious prima-facie difficulties. The present essay is devoted to explaining and disposing of one of these.

The first difficulty consists of the following pair of problems. In seeing Hume's theory of justice in the light of Grotius's theory of rights, I am in effect aligning the former with a theory which, in the seventeenth and early eighteenth centuries, was often assailed as a form of scholastic realism or essentialism—not least by Samuel Pufendorf. At the same time I might be seen to reinforce the puzzlement which has often been expressed over the fact that Hume so studiously avoids the language of rights, a puzzle which may appear to approach paradox when Hume's theory of justice is seen as leading to Smith's explicit theory of rights. While it is not my intention to deal with this cluster of problems here, it will become clear in the sequel that the concept of moral realism is complex, and it would not be surprising if, having used it, we should

---

[4] R. B. Sher, *Church and university in the Scottish Enlightenment: the moderate literati of Edinburgh* (Princeton 1985).

[5] K. Haakonssen, 'Introduction', in Thomas Reid, *Practical ethics*, ed. Haakonssen (Princeton 1989); id., 'From moral philosophy to political economy: the contribution of Dugald Stewart', in *Philosophers of the Scottish Enlightenment'*, ed. V. M. Hope (Edinburgh 1984), 211–32; id., 'The science of a legislator in James Mackintosh's moral philosophy', *History of political thought* 5 (1984), 233–66; id., 'James Mill and Scottish moral philosophy', *Political studies* 33 (1985), 628–41.

decide eventually to discard it, ladder-like, from our historical interpretations.[6] This may lend some flexibility to our understanding of the ontological implications of moral theories such as those of Grotius and Hume. In any case, the connection claimed here is limited[7]—not least because there is a good deal more to Grotius's theory of justice than his theory of rights.[8] Also, the virtual absence of the term 'right' from Hume's writings requires a thorough consideration separate from the present discussion. It may, however, be in place to point out that there is evidence that Hume thought of rights in conventional terms as derivative from a concept of duty; that is to say, he took "rights" in the same basic sense as the Pufendorfian tradition which we will meet below, and this is clearly a concept for which no room could be found in his scheme of morals.[9] Or, to make the point more cautiously, if Hume did have an idea of subjective rights, he may well have thought it unwise to use it in the formulation of his theory of justice because he clearly thought the conflicting, "Pufendorfian", concept of rights to be the established one. As for Smith, I have offered an extensive explanation in *The science of a legislator*.

The other major difficulty I have referred to occurs on the other side of the divide by means of which I try to sort out some main lines in the moral thought of the Scottish Enlightenment, and this is the topic I shall proceed to address. In claiming both that the mainstream of Scottish moral thought was, in our modern terms, cognitivist and realist, and that it was significantly dependent upon a Pufendorfian natural jurisprudence, I must inevitably appear to be combining the incompatible. The heart of Pufendorf's theory is the notion of a law which institutes the moral realm by imposing duties upon agents possessed of free will. By contrast, the central concern of the moral realists is to show that there are moral values independent of any law. The crucial figure in this situation is Francis Hutcheson.

II. NATURAL LAW V. MORAL REALISM IN HUTCHESON

It is incontrovertible that Hutcheson in his published work both presents a front against the theory that morality is dependent upon law

---

[6] For a general defence of such apparent anachronism in the history of ideas, see K. Haakonssen, 'Introduction: Liberal traditions and the history of ideas', in *Traditions of liberalism*, ed. Haakonssen (Sydney 1988), xi–xxi.

[7] Apart from Haakonssen, 'Grotius and the history of political thought', see especially D. Forbes, *Hume's philosophical politics* (Cambridge 1975), chap. 1.

[8] R. Tuck, *Natural rights theories* (Cambridge 1979), chap. 3.

[9] For a brief consideration of this point, see K. Haakonssen, 'Jurisprudence and politics in Adam Smith', in *Traditions of liberalism*, p. 111.

and expounds a system of natural jurisprudence which is largely
derivative from that of Pufendorf. It has, however, been argued with
considerable force that Hutcheson never manages to integrate these two
strands of his work—that he in fact presents two incompatible systems.[10]
The first is that of his early work, published in the 1720s, in which he
developed a moral theory which is realist and cognitivist in character. It
is realist in maintaining that moral judgements have truth-value; that
there are facts about which some moral judgements are true; and that
these facts are the presence of certain qualities in persons, which cannot
be reduced to subjective states of the person who judges. Hutcheson's
theory is thus primarily concerned with qualities in persons, that is to
say, virtues, which he considers to be natural to man. This is combined
with a moral-sense cognitivism; that is, the idea that man is naturally
supplied with a special moral sense which simultaneously approves or
disapproves of, and occasions the apprehension of, moral qualities.
Without committing himself to a doctrine of innate ideas, Hutcheson
thus puts forward a moral theory according to which morals, in the sense
of both sentiments and ideas, come naturally to man.[11]

   This simple nucleus of ideas, around which a fairly elaborate moral
and political theory is built, has a critical edge against a number of what
were then contemporary doctrines, the most important of which are the
following.[12] First, Hutcheson denies that postlapsarian man is inherently sinful, and that all apparent morality can be reduced to a more or
less complicated function of this sinfulness. More particularly, he denies
that man's moral institutions can be understood to arise from the
prescriptions of an avenging God, whom His creatures follow in terror
and in hope. It was exactly this kind of authoritarian voluntarism,
legalism, and egoism which Hutcheson saw as the foundation of the
natural jurisprudence of Pufendorf (and Locke), and which he rejected
in his early works. Yet in his later works on morals Hutcheson put
forward a complete system of natural jurisprudence, which owes a good
deal to Pufendorf and something to Locke. Not only that, but in a series
of Latin textbooks for students he backed this second system of morals
with a logic and a metaphysics which was entirely conventional in its
dependence upon the sort of Augustinianism that was developed within
reformed scholasticism in the Netherlands and Switzerland and
imported into the Glasgow curriculum by Carmichael and others.[13]

   [10] James Moore, 'The two systems of Francis Hutcheson' (the preceding paper in this
collection).
   [11] This summary of Hutcheson's "first system" is not Moore's, but mine.
   [12] Moore, 'Two systems'.
   [13] For Carmichael, see J. Moore and M. Silverthorne, 'Gershom Carmichael and the natural
jurisprudence tradition in eighteenth-century Scotland', in *Wealth and virtue*, ed. I. Hont and
M. Ignatieff (Cambridge 1983), 73–87; id., 'Natural sociability and natural rights in the moral
philosophy of Gerschom Carmichael', in *Philosophers of the Scottish Enlightenment*, 1–12.

According to the proponent of the two-systems thesis it is an error to intepret this "second system" as an integral part of Hutcheson's philosophical writing. While the first system is Hutcheson's serious contribution to philosophy, the second is largely pedagogical in intent; a conventional philosophy suited for the moral breaking in of youth, and one which was acceptable to the academic, civil, and ecclesiastical authorities in Glasgow and in Scotland at the time. The interpretation of Hutcheson presented below is in fact headed this allegedly erroneous way, and we shall thus see whether we need to be quite so rigidly dualistic in our reading of him.

My main concern is with Hutcheson's moral thought, and I argue that it does manage to achieve a basic coherence between the moral realist and the natural law elements. In a companion essay to the present one I have tried to relate Hutcheson's attempted synthesis to a clear precedent, that of Richard Cumberland.[14] On this occasion I am setting Hutcheson against the background of the thinker who is traditionally seen as the main representative of voluntarist natural law, Samuel Pufendorf. However, while acknowledging that Pufendorf in one sense was a voluntarist and that Hutcheson saw him as such, I want to show that one can easily in another sense see the German thinker as a realist. The purpose of this apparently perverse reading is twofold. I want to indicate that the problem situation faced by Hutcheson was volatile and less than clear-cut, and that his synthesis was closer to hand than might otherwise appear; and I want to maintain an awareness that a sharp separation between voluntarist constructivism and realism may eventually prove to be a hindrance rather than a help in the interpretation of early modern moral thought.

III. REALISM AND VOLUNTARISM IN PUFENDORF

We need not concern ourselves with the vexed question of the extent to which Book I of Pufendorf's *De iure naturae et gentium*[15] is to be seen as simply the latest of a long line of nominalist arguments, and the extent to which it is to be understood as an attempt to accommodate moral philosophy to the new modes of natural philosophy.[16] Whatever

---

[14] K. Haakonssen, 'Moral philosophy and natural law: From the Cambridge Platonists to the Scottish Enlightenment', *Political science* 40 (1988), 97–110.

[15] Samuel von Pufendorf, *De iure naturae et gentium libri octo* [1672], 1688 edn. reprinted with introd. by W. Simons (Oxford 1934). In the present context I generally cite Pufendorf, *Of the law of nature and nations . . . Done into English by Basil Kennet . . . To which are . . . added . . . the notes of Mr Barbeyrac translated from his last edition . . . in 1712 . . . Fifth edition* (London 1749).

[16] See, however, H. Denzer, *Moralphilosophie und Naturrecht bei Samuel Pufendorf* (Munich 1972), pp. 53–5. Much of Pufendorf's defence against his critics is directly relevant here; see esp. the Appendix to 'Epistola ad . . . Joh. Adamum Scherzerum', in *Eris Scandica, qua adversus Libros de jure naturali et gentium objecta diluuntur* (Frankfurt 1706), pp. 72ff.

Pufendorf's intentions, it was undoubtedly in the latter light that the book was seen and had its influence.

Stripped to its essentials Pufendorf's case is simple.[17] In itself the natural world is a value-free realm; neither things nor events have value in themselves. Values are not amongst the natural qualities or properties. In order for things or events in nature to acquire value, they have to be related to a norm, and such relating can only be undertaken by beings who can *understand* norms as prescriptions for action, and who can act upon this understanding—i.e. beings of intellect and will, who may or may not follow the prescription and thereby do either right or wrong. Value is thus imposed upon that which in itself is morally neutral, when a rule is prescribed to guide a will. The human will can give such guidance to itself when it enters into pacts and promises and thus undertakes obligations; and one human will can guide another by legislating for it. These human impositions are, however, no more than extensions of the moral world created by the will of God in the law of nature. Without the guidance of natural law, human volition and human action would be natural, non-moral, phenomena like those we find amongst the rest of the animal creation. In words which foreshadow both Hutcheson and Hume, Pufendorf says,

we see Beasts every Day doing such Things without Fault or Sin, in committing which, Men would have been guilty of the highest Wickedness. Yet are not the natural Motions of Men and of Beasts in themselves different, but some Actions of Men are by the Authority of a Law invested with a moral Quality, which does not at all touch or affect the Proceedings of Brutes. (*Law of nature*, I. 2. vi)

This is then illustrated by adultery, theft, murder, and incest, which, he says, "in a natural and absolute Sense", that is, without reference to law, "are altogether indifferent Things".

It is hardly necessary to point out the general similarity between Pufendorf's and Hume's basic idea—and exemplifications—of a natural world in itself amoral, upon which the phenomena of morals *somehow* have to be imposed. The task here is to think through some of the steps in the transition from Pufendorf to Hume, and especially how Pufendorf's particular solution to the problem of the creation of morals, viz. his theological voluntarism, was rejected and replaced. The critical edge of Pufendorf's argument was, of course, against all forms of essentialism in general and what he saw as Grotius's in particular. As he put it,

we do not think it necessary to assert, with some Writers, that there are several Things honest or dishonest of themselves, and antecedent to all Imposition . . .

---

[17] For this paragraph, see Haakonssen, 'Natural law and the Scottish Enlightenment', pp. 56–7. The best general overview of Pufendorf's ethics in English is J. B. Schneewind, 'Pufendorf's place in the history of ethics', *Synthèse* 72 (1987), 123–55.

And truly, as for those who would establish an eternal Rule for Morality of the Actions, without Respect to the Divine Injunction and Constitution, the Result of their Endeavours seems to us to be the joining with God Almighty some coeval extrinsecal Principle, which He was oblig'd to follow, in assigning the *Forms* and *Essences* of Things . . . From all that we have urg'd on this Head, it may appear, that the Sentence which is frequently in the Mouths of most Men, *That the Precepts of natural Law are of eternal Verity*, is so far to be restrain'd and limited, that this Eternity ought to reach no farther than the Imposition and Institution of GOD ALMIGHTY, and the Origin of human Kind. (*Law of nature*, ibid.)[18]

The final point here is perhaps brought out with greater clarity in the early work, the *Elementa*, in which Pufendorf goes out of his way to stress that the voluntarist element is in fact not primarily the law, but human nature. It was in the choice of the latter that God exercised his free will and, once he had chosen human nature as he did, a certain law was naturally fit to provide guidance.[19] The standard charge against voluntarism, that it made God's prescription of natural law appear an arbitrary imposition, was thus misconceived as far as Pufendorf is concerned; and a parallel complaint about the arbitrary choice of human nature would be impossible because it would be an impious questioning of God's motives behind the creation. It is in this context that Pufendorf insists on the Lutheran idea of the complete incommensurability between God and man.[20] We cannot know God's motivation in creating us, but accepting, as we must, creation as empirically given, we can investigate the law appropriate to it, i.e. the law which is natural and certainly not arbitrary. Pufendorf's formulation of the Lutheran notion of the gulf between God and man provides a rationale for treating morals as part of the naturally given world, and thus the subject of empirical investigation without reference to revealed insights. The importance of this lesson for Enlightenment ideas of a science of morals is obvious, even though those who took the lesson did not always understand the true nature of the voluntarism behind it.

Against this background it is obvious that we cannot consider moral phenomena in any sense less real than physical nature in Pufendorf's theory. This is underlined by Pufendorf's nomenclature, according to which the elements of morals are *entia moralia*, by analogy with the *entia naturalia* of the material world. The whole purpose of the first two chapters in Pufendorf's major work is precisely to establish that morals

[18] Concerning Grotius, see also *Law of nature*, II. 3. iv, and 'Apologia pro se et suo libro', *Eris Scandica*, p. 26.

[19] Pufendorf, *Elementorum jurisprudentiae universalis libri duo* [1660], 1672 edn. repr. with introd. by H. Wehberg (Oxford 1931), I. xiii. 14.

[20] Pufendorf, *Elementa*, ibid.

are such an objective feature of God's creation that they can form the object of a properly scientific treatment. The fact that morals are created for man and thus cotemporaneous with humankind does not in itself mean that they are less real than anything else in the finite creation. Pufendorf's concern is the *origin* and *nature* of an objective moral realm, not whether there is one or not. In this sense at least, his discussion with Grotius and others may thus be seen as a discussion *within* moral realism, not about moral realism. Both parties without doubt would subscribe to the following points which, as I have implied earlier, may be taken to constitute moral realism in the sense relevant to the present discussion— which is not to deny other possible senses of the phrase. First, that moral judgements have truth-value; second, that some moral judgements are true, i.e. that there are facts about which moral judgements are true; third, that such facts in no sense of the term are reducible to subjective states, whether cognitive or affective, of the person judging morally about them.[21]

IV. THE DEBATE ABOUT PUFENDORF AS A SETTING FOR HUTCHESON

Although Pufendorf's intention clearly was to show that the reality or objectivity of moral objects could be compatible with a theological voluntarism and thus avoid what he saw as Grotius's essentialism, his solution was, in the eyes of his successors, beset with fundamental difficulties. The most important was that, by appearing to rest morality upon a voluntaristic theory of law, he was seen to run into problems concerning the moral status of this law itself, and his solution to these problems was considered to undermine his assertion of the objective reality of morals because it landed him in egoism. In order to see this, we first have to look at the early reactions to Pufendorf by Leibniz and Carmichael. This ground has, however, been laid out with particular care in recent scholarship, and we can, therefore, traverse it quickly.[22]

The heart of the matter is that Pufendorf was seen to be caught in the following dilemma. If the moral realm is imposed by God's will in the form of natural law, then this will can be authoritative for one of two reasons: either because it is backed by a superior power, or because it has some moral force. If, however, God is authoritative because he can know all and punish all, then the resulting obligation is not moral at all, but

---

[21] The formulation of the first two points is indebted to G. Sayre McCord, 'The many moral realisms', *Southern journal of philosophy* 24 (1986), Supplement, pp. 6–10.

[22] See Moore and Silverthorne, 'Carmichael and the natural jurisprudence tradition' and 'Natural sociability and natural rights'.

merely prudential in character, and Pufendorf has thus hardly advanced beyond Hobbes, as he obviously wanted to do. If alternatively God's authority is moral in character, then we must have moral criteria or principles by means of which we recognize the goodness of God's will and which hence cannot simply be a matter of God's will. As Leibniz sums it up,

if the source of law is the will of a superior and, inversely, a justifying cause of law is necessary in order to have a superior, a circle is created, than which none was ever more manifest.[23]

Pufendorf tries to escape the dilemma in the following way:

It must be acknowledg'd therefore as a certain Truth, That neither Strength, nor any other natural Pre-eminence, is alone sufficient to derive an Obligation on me from another's Will; but that it is farther requisite, I should either have receiv'd some extraordinary Good from him, or should voluntarily have agreed to submit my self to his Direction . . . For, as we naturally yield and give up ourselves to some singular Benefactor, so if it appears that this Benefactor both intends my Good, and can consult it better than I my self am able, and, farther, doth actually claim the Guidance of me, I have no Reason in the World to decline his Government and Sway. Especially if it so happen, that I am beholden to him for my very Being, *Acts* xvii. 24 *&c.* (*Law of nature*, I. 6. xii)

Since natural theology leaves no room for covenants with God, and since covenants in any case derive their moral force from the basic law of nature, Pufendorf's conclusion must of course be that God's will is morally obligatory upon men because of the extraordinary good—not least their very existence as free beings—which God has bestowed upon them.

The trouble with this argument was that it did not appear to evade the second horn of the dilemma which I sketched above, namely the vicious circle alleged by Leibniz—which is, rather, an infinite regress—for it seemed to lay itself open to a legitimate open question, as it were, as to whether each man's own good is a moral good, and what lends it a moral quality. It is precisely this question which was implicitly posed by Pufendorf's successors, and especially by Hutcheson, as we will see below.

That this up to a point is a fair interpretation of Pufendorf becomes much clearer when, in the second Book of the *Law of nature*, he draws a distinction between the foundation of natural law as such and the thence-derived basic law of nature. The former is each man's self-love and concern for himself. The egoistic *foundation* for morals, or natural law,

[23] G. W. Leibniz, 'Opinion on the principles of Pufendorf', in *The political writings of Leibniz*, ed. P. Riley (Cambridge 1972), pp. 73–4. I am here greatly indebted to Moore and Silverthorne, 'Carmichael and the natural jurisprudence tradition', pp. 77–8.

does, however, not imply that the basic law of nature, let alone all morality, is egoistic in character. For from man's egoism and his general weakness and natural needs follows his dependence upon his fellow men and hence the requirement to be sociable—which is the basic law of nature (II. 3. xiii–xv). In other words, the bridge between our own good and that of others, and thus the basis for morals, is our natural weakness. Only when we contemplate the goodness of God in creating us weak and interdependent, as well as egoistic, can we see that this goodness has a moral potential, namely our potential for creating moral institutions to make up for some of these weaknesses.

To a generation which was still shocked by Hobbes, this attempt to confine the effects of the alleged egoistic foundation of morals was less than persuasive; to the following generation, which experienced the outrage of Mandeville, the need to maintain the reality of virtue against egoism as the paramount form of moral scepticism had become *the* basic problem of moral philosophy. Thus Hutcheson is quite prepared to acknowledge that when men act in accordance with Pufendorf's basic law of nature, their behaviour appears moral. The good produced is, however, a natural and not a moral good as long as the obligation to this pattern of behaviour is prudential rather than moral.[24] We shall return to this point below.

Furthermore, the link between a voluntaristic or law-based ethics and egoism had—whether rightly or wrongly—been further strengthened by Locke's account in the second Book of the *Essay*: "Good and Evil . . . are nothing but Pleasure or Pain, or that which occasions, or procures Pleasure or Pain to us. *Morally Good and Evil* then, is only the Conformity or Disagreement of our voluntary Actions to some Law, whereby Good or Evil is drawn on us, from the Will and Power of the Law-maker; which Good and Evil, Pleasure or Pain, attending our observance, or breach of the Law, by the decree of the Law-maker, is that we call *Reward* and *Punishment*."[25]

In the light of this it is hardly surprising that law-based ethics is seen invariably as egoistic by Hutcheson. From the beginning to the end of his moral philosophical *oeuvre* an important feature of his argumentative strategy is to show "that we have Ideas of *Virtue* and *Vice*, abstractly from any *Law, Human* or *Divine*", and that these are presupposed or implied by all "Writers upon opposite Schemes, who deduce all Ideas of *Good* and *Evil* from the *private Advantage* of the *Actor*, or from Relation

---

[24] See e.g. Hutcheson, *An inquiry into the original of our ideas of beauty and virtue*, first edn. (Dublin 1725), p. 251; id., *De naturali hominum socialitate oratio inauguralis* (Glasgow 1730), p. 11. Unless otherwise indicated, I refer always to the first edn. of the *Inquiry*.

[25] John Locke, *An essay concerning humane understanding*, ed. P. H. Nidditch (Oxford 1975), II. xxviii. 5.

to a *Law* and its *Sanctions*, either known from *Reason* or *Revelation"* (*Inquiry*, pp. 249 and 247). Further, that all attempts to reverse this order and make law basic to morals must end with a purely prudential obligation to this law, that is, an egoistic or self-interested foundation for morals, as we see especially in "the definitions of *Puffendorf*, and of *Barbeyrac"*.[26]

The above quotation from Locke brings us to another difficulty which it is reasonable to see as part of the complex of problems that Hutcheson is addressing. Locke is saying that morality falls into the category of complex ideas called relations; morality is a relation of actions to rules or laws (*Essay*, II. xxviii. 6–16). This has its problems, and those are problems which might be seen also to beset Pufendorf's moral theory.

Although Pufendorf, as noted earlier, talks of the furniture of the moral realm as *entities*, he is quite explicit that the similarity with physical things is purely analogical. In stricter metaphysical terms the moral entities are *modi* of the substance, human being (*Law of nature*, I. 1. vi). However, from his whole account it is quite obvious that the only way in which human beings are, as it were, modified by moral entities is that they are subjected to some law and, ultimately, the law of nature: this is the only way these so-called *modi* can be described. This should, though, make it apparent that the basic ontological category in Pufendorf's moral theory is that of *relation*, namely that of the relations between persons and laws, especially the law of nature. Apart from being an obvious inference from the text itself, it would certainly lie near to hand for subsequent thinkers like Hutcheson, who read Pufendorf with an empiricist epistemology in mind.

However, if one subscribes to a Lockean theory of knowledge, as Hutcheson did, and if one takes morals to be a relation between persons and laws, as we have seen Locke do explicitly, and Pufendorf by implication, then one runs into the following difficulty. Both "person" and "law" are in Lockean terms mixed modes, but since mixed modes are made "arbitrarily", the conclusion must be that the relations themselves and thus morals are "arbitrary".[27] It is not part of my present design to discuss Locke's attempt to get round this conclusion.[28] It is possible that he took 'arbitrary' to mean simply *by choice*, but even then the doctrine would have appeared like pure Mandevillian scepticism to Hutcheson's generation.

[26] Hutcheson, *A short introduction to moral philosophy* (Glasgow 1747), pp. 121–2. Cf. *Inquiry*, pp. 251, 254–5; *A system of moral philosophy*, vol. 1 (Glasgow 1755), pp. 264ff.; *An essay on the nature and conduct of the passions and affections, with Illustrations on the moral sense* (London 1728), pp. 229–30.

[27] I am here indebted to W. Leidhold, *Ethik und Politik bei Francis Hutcheson* (Munich 1985), pp. 57–8.

[28] But see Leidhold, pp. 58ff.

We have sufficiently established some of the central elements in a set of problems, against the background of which a moral realism like the one ascribed to Hutcheson by recent commentators makes perfect sense.[29] The relevant problems may be summarized in the following manner. Modern philosophy's criticism of what was seen as scholastic essentialism had made it difficult to see how morality could be a matter of qualities in persons. As far as natural jurisprudence is concerned, this is clearly exemplified by Pufendorf's criticism of Grotius. Nevertheless, Pufendorf's attempted solution was clearly intended to maintain a kind of realist framework, indicated by his language of entities and modes, and the difficulties he ran into must be seen within this framework. It is precisely because they appeared to endanger a realist view of morals that they were perceived as problems. The traditional dilemma facing a voluntarist, law-based ethics was considered fatal. One of its horns appeared to leave morality without any other foundation than, at best, an infinite regress of justification, and this was no foundation at all (except within a mitigated scepticism which seeks no ultimate justifying ground); while the other horn of the dilemma would gore morality by reducing it to mere prudence or egoism.

Furthermore, Carmichael's attempt to resolve this by reducing the basis of morals to a divine injunction of love brought with it problems of a different dimension. For by making love a matter of divine prescription, it made natural theology fundamental to morals, as Carmichael himself strongly emphasizes.[30] It is one of the most important points in Hutcheson that he attempts a reversal of this order of priority, in the sense that some sort of morality is possible without a theological starting-point and that a theological perspective on morality is, so to say, the *completion* of morality.[31] In order to do so he had to show that morality is an empirically ascertainable part of the world and, as we have seen, this excluded the possibility that morals could be relational in character. This threw him back on a renewed attempt to show that morality was a matter of qualities in persons, but empirically ascertainable ones. This is, I submit, the philosophical core of the turn to a language of *virtues* in Scottish moral philosophy.

[29] D. F. Norton, 'Hutcheson's moral sense theory reconsidered', *Dialogue* 13 (1974), 3–23; id., 'Hutcheson on perception and moral perception', *Archiv für Geschichte der Philosophie* 59 (1977), 181–97; id., *David Hume: Common-sense moralist, sceptical metaphysician* (Princeton 1982), chap. 2; id., 'Hutcheson's moral realism', *Journal of the history of philosophy* 23 (1985), 392–418. Also, though more indistinctly, Leidhold, IV, 2. This reading of Hutcheson is controversial; for criticism, see K. Winkler, 'Hutcheson's alleged realism', *Journal of the history of philosophy* 23 (1985), 179–94.

[30] Moore and Silverthorne, 'Carmichael and the natural jurisprudence tradition', p. 78.

[31] The two points are to be found in several places, but see esp. sect. VI of the *Illustrations* (*Essay*, pp. 301ff.) and, for the latter point, *Short introduction*, pp. 101–2.

V. HUTCHESON'S MORAL REALISM AND COGNITIVISM

In the present context there is no reason for going over Hutcheson's efforts to show that disinterested behaviour is an empirical fact, nor for giving a detailed account of his theory of the mental powers by which we judge such behaviour to be moral. This has been done by a succession of scholars with great thoroughness and analytical sharpness, and I have nothing to add to it.[32] All I need to establish for present purposes is that for Hutcheson our putative moral judgements are in fact real judgements; that the putative objects of such judgements are in fact real objects; and that these objects are empirically ascertainable features of human nature. Even on these points I can be brief for, although his perspective is different, the basic work has been done by another recent commentator.[33] The issues can in fact be settled by means of a few central passages from Hutcheson himself.

That we may discern more distinctly the Difference between *moral Perceptions* and others, let us consider, when we taste a pleasant Fruit, we are conscious of Pleasure; when another tastes it, we only conclude or form an Opinion that he enjoys Pleasure; and, abstracting from some previous *Good-Will* or *Anger*, his enjoying this Pleasure is to us a Matter wholly indifferent, raising no new *Sentiment* or *Affection*. But when we are under the Influence of a virtuous Temper, and thereby engaged in virtuous Actions, we are not always conscious of any Pleasure, nor are we only pursuing private Pleasures, as will appear hereafter: 'tis only by *reflex Acts* upon our Temper and Conduct that we enjoy the Delights of Virtue. When also we judge the Temper of another to be virtuous, we do not necessarily imagine him *then* to enjoy Pleasure, tho' we know *Reflection* will give it to him: And farther, our Apprehension of his virtuous Temper raises Sentiments of *Approbation, Esteem* or *Admiration*, and the Affection of *Good-will* toward him. The Quality approved by our moral Sense is conceived to reside in the Person approved, and to be a Perfection and Dignity in him: *Approbation* of another's virtue is not conceived as making the Approver happy, or virtuous, or worthy, tho' 'tis attended with some small Pleasure. Virtue is then called *amiable* or *lovely*, from its raising *Good-will* or *Love* in Spectators toward the Agent; and not from the Agent's perceiving the virtuous Temper to be advantageous to him, or desiring to obtain it under that View. A virtuous Temper is called *good* or *beatifick*, not that it is always attended with Pleasure in the Agent; much less that some small Pleasure attends the

---

[32] Apart from the works of Norton and Leidhold, see J. D. Bishop, *The moral philosophy of Francis Hutcheson* (Ph.D., University of Edinburgh 1977); W. T. Blackstone, *Francis Hutcheson and contemporary ethical theory* (Athens, Ga. 1965); H. Jensen, *Motivation and the moral sense in Francis Hutcheson's ethical theory* (The Hague 1971); B. Peach, 'Introduction', in Hutcheson, *Illustrations on the moral sense*, ed. Peach (Cambridge, Mass. 1971); D. D. Raphael, *The moral sense* (London 1947).

[33] Leidhold, pp. 146–64.

Contemplation of it in the Approver: but from this, that every Spectator is persuaded that the *reflex Acts* of the virtuous Agent upon his own Temper will give him the highest Pleasures. The admired Quality is conceived as the Perfection of the Agent, and such a one as is distinct from the *Pleasure* either in the Agent or the Approver; tho' 'tis a sure Source of Pleasure to the Agent. The Perception of the Approver, tho' attended with Pleasure, plainly represents something quite distinct from this Pleasure; even as the Perception of *external Forms* is attended with Pleasure, and yet represents something distinct from this Pleasure. This may prevent many Cavils upon this Subject.[34]

Hutcheson might well be hopeful that this passage would prevent further cavils, for he could hardly have been more explicit. Moral perception is *not* a subjective affective experience; and moral judgements are thus not simply the expressions of such experiences. Whether we make moral judgements of our own behaviour or that of others, our moral perception and thus our moral judgement is explicitly *representative*, and thus either true or false. Further, moral judgements are emphatically representative of something quite distinct from the pleasures which moral behaviour may and, upon reflection, will occasion in the agent as well as the spectator.

The question is now what this something is, which our moral judgement represents or which makes it true or false. On this point Hutcheson is equally clear. It is love or benevolence which "excites toward the Person in whom we observe it" an "Esteem, or Perception of moral Excellence" (*Inquiry*, p. 108). Benevolence, which is one of the two basic forms of human motivation (self-love being the other), is the quality of human nature which forms the object of moral judgement.

However, for a Lockean theory of knowledge like Hutcheson's, this solution to the problem of moral ontology does give rise to an obvious epistemological problem, viz. how can we know the motivation of other people and thus distinguish genuinely moral behaviour from counterfeits which spring from self-interest?[35] It has rightly been suggested that Hutcheson's intention is that we find the proper object of moral judgement by means of reason. First we identify moral-looking behaviour by calculating the consequences of the action in question in accordance with the well-known greatest happiness principle. Secondly, we try to reconstruct the motivation for such behaviour by drawing on our own experience—a point that was to be of particular interest to Hume and Smith:

We judge of other rational Agents by our selves. The human Nature is a lovely Form; we are all conscious of some morally good Qualitys and Inclinations in

---

[34] This passage is quoted from the fourth edition of the *Inquiry* (1738), pp. 129–31. It was first added in the third edition (1729), pp. 128–30.

[35] I am here and in the following indebted to Leidhold, pp. 155–6.

our selves, how partial and imperfect they may be; we presume the same of every thing in human Form, nay of every living Creature. (*Inquiry*, pp. 131–2)

Finally and more particularly, we seek out any available evidence that the agent may have had to surmount his self-interest in order to behave morally, though, while this is a sufficient reason for judging the motivation to be benevolent, it is not a necessary condition.[36]

Once reason has performed these preparatory tasks, which would bear some comparison with those allotted it by Hume and Smith, the moral sense has as good a chance as we can hope for of forming an adequate perception of the moral quality of the agent concerned. While reason prepares moral judgements by establishing the subject of such judgements, viz. the (likely) motivation to moral behaviour in each particular case, the moral sense perceives the moral quality of this motivation, when it approves or disapproves the motivation; and this perception occasions an idea of the moral quality. This is a so-called "concomitant" idea which constitutes a non-pictorial representation of the quality which is being predicated of the subject of the moral judgement.[37]

VI. THE POLITICAL AMBIGUITY OF HUTCHESON'S MORAL THEORY

From what has been said in the previous section, it should be clear that moral perception, and hence moral judgement, is inherently fallible.[38] This fallibility follows directly from the combination of a Lockean theory of knowledge—in this case, a theory about our knowledge of other

---

[36] See *Inquiry*, p. 171, and Leidhold, pp. 162–3. On the role of reason in Hutcheson's theory of moral judgement, see also Norton's summary in 'Hutcheson's moral realism', pp. 404–5.

[37] Norton's ascription to Hutcheson of a theory of concomitant ideas in moral perception in analogy with those in external perception has caused some controversy. See Winkler, 'Hutcheson's alleged realism', and Leidhold, *Ethik und Politik*, pp. 156–7, note 79. Winkler has been adequately answered by Norton in 'Hutcheson's moral realism', pp. 405–11. The solution I sketch here is a hesitant synthesis of Leidhold and Norton. Leidhold entirely rejects the suggestion of concomitant moral ideas in Hutcheson, but he does so on the basis that Norton in his earlier writings had included in this concept the ideas of agency, motivation, etc., which Leidhold sees as conclusions of reasoning and not as matters of perception at all. I agree that it is hard to understand these as concomitant ideas, and there is little hard evidence that Hutcheson did so. At the same time Norton has provided very strong evidence that Hutcheson did operate with a notion of concomitant moral ideas ('Hutcheson's moral realism', pp. 407–11) and, in the absence of a clear list of these in his text, the most obvious reading seems to me the one indicated here, namely that the ideas of the actual moral qualities (virtue and vice) are concomitant with the moral sense's approval/disapproval of the motivation of which these moral qualities are being predicated.

[38] "In most Cases it is impossible for Men to know how far their Fellows are influenc'd by the one or the other of these Principles", i.e. self-love or benevolence (*Inquiry*, p. 130; cf. p. 171).

minds—with a moral-sense cognitivism and a moral realism according to which the objects of moral judgement are the motives behind moral behaviour.[39]

The fallibility of moral judgement is of crucial importance for our understanding of some basic features of Hutcheson's political theory. First of all, since there is no certain way of settling that any man (in contrast to God) genuinely intends the good of others, there is no natural right in one to rule over others. Such a right has to be constructed by means of the consent of all concerned. Furthermore, it is not only the basis but also the form of civil society which must be shaped by the fallibility of our moral judgement; since we cannot have certainty about other persons' moral judgements, we must rely on our own. As Hutcheson explains, in reference to "the existence, goodness, and providence of God, and all the social duties of life, and the motives to them":

Every rational creature has a right to judge for it self in these matters: and as men must assent according to the evidence that appears to them, and cannot command their own assent in opposition to it, this right is plainly unalienable: it cannot be matter of contract; nor can there be any right of compulsion as to opinions, conveyed to or vested in any magistrate. He can have no right to extort mens sentiments, or to inflict penalties upon their not agreeing to the opinions he thinks just; as such penalties are no evidences to convince the judgement, and can only produce hypocrisy . . . (*System*, vol. 2, p. 311).

Moral fallibility and the consequent necessity of self-judgement constitute the principles of what we may call the restraining aspect of Hutcheson's politics. It is because of them that political power should not be concentrated but, rather, distributed in a Harringtonian balanced system; that there should be a comparatively wide religious toleration, freedom of opinion and of the press, etc.[40]

Hutcheson's moral philosophy is, however, politically Janus-faced. At the same time as his moral fallibilism, which followed from his moral realism, is restrictive upon the exercise of political power, his realism is politically expansive in the following way. Morality is ultimately a

[39] As an aside it may be suggested that this fallibilism concerning moral judgement could be a fruitful point of departure, if we were to seek an understanding of Hume's and Smith's moral ontology. For in order to show how it is that, despite such fallibility, we can have a *common* moral world—a world so common that Hume can maintain that the ordinary person's moral judgement on the whole is *in*fallible—they had to construct a theory of how the objects of fallible moral judgements, i.e. other people's motives, in themselves are shaped by the same kind of preparatory reasoning which enables the observer to judge morally. This was the theory of the search through sympathy for the impartial standpoint.

[40] *System*, vol. 2, pp. 310ff. For this side of Hutcheson's politics, see D. Winch, *Adam Smith's politics* (Cambridge 1978), chap. 3; C. Robbins, ' "When it is that colonies may turn independent" ', *William and Mary quarterly*, 3rd Ser., 11 (1954), 214–51; id., *The eighteenth-century commonwealthman* (Cambridge, Mass. 1959), pp. 185–96. Also Leidhold, chaps. 9–10.

matter not of maximizing happiness, but of doing so intentionally, i.e. with such maximization as the leading motive. This I take to be one of the ways in which a utilitarian moral theory is distinguished from what, drawing on theological language and Hutcheson's own usage,[41] may be called a beatific moral theory; the latter is concerned with the creation of happiness as a consequence of the beatitude of its agent's soul. Consequently, our individual as well as our collective efforts, especially our political and institutional arrangements, must be centrally concerned with the motivation to moral behaviour, or, in other words, with virtue. This is precisely what we find in Hutcheson's politics. Civil society is essentially an institution for the moral improvement of mankind, and it is only limited in this regard to the extent that our moral fallibility, as indicated above, puts such improvement outside our reach. Subject to this restriction, civil society exists not just to maximize happiness, but to inculcate the benevolent or beatific motivation of the citizenry. Thus morality and its extension in religion must be taught, partly by instruction, not least the instruction of public-minded teachers and writers like Hutcheson himself; partly by the practice of participation by the citizens at large in the civil, the military, and the productive life of the commonwealth. In other words, the qualities which form the objects of moral judgements in Hutcheson's realism, far from constituting a timeless, Platonic realm, are historically conditioned in the sense that they can be expanded by suitable institutional arrangements.

VII. NATURAL JURISPRUDENCE IN HUTCHESON'S SYSTEM

(a) *Natural law and the common good*

If Hutcheson's moral theory is basically a theory of virtue, how can he accommodate a system of natural jurisprudence and, especially, a theory of rights, as he clearly attempts to do? We may approach this issue by considering the difficulties which a recent commentator has found in Hutcheson, and in the following passage in particular:

Precepts of the law of nature . . . are deemed immutable and eternal, because some rules, or rather the dispositions which gave origin to them, and in which they are founded, must always tend to the general good, and the contrary to the general detriment, in such a system of creatures as we are. (*System*, vol. 1, p. 273)[42]

---

[41] See the long quotation at pp. 73–4 above.
[42] The passage is misquoted in Leidhold, p. 210.

Hutcheson's supposed difficulties in combining moral sense and natural law are, it has been suggested, particularly evident here, where

> the expressions 'rules' and 'dispositions' appear next to each other: Hutcheson cannot make up his mind whether natural law consists of rules or dispositions. He himself seems rather inclined to interpret them as dispositions. That would, however, make natural law identical with the divinely created natural order, which is subject to immutable and eternal laws of nature. Does the teleological concept of nature in the end turn out to be mechanistic?[43]

Whether or not there is some tension in Hutcheson between a teleological and a mechanical conception of nature, it is hardly to be found here. Hutcheson is not saying that the laws of nature may be seen either as rules or as dispositions, but, rather, that it consists of rules which have their origin and foundation in certain dispositions. These dispositions are our moral abilities, essentially our capacity for benevolent motivation, and the law of nature is "founded" in these because they "must always tend to the general good . . . in such a system of creatures as we are". The reasoning behind this is briefly as follows. Our moral experience will show that individual moral phenomena, i.e. particular moral dispositions as judged by our moral sense, tend towards the general good, namely, towards a moral system of humanity in which the human moral potential is fully realized, i.e. in which happiness is maximized intentionally, or in which all agents are effectively beatific. Our experience of this potential moral system of all humanity will, through a reasoning process analogous to the one which prepares our moral judgement of men, lead us to the conclusion that there is a superior moral motivation behind this system, namely the divine benevolence, which our moral sense will judge in the same way as it judges the moral qualities of men. In this way piety towards God is the completion of our moral life rather than its starting-point, though natural religion of course underwrites our natural moral ability.[44]

We may see the point in a different perspective. Having gained the insight that the moral system of humanity is not simply the aggregate of men's individual moral endeavours, but in itself a moral good because it flows as a whole from God's moral motivation, we morally approve of, i.e. feel an obligation to, the rules which our reason works out to be God's prescriptions for realizing the sytem.[45] In this way the moral sense is the basis for natural law and thus Hutcheson's means of solving the dispute

---

[43] Translated from Leidhold, p. 211.

[44] *Inquiry*, pp. 272–6; *Illustrations*, sect. 6; *Short introduction*, pp. 59–60, 72–7, 100–101, 112; *System*, vol. 1, pp. 69–70, 168ff., 239.

[45] *Short introduction*, p. 112; *System*, vol. 1, pp. 264–5; *Inquiry*, 4th edn., pp. 267–77 (based on the recasting in the second edn.).

between Pufendorf and Leibniz, as he himself points out (*System*, vol. 1, p. 264).

(b) *Natural law and natural rights*

The consequences of seeing natural religion as the connecting link between the moral sense and natural law do, however, go much further. Just as the concept of the common good, which ultimately must be understood in natural religious terms, is the foundation for natural law, so it is from this that natural rights must be derived. We may approach this point in the following, perhaps slightly unusual, way.

Once we have realized that the general good of humanity and its constituent parts are a moral good, in the strict sense that it flows from a motive judged to be morally good by our moral sense, we must reckon with the possibility that goods which are not perceived as morally relevant by the moral sense nevertheless have a moral aspect by being part of God's intention, i.e. part of the common good. The typical and most important example is the pleasure derived from the satisfaction of our various needs. The actions involved here may often be considered morally neutral by the moral sense. Yet the fact that such actions have enough potential satisfaction in them to make them the object of the agent's intention means that they have a prima facie claim to be contributors to the sum of good in God's creation. Further investigation may, of course, reveal this not to be the case, but, in the absence of such evidence, any action which carries with it some pleasure, however modest, must be given some sort of moral position. In this way even actions which to the moral sense appear morally neutral gain a moral status as rights,

as in fact it is for the good of the system that every desire and sense natural to us, even those of the lowest kinds, should be gratified as far as their gratification is consistent with the nobler enjoyments, and in a just subordination to them; there seems a natural notion of *right* to attend them all. (*System*, vol. 1, pp. 254–5; cf. *Short introduction*, pp. 118–20, and *Inquiry*, p. 256)

The inclusion of that which in itself is morally neutral in the moral realm of rights, without its being imposed through law, may also be seen from the following. Rights can, according to Hutcheson, be ascribed to creatures which are incapable of moral motives and which, therefore, cannot possibly be the objects of the moral sense and moral judgement. This applies to animals and to unborn children. Along with the contemporary Danish philosopher, Frederik Christian Eilschow, Hutcheson was the most consistent animal rights theorist of his age, and helped establish a pattern of argument which became commonplace later in the century; he maintained that the capacity of animals for pleasure and pain clearly includes them in the moral community instituted by God, to the extent that men have an obligation to respect their right to the seeking of pleasure and the avoidence of pain, even though animals themselves are incapable of undertaking obligations. Similar reasoning applies to the foetus. (*System*, vol. 1, pp. 309–16; *Short introduction*, pp. 147–9)

The point in approaching Hutcheson's theory of rights in this way is to illustrate how entirely the concept of rights is derivative from the concept of the common good, and hence how wide the former concept is. A person has a natural right to perform any action by which he can best maximize the common good. This test applies not only to actions which are perceived by the moral sense to be morally neutral, but likewise to actions which are judged morally good when seen in isolation. This is the argument with which Hutcheson begins his exposition of rights in both the *System* and the *Short introduction*. "From the constitution of our *moral faculty* . . . we have our notions of *right* and *wrong*, as characters of affections and actions." (*System*, vol. 1, p. 252; cf. *Short introduction*, pp. 109–10, 119.) However, "This is the *rectum*, as distinct from the *jus* . . .: the *jus* ensues upon the *rectum*." (*System*, vol. 1, p. 252, note.) Hutcheson then proceeds to show how the subjective rights, *iura*, "ensue upon" that which is right, *rectum*, when the latter contributes to the common good. (*System*, vol. 1, pp. 253–6; *Short introduction*, pp. 118–20.) Since the common good is enjoined by the law of nature, he can also express the matter by saying that "*rights* as moral qualities, or *faculties*", i.e. *iura*, are "granted by the law of nature" (*Short introduction*, p. 119). This relationship between law and right, apart from being evident from the presentation as a whole, is expressed in a phrase in the original Latin version of the *Short introduction* which is left out in the English translation, "*Ut juri omni respondet lex quaedam, jus illud constituens aut confirmans, ita etiam* obligatio."[46]

In view of this, it seems impossible to see a "Grotian" theory of subjective rights as the foundation for Hutcheson's natural jurisprudence. This is further underlined by the fact that he himself does not see in Grotius a subjective rights theory but, rather, a precursor of his own line of argument:

---

[46] Hutcheson, *Philosophiae moralis institutio compendiaria* [1742], second edn. (Glasgow 1745), p. 126. The phrase '*jus . . . confirmans*' is not rendered in the English version. The deviations between the Latin and the English versions of this work are sufficiently numerous to cast doubt upon the claim that Hutcheson himself was responsible for the translation: see A. Bower, *The history of the University of Edinburgh*, vol. 2 (Edinburgh 1817), p. 340; T. E. Jessop, *A bibliography of David Hume and of Scottish philosophy from Francis Hutcheson to Lord Balfour* (London 1938), p. 145. This claim is anyway highly unlikely in view of the formulation of the 'Advertisement by the translator' in the *Short introduction*.

[Grotius] deduces the notion of right from these two; first, the *initia naturae,* or the natural desires, which do not alone constitute right, till we examine also the other, which is the *convenientia cum natura rationali et sociali.* (*System,* vol. 1, p. 255n.)[47]

For Hutcheson subjective rights, *iura,* are derived from natural law when our spontaneous notions of right action, *rectum,* are trimmed by considerations of the common good, into which natural theology gives us insight:

Thus we have the notion of *rights* as moral qualities, or *faculties,* granted by the law of nature to certain persons. We have already sufficiently explained how these notions of our *rights* arise from that *moral sense* of right and wrong, natural to us previous to any considerations of law or command. But when we have ascended to the notion of a divine natural law, requiring whatever tends to the general good, and containing all these practical dictates of right reason, our definitions of moral qualities may be abridged by referring them to a law; and yet they will be of the same import; if we still remember that the grand aim of the law of nature is the general good of all, and of every part as far as the general interest allows it. (*Short introduction,* pp. 119–20)[48]

(c) *Rights perfect and imperfect*

Once we have focused sharply on this order of justification and, especially, on the primacy of the common good, we can provide some further clarification of Hutcheson's politics. Since the concept of the common good is that of the beatitude of God's creation, it encompasses the whole of human morality, or all the virtues. Consequently all rights the exercise of which contributes to the common good are morally well founded. When some rights are considered to have priority over others, this can only be based upon considerations of what in concrete situations

[47] My denial that Hutcheson is in any strong sense a rights theorist has recently been reinforced by T. Mautner, 'Pufendorf and 18th-century Scottish philosophy', in *Samuel von Pufendorf 1632–1982,* ed. K. A. Modéer (Lund 1986), pp. 125–7. Mautner does, however, deny the Pufendorfian ancestry to this.

[48] The dependence of all *iura* upon the law of nature and thus upon the common good of course extends to property rights. This must be borne in mind when considering the claim that Hutcheson (and Carmichael) is a precursor of Adam Smith in transforming the labour theory of property into "a theory of the natural and moral sentiments" (J. Moore, 'Locke and the Scottish jurists', paper presented to the conference on "Locke and the political thought of the 1680s" sponsored by the Conference for the Study of Political Thought, Folger Shakespeare Library, Washington, DC, March 1980). In a sense this is quite true, but the important point is that this proto-Smithian theory—which in Hutcheson is simply an extension of the general moral sense concept—occurs within the framework of the theory of natural law and the common good. In Smith property rights, like all other subjective rights, are precisely *not* dependent upon a morally comprehensive concept of the common good. For other discussions of this point in Hutcheson, see Teichgraeber, p. 71, and T. A. Horne, 'Moral and economic improvement: Francis Hutcheson on property', *History of political thought* 7 (1986), pp. 122–3.

will contribute most to the common good. Mankind being what it is, this will on the whole mean that the negatively defined rights—rights not to be injured—or perfect rights, have practical priority over the positively defined rights—rights to receive some good—or imperfect rights.

Yet the boundaries between perfect and imperfect rights are not always easily seen. There is a sort of scale or gradual ascent, through several almost insensible steps, from the lowest and weakest claims of humanity to those of higher and more sacred obligation, till we arrive at some imperfect rights so strong that they can scarce be distinguished from the perfect . . . (*Short introduction*, pp. 122–3; cf. *System*, vol. 1, pp. 262–3)

This being so, we cannot use the distinction between perfect and imperfect rights as a boundary-line for the legitimate exercise of political power. Indeed, as indicated above, Hutcheson does in fact charge government with the promotion of a wide field of positive goods, and he does not see claims to perfect rights as a barrier to government intervention.[49]

Just as the framework for the exercise of political power is the concept of the common good, so the latter is the basis for this power. The rationale for the institution of civil society is the promotion of the common good, and political government is the trustee for this. At the same time, Hutcheson is, of course, a well-known contractarian: "all human *Power*, or *Authority*, must consist in *a Right transferr'd to any Person or Council, to dispose of the alienable Rights of others*" (*Inquiry*, 4th edn., p. 294). As we have already seen, this is based upon the fallibility of our judgement of the moral motivation of others. Hutcheson's politics is characterized by a balance between the politically expansive claim to knowledge about the common good and the politically restraining fallibility of our individual moral judgement. The balance is in general achieved by the consoling thought that we can be assured by natural theology that in principle there is no conflict between common good and individual good.

VIII. THE COHERENCE OF HUTCHESON'S THOUGHT

The interpretation of Hutcheson offered here has consequences in a number of areas. By way of conclusion I return to the two topics with which I opened, the coherence of his thought and the overall development of the moral thought of the Scottish Enlightenment.

---

[49] Cf. T. D. Campbell, 'Francis Hutcheson: "father" of the Scottish Enlightenment', in *The origins and nature of the Scottish Enlightenment*, ed. R. H. Campbell and A. S. Skinner (Edinburgh 1982), pp. 176–7.

Hutcheson's moral thought exhibits a basic coherence. By incorporating natural jurisprudence in his moral theory he made a serious attempt to solve the issues which had been brought to a head in the debate about moral scepticism and the clash between a long tradition of moral realism, especially in England, and a renewed voluntarism, especially within natural jurisprudence. Given his premises, the attempt makes sense, nor is there any direct evidence that he was dissatisfied with this particular aspect of his system. Apart from some unspecific dissatisfaction in the later part of his life at his inability to write up a systematic synthesis of his moral thought, his expressed dissatisfaction was with the *Synopsis metaphysicae*, and particularly with the first edition of it, which had been published without his knowledge. Here again we have no evidence of where he saw the deficiencies; he did, however, find it worth while to revise the book and reissue it in a properly authorized version.

In general terms it is not hard to imagine Hutcheson's unhappiness at having to keep his textbooks within a systematics which was directly transferred from the reformed scholastic curriculum and, at least to that extent, there is a division between these textbooks and the rest of his *oeuvre*. However, once we go beyond this to specific doctrines, the lines become blurred. Only a detailed comparison of Hutcheson's Latin texts with their Continental models can reveal the degree of their orthodoxy, but it is worth picking up a couple of central points.

A cornerstone in any version of the sort of Augustinian dualism from which the Latin textbooks are derivative is a strong notion of man's sinfulness and moral incapacity. On this point, however, the most striking feature of the *Synopsis metaphysicae* is an, admittedly poorly formulated, version of the idea of man's natural moral sense, or capacity for moral judgement.[50]

The second point, which has been cited as particularly strong evidence for the orthodoxy of the *Synopsis metaphysicae*, is Hutcheson's adoption of the traditional division between God's communicable and incommunicable attributes: "Some attributes of God, such as omniscience, omnipotence, infinity, were described as 'incommunicable', i.e. were possessed by God alone. Other attributes, such as knowledge, volition, majesty, were described as 'communicable', or common to God and men; provided these men were redeemed from their sinful condition through the mediation of Jesus Christ."[51] The importance of this distinction thus lies in its connection with "the dogma of the Incarnation: that God became man in Jesus Christ while remaining

---

[50] Hutcheson, *Synopsis metaphysicae, ontologiam et pneumatologiam complectens*, second edn. (Glasgow 1744), pp. 53–5.

[51] This and the next quotation are Moore's concise résumé of reformed scholastic doctrine. Hutcheson introduces the distinction in *Synopsis metaphysicae*, pp. 97–8.

God''. This flew in the face of the Arminian theology which Hutcheson taught in his public Sunday lectures, based on Grotius's *The truth of the Christian religion.*

There is no doubt that the introduction of the distinction between God's attributes is a significant concession on Hutcheson's part. Yet the edge of it is completely blunted by the absence in the *Synopsis metaphysicae* of a clear commitment to the Incarnation; without that the distinction becomes trite. It becomes even more innocent when it is not combined with the usual idea of selection of those to whom the communicable attributes are communicated as a sign of their task as moral and civic leaders. Add the notion of man's natural moral ability, and the *Synopsis metaphysicae* begins to look like an Arminian sheep in orthodox wolf's clothes. At least it seems worth pursuing the possibility that a text which, from one point of view, undoubtedly was a major concession to the orthodox moral theology which Hutcheson in general fought, from another point of view is an attempt to empty the latter of some of its distinctive doctrines. Despite or, perhaps, because of the muddled result, it may have contributed to the theological compromises characteristic of that mainstream of Scottish moral thought which Hutcheson's moral theory proper established.

IX. HUTCHESON AND THE DEVELOPMENT OF SCOTTISH MORAL THOUGHT

Just as Hutcheson's moral theology helped set the tone for subsequent Moderatism, so the duality which we found in his politics can be seen as a pointer for the development of Scottish political thought. When the fallibility of moral judgement is weakened by Reid's replacement of the moral sense with Common Sense, we see a tendency to weaken the restraints on political power, resulting eventually in a strong temptation towards the total politics of Utopia. Here traditional social relations, and especially market and property relations, would be replaced by a system of public moral accountancy establishing moral merit as the basis for social standing.[52] If, on the other hand, we raise sceptical questions about the deity of natural religion, as Hume did, then the first casualty is our purported knowledge of this deity's good moral intentions and, hence, the concept of the common good in the morally wide sense adopted by Hutcheson. Once the guarantee of an—in principle—all-encompassing harmony between individual goods has disappeared, the concept of the

---

[52] See Reid's remarkable paper delivered to the Glasgow Literary Society in November 1794, 'Some thoughts on the utopian system', in Reid, *Practical ethics*, sect. XVIII.

common good becomes an empirical and historical one. That is to say, it becomes a question of what sort of common good we can create in human society. The only common good about which we can have some certainty, according to Hume, amounts to a good deal less than it did in Hutcheson, viz. the enforcement of the rules of the negative virtue of justice. Any further common goods are not a matter of the principles of law but of the expediency of politics, and thus, for a philosopher, mostly fit for empirical investigation as they occur in the progress of society. This is the message of Smith's combination of jurisprudence and political economy.

In short, for Hutcheson the whole realm of law, rights, and duties described by natural jurisprudence is dependent upon a collective view of mankind and a concept of the common good. This separates it from the individualistic morality of the moral sense. However, the two are tied together by Hutcheson's theory of natural theology. Once Hume had destroyed the latter, individual moral claims were, unnervingly, without a guarantee of mutual—even if only eventual—harmony. This is an idea which Hume and Smith may well have seen as a possibility in Grotius's theory of subjective rights. At the same time it is very close to the scepticism in morals against which Pufendorf's natural law theory was deployed by writers like Barbeyrac, Carmichael, and Hutcheson. This is worth remembering, when we talk of "the" natural jurisprudence tradition in Scotland.[53]

History of Ideas Unit
Research School of Social Sciences
Australian National University

[53] A major part of this paper was presented to the conference on "The political thought of the Scottish Enlightenment in its European context" (Edinburgh, August 1986), sponsored by the Conference for the Study of Political Thought. The original was written while I was a fellow at the Institute for Advanced Studies in the Humanities, University of Edinburgh. The final version was written while I was a fellow at the Woodrow Wilson International Center for Scholars, Washington, DC. I am indebted to both for their generous support.
 A. C. MacIntyre's *Whose justice? Which rationality?* (Notre Dame 1988) arrived too late for its substantial discussion of Hutcheson and the Scottish Enlightenment to be considered here.

PROFESSORS OF VIRTUE: THE SOCIAL HISTORY OF THE EDINBURGH MORAL PHILOSOPHY CHAIR IN THE EIGHTEENTH CENTURY

RICHARD B. SHER

Thomas de Quincey once observed, with the professorial practice at Edinburgh particularly in mind, that "Moral Philosophy, in the large and popular use of that term by the Scotch, offers so immeasurable an expanse, that two people might easily wander there for a whole life and never happen to meet".[1] Those who have tried to make sense of eighteenth-century academic moral philosophy will be inclined to agree. Elements of what would now be called psychology, religion, epistemology, metaphysics, logic, ethics, jurisprudence, sociology, history, economics, political science, philosophy of history, rhetoric, literary criticism, and more, all found their way into Scottish moral philosophy classes during the age of the Enlightenment. Given the vastness of the field and the disciplinary boundaries separating scholars today, it is no wonder that investigators of this subject often feel like de Quincey's wanderers.[2]

This essay seeks to make a modest contribution towards cultivating more of the land in de Quincey's "expanse" by examining the important roles played by two extra-philosophical factors. One concerns institutional matters, such as the size and number of classes, the ages and backgrounds of students, the language and method of instruction, the manner and amount of remuneration, the ways and means of filling vacant chairs, and the demand and expectations placed upon professors of moral philosophy. Investigation of such matters helps to elucidate the economic, political, and pedagogical incentives and constraints that Scottish moral philosophy professors experienced. The second factor to be considered is ideology, in the broad sense of values and beliefs about

[1] *Testimonials of J. F. Ferrier, B. A. Oxon. . . . now a candidate for the chair of Logic and Metaphysics in the University of Edinburgh. First series* (1856), p. 48.

[2] Despite its limitations, G. Bryson, *Man and society* (Princeton 1945) remains the most comprehensive and perceptive treatment of the intellectual content of Scottish moral philosophy courses.

the organization of social, political, economic, and religious life. The comprehensive nature of the discipline allowed particular professors to express their ideological beliefs about points of special concern to them—James Beattie against the slave trade, Adam Ferguson against standing armies unsupported by militias, Adam Smith for economic liberty, and so on. Beyond these particulars, all eighteenth-century Scottish moral philosophy courses operated within a general ideological framework which was fundamentally Whig-Presbyterian. Professors of this subject were expected to teach natural religion and instil conventional moral and religious principles, as well as respect for the Hanoverian establishment and the "constitution". Conversely, a professor who advocated Jacobite or Jacobin ideals, or moral or religious scepticism, would have raised serious problems.

Here attention will be focused particularly on the interplay of these two extra-philosophical factors during the first century of the chair of moral philosophy at the University of Edinburgh. This chair presents a revealing case study in the social history of Scottish academic moral philosophy. It is well known that it constituted one of the college's major attractions during the last three and a half decades of the eighteenth century, when Adam Ferguson and Dugald Stewart filled their lecture halls with eager pupils and their pockets with lucrative student fees that they collected for their services. But what of the preceding years, when mediocrity or obscurity often prevailed? Of the five persons who occupied the moral philosophy chair from its inception in 1708 until the appointment of Ferguson in 1764—William Law (1708–29), William Scott (1729–34), John Pringle (1734–45), William Cleghorn (1745–54), and James Balfour (1754–64)—none can be said to have made a sufficient name as a moral philosopher to attract significant numbers of students to Edinburgh, and on at least one occasion the chair nearly degenerated into a sinecure. This was at a time when the university was rapidly expanding and self-consciously striving to become a first-rate academic institution, a time, moreover, when the rival chair at Glasgow was occupied by a succession of internationally known thinkers—Gershom Carmichael, Francis Hutcheson, and Adam Smith, as well as Ferguson's professorial contemporary Thomas Reid—who brought a reputation for scholarly excellence to their discipline and their university. The specific questions to be investigated in this essay are: why was the reputation of the Edinburgh chair so unimpressive before 1764, and why did it improve so dramatically after that date?

I

The problems besetting the moral philosophy chair at Edinburgh prior to 1764 have much to do with the fact that the university there was, to a greater degree than most other Scottish universities, under the jurisdiction of the local town council, a self-perpetuating oligarchy of merchants and tradesmen whose interest in philosophical matters was not always evident. At times the magistrates could be persuaded by a "great man", such as the third Duke of Argyll, by a particularly powerful principal, such as William Carstares, or by an influential leader from their own ranks, such as Lord Provost George Drummond, to pursue an enlightened policy in college affairs. At other times, however, they were factious, self-interested, indifferent, narrowly parochial, or generally inefficient as university administrators. Not only were academic appointments often made on the basis of kinship ties and political connections—a common eighteenth-century practice—but, in the area of moral philosophy specifically, preference was sometimes given to undistinguished philosophers with the "right" moral and religious values, occasionally at the expense of a brilliant philosopher like David Hume. It will be shown that these factors, along with the moral philosophy professors' ambiguous status and unusual financial situation, had much to do with the ills that plagued the Edinburgh chair for more than fifty years.

The major academic reorganization which brought the chair of "Pnewmaticks and Morall Philosophy" into being in 1708 provides an example of the town council at its most and least efficient.[3] The fundamental idea behind the reorganization—the establishment of specialized professorships in the arts and sciences in place of the old regenting system—was pedagogically sound and deserving of the accolades it has received from numerous commentators, but the wording of the new regulations was so ambiguous that it is difficult to say exactly what role was intended for the new position. Since the regulations specified that all parts of philosophy were to be taught in the two-year sequence of "Logick and Metaphisick" and "Ethicks and Natural Philosophy" by just two designated professors, the additional professor of "Pnewmaticks and Morall Philosophy" was something of an anomaly: he was to supplement the other two "at such times as the Students are not obliged to be in their Classes", and might, in addition, "have publick Lessons of philosophy in the Common hall where all the students may be present at such times as shall be most convenient".[4] Such wording implies that moral philosophy was originally added to the

---

[3] On the reorganization of 1708, see A. Bower, *The history of the University of Edinburgh*, vol. 1 (Edinburgh 1817), pp. 70–75; A. Grant, *The story of the University of Edinburgh*, vol. 1 (London 1884), pp. 258–64. Pneumatics (or pneumatology) was usually defined as the science of mind, both human and divine.

[4] City Chambers, Council minutes, vol. 39, p. 105 (16 June 1708).

Faculty of Arts to tie up loose ends in the curriculum by means of non-compulsory lectures delivered at odd hours. Yet the regulations also stressed the "great importance" of thorough training in pneumatics and moral philosophy, and gave the professor of that subject a unique financial arrangement which was clearly considered desirable at the time. Each of these points must be briefly addressed in order to understand the early development of the chair.

The tradition of supplementing professors' salaries with student fees has often been praised as an effective means of providing incentive for academic excellence in the Scottish universities of this period. Eighteenth-century commentators noted that wherever such incentives were lacking, such as at Oxford and in a handful of Regius chairs at Edinburgh, professors tended to give up lecturing and regard their chairs as sinecures.[5] Student fees were also popular with the town council because they justified low academic salaries. Since the interests of the council and the college coincided in this matter, it is not surprising that the regulations of 1708 granted the professors of humanity (Latin), Greek, logic and metaphysics, and natural philosophy and ethics, modest salaries of £52 sterling per annum along with the right to collect student fees. Those four professors were assured of respectable enrolments because their classes met at regular hours and were normally taken in a fixed sequence by every arts student.

The ambiguous teaching role of the professor of moral philosophy required a different arrangement. He alone was to be paid an extra £50 in salary with the understanding that no additional fees would be permitted (Bower, vol. 2, pp. 73–4). In the early part of the century, when student fees averaged a guinea or less per class and the entire college had no more than about four hundred students, this state of affairs favoured the professor of moral philosophy. It is probably for this reason that the first two Edinburgh professors of that branch of learning invoked seniority to obtain the moral philosophy chair. As the years passed, however, inflation, the rapid growth of the college, and the increase in real income from student fees that came with rising prosperity, greatly decreased the value of this chair relative to others, so that what had begun as a generous arrangement soon became a less desirable one.[6]

[5] Adam Smith, *An inquiry into the nature and causes of the wealth of nations*, ed. R. H. Campbell and others (Oxford 1979), V.i.f. 4–8; Thomas Reid, 'A statistical account of the University of Glasgow', in *Philosophical works of Thomas Reid*, ed. W. Hamilton, vol. 2 (repr., Hildesheim 1967), p. 733.

[6] On the rapid growth of the university and the intricacies of the fee system, see R. L. Emerson, 'Scottish universities in the eighteenth century, 1690–1800', *Studies on Voltaire and the 18th century* 167 (1977), 453–74; J. B. Morrell, 'The University of Edinburgh in the late eighteenth century: its scientific eminence and academic structure', *Isis* 62 (1971), 158–71. By the second half of the century students could be charged two or three guineas per class, but less

As for the council's insistence on the "great importance" of moral philosophy instruction, it is necessary to keep in mind that in the eighteenth century moral and religious training were considered essential functions of the university. Since university students were boys in their middle teens—frequently as young as twelve or thirteen years old when they initially enrolled and usually about sixteen when they took the moral philosophy class—the university's role was thought to be normative as well as intellectual. The university reflected the values of the presbyterian burghers who governed it and the presbyterian churchmen who served as its administrators and supervised its curriculum with careful scrutiny. If, as Principal Robertson stated publicly at the close of the century, the primary purpose of the university was not only to impart knowledge and train young men for professional careers, but also to instil a "love of religion and virtue" in every student,[7] then moral philosophy lay at the heart of the curriculum. Even as the Church of Scotland grew steadily less rigid during the century, academic moral philosophy was never regarded as a purely secular or "scientific" discipline by magistrates and churchmen. It was also a means of integrating piety, politeness, propriety, and knowledge, with a view to producing learned, genteel, virtuous young men whose religious, social, and political views would prepare them for happiness and success in post-Revolution, post-Union, presbyterian Scotland.

The problem was that in their zeal for morality the town fathers had divided responsibility for teaching it among the new chair-holders without specifying the precise duties of each. So long as the professor of "Ethicks and Natural Philosophy" was officially responsible for teaching the former topic in his class, the professor of moral philosophy performed a supplementary function. But as ethics lost its place in the natural philosophy class during the first half of the century—for reasons and in ways that are not yet clear[8]—the full responsibility for moral instruction fell to the professor of moral philosophy, whose uncertain

---

affluent students and students repeating a class for a second or third time might be allowed to attend for less or gratis. The fact that Ferguson complained of his fee income being cut in half as a result of the financial crisis of 1773–74 indicates the extent to which the system depended in practice upon the general state of the economy.

[7] William Robertson's address on the occasion of the laying of the foundation stone of the new Edinburgh University buildings, 1791, in Henry, Lord Brougham, *Lives of men of letters and science who flourished in the time of George III*, vol. 2 (London 1845), p. 319.

[8] Though this development seems to have taken place early in the century, there are signs that the old pedagogical tradition of treating ethics within an integrated philosophical context did not entirely die out. For example, in 1786 John Bruce, the professor of logic, who had once deputized in the moral philosophy class, published *Elements of the science of ethics, on the principles of natural philosophy* in order to demonstrate that "the method of Natural Philosophy might be applied to [ethics] with success" (p. vii).

teaching status and restricted financial incentive discouraged strenuous exertion. As will be shown, Ferguson's appointment in 1764, and the simultaneous extension of the privilege of collecting fees in the lecture class, did more than anything else to elevate the Edinburgh chair of moral philosophy to an exalted position at "the apex of the whole teaching establishment".[9]

II

The first professor, William Law, illustrates the mixture of didactic moralizing and presbyterian piety that was expected from holders of the chair. Law was the son of an Edinburgh minister and the patron of another presbyterian clergyman, the poet Robert Blair. Blair eulogized him in a long poem which included the following tribute to his teaching:

> Learn'd were thy lectures, noble the design,
> The language *Roman*, and the action fine;
> The heads well rang'd, the inferences clear,
> And strong and solid thy deductions were:
> Thou mark'd the bound'ries out twixt right and wrong,
> And show'd the land-marks as thou went along.
> Plain were thy reasonings, or if perplext
> Thy life was the best comment on thy text.[10]

Coming from the pen of Law's future son-in-law, these lines must be read with caution. But whether accurate or not, they express the idealized vision of what a moral philosophy professor was supposed to do during the first quarter of the eighteenth century. He was to deliver clear, well-organized, sensible lectures in Latin ("the language *Roman*"), which would provide his young students with moral "bound'ries" and "land-marks", and he was to live his life in accordance with the moral, and presumably also religious, principles he taught.

   That Law probably did conform to these ideals is suggested by the comments of another of his students, William Wishart *secundus*, who praised "my great Master Mr. Law" for successfully imparting "both the principles of Natural Religion and Morality and the Truth of the Christian Religion".[11] Similarly, the pious ecclesiastical historian

[9] Grant, *University of Edinburgh*, vol. 1, p. 262. Grant's phrase reflects the typical nineteenth-century view. De Quincey likewise referred to this as "the supreme chair of philosophy" (quoted in *Testimonials*, p. 49).

[10] Robert Blair, *A poem dedicated to the memory of the late learned and eminent Mr. William Law, professor of philosophy in the University of Edinburgh* (Edinburgh 1728). Ten years later Blair married Law's daughter Isabella.

[11] Transcription from shorthand quoted from an unpublished paper by M. A. Stewart, 'David Hume and the Edinburgh chair'; this is to be incorporated in a forthcoming book, provisionally titled *Warmth in the cause of virtue*, under contract with Edinburgh University Press.

Robert Wodrow described Law in his memoirs as a "person of great learning and solidity in his business, and much gravity and piety", and "a great ornament to that university". It would be a pity, wrote Wodrow, if some part of Law's lectures were not published, particularly his "excellent prelections upon Naturall Religion".[12] But nothing of Law's ever was published, and no lecture notes are known to have survived from his two decades as professor of moral philosophy.[13]

As little is known about the teaching of his successor, William Scott. Like Law, Scott was a former regent who claimed the moral philosophy chair on grounds of seniority. He was a Scottish patriot who had zealously defended the disastrous Darien scheme in 1699, and eight years later published a Latin compendium of Grotius, indicating some familiarity with at least one of the fields of inquiry classed under moral philosophy.[14] Apart from this, Scott's qualifications for teaching this subject were not impressive when he succeeded Law in 1729. He was then more than sixty years old and had been confined to the chair of Greek for more than twenty years (Grant, vol. 2, p. 336). In the latter capacity he had infuriated Wodrow and other Calvinists by supposedly declaring the epics of Homer to be second only to the New Testament as works of religion. Upon hearing that Scott would be invoking seniority to switch from Greek to moral philosophy, Wodrow remarked that "if all be true, or the half, that is said of Mr S, he does not seem qualifyed to be a Professor of that part of learning" (*Analecta*, vol. 4, p. 23). Similar concerns may have motivated former Provost Thomas Fenton's unsuccessful attempt to block Scott's transfer at a town council meeting on 12 February 1729. Though Fenton did not attack Scott personally, his anger was clearly directed against regulations that made it possible for an ill-qualified former regent to claim the relatively lucrative chair.[15]

[12] Robert Wodrow, *Analecta*, vol. 4 (Edinburgh 1843), p. 23. That Law's teaching was known and well regarded in England is suggested by a letter from Christopher Taylor to William Carstares, 5 March 1706: EUL, Dk.1.1², fol. 50.

[13] Several sets of Latin dictates and one set of graduation theses from Law's classes have been preserved, but they date from his tenure as a regent and are not necessarily representative of his specialized moral philosophy teaching in the period after 1708. Christine Shepherd has studied these sources and discovered a strong Ciceronian and Aristotelian influence (*De officiis* and *Nicomachean ethics* were his texts), coupled with respect for Pufendorf and a noticeable religious orientation (e.g. true happiness is defined as contemplation of God, and Hobbes is condemned for atheism).

[14] C. P. Finlayson, 'Edinburgh University and the Darien scheme', *Scottish historical review* 34 (1955), 97–102. According to Finlayson (p. 100), Scott states early in the compendium that he lectured on Grotius extensively while a regent and that he considered philosophy and the classics to be preparatory studies for more useful subjects such as the law of nations.

[15] In particular, Fenton took issue with (1) the 1708 resolution enabling regents then in office to transfer later to other vacant philosophy chairs without a public competition, and (2) the arrangement that provided the professor of moral philosophy with a greater salary than other philosophy professors. On these grounds he objected against any professor of ethics being appointed "untill the Councill as Patrons and masters of the Colledge make a visitation to the Colledge in order effectually to reform the many abuses and Irregularitys that have so notourly

There is no reason to believe that once in office Scott did anything to dispel Wodrow's and Fenton's fears.

Scott's undistinguished tenure was all the more embarrassing to the town fathers of Edinburgh because it coincided with the beginnings of the brilliant career of Francis Hutcheson at Glasgow. In almost every conceivable sense Hutcheson was the embodiment of what a professor of moral philosophy was supposed to be. Having established an international reputation in the late 1720s with two works on moral-sense philosophy, *An inquiry into the original of our ideas of beauty and virtue* (1725) and *An essay on the nature and conduct of the passions and affections* (1728), he narrowly defeated Frederick Carmichael, son of the deceased incumbent, in December 1729, and came to Glasgow University from his native Ireland the following year. Learned and liberal-minded, Hutcheson was a firm Whig in politics, a moderate presbyterian in religion, and a dedicated moralist in the class-room. He immediately set about establishing and enforcing "rules, catalogues, exact hours, etc." for his classes, which attracted large numbers of English, Irish, and Scottish students.[16]

In the traditional, "internalist" historiography of Scottish philosophy, Hutcheson's major contribution was his formulation of the concept of the moral sense, particularly as it was developed in his youthful treatises of the 1720s. The great bulk of philosophical scholarship on Hutcheson deals with this subject in a highly technical manner. Yet from 1730 until his death in 1746, Hutcheson devoted nearly all his philosophical energies to didactic, systematic, and primarily pedagogical activities and writings which greatly transcended moral-sense philosophy, most notably his Latin *Compend* of moral philosophy (1742, 2nd edn. 1745),[17] and posthumous *System of moral philosophy* (1755). Besides following the earlier treatises by employing the doctrine of the moral sense in the "Stoick" cause of virtue for its own sake, drawing upon Shaftesbury and opposing the supposed selfish systems of Hobbes and Mandeville, these later writings followed Cicero's *De officiis* in insisting upon the importance of right action in "the external duties of life", even

Crept in and there publickly practised to the Dishonour of the Councill and Discouradgement of Learning" (Council minutes, vol. 52, p. 191).

There is circumstantial evidence that Scott was in declining health and had opted for the moral philosophy chair as a less arduous position (EUL, MS. Dc 1.4¹, fol. 121). On Scott's death in 1735 his ageing successor in the Greek chair, Colin Drummond, also tried, apparently from pecuniary motives, to make the same transfer (EUL, MS. La. II. 236).

[16] Wodrow, *Analecta*, vol. 4, pp. 190–91; W. R. Scott, *Francis Hutcheson* (Cambridge 1900), chaps. 3–4.

[17] I follow the posthumous English translation, which appeared under the title *A short introduction to moral philosophy* in 1747. Hutcheson observed in the Preface that this work was "for your use who study at Universities, and not for the learned".

if those duties would be classified from a Stoic point of view as *"things indifferent*, neither morally good nor evil" (*Short introduction*, p. iii).[18] Much of Hutcheson's course consisted of prelections on rights and duties with practical applications in "real life" situations—the nature of contracts and property; the duties of husbands and wives, parents and children, masters and servants; the need to avoid what Leechman in his Preface to the *System* called "fashionable vices and follies in the upper part of the world"; and the laws of war.

In treating these and other topics Hutcheson drew heavily upon modern natural-law writers to whom he paid tribute, including Grotius, Pufendorf, Barbeyrac, and his own predecessor Carmichael. Yet in the Preface to *A short introduction* he had the natural-law writers in mind when he commented that "the method and order which pleased me most is pretty different from what has of late prevailed" in moral philosophy compends. Hutcheson was too eclectic to be confined to the natural-jurisprudence mould in the manner of Carmichael.[19] Another idiom to which he was attracted was that of Harrington and the classical republican tradition, particularly in its eighteenth-century "real Whig" or commonwealthman manifestation. In this mode he is to be found recommending a militia in place of a standing army and a mixed government in place of a simple one, as well as proposing a thoroughly republican vision of Utopia (*System*, vol. 2, pp. 259–66, 323–7).[20] There was a further debt owed to Locke and other Whig writers in regard to the social contract and the right of resistance, a debt acknowledged in the Preface to *A short introduction*. Hutcheson's Whig ideas of civil and religious liberty were so persuasively presented in the class-room that, according to Leechman, no student ever left the course "without

[18] Hutcheson's intimate friend and biographer William Leechman observed that his lectures "were not confined to high speculations, and the peculiarities of a scheme, but frequently descended to common life". See the biographical Preface to Hutcheson's *System of moral philosophy*, vol. 1 (Glasgow 1755), p. xxxiv. Leechman's biography carries more weight than such accounts normally do because of Hutcheson's pronouncements on their close friendship and similar viewpoints, notably in his letters to Thomas Drennan (GUL, MS. Gen. 1018). On 15 June 1741, for example, Hutcheson wrote of "one of my Scotch Intimates, who sees all I do, Mr Leechman" (ibid., item 8).

[19] On Carmichael see J. Moore and M. Silverthorne, 'Natural sociability and natural rights in the moral philosophy of Gerschom Carmichael', in *Philosophers of the Scottish Enlightenment*, ed. V. M. Hope (Edinburgh 1984), 1–12; id., 'Gershom Carmichael and the natural jurisprudence tradition in eighteenth-century Scotland', in *Wealth and virtue*, ed. I. Hont and M. Ignatieff (Cambridge 1983), 73–87. There is some dispute about the nature and extent of Hutcheson's contacts with Carmichael, but in 1808 James Wodrow, recalling his days as a student in Hutcheson's class, told the Earl of Buchan that "Hutcheson his [i.e. Carmichael's] Scholar & Successor frequently spoke of him to us, with esteem gratitude & affection" (Mitchell Library, MS Baillie 32225, fol. 47). On the relationship between their philosophies, see James Moore's paper in this volume.

[20] See D. Winch, *Adam Smith's politics* (Cambridge 1978), chap. 3; C. Robbins, *The eighteenth-century commonwealthman* (Cambridge, Mass. 1959), chap. 6, esp. pp. 185–96.

favourable notions of that side of the question which he espoused and defended" (*System*, vol. 1, pp. xxxv–vi). One such student recalled that "By his Lectures on Government, he revived the principles & spirit of Whigism in this part of the kingdom, and infused them into the minds of his Scholars so deeply, that scarcely one of them disserted them afterwards".[21] Hutcheson also spoke the language of empirical science: he wished, as he stated in the opening sentence of his *System*, to discover the "laws of nature" by means of empirical "observations and conclusions". And then there was Hutcheson the presbyterian moralist, teaching the principles of natural religion, comparing the lessons of moral philosophy to those found in the New Testament, advocating laws against "direct Atheism", advising his students to proceed from his compend to the ancient classics and then to "yet purer fountains, *the holy Scriptures* which alone give to sinful mortals any sure hopes of an happy immortality", and stating—in an extraordinary and totally overlooked passage that might have been written by any good Calvinist divine of his day—that "we are spirits carrying about with us frail decaying putrifying carcases; that as yesterday were embryoes, and shall in a few days be earth and bones" (*Short introduction*, p. iv; *System*, vol. 1, p. 228; vol. 2, pp. 313, 378).[22]

The grand "farrago" of philosophical ideas and practical teachings that made up Hutcheson's so-called "system"[23] was the fountainhead of most Scottish academic moral philosophy during the second half of the eighteenth century.[24] It was not always consistent, either in the ideals it espoused or in the idioms it employed, but it was remarkably wide-

---

[21] James Wodrow to the Earl of Buchan, 4 May 1808: Mitchell Library, MS Baillie 32225, fols. 59–60.

[22] In *A vindication of Mr. Hutcheson from the calumnious aspersions of a late pamphlet* ([Glasgow] 1738), several of Hutcheson's students offered this defence of their master's classroom teachings against charges made by a strict Calvinist critic: "He never said there was any Salvation to any of fallen Mankind, except by the Merits of Christ, but often said, he saw no Proof, that none could reap the Benefit of his Merits, but those who actually knew him." (p. 15.)

[23] Like Montesquieu's *Spirit of the laws*, Hutcheson's *System* was written over a long period in a generally unsystematic fashion. In a discussion of the manuscript in the letter to Drennan cited at n. 18 above, Hutcheson observed that he was "Adding confusedly to a confused Book all valuable Remarks in a Farrago, to refresh my Memory in my class Lectures on the several Subjects". In his perceptive paper earlier in this collection, James Moore has suggested that the *System*'s lack of coherence was the necessary result of attempting to combine two distinct bodies of Hutcheson's writings: the "public" philosophy in his Dublin treatises of the 1720s and "a parallel academic philosophy" in the Latin textbooks he published for students at Glasgow during the 1740s. It is worth noting, however, that the work's lack of coherence is not limited to clashes between the early "public" and later "pedagogical" traditions, and that, as the passage quoted above suggests, the *System* was itself largely pedagogical and didactic.

[24] P. B. Wood in the next essay in this volume shows that academic moral philosophy in Aberdeen tended to have a stronger metaphysical component than was the case elsewhere in Scotland and may have been more heavily influenced by George Turnbull than by Hutcheson. But as Wood acknowledges, there is much evidence of fervent moral teaching in Turnbull's work.

ranging, thoroughly moralistic, and full of sound Whig-Presbyterian values and sensible moral advice. People are equipped with a faculty for appreciating benevolence; slavery and torture are bad; Providence and religious tolerance are good; servants are to receive humane treatment from their masters; contracts are to be honoured; liberty is to be cherished. When certain controversial matters were discussed, such as whether suicide or lying can ever be justified, the professor was careful "to represent what is said on both Sides, in a fair and just Light", leaving the students themselves to make up their own minds (*Vindication of Mr. Hutcheson*, pp. 9, 11). The idea was not so much to produce expert philosophers as polite, virtuous, thoughtful, well-rounded, liberal Christian gentlemen with Whiggish sentiments. Beyond this, Hutcheson aimed at the establishment of a truly virtuous society, in which the well-known goal of the greatest happiness for the greatest number would be achieved through the intentionally or self-consciously moral actions of the citizenry.[25]

Hutcheson's teaching methods were crucially important for achieving these ends. As his modern biographer remarked, Hutcheson was above all else "a teacher who *preached* Philosophy" (Scott, p. 65; cf. 286). His avowed intention was "to direct men to that course of action which tends most effectually to promote their greatest happiness and perfection" (*System*, vol. 1, p. 1). Hutcheson shattered the tradition of reading dry, scholastic, Latin lectures by delivering instead lively, extemporaneous discourses in English while pacing back and forth in front of the class, and his moralizing mission was probably one reason for this change.[26] The success of his teaching method is indicated by his widespread fame and popularity as a teacher. Alexander Carlyle, who attended the moral philosophy class "with great satisfaction and improvement" in 1743 and

---

[25] In the preceding essay, Knud Haakonssen distinguished between a "utilitarian" moral theory which views the maximization of happiness as its end, and a "beatific" moral theory like Hutcheson's which seeks the same end but insists that it be achieved through the moral goodness or "beatitude" of each agent. This distinction is useful for appreciating the difference between the Hutchesonian tradition of academic moral philosophy and the utilitarian tradition represented by Bentham.

[26] Hutcheson "was the first who introduced the custom of lecturing in English into [Glasgow] university", wrote his former student James Wodrow. Recording this in the biographical preface to William Leechman's *Sermons* (London 1789), Wodrow went on to describe how Hutcheson "lectured, to appearance, *extempore*, walked up and down his class-room, and spoke with an animation of countenance, voice, and gesture, which instantly went to the heart" (vol. 1, p. 28). Further evidence appears in letters written by Wodrow and another former student, Samuel Kenrick, in 1808 (Mitchell Library, MS. Baillie 32225, fols. 53, 55), where among other details Kenrick recalled that "Profsr. Hutcheson was I believe the first who introduced lecturing in English in that University. We know it had not reached the Logic Class in our time when the formal & venerable Mess: John Loudon used in solemn peripatetic step to illustrate his own mysterious Compend, and the still more metaphysical subtleties of De Vries."

1744, remarked that the professor "raised the attention of his hearers at all times; and when the subject led him to explain and enforce the moral virtues and duties, he displayed a fervent and persuasive eloquence which was irresistible".[27] Leechman remarked that when Hutcheson employed his oratorical skills to portray the beauty and dignity of virtue, his students "were charmed with the lovely forms, and panted *to be* what they beheld" (*System*, vol. 1, pp. xxxii–iii). The anonymous Calvinist who attacked Hutcheson's teaching in 1738 described the great difficulty of resisting the powerful current of the lectures and lamented "the vast Number of Proselytes you have made" and "the quick Progress your Principles are daily making" among prospective clergymen and others.[28] For Hutcheson, a presbyterian minister and staunch Whig, the discipline of moral philosophy fulfilled a didactic function for which a vibrant, vernacular mode of academic "preaching" was highly appropriate.

Along with Colin MacLaurin's *Account of Sir Isaac Newton's philosophical discoveries* (1748), which celebrated the triumph of Newtonian science among the learned throughout Great Britain, Hutcheson's *System of moral philosophy* was a book with enormous significance for understanding the prevailing outlook in mid-eighteenth-century Scotland. Both books reflected the views of their progressive Scottish Whig-Presbyterian authors as well as the hundreds of people, English and Scottish, whose names appeared on their impressive subscription lists. Among the more than four hundred individuals who subscribed to Hutcheson's *System* were numerous Scottish men of letters, lawyers, judges, baronets, peers, professors, and clergymen of all ages. They included Adam Smith, Lord Kames, William Cullen, Sir David Dalrymple, Robert Wallace, John Stevenson, Thomas Reid, Alexander Wedderburn, Lord Milton, Lord Minto, William Mure of Caldwell, the Earl of Glasgow, and the Earl of Selkirk (who purchased twelve sets). Among them also were two future Edinburgh professors of moral philosophy: James Balfour of Pilrig and the "Rev. Adam Ferguson, A.M.". In publicly expressing their support for Hutcheson's "system", these and other subscribers were not committing themselves to the notion of "moral sense" or any other specific philosophical doctrine. Rather, they were making a statement on

---

[27] *The autobiography of Dr. Alexander Carlyle of Inveresk, 1722–1805*, ed. J. H. Burton, new edn. (London 1910), p. 78. Carlyle also corroborates Wodrow's claims that Hutcheson lectured without notes while moving around the front of the class-room.

[28] "I was almost carried down the Stream, and my Feet had well nigh slipt", said this author of the two sessions of Hutcheson's lectures he attended. (*Shaftsbury's ghost conjur'd: or, A letter to Mr. Francis Hutcheson, professor of moral philosophy in the University of Glasgow. Wherein several gross and dangerous errors, vented by him in the course of his teaching, are brought to light, and refuted* ([Glasgow] 1738), pp. 4–5.)

behalf of Hutcheson's "farrago" of moral philosophy as a didactic, pious, scientific, liberal, Whiggish, humane, character-building, academic discipline which was to be taught in a lively and forceful manner. The book's publisher, Hutcheson's disciple Robert Foulis, was well aware of the work's significance, for as it was being printed he wrote to a friend: "I look upon this as a capital work for promoting the cause of virtue, accompanied with just notions of government and Liberty."[29]

Hutcheson's achievement at Glasgow during the 1730s and 1740s set a new standard for moral philosophy teaching. It made a strong impression on the members of the Edinburgh town council, who would twice try unsuccessfully to woo Hutcheson to their college shortly before his death. Meanwhile, when ailing and elderly William Scott requested that young John Pringle, an aspiring physician, be hired as his teaching assistant, the council seized the opportunity to reform the Edinburgh position so as to ensure Hutchesonian diligence and piety. Pringle was required to demonstrate his competence as a moral philosopher and orator at a public trial.[30] The council insisted that "punctual attendance shall be given at least by one of them" (thereby suggesting that punctual attendance had not previously been the rule) and that both men follow teaching regulations set down by the council.[31] The Lord Provost had then taken the unprecedented action of asking the Senatus Academicus to formulate official "regulations for teaching Pneumaticks and Moral Philosophy". At a meeting of 19 February 1734, the Senatus accordingly named Principal James Smith and six professors "as a Committee to prepare regulations for that purpose, and to report to the University".

Six days later the committee presented its report, and "after some reasoning and amendments" the following set of regulations was approved:

The University meeting having at the desire of my Lord Provost taken into Consideration what shall be the regulations under which the Professour of Pneumaticks and moral Philosophy shall be oblig'd to teach in that profession did aggree by a majority on these following

1st He shall teach the Pneumaticks, that is, the being and perfections of the one true God, the nature of Angels and the Soul of man, with the duties of natural religion to which rational Creatures are bound towards the Supreme being.

2ly He shall teach Moral Philosophy.

3ly Every Munday he shall praelect upon the truth of the Christian religion.

[29] *Notices and documents illustrative of the literary history of Glasgow, during the greater part of last century* (Glasgow 1831), p. 21.

[30] EUL, Senatus minutes, vol. 1, 10 Jan. and 19 Feb. 1734.

[31] Council minutes, vol. 55, p. 38 (20 Feb. 1734). On 8 January Scott had written to the council that poor health prevented him from continuing to teach his class.

4ly He shall have prelection for an hour betwixt the hours of ten and eleven in the forenoon within the Colledge five days of the week to all who shall think fit to hear him, and this for six months, to wit from the first of Novr to the first of May next ensuing.

5ly For securing the attendance and engaging the attention of his Schollars, all Students in any of the classes of the Colledge who shall attend upon his lessons shall for the first year of their attendance be inroll'd in a Catalogue and examin'd by him at least once a week.

6ly If any book from which he shall teach shall contain any thing contrary to the Scriptures or the Confession of faith or to good manners, he shall confute the Same to prevent the youth's being corrupted with errour or immorality.

7ly Dr John Pringle being at present named to that Profession as asistant to Mr Scot, if his busyness as a Physician shall at any time hereafter so increase as to hinder him from discharging aright the office of a Professour of the University, in that case he shall be obligged to give over either his practise of medecine or his profession in the University, and this rule shall hold as to all Professours of that part of learning in time coming mutatis mutandis.

8ly If he shall see fit to give private lessons for which he shall take fees, it shall be free for him to doe so at any hour and place different from these of his publick prelections, and in that case the faculty shall have power to dispense with such hours of his publick teaching as they shall see fit. (Senatus minutes, 25 Feb. 1734)

By prohibiting professors from spending too much time on outside occupations, permitting them to accept student fees in their private classes, ordering them to enrol first-year pupils in a "Catalogue", and requiring them to give daily lectures on moral philosophy (including natural religion and pneumatics) at a fixed time and place, weekly lectures on the truth of Christianity, and frequent student examinations in a class running a full six months, these regulations were apparently designed to prevent any further deterioration of the chair. They were also intended to ensure that students would receive a sufficient dose of religious instruction along with their Pufendorf and Cicero, or at the very least that nothing taught in the class-room would be inconsistent with the Bible, the Westminster Confession, or "good manners". Like Hutcheson, who also lectured five days a week on moral philosophy (including natural religion) and once a week on the "truth and excellency of Christianity", in addition to his thrice-weekly private class on ancient ethics (*System*, vol. 1, p. xxxvi), the people who formulated and instituted these regulations viewed moral philosophy as a didactic discipline with an important social function. Their emphasis was at least as much on the word 'moral' as the word 'philosophy'.

Towards the end of 1734 the Senatus Academicus voted to reintroduce annual public examinations in the philosophy curriculum and to add moral philosophy to the philosophy classes subject to that requirement.[32] In retrospect, however, it appears that the council and Senatus did not go far enough in their efforts at reform in 1734. Although attendance records and weekly and annual examinations, if enforced, may have helped to maintain the interest of those students who elected to take the class, moral philosophy remained, at least officially, an optional part of the curriculum until 1738, when the Senatus declared it and mathematics to be official requirements for an arts degree.[33] A more serious problem concerned financial arrangements. Though the right to collect student fees in "private" classes may have provided additional incentive to excel in the class-room,[34] such fees were still prohibited where they mattered most—in the potentially large lecture class that met five mornings a week at ten o'clock. Thus the regulations of 1734 did not remove the danger that the moral philosophy chair would lapse into a virtual sinecure, as it nearly did in the years to come.

As Scott's assistant and eventual successor, Pringle seems to have begun his tenure by taking the regulations of 1734 quite seriously.[35] He lectured from early November to early May, first on pneumatics and natural theology and then on "ethics or Moral Philosophy", using Cicero, Marcus Aurelius, Pufendorf, and Bacon as his main sources for the latter. The sole surviving sample of his teaching, a set of student notes from 1741, reveals strong commitments to Cicero, Stoicism, and Christianity.[36] A warm Whig in politics, Pringle covered "the origins and principles of Civil Government" by treating ancient Greece and

[32] EUL, Senatus minutes, vol. 1, 8 Nov. 1734.

[33] Senatus minutes, vol. 1, 30 Nov. 1738. (This reference courtesy of Roger Emerson.) Most arts students at Edinburgh did not take a formal degree during the eighteenth century, but most did follow a prescribed sequence of courses which was a good deal less flexible than some commentators have claimed.

[34] It is not known, however, whether any Edinburgh professor of moral philosophy ever offered a private class during the eighteenth century. This situation contrasts with the one at Glasgow, where Hutcheson, Craigie, Smith, and Reid are all known to have given private classes or "colleges" on particular subjects of interest to them.

[35] On Pringle's class see Robert Henderson's account in the *Scots magazine* 3 (Aug. 1741), 371–4; John Erskine, 'The agency of God in human greatness', in *Discourses preached on several occasions*, 2nd edn., vol. 1 (Edinburgh 1801), pp. 266–7; Bower, *University of Edinburgh*, vol. 2, pp. 288–91; Andrew Kippis, 'Life of Sir John Pringle', in Pringle's *Six discourses* (London 1783), pp. vi–vii; *DNB*, vol. 16, p. 387.

[36] In his lecture of 13 March 1741, for example, Pringle spoke of the close connection between the study of nature and the scriptures and argued that the sentiments of the Stoics "are far from being a disgrace to Xianity" ('Lectures from Cicero by Dr John Pringle Professor of Morall Philosophy att Edinr': EUL, MS. Gen. 74D, fol. 59). If, as seems likely, the rest of the writings in this student notebook are also drawn from lectures or assigned readings in Pringle's class, then there was much in that class to satisfy the religious component in the teaching regulations of 1734. See especially 'Argument for the Xian Religion' (fols. 90–94), 'A Lecture upon the 1st Epistle of Paul to the Corinth:' (fols. 129–46), and 'A Scheme of Naturall Religion' (fols. 147–80). For commentary on the 'Lectures on Cicero' and related topics, see J. C. Stewart-Robertson, 'Cicero among the shadows: Scottish prelections of virtue and duty', *Rivista critica di storia della filosofia* (1983), 25–49.

Rome as well as the rise of modern European political establishments. Students regularly wrote essays in both Latin and English, which were delivered in public sessions attended by Principal Wishart, and private discussion sessions were held with deserving pupils. Accounts by former students were generally positive about Pringle's lecturing; as a teacher he appears to have represented a vast improvement over Scott. But his true love was medicine, and though "an aggreeable lecturer" and competent Latinist he was apparently "no great master" of moral philosophy.[37] He never published on the subject, and as far as we know did not draw any students to Edinburgh University for their studies. As his medical career began to thrive during the early 1740s, Pringle devoted less and less time to his academic chair, which he nevertheless sought to retain by means of paid substitutes, in direct violation of the regulations of 1734. In March 1745 the town council finally succeeded in getting him to resign after three years' absence.[38] During that time the class was entrusted to two young presbyterian probationers (licensed preachers who were not yet ordained) with academic ambitions, William Cleghorn and George Muirhead.

It was during Pringle's tenure as professor of moral philosophy that Hume published his *Treatise of human nature* (1739–40), which constituted an implicit challenge to the Hutchesonian mode of academic moral philosophy. While Book III ('Of morals') was being readied for publication, Hume sent portions of the manuscript to Hutcheson for comment and criticism. Judging from Hume's surviving letters, it is clear that one of Hutcheson's chief objections was that this book "wants a certain Warmth in the Cause of Virtue" (HL i. 32). This characterization Hume not only admitted but defended, clarifying his design in a revealing metaphor:

There are different ways of examining the Mind as well as the Body. One may consider it either as an Anatomist or as a Painter; either to discover its most secret Springs & Principles or to describe the Grace & Beauty of its Actions. *I imagine it impossible to conjoin these two Views.* . . . Any warm Sentiment of Morals, I am afraid, wou'd have the Air of Declamation amidst abstract Reasonings, & wou'd be esteem'd contrary to good Taste. (HL i. 32–3, emphasis added)

Here was the crux of the difference between Hume's and Hutcheson's approaches to the discipline—the one "abstract" and coolly analytical,

---

[37] Carlyle, *Autobiography*, p. 55. Carlyle complained that Pringle devoted so much class time to the works of Bacon that students received too little training in the fundamentals of moral philosophy. Noting that Pringle published an important medical article in 1742, D. W. Singer has claimed that Pringle's appointment to the moral philosophy chair "cannot have interfered with his medical practice" ('Sir John Pringle and his circle', *Annals of science* 6 (1949), p. 131).

[38] Fuller details are contained in Stewart (above, n. 11).

the other warm and didactic. Hutcheson's own scientific model for moral philosophy was not anatomy but curative medicine. "Let not philosophy rest in speculation," he advised students; "let it be a medicine for the disorders of the soul." (*Short introduction*, p. iv.) Though Hume did not deny that the metaphysician might ultimately be as helpful to the moralist as the anatomist to the painter, he insisted that the two characters be kept distinct. He wondered if Hutcheson were not being "a little too delicate" concerning points of prudence. "Except a Man be in Orders, or be immediatly concern'd in the Instruction of Youth, I do not think his Character depends upon his philosophical Speculations, as the World is now model'd." (HL i. 34)

Five years later, however, when he attempted to become personally "concern'd in the Instruction of Youth" by competing for Pringle's decaying position at Edinburgh, Hume learned to his regret that the *Treatise* had indeed stamped his character as an enemy of virtue. Among those who opposed his candidacy were Principal Wishart, most of the ministers of Edinburgh, and, to Hume's embarrassment and dismay, Hutcheson and Leechman of Glasgow. "What can be the Meaning of this Conduct in that celebrated & benevolent Moralist, I cannot imagine", Hume commented with characteristic naïveté upon hearing that Hutcheson considered him "a very unfit Person for such an Office" (HL i. 58). He does not seem to have realized how far and how fundamentally his "anatomical" approach to moral philosophy was at variance with the preachy, moralizing style of Hutcheson and his followers.

Hume's pride would have suffered a further blow had he been privy to the list of candidates whom Hutcheson had privately recommended in the name of "zeal for promoting virtue & literature". Writing to Lord Minto in July 1744, Hutcheson first explained why he himself was not interested in the Edinburgh chair (advanced age and poor health) and then named seven individuals—Thomas Craigie, Robert Trail, Robert Pollock, James Moor, William Rouet, William Cleghorn, and George Muirhead—whom he considered qualified.[39] All seven were bright young men who would eventually secure positions in Scottish universities. Two of them (Cleghorn and Muirhead) had experience teaching moral philosophy as Pringle's substitutes, and another (Craigie) would perform competently as the holder of the Glasgow chair for a short

[39] Hutcheson to Lord Minto, 4 July 1744: NLS, MS. 11004, fol. 57. In spite of Hutcheson's refusal, the council formally conferred the position on him the following April, at which time he again refused it. The ministers of Edinburgh on this occasion strongly supported Hutcheson's candidacy, notwithstanding some concern about their not being formally consulted before the offer was made.

period after Hutcheson's death.[40] Two (Muirhead and Moor) had signed their names to the previously mentioned *Vindication* produced by Hutcheson's "scholars" in 1738, and four years later Moor had collaborated with Hutcheson on an annotated translation of Marcus Aurelius. In obvious contrast to Hume, however, none of these seven men had yet produced, or ever would produce, a single publication of their own in the field for which they were being recommended. If Hutcheson's list of suitable candidates revealed a common pattern, beyond the fact that most of them came from the Glasgow region with which he was most familiar, it was the possession of sound Whig-Presbyterian credentials.[41] This was the unspoken ideological component in the terms 'virtue' and 'morality' as those words were used by Hutcheson and other members of the academic and ecclesiastical establishment in mid-eighteenth-century Scotland. When judged by such ideological standards, the religiously and politically "impartial" Hume must have seemed a thoroughly unacceptable candidate, not only because the *Treatise* exposed him to charges of "Scepticism, Heterodoxy, & other hard Names" (HL i. 59), but also because he displayed none of that "zeal for promoting virtue" which Hutcheson valued so highly. Though the appearance of Hume's *Essays, moral and political* in 1741 and 1742 showed a lighter, less abstruse side of Hume than the *Treatise*, the anti-clericalism and political scepticism in some of the essays would have done no good for his academic campaign.

It was therefore quite naïve of Hume to suppose that by adding to the end of the *Treatise* a brief 'Conclusion' about the usefulness of the anatomist to the painter, and the subservience of "the most abstract speculations concerning human nature" to "practical morality", he should have been able "to keep on good Terms even with the strictest & most rigid" (T. 620–21; HL i. 37). Hume well knew that a distinguishing feature of the Scottish political context at this time was the strict correspondence of religious and political parties.[42] When Hutcheson

[40] Craigie's efforts to emulate Hutcheson's style, by lecturing "without Papers, following in a great measure H's plan", but without his predecessor's animation and success, are described in a letter from James Wodrow to the Earl of Buchan, of June 1808: Mitchell Library, MS. Baillie 32225, fol. 49.

[41] Five of the seven whom Hutcheson recommended were either probationers or ministers in the Church of Scotland and a sixth (Rouet) was a son and grandson of presbyterian ministers. On the strong Whig principles of the remaining figure, Moor, during the Jacobite rebellion of 1745, see the account by W. J. Duncan in *Notices and documents illustrative of the literary history of Glasgow*, p. 129.

[42] "Our political and religious divisions in this country have been, since the *revolution*, regularly correspondent to each other. The PRESBYTERIANS were all WHIGS, without exception: Those who favoured *episcopacy*, of the opposite party." (Hume, *Essays, moral, political and literary*, ed. E. F. Miller (Indianapolis 1985), p. 615.) The passage appeared in early editions of 'Of the parties of Great Britain'. Perhaps the transformation of political terminology since the 1740s made the note seem dated. In 1770 Hume cut out the entire footnote in which it appeared, having in 1758 already indicated at this point that he was reconsidering some of his historical judgements in the light of further work on his *History*.

charged that Book Three of the *Treatise* lacked "Warmth in the Cause of Virtue", he probably had in mind political ideology as well as ethics. The two sections dealing with the measures and objects of allegiance (Part II, sections ix and x) would have been very unsatisfactory to a firm Whig like Hutcheson. True, the right of resistance was admitted in extreme circumstances (T. 552), and there was a passing nod to the legitimacy of the "Glorious" Revolution (T. 563–4). But the contract theory of government was eliminated (soon to be demolished), and the thrust of Hume's theory of allegiance was the heterodox notion that "time and custom give authority to all forms of government, and all successions of princes" (T. 566).[43] In an age when insurrectionary Jacobitism was still very much alive, could Hume seriously have expected to obtain a chair of moral philosophy with such sceptical political opinions?

The story of Hume's unsuccessful bid for the Edinburgh chair in 1744–45 was first subjected to a detailed investigation by Ernest Mossner and John Price. Their account looked at the affair from the point of view of political interest and influence.[44] In so doing it offered an interesting and original interpretation, centring on the claim that Hume lost the chair because the council was at this time controlled by the "Squadrone" Whig faction rather than by members of the "Argathelian" Whig faction who supported Hume. The competition was therefore a political contest in a narrow sense. This interpretation, like Mossner's pioneering biography of Hume, broke new ground by viewing Hume's career in terms of extra-philosophical factors. But this interpretation was so closely focused on one particular factor that it lost sight of all others. Above all, it ignored institutional and ideological considerations that must be taken into account along with narrowly political ones.

When this is done, and when archival sources are utilized to a greater extent than previously, the whole affair takes on a different appearance. It is quite true that the Argathelian and Squadrone factions then vying for control of Edinburgh were narrowly political in outlook and generally unconcerned with philosophical and ideological questions. There is no reason to doubt Mossner's contention that Squadrone manager Thomas Hay "viewed the election in a purely political light". Yet the affair was not so simple as the correspondence of a one-dimensional politician like Hay would suggest. Factional rivalries cannot explain why Wishart, who owed his office to the Duke of Argyll, led the almost fanatical opposition to the Argathelian candidate, Hume, and became so preoccupied with the matter that he revived old dreams of

---

[43] Cf. D. Forbes, 'Sceptical whiggism, commerce, and liberty', in *Essays on Adam Smith*, ed. A. S. Skinner and T. Wilson (Oxford 1975), p. 181.

[44] E. C. Mossner and J. V. Price, Introduction to *A letter from a gentleman to his friend in Edinburgh* [1745] (Edinburgh 1967), pp. vii–xxv.

winning the chair himself. Nor can they explain the opposition to Hume's candidacy from such enlightened presbyterian professors as Hutcheson and Leechman. Nor can they explain why the ministers of Edinburgh voted Hume down by an overwhelming margin (12 to 3) in mid-May 1745. For these clergymen and academics, Hume's philosophical acumen and factional attachments were a good deal less important than his lack of moral fervour and his political and religious scepticism. Indeed, Wishart's passionate concern with the danger Hume represented drove him to adopt a thoroughly reactionary position which called for the return of Latin as the language of instruction and a redefinition of the moral philosophy chair as "a Professorship of Divinity". Though ultimate responsibility for filling academic chairs at Edinburgh rested with the town council, the authority of the clergy was still such that Hume lost the support of his primary patron, the Argathelian magistrate John Coutts, once the ministers of Edinburgh passed their formal judgement or *avisamentum* against him.[45] As it turned out, Hume was defeated not by the council for narrowly political reasons, as Mossner and Price have contended, but rather by the Whig-Presbyterian clerical and academic establishment for moral, religious, and ideological reasons.[46]

The successful candidate, Cleghorn, owed his appointment to a variety of factors. His family ties to Robert and Gavin Hamilton—Edinburgh minister and presiding magistrate, respectively, at the time of the election—were apparently of great service to him. So was the fact that he had been teaching the class successfully since the early 1740s as Pringle's primary substitute.[47] He had fewer enemies than Wishart and, as Mossner and Price have demonstrated, he was supported by the Tweeddale or Squadrone faction which happened to be dominant at this time. But all these assets would have been insufficient if Cleghorn had not also held acceptable views in religion and politics and possessed a suitably didactic, moralistic conception of the function of moral philosophy.

If one were to examine surviving student lecture notes from Cleghorn's course in terms of traditional notions of philosophical "schools", one might conclude that he was less like Hutcheson than

[45] No one disputed the right of the clergy to pass judgement on the council's nominees for academic chairs, but by the middle of the eighteenth century there was disagreement about whether this *avisamentum* was to be taken as advice or a binding veto. See the letter on Hume's candidacy in the *London chronicle* 40 (5–7 Nov. 1776), p. 444.

[46] I have drawn on the excellent account of this affair in Stewart (above, n. 11), to which I am particularly indebted for information about Wishart's role.

[47] William Adam, whose family knew Cleghorn well, stated that Cleghorn had won the moral philosophy chair because he "had so distinguished himself" as Pringle's substitute (W. Adam, Preface to *Two short essays on the study of history and on general reading . . . the gift of a grandfather* (Blair Adam 1836), p. v).

Hume was. On the issue of the foundation of morals, for example, Cleghorn seems to have looked to reason rather than sense or sentiment.[48] Had this issue been a matter of pressing concern to Hutcheson, he might have recommended Hume, who was closer to his own position on this matter. In his letter to Minto, however, Hutcheson omitted Hume and praised Cleghorn, whom he scarcely knew, as "a very acute man from some few days conversation". Among the attributes which probably contributed to Hutcheson's positive assessment of Cleghorn was the overall similarity of their ideological, moral, and religious outlooks. Both Hutcheson and Cleghorn were trained for the ministry; both were apparently members of the Revolution Club, which met at Edinburgh to sing Whig songs and express patriotic sentiments; and both were committed to moral instruction as a didactic enterprise.[49] As the following passage from the later part of his dictates demonstrates, Cleghorn was well aware that class-room instruction in moral philosophy had an essentially pedagogical function which made it quite different from scholarly philosophical investigations:

I hope you are sufficiently aware that the intention of an academical course such as this is not to give any full representation of things; for this would neither be possible considering the shortness of our time nor would it be the most proper course as it would be leaving too little to your selves. The design of this course is to set you a thinking by your selves, to cut out a channel as it were for the streams of your own thoughts to flow in, and is of great consequence for promoting your industry and instruction. So a course of this kind is like the chart of a country where one has a general idea of the coastings, high ways, cities, remarkable places etc. by the assistance of which he may travel thro' it with the greater ease safety and pleasure. Hence I have insisted at greatest length on the principles and ordannences for when these are thoroughly understood most of the other difficulties will disappear. (Cleghorn dictates, Dc 3.6, fol. 327)

Hutcheson would have approved of these words, as Cleghorn approved of Hutcheson's teaching methods. In a discussion of ethics and politics, for example, Cleghorn disagreed with Hutcheson on particular points but told his students that "the compend of Mr Hutcheson is an excellent treatise on this subject and will be of great use to you" (fol. 343). On the other hand, the fact that Hutcheson is known to have admired Hume's

---

[48] Cleghorn dictates: EUL, MS. Dc 3.3, fols. 219–23. Here, as elsewhere in his lectures, Cleghorn explicitly takes issue with "the late Mr Hutcheson" on philosophical points such as the idea of the moral sense.

[49] 'List of the Members of the Revolution Club at Edinburgh': EUL, MS. Dc 8.37. It seems likely that the Francis Hutcheson whose name appears in this list is the famous philosopher, though this is not certain. On Cleghorn's moral and political teachings, respectively, see Stewart-Robertson, 'Cicero among the shadows', and D. Nobbs, 'Political ideas of William Cleghorn, Hume's academic rival', *Journal of the history of ideas* 26 (1965), 575–86, both of which draw upon the dictates from Cleghorn's 1746–47 session.

philosophical genius[50] suggests that the omission of Hume's name from his recommended candidates stemmed from his doubts and fears about the extent of Hume's commitment to the political, religious, and moral values that Hutcheson held dear.

The importance of political ideology in the contest is illustrated by an anecdote attributed to the Episcopalian-Jacobite classicist Thomas Ruddiman. Cleghorn had been the proper choice for the appointment, Ruddiman is supposed to have quipped, because a deist like Cleghorn might some day become a Christian, whereas a Jacobite like Hume could not possibly become a Whig (Grant, vol. 2, p. 338). Hume, of course, was not really a Jacobite, just as Cleghorn, a licensed probationer, was almost certainly no deist. But Hume and his patron, John Coutts, were thought by some zealous Whig-Presbyterians of the day to be untrustworthy. In this light it is significant that when the Forty-Five broke out scarcely two months after Cleghorn's appointment, the professor of moral philosophy was, according to Carlyle and John Home, respectively, "very fiery" and "one of the most zealous" in his support of the Hanoverians, whereas his former rival's support for the government was decidedly more restrained.[51]

Owing, perhaps, to his poor health and a premature death at age thirty-six, Cleghorn appears never to have published a scholarly work or to have achieved eminence as a moral philosopher. Extant dictates from his class provide modest support for Adam's depiction of Cleghorn as "a man of superior genius and of great learning", and Hugh Cleghorn was told by "many eminent men" that his uncle's lectures "were universally esteemed & . . . attended by Men of all Ages & the most Liberal Professions".[52] Yet for a capable man who dominated moral philosophy teaching at Edinburgh, as substitute and professor, for more than a decade during the fertile years of the mid-eighteenth century, Cleghorn appears to have exerted little lasting influence on anyone except Adam Ferguson. An imaginary dialogue by Ferguson hints that it was Cleghorn who provided him with his "first Draughts of Moral

---

[50] I. S. Ross, 'Hutcheson on Hume's *Treatise*: an unnoticed letter', *Journal of the history of philosophy* 4 (1966), 69–72.

[51] Carlyle, *Autobiography*, p. 131; John Home, *The history of the rebellion in the year 1745*, in *The works of John Home*, ed. H. Mackenzie, vol. 2 (Edinburgh 1822), p. 54; E. C. Mossner, *Life of David Hume*, 2nd edn. (Oxford 1980), chap. 14. From an examination of the correspondence of Cleghorn's nephew Hugh with Principal John Lee in 1836 (NLS, MS. 3441, fols. 84–5, 122–3), Dr Stewart and I have discovered that during his tenure in the chair Cleghorn published a conservative Whig pamphlet, perhaps with the title or subtitle 'Address to some Gentlemen immediately after the Rebellion'. If it can be located, this pamphlet should reveal more about Cleghorn's political and ideological beliefs at this time.

[52] Adam, p. v; Hugh Cleghorn to Lee, 13 March 1836: NLS, MS. 3441, fol. 84.

Science".[53] Ferguson presumably attended Cleghorn's class some time between 1742 and 1745, when the former was a divinity student and the latter a substitute instructor. The nature and full extent of his debt to Cleghorn will probably never be known, but one suspects that among other things Cleghorn helped to nurture Ferguson's commitments to the defence of the Whig-Presbyterian establishment in Scotland and the practice of a didactic, moralistic style of teaching. Respect between teacher and pupil was apparently mutual, for in later years Ferguson related "with much emotion" Cleghorn's dying words: "I can only say of you, as Hamlet did of Fortinbras, *He has my dying voice.*"[54]

Unfortunately for Ferguson, Cleghorn's dying voice was not strong enough to win the chair for him at this time. While Cleghorn lay on his deathbed in August 1754, his uncle Gavin Hamilton is said to have arranged his resignation in order to push through the election of Hamilton's brother-in-law, James Balfour of Pilrig.[55] Balfour was a landed gentleman, advocate, devout presbyterian, and Revolution Club member with remarkably extensive kinship ties within the Whig-Presbyterian world of mid-eighteenth-century Scottish clergymen and professors. His several sisters married respectively Dr Robert Whytt of the university medical faculty; the surgeon James Russel, who was Ferguson's first cousin and would later occupy the chair of natural philosophy; the Rev. William Leechman of Glasgow University; the Rev. Patrick Wodrow, son of the previously mentioned memorialist and historian Robert Wodrow; and the influential bookseller and magistrate Gavin Hamilton, who was also a cousin on his mother's side. Through the Hamilton connection—which was further strengthened by the publishing partnership between Gavin Hamilton and James Balfour's brother John (himself a member of the town council in 1754)—Balfour

[53] E. C. Mossner, 'Adam Ferguson's dialogue on a Highland jaunt with Robert Adam, William Cleghorn, David Hume, and William Wilkie', in *Restoration and eighteenth-century literature: essays in honour of Alan Dugald McKillop*, ed. C. Camden (Chicago 1963), p. 301.

[54] John Lee, 'Adam Ferguson', *Supplement to the 4th, 5th, and 6th editions of the Encyclopaedia Britannica*, vol. 4 (London 1824), p. 241. See also Hugh Cleghorn to Lee, 13 March 1836: NLS, MS. 3441, fol. 84: "I got many anecdotes concerning [Cleghorn] from our friend Dr. A. Ferguson who retained to the last the most affectionate remembrance of his Talents & his Virtues."

[55] In the letter cited in the previous note, Hugh Cleghorn wrote: "He was Urged to resign his Office a very short time before his death, to secure its Succession to Mr. Balfour, who commanded a Majority of the Patrons by the Influence of his Brother in Law Baillie Hamilton, who was also the Brother of my grandmother. By a private Bargain Mr Balfour also got the Lectures of my Uncle for the trifling sum of £100 though I believe he never availed himself of them." Warren McDougall has informed me that correspondence in the Saltoun Papers (NLS) demonstrates involvement by Lord Milton and the Argathelian interest in the Cleghorn-Balfour arrangement. For example, on 20 August 1754—shortly before Cleghorn's death and eight days before Balfour's appointment—Milton received a letter from his agent William Alston stating that "Professor Cleghorn cannot live long, so that Mr. Balfour's Prospect is very near".

was related to Gavin's clerical brothers Robert, who was professor of divinity, and Gilbert, who was minister of a nearby parish, as well as to their sister's son William Cleghorn. Gavin Hamilton and his siblings were the children of William Hamilton, a former professor of divinity at Edinburgh, and briefly principal, who had trained Leechman's circle of progressive presbyterian clergymen. Finally, Balfour's uncle on his father's side was the Rev. Neil MacVicar, a Highlander who became minister of one of Edinburgh's churches and dared to preach a patriotic Hanoverian sermon while Bonnie Prince Charlie's forces were occupying the town during the Forty-Five.[56]

With family connections like these it is no wonder that James Balfour won the moral philosophy chair. But Balfour was also the author of a critique of Hume's moral philosophy, which his family's publishing firm issued anonymously in 1753. Like his predecessor, Balfour defended reason against the sentimental theory of morals propounded by Shaftesbury, Hutcheson, and Hume.[57] The main thrust of the *Delineation*, however, was directed against Hume alone, with Hutcheson appearing as an ally rather than an opponent. Branding Hume an Epicurean, Balfour took issue with his reduction of virtue to "utility" or "humanity . . . in the observer" (pp. 123, 144). His aim was to show that the key to virtue lies in humanity in the *actor*, which is to say, benevolence, and that virtue so defined "is our truest happiness" (p. 7). Addressing the problem of a potential conflict between self-love and virtue, Balfour contended that "it is religion alone, that, by uniting duty and happiness, can forever bind self-love to the interests of virtue" (p. 162). Religion is "a natural and universal principle" and there is an "indissoluble connexion betwixt religion and virtue" (pp. 164, 205).

Hume's reaction to Balfour's *Delineation* was characteristic of *le bon David*. Not knowing (or affecting not to know) the identity of the author, he nevertheless sent a letter in care of the publisher in which he all but expressed thanks for the criticisms levelled against his second *Enquiry*. Acknowledging fundamental points of disagreement between them, Hume called for friendship between them all the same, as in "the happy times, when Atticus and Cassius the Epicureans, Cicero the Academic, and Brutus the Stoic, could, all of them, live in unreserved friendship together, and were insensible to all those distinctions, except so far as

---

[56] Barbara Balfour-Melville, *The Balfours of Pilrig* (Edinburgh 1907). Gavin Hamilton was also one of Edinburgh's fiercest Whigs during the Forty-Five, and when Charles's forces entered the city he was supposedly forced to "flee for his life" (p. 106).

[57] James Balfour, *A delineation of the nature and obligations of morality, with reflexions upon Mr Hume's book, entitled, An inquiry concerning the principles of morals* [1753], 2nd edn. (Edinburgh 1763), esp. 'Appendix concerning the office of reason in morals, and the superiority of that principle to sentiment', 208–40. On the professional relationship between Hume and Balfour around this time see J. V. Price's note in *Etudes anglaises* 41 (1988), 185–7.

they furnished agreeable matter to discourse and conversation" (HL i. 173). In a polite but cool reply which maintained his anonymity, Balfour accepted this principle of intellectual tolerance up to a point but noted the inadequacy of Hume's philosophy "for all the purposes of life".[58] Such a philosophy, he charged, was "not powerful enough to govern the generality of mankind. As virtue is a matter of the greatest importance to us, and yet its obligation is often contested, to me it appears reasonable to support it by every proper Principle, and when all are united they have often enough to do." Towards the end of the letter Balfour criticized Hume for having "turned your Thoughts too much inward upon your own Particular Temper; and been less attentive to the condition of the great Bulk of Mankind". The issue once again was chiefly a matter of differing values and objectives. For a confirmed and somewhat self-righteous moralist like Balfour, the proper function of moral philosophy was not to pose disturbing questions or formulate perplexing paradoxes about the human intellect on the basis of introspective—and therefore idiosyncratic—evidence, but to spread just principles of religion and virtue among "the great Bulk of Mankind".

As a professor of moral philosophy Balfour carried his opposition to Hume into the class-room. Each academic session is said to have concluded with six lectures directed against the errors in Hume's philosophy.[59] Some of this class-room material is supposed to have found its way into Balfour's *Philosophical essays* (1768), a work that prompted Hume to quip that the author "woud fain, I see, be candid, and civil, as in his other Book; if his Zeal for the House of the Lord woud permit him" (HL ii. 185). This remark is hard to fathom, since the *Philosophical essays* was written in the same politely critical tone as Balfour's other books and the previously mentioned letter to Hume. There was a good deal of religion in it, to be sure: claims that the gist of Plato's admirable philosophy could be found in the Old Testament; praise for the biblical account of Creation; and frequent allusions to the critical role of God and Providence in providing the foundations of virtue, liberty, and knowledge. There was still more religion in the concluding essay in Balfour's last book, *Philosophical dissertations* (1782), which one hostile reviewer called "a faithful picture of his mind" that "confirms the unenvied obscurity of his life".[60]

But Balfour freely admitted the "acuteness" of Hume ("this very subtile author", he calls him in *Philosophical essays*, p. 37), and was not all that uncivil in his attacks on him. 'Persistent' would perhaps be a better word. Besides the view that the foundation of morality was to be

---

[58] Balfour to Hume, [March 1753], in Balfour-Melville, pp. 113–16.
[59] Thomas Somerville, *My own life and times, 1741–1814* (Edinburgh 1861), p. 17.
[60] *The European magazine and London review* 3 (Jan. 1783), p. 40.

found in reason rather than sentiment, the overriding theme of Balfour's writings against Hume was that the latter's philosophy was dangerously sceptical because it was rooted in an egoistic methodology—the same point emphasized in his letter to Hume of 1753. When such a methodology is employed, "we are apt to ascribe a kind of infallibility to our own understanding, and to place the rash conclusions of our own reason in direct opposition to the common sense of mankind" (*Philosophical dissertations*, p. v). Balfour's solution to Hume's alleged "Pyrrhonism" was a modest, probabilistic epistemology which sounded suspiciously like Hume's own concept of "mitigated scepticism". Being unwilling, however, to surrender to his adversary the hallowed ground of "modesty, caution, and reserve", Balfour refused to recognize the similarity of their positions, and in one of his least civil moments he denounced Hume's concept of "mitigated scepticism" as "a palpable piece of sophistry" (*Philosophical essays*, pp. 44–5).

Balfour's published attacks on Hume's scepticism and the necessitarianism of Lord Kames (another popular target of strict Presbyterians) attracted little attention in Britain.[61] But as undistinguished as was Balfour's career as a writer on moral philosophy, it was considerably more successful than his feeble efforts as a teacher of that subject. The previously cited review of the *Philosophical dissertations* reported that Balfour performed even worse as a professor than he had done in an earlier job as sheriff depute: "As Professor of Moral Philosophy in the University of Edinburgh, he was still, if possible, less meritorious. He could not reflect himself, and the transcriptions from printed books, which composed his lectures, were ill chosen, and without either usefulness or propriety." The memoirs of Thomas Somerville, who attended Balfour's class in the late 1750s, confirm that he was an ineffective and dull lecturer whose classes were but sparsely attended. When not stalking Hume or Kames, Balfour either read straightforward lectures on Pufendorf or did not lecture at all. "No [student] fees were paid", Somerville noted. "The professorship was considered, indeed, a sinecure office, and did not call forth the exertions of the teacher, Mr. Balfour of Pilrig." (Somerville, pp. 16–17.)

III

By the early 1760s the dismal state of moral philosophy teaching was an

[61] David Raynor has brought to my attention, however, a very positive review of the *Delineation* in the *Monthly review* (May 1753) as well as favourable notices in two French periodicals. The *Monthly*'s notice of the *Philosophical essays* was sharper, observing that though the author was apparently "a sincere friend to the interests of virtue and religion" he had "little, if any thing new" to say.

embarrassment among the literati and concerned citizenry of Edinburgh. The university as a whole had undergone significant expansion and improvement since the reorganization of 1708, yet its professors in this subject made a sorry comparison with their illustrious counterparts at Glasgow during roughly the same period. The chair's initially ambiguous status had been clarified during the 1730s; Law, Pringle, and Cleghorn seem to have been at least competent in the class-room when they applied themselves; and Balfour ventured into print from time to time as an adversary of Hume. But no holder of the chair in this period is known to have published anything remotely related to the subject during his actual tenure, and the financial arrangements did not hold out much incentive for professors to distinguish themselves as teachers. If Edinburgh were to compete successfully for students and academic reputation, it would be necessary to reform the moral philosophy chair. To leaders of the cultural establishment this meant not only changing institutional regulations but, equally important, filling the post with a professor possessing that rare blend of learning and scholarship, pedagogical dedication and charisma, enlightened principles, polite manners, and Whig-Presbyterian values that Francis Hutcheson had established as the standard at Glasgow.

The reformers were convinced they had their man in the person of Adam Ferguson, then professor of natural philosophy. Like Hutcheson, whose writings he admired, Ferguson's personality combined, in the words of a close friend, "all the decorum belonging to the clerical character" with "the manners of a gentleman".[62] Like Hutcheson also, he was a presbyterian minister with a passion for virtue, a strong attachment to the Hanoverian establishment, an impressive intellect, and a reputation for superb teaching. He was closely connected with the Moderate party in the church and the causes for which it then stood: freedom of expression, religious tolerance, ecclesiastical and civil order, polite learning and virtue, and the establishment of a Scots militia.[63] He was prominent among Edinburgh men of letters and intimate with the most powerful local political figure of the day, Andrew Fletcher, Lord Milton. It was chiefly by means of Milton's patronage that Ferguson had bested a much more qualified candidate—his cousin and friend James Russel—to obtain the natural philosophy chair in 1759 (Sher, pp. 106–8). At that time there had been talk of an ambitious "double scheme" to secure Balfour's moral philosophy chair for Ferguson and the natural philosophy chair for Russel, but Ferguson and Russel's mutual friends had agreed it would be wiser first to procure the natural

[62] Carlyle, *Autobiography*, p. 296. Cf. Hugh Blair's laudatory account of Hutcheson's character in the *Edinburgh review* 1 (July 1755), pp. 11–12.

[63] R. B. Sher, *Church and university in the Scottish Enlightenment* (Princeton 1985).

philosophy chair for Ferguson, the needier candidate, with the understanding that the "double scheme" so desirable to both men might be attempted later.[64]

As disenchantment with Balfour's performance mounted, plots were hatched in an effort to implement the double scheme. The matter was first raised by Provost George Lind, writing to Lord Milton in March 1761: "It's certain Mr Balfour has made no figure in his present Situation. Mr Ferguson it's thought would make an excellent Professor of moral Philosophy, & everybody agrees that in all Europe there could not be a better man found than Mr Russel for Professor of natural & experimental Philosophy."[65] The problem was that "Mr Balfour refuses to resign, (for which all the Town are exclaiming against him)", despite the prospect of an appointment as commissary clerk, plus additional compensation from Russel, who was his brother-in-law. That Lind's letter was written at the behest of "several Gentlemen, some of the professors in the Colledge, & some of my Brethren in the Magistracy" is significant, because it shows that the Provost's plan had widespread support among the people who controlled town and university affairs. But professorships were good for life, and the combined pressure brought to bear by Milton and the council was not sufficient to budge Balfour at this time.

Balfour's stubbornness was such that Ferguson and his supporters temporarily turned their attention away from the chair of moral philosophy when the office of principal became vacant early in 1762. Soon after the principalship was won by Ferguson's friend William Robertson,[66] however, the double scheme was revived in a slightly different guise. Since local patronage could not offer Balfour enough financial inducement to resign his chair, it was decided to employ political connections in London to land the reluctant professor a lucrative office that would make it worth his while to give up moral philosophy. Robertson emphasized the need for such a policy in a revealing letter to Gilbert Elliot, then political agent of the powerful third Earl of Bute:

You know of how much importance the Class of Moral Philosophy is in a Scotch College; unfortunately your friend Mr Balfour tho' a man of great integrity, & well-skilled I am told in his own profession of law, teaches that Class in such a manner that it has dwindled to nothing, which is a cruel circumstance to the College, & a real & essential loss to the country, as there are more Gentlemen & Clergymen educated here than in any other College.[67]

[64] Hume to William Robertson, 29 May 1759: NHL 56–8; George Drummond to Milton, 26 June 1759: NLS, MS. 16709, fol. 252; Ferguson to Milton, 12 July 1759: NLS, MS. 16710, fol. 20.

[65] Lind to Milton, 19 March 1761: NLS, MS. 16721, fol. 108.

[66] Sher, *Church and university*, pp. 113–14.

[67] Robertson to Elliot, 8 January 1763; NLS, MS. 11009, fols. 163–4. Cf. Somerville, p. 16.

Restated more bluntly, Robertson's message was that moral philosophy was a vital component in the Scottish system of higher education, that Balfour was not equipped to teach it, that his class had deteriorated into a virtual sinecure, that the reputation of the university was suffering from his ineptitude, and that Scotland as a whole was being cheated because so many of its future social, political, and religious leaders were not receiving proper instruction in this important field of study.

The triumph of the campaign to reform the moral philosophy chair had to wait another year. At a meeting of the town council on 22 February 1764, Provost George Drummond read a letter from Robertson proposing a two-part plan.[68] First, Robertson proposed that Balfour be appointed to the chair of public law—a £200 a year sinecure in the gift of the crown—and that Ferguson and Russel then be placed in the chairs of moral and natural philosophy, respectively. In the second part of his letter Robertson recommended that moral philosophy be converted into a fee-paying class, because the experience of the past fifty years had amply demonstrated that teaching quality and student attendance were both noticeably lower when student fees were prohibited. Thus, Robertson's vision extended beyond a particular change in teaching personnel, however desirable such a change might be. In his view, an equally important *institutional* reform would have to be made if moral philosophy teaching were to fulfil its proper function on an on-going basis.[69]

The council approved both of Robertson's proposals and appointed Provost Drummond to write letters to the Lord Privy Seal (Bute's brother James Stuart Mackenzie, who was then government manager of Scottish business) and the Edinburgh member of Parliament (James Coutts), recommending Balfour for the public law chair as a means of implementing the Ferguson-Russel double scheme. The next day Lord Milton wrote to Mackenzie in support of the same cause, and within a fortnight Mackenzie replied that he was "most willing and ready" to facilitate any scheme beneficial to the university, the town, and "the Publick in general".[70] While it is unlikely that even a relatively enlightened London politico fully comprehended the scope and importance of the Edinburgh moral philosophy class, Mackenzie seems to have understood that more was at stake in this case than an ordinary

---

[68] Council minutes, vol. 79, pp. 283–5 (22 February 1764).

[69] Two years earlier another member of Robertson and Ferguson's circle of Moderate literati, Hugh Blair, had used similar logic in regard to his appointment as Regius professor of rhetoric and belles lettres: "You can never have any Security for a Professor's exerting himself, without some Spurr from Interest; nor any Prospect of Students applying with care, where the doors are open att all times to all." (Blair to Gilbert Elliot, 3 Sept. 1761: NLS, MS. 11009. fols. 87–8.)

[70] Milton to Mackenzie, 23 Feb. 1764 (copy): NLS, MS. 16731, fol. 95; Mackenzie to Milton, 5 March 1764: NLS, MS. 16731, fol. 105.

patronage job. Once he had approved it, the scheme proceeded without incident (Sher, pp. 117–18). All parties can be assumed to have been well pleased with the final arrangement. Balfour doubled his salary and freed himself from teaching responsibilities. Ferguson and Russel gained the particular chairs they desired. Politicians and professors who had been involved in the affair received the satisfaction of having instituted a major academic improvement that would be likely to attract more students to Edinburgh.

In the autumn of 1764 Hugh Blair reported with obvious pleasure that both Ferguson and Russel "are beginning their new Courses with much applause".[71] Ferguson's class-room style was undoubtedly one major reason for his great success. His lectures were lively and were usually spoken from outlines or unpolished lecture notes rather than read in a formal manner.[72] Each session a great deal of time and effort was devoted to revising the lectures.[73] Course outlines were also periodically revised and published for the benefit of students, who were regularly reminded to consult and study them in order to make sense of the lectures.[74]

Another significant pedagogical feature was the assignment and discussion of essays. At the beginning of his course in November, Ferguson would announce that he expected "at Different Periods to receive [written] specimens . . . which may prove an useful Excercise to you and give me some satisfaction with respect to the Proficiency you are making" (Lectures, vol. 1, fol. 20).[75] A few weeks later he would add words such as the following, spoken on the eve of the holiday recess:

You are now acquainted with the manner of proceeding in this Place. To such as have their habits of Inquiry & Disquisition to Form I would gladly become a Prompter and an Assistant. To those who are Already become Inquisitive I would willingly point out the preferable Object & the Road to arrive at it. . . . If I

---

[71] Blair to Hume, 15 November 1764: NLS, MS. 23153, item 54.

[72] *Principles of moral and political science*, vol. 1 (London 1792), p. v.

[73] Ferguson's own lecture notes (EUL, vol. 1, Dc 1.84; vol. 2, Dc 1.85) are usually dated, revealing an almost obsessive concern with revision of course material between 1775–76 (the earliest session for which the notes are available) and his retirement in 1785. This source is cited hereafter as 'Lectures'.

[74] Ferguson, *Analysis of pneumatics and moral philosophy* (Edinburgh 1766) and *Institutes of moral philosophy* (Edinburgh 1769). The *Institutes* was revised for new editions in 1773 and 1785, and was translated into German, French, and Russian. It was to be used "as your Principal Aid in recollecting & possessing yourselves of the Observations that may be made in the course of our Lectures", and students should "get the devisions and definitions . . . by heart" so that "what may possibly appear Obscure at present will afterwards recur with a Clear & Obvious meaning" (Lectures, vol. 1, fol. 15). Ferguson was opposed to traditional dictates, and expected students to take only "some short notes in Aid of the memory" during lectures.

[75] The lecture notes are corroborated on this point by a former student, Robert Bisset, who recalled that "the Doctor proposed, periodically, themes for discussion to his pupils". Bisset was particularly impressed by one of these student themes, an essay on the advantages of travel by the future Earl of Lauderdale (R. Bisset, 'Dr. Adam Fergusson', in *Public characters of 1799–1800* (London 1799), p. 437).

present Objects, if I arouse Curiosity, if I excite any just Degree of Ardour, a great Point is gained. The mind that Exerts itself will acquire a Force which no external Information can give. Part of your Exertion in attending this Course I hope will be to accompany the progress of it with your thoughts. To commit those thoughts to writing from Day to Day And to enure yourselves to state Facts and to draw Inferences whether those that occur to Yourselves or are suggested by Others. And I must Request that you will communicate to me from time to time your Essays on chosen Subjects. And I mention this matter now as we are about to have a recess of some Days which you may Employ in furnishing some such Species of your Attention and Proficiency. (24 Dec. 1779: Lectures, vol. 1, fol. 292)

Around February Ferguson might devote an entire class hour to a detailed discussion of "some Essays on Different Subjects that have been delivered to me" (vol. 2, fols. 13–17). At such times he was extremely thorough and encouraging, characteristically concluding one such session by noting his "great Satisfaction in the Proofs of Ingenuity, Application & respectable Proficiency which I have received". On this occasion Ferguson discussed—in order of merit though without identifying the authors—seven essays dealing with the following topics: the general history of the human species; the state of nature; population; man's disposition to social states; political establishments; the ancient and present state of the British constitution; and a second essay on political establishments.[76] Still later in the session he might resort to other tactics: on 4 April 1776, for example, he praised an essay he had received on friendship but added that "*Numbers however are yet wanting and I woud willingly flatter myself that some may yet favour me before I shall have concluded the last part of our Course on which I am now to enter*" (ibid., fol. 435). On 24 April 1776 he began his lecture by noting that the course would already have ended "if the Duty I owe to some Gentlemen who have furnished me with papers on different Subjects had not determined me to entreat your Attendance for one Day longer" (fol. 540).

That final lecture of the 1775–76 academic year provides an excellent illustration of the didacticism which Ferguson brought to the moral philosophy chair. Having spent five months introducing his students to the rudiments of the natural history of man, the theory of mind, the knowledge of God, moral laws, jurisprudence, casuistry, and politics—the seven major parts of his course—Ferguson now emphasized the practical value of these studies for the business of life: "Now is your time to begin Practices & lay the Foundation of habits that may be of use to you in every Condition and in every Profession at least that is founded on

---

[76] He added that he had received "a Moral Essay without a Name on the Government of the Heart". Some pedagogical problems are apparently universal!

a literary or Liberal Education. Sapere & Fari quae sentiat[77] are the great Objects of Literary Education and of Study." He hoped he had given his students much valuable information, but added that

mere knowledge however important is far from being the only or the most important Attainment of Study.

The Habits of Justice, Candour, Benevolence, and a Courageous Spirit are the first Objects of Philosophy the Constituents of happiness and of personal honour, & the first Qualifications for human Society & for Active life.

While I endeavoured to set the example of Fair and unexceptionable Argument on Particular Subjects I have addressed my weak endeavours to the feelings of the mind as well as the Understanding. And shall be happy if you perceived and approve of my Intentions.

If I have failed in the execution I am sensible it is now too late to supply any defects. And must flatter myself from the manner of your Attendance in this place that the Subject at least has Fixed the Attention of many of you. And this Introduction may in some Measure facilitate your way to a life of useful Observations & worthy Conduct. (fols. 540–41)

Ferguson's approach to the teaching of moral philosophy was firmly in the tradition of Hutcheson. This is not to say that he was a consistent disciple on most philosophical issues. On the source of moral approbation, for example, Ferguson endorsed neither Hutcheson's "moral sense" nor the rational moral faculty championed by his own predecessors Balfour and Cleghorn. He thought the question was of little significance and breezily asserted that "Reason, Conscience, and Moral Sense" are "so many different names" for the same thing.[78] In regard to political theory, similarly, Ferguson broke from Hutcheson by dismissing the concept of the social contract as "a mere fiction in theory". Numerous other differences on particular points could easily be cited. But such differences appear insignificant when compared to the similarities in the styles and ultimate objectives of these men. Both were moralists, clergymen, ideologists, and teachers as well as philosophers. Their primary goal was to mould teenage boys into virtuous, polite, tolerably learned, self-confident, upstanding, patriotic young gentlemen. They were to be moderate Christians, benevolent and responsible but also prudent and proper, in accordance with the teachings of Cicero and the Stoics. They were also to be firm Whigs and good British citizens, loyal to the Hanoverian regime and the "constitution" on which it was thought to be founded. These objectives called forth a variety of pedagogical techniques, including a dynamic class-room style, publishing and revising course outlines or compends for student use, and careful

---

[77] "To be discerning, and to express what one thinks" (Horace, *Epistles*, I. iv. 9).

[78] Ferguson, *Institutes of moral philosophy*, 3rd edn. (Edinburgh 1785), pp. 108–9.

attention to the cultivation of students' moral and philosophical sensibilities by means of essay assignments.

By following in Hutcheson's footsteps as a dynamic teacher of moral philosophy, Ferguson aroused the same kind of enthusiasm in his students. Many years later one of them remarked that "the recollection of the manner in which he discharged the high and important calling of a teacher of moral science was deeply imprinted on the minds of all his disciples". Another was quoted as saying:

> I have always considered Adam Ferguson as the first philosopher of his day. His was a manly, spirited, practical philosophy, intended to rear active, useful, and disinterested citizens, to attend to and to promote the welfare of their country, in preference to every other object.[79]

Still another, commenting later on the two sessions of lectures he had attended during the mid-1770s, stated that he

> was so deeply impressed with their excellence, that though then not much addicted to study, he took accurate notes both of the general principles and illustrations, and can say for himself, from experience, and for others, from their concurrent testimony, that from no other system of literary discipline, at any stage of their education, they received so much advantage as from the lectures of Fergusson; that from him they learned the objects of pursuit, and the means of attainment, in moral and political science; so that if they did not succeed, it must have been for want of either the power of investigation, or of its direction to these objects.[80]

It was probably a former student who observed in an Edinburgh newspaper that "Ferguson, taking a route different from his contemporaries, has directed philosophy to the heart: has endeavoured to animate the coldness of modern times with the ardent spirit of antiquity; and, to a mercenary and luxurious age, has lifted up the voice which called the Greeks and Romans to virtue and glory."[81] Yet another former student, the Indian civil servant Sir John Macpherson, sent Ferguson a long letter asserting that his policy as Governor-General of India was rooted in the three "favourite positions" of his master:

> 1st. That the pursuits of an active mind are its greatest happiness, when they are directed to good objects, which unite our own happiness with that of our friends and the general advantage of society. . . . 2nd. I have likewise experienced that he who has not been in contact with his fellow creatures knows but half of the

---

[79] Both quotations are from Adam's Preface to *Two short essays*, p. vi, the latter quoting a letter from Rutherford of Egerston.

[80] Bisset, 'Dr. Adam Fergusson', pp. 436–7. Bisset added that Ferguson's "mode of communicating his knowledge was firm, manly, and impressive, but mild and elegant; he was delicate, but justly severe, in his rebukes to the inattentive and negligent".

[81] *Caledonian mercury*, 17 February 1777. (This reference courtesy of John Dwyer.)

human heart. . . . 3rd. That all that rests with us individually, is to act our own parts to the best of our ability, and to endeavour to do good for its own sake, independent of events, disappointments, or sufferings.[82]

Backed by God rather than fate, these essentially Stoic beliefs had also been insisted upon by Hutcheson.[83] They represented a commitment to pure and selfless virtue that set off didactic moralists from adherents of the supposed "selfish school" like Mandeville, as well as from strict utilitarians like Bentham and cool philosophical "anatomists" like Hume. Ferguson's subscription to Hutcheson's *System of moral philosophy* in 1755, inclusion of Hutcheson among the few modern authors recommended at the final lecture of the academic year,[84] and praise (in the *Principles* of 1792) of Hutcheson for helping to revive Stoicism, all take on greater significance when seen from this perspective.

It is also significant that the one person known to have disapproved of Ferguson's shift from the natural philosophy to the moral philosophy chair was David Hume. "Between ourselves", Hume wrote to Hugh Blair from Paris, "I know not whether I ought to rejoice at Ferguson's getting the Class of moral Philosophy. He succeeded perfectly in his former Department." (HL i. 438.) In a section of a common letter to several of his "Protestant Pastors" that was addressed to Ferguson himself he was equally candid: "I am glad of the Change of your Class, because you desir'd it, and because it fitted Russell. *For otherwise I shou'd have lik'd better the other Science.*" (HL i. 496, emphasis added.) Since Ferguson was at best a makeshift natural philosopher, with no special training or expertise in that subject,[85] Hume's remarks suggest that he

---

[82] Sir John Macpherson to Ferguson, 12 Jan. 1786, in J. Small, 'Biographical sketch of Adam Ferguson', *Transactions of the Royal Society of Edinburgh* 23 (1864), pp. 644–5. The fact that Macpherson failed to live up to these lofty principles raises interesting questions about the relationship of moral philosophy and political practice but does nothing to weaken the point being made here about the impact of Ferguson's teaching on his students.

[83] On the Christian-Stoic ethical thought of Ferguson and its Hutchesonian roots, see Sher, *Church and university*, pp. 175–86. See also the introduction and notes to Hutcheson and Moor's 1742 translation of the *Meditations* of Marcus Aurelius.

[84] Volume 2 of the Lectures contains three versions of Ferguson's concluding recommendations to students. In the earliest of these, dated 1776 (fol. 551), Shaftesbury (moral philosophy), Montesquieu (politics), and Smith (political economy) are cited, and 'Dr Reid' is written in the margin. In a somewhat later, undated version (fol. 532), Hutcheson is joined with Shaftesbury as "principal founders of moral philosophy in this Country", and the page breaks off during the discussion of Montesquieu. In the last version, dated 1785 (fol. 538), only Shaftesbury, Hutcheson, and Montesquieu are mentioned. According to the set of student notes in Edinburgh Public Library (MS. YB1413M/81311A), Hutcheson, Shaftesbury, Montesquieu, and Smith were the modern thinkers recommended by Ferguson at the conclusion of the 1779–80 session.

[85] My contention that natural philosophy was an unfamiliar subject to Ferguson at the time of his appointment to that chair is supported by a passage from Carlyle's *Autobiography* which merits re-examination in the light of Roger Emerson's charge, in the opening paper in this

disapproved of his friend's approach to moral philosophy. He knew that Ferguson was at least as much moralist as philosopher, and his worst fears were realized when he received portions of the manuscript of Ferguson's highly moralistic *Essay on the history of civil society*, which he tried his best to keep from being published on account of alleged deficiencies of "Style" and "Reasoning", "Form" and "Matter". The situation was "very serious", Hume warned Blair, because an unsuccessful publication by Ferguson would discredit not only his personal reputation but his class and, indirectly, the entire university (HL ii. 12).

Blair agreed that "much depends on the Success of this work, for Ferguson's reputation, and Class, and indeed for our College in general", and he was willing to concede that he and Robertson had probably overlooked a few flaws owing to their "partiality" for the author. Nevertheless, Blair and Robertson remained convinced that the "Blemishes" were "far outweighed by the Beauties", and that "the Rousing and animating Spirit, which runs thro' it" would soon attract "a high degree of publick Attention".[86] They were quite right, of course. Ferguson's *Essay* immediately became a best-seller, largely because it was read as a passionate attack on "selfishness and luxury" in the name of virtue.[87] Far from disgracing the professor or his college, the book increased Ferguson's fame and fortune and further enhanced the reputation of Edinburgh University as a northern bastion of enlightened education.

Ferguson was the first Edinburgh professor of moral philosophy to achieve eminence both as a teacher and as an author, and in the process to place the reputation of the Edinburgh chair on a par with the chair at Glasgow. Scarcely one year after Ferguson had assumed his new position, his Glasgow counterpart Thomas Reid commented to a friend that the moral philosophy class at Edinburgh "is more than double ours".[88] At that time Ferguson's class had at least eighty-nine formally

volume, that I have trivialized the thought of Ferguson, and the Moderates generally, out of a failure to appreciate the importance of science in the Scottish Enlightenment. "David Hume said Ferguson had more genius than any of them," Carlyle wrote, referring to his circle of Edinburgh literati, "as he had made himself so much master of a difficult science—viz., Natural Philosophy, *which he had never studied but when at college*—in three months, so as to be able to teach it." (pp. 297–8, emphasis added.) I see no contradiction between my belief that science was a secondary concern for most of the Moderate literati and my belief that it "played a vital role during the heyday of the Scottish Enlightenment" (Sher, p. 308; see also pp. 3–19). My contention that the Moderate literati were central to the Scottish Enlightenment does not involve the claim that they played a leading role in every branch of Enlightenment thought.

[86] Blair to Hume, 24 February 1766: NLS, MS. 23153, item 56.

[87] See Lord Kames's praise for the *Essay*'s blatant moralizing in a letter to Elizabeth Montagu of 6 March 1767 and Mrs. Montagu's similar reply of 24 March, both in A. F. Tytler, *Lord Woodhouselee, Memoirs of the life and writings of the honourable Henry Home of Kames*, vol. 2 (Edinburgh 1807), pp. 48–51.

[88] Reid to David Skene, 20 Dec. 1765, in Reid, *Philosophical works*, vol. 1, pp. 42–3.

matriculated pupils, in addition to undisclosed numbers of students and "gentlemen of rank in the literary world" who attended lectures without signing the matriculation book.[89] The next year the number of formally matriculated students rose to an impressive one hundred and fourteen—by far the highest of his entire tenure. As student enrolment soared, so too did Ferguson's income. Although he is said to have allowed an unusually large number of needy students to attend his lectures without charge (Bisset, p. 454), in a good year Ferguson took in about £200 sterling—or roughly twice his fixed salary—from student fees.

The importance to Ferguson of the economic incentive from student fees is made clear in a letter he wrote to Adam Smith during a period of economic recession in 1774, when he was considering taking a leave of absence to accept a lucrative position as travelling tutor to the young Earl of Chesterfield:

My place here, a few years ago, was worth about £300 a-year, but this and the preceding year it has fallen considerably short; and while the present alarm of the scarcity of money, and the expense of education at Edinburgh, continues, it may not rise again to its former value. To this I may add, that in case of debility or old age, I shall probably be reduced to my salary, which is no more than £100 a-year. For these reasons I think that I can fully justify myself to my family in accepting of £200 a-year certain, with the privilege of choosing my place and my occupations . . .[90]

When Ferguson accepted this offer and his class was taught for a year by the logic professor John Bruce, the number of formally matriculated students fell almost in half—from fifty-eight in 1773–74 to thirty-one in 1774–75.[91] Indeed, during the four years in which the class was taught by a substitute owing to Ferguson's absence for private tutoring (1774–75), for American diplomacy (1778–79), and for illness (1780–82), the average number of students signing the roster each year fell under forty. When Ferguson was teaching, however, average class size rose to sixty-four. It stood at sixty-one in November 1782, when the professor of Greek, Andrew Dalzel, sent the following account to a friend:

Ferguson is teaching his own class this session, after a vacation on his part of two

---

[89] Bisset, 'Dr. Adam Fergusson', pp. 447–8. All references to class size are drawn from the typed copies of matriculation lists in the EUL Rare Book Room. Students who had matriculated in another class in an earlier year did not always sign the register a second time.

[90] Ferguson to Smith, 23 Jan. 1774, in *The correspondence of Adam Smith*, ed. E. C. Mossner and I. S. Ross, 2nd edn. (Oxford 1987), p. 170. The arrangement called for Ferguson to receive £400 per annum while accompanying Chesterfield on the Continent and £200 per annum for life after his services were completed. The fact that such a generous offer was made is yet another testimony to Ferguson's reputation as a first-rate pedagogue.

[91] Cf. Sher, pp. 138–9. The severe decline in enrolment in the moral philosophy class was probably one of the factors that caused the town council to take a hard line against Ferguson on this occasion.

years. The effect of it is curious. Ferguson has the pleasure to find that his former fame is again revived. He has got a most crowded class. The students are sitting, some of them, in the gallery, in the manner they did when we attended him in his vigorous days; and though he is living on vegetables and water, he is lecturing with uncommon spirit.[92]

It would be foolish to suggest that a dedicated moralist like Ferguson was motivated to excel in the class-room solely, or even chiefly, by pecuniary incentives. But it would be equally foolish to ignore this factor. As a result of the important reform made by the town council in 1764 in response to Principal Robertson's request, Ferguson enjoyed the opportunity—denied to his predecessors—of substantially increasing his income by attracting more students. With so much additional income available as an incentive, the Edinburgh moral philosophy chair would not soon be in danger of becoming a sinecure.

In fact, Dugald Stewart regularly attracted even larger numbers than Ferguson, and earned proportionately more income, during his quarter of a century in the chair (1785–1810).[93] This is partly attributable to the general growth of Edinburgh University at the end of the eighteenth century—the total number of students seems to have doubled between the mid-1760s and the early 1790s[94]—but it also owed much to an institutional framework that rewarded excellent teaching and to Stewart's ability to fuse the "scientific" and didactic components of academic moral philosophy in a harmonious whole. A staunch Whig, son of a presbyterian clergyman-professor, and for many years a lay elder in the General Assembly, Stewart possessed not only sufficient intellect and diligence but also the right family background and ideology to win the chair and succeed in it.

Stewart's debt to Ferguson as a didactic moralist has not received its due among modern commentators. At seventeen years of age he attended Ferguson's class during the 1770–71 session. The following year he was sent by Ferguson to study with Reid at Glasgow. When Ferguson went

---

[92] Dalzel to Sir Robert Liston, 30 Nov. 1782, in Andrew Dalzel, *History of the University of Edinburgh*, vol. I (Edinburgh 1862), p. 39.

[93] Statistics cited in Morrell, 'University of Edinburgh', p. 165, show that in the 1790s the average size of Dugald Stewart's class exceeded one hundred students. Recent studies of Stewart as a professor of moral philosophy include N. T. Phillipson, 'The pursuit of virtue in Scottish university education: Dugald Stewart and Scottish moral philosophy', in *Universities, society and the future*, ed. Phillipson (Edinburgh 1983), 575–86; D. Winch, 'The system of the north: Dugald Stewart and his pupils', in *That noble science of politics*, ed. S. Collini and others (Cambridge 1983), 23–62; K. Haakonssen, 'From moral philosophy to political economy: the contribution of Dugald Stewart', in Hope, *Philosophers of the Scottish Enlightenment*, 211–32.

[94] A pamphlet generally attributed to William Robertson, *Memorial relating to the University of Edinburgh* (Edinburgh 1768), put the student population between six and seven hundred in the late 1760s. William Creech, *Letters addressed to Sir John Sinclair* (Edinburgh 1793), p. 15, stated that the student body had grown from about five hundred in 1763 to more than thirteen hundred in 1792.

abroad in 1778 he chose Stewart for his substitute, and it seems highly likely that Ferguson was also instrumental in recommending Stewart for the moral philosophy chair when he retired from active teaching in 1785.[95] Three years later Stewart was still widely regarded as Ferguson's disciple: the description of his class in a book published that year stated that "the present Professor gives a course of lectures on moral philosophy, following chiefly the arrangement of Dr Ferguson's institutes of that science."[96] In 1792 Stewart published his own course outline for the benefit of his students, and perhaps a desire to free himself from Ferguson's shadow led him to insist a bit too strenuously on the originality of his scheme.[97]

To be sure, the content and structure of Stewart's course did differ increasingly from Ferguson's, due in large part to the strong influence of Smith and Reid. From Smith, Stewart took over a penchant for political economy; from Reid he obtained proficiency in the philosophy and "culture" of the mind. Even for Smith and Reid, however, these highly technical subjects formed parts of a broader moral vision that drew upon the ancient moralists, Bacon, Pufendorf, and Hutcheson.[98] Stewart drew upon Ferguson in other parts of his course, such as in his moralistic treatment of Stoic philosophy.[99] Moreover, he seems to have deliberately emulated Ferguson's dynamic teaching style.[100] On the five days a

[95] The arrangement that sent Stewart to the moral philosophy chair gave Ferguson the income from Stewart's mathematics chair for life, while John Playfair took over the latter teaching responsibilities in exchange for the right to collect class fees. In all probability Ferguson, Stewart, and Playfair fixed the matter before approaching the council.

[96] Hugo Arnot, *The history of Edinburgh* (Edinburgh 1788), p. 410. Stewart had used Ferguson's *Institutes* successfully while substituting in the 1778–79 session. His marked copy of the second edition (1773) has just been acquired by EUL.

[97] Dugald Stewart, *Outlines of moral philosophy* (Edinburgh 1793), pp. vii–viii: "With respect to my general plan, those who are in the smallest degree conversant with Ethical writers, will perceive, that, in its formation, I have been guided almost entirely by the train of my own speculations."

[98] On Smith see R. F. Teichgraeber III, *"Free trade" and moral philosophy* (Durham, NC 1986). It is significant that when Smith took over the Glasgow moral philosophy chair in the early 1750s he made, according to one former student, "a laudable attempt at first to follow Hutcheson's animated manner, lecturing on Ethics without Papers walking up & down his Class room", though his inability to match the master in this enterprise soon caused him to give it up (James Wodrow to the Earl of Buchan, June 1808: Mitchell Library, MS. Baillie 32225, fols. 47–51). Recent scholarship on Reid suggests that there was more to him *qua* moral philosophy professor than the concern with pneumatology that so dominates his published writings. See, for example, J. C. Stewart-Robertson, '*Sancte Socrates*: Scottish reflections on obedience and resistance', in *Man and nature* 1 (London, Ont. 1982), 65–80; id. 'The pneumatics and georgics of the Scottish mind', *Eighteenth-century studies* 20 (1987), 296–312; and above all, Thomas Reid, *Practical ethics*, ed. K. Haakonssen (Princeton 1989).

[99] Stewart, *Outlines of moral philosophy*, pp. 155–226.

[100] As Stewart's contemporary biographer put it: "Like his predecessor in the Chair, whom Mr. Stewart resembled in many features of character, intellectual and moral, and whose modes of teaching he appears in great measure to have followed, he was in the habit of speaking from notes, not reading lectures formally prepared and fully committed to writing." (J. Veitch, 'A memoir of Dugald Stewart', in *Collected works of Dugald Stewart*, ed. W. Hamilton, vol. 10 (Edinburgh 1858), p. xxxviii.)

week that he taught, Stewart was in the habit of rising at 3 a.m. in order to rehearse the lecture he would deliver seven hours later! (Veitch, p. xxx). His biographer observed that "Stewart's aim and influence as a teacher of philosophy was doubtless less purely speculative than moral and practical" (p. xxxix). One of his best-known students characterized him as a teacher who "breathed the love of virtue into whole generations of pupils".[101] Like Ferguson, Stewart assigned essays early in his career, though as time passed the large size of his class may have caused him to stop this practice. If so, it is certainly ironic that the very success of Ferguson's and Stewart's pedagogical practices was largely responsible for opening Edinburgh to the charge of being "merely a lecturing University".[102]

But what lecturing it was! After decades of playing second fiddle to Glasgow as a place to study moral philosophy, Edinburgh caught up after Ferguson won the chair in 1764, and took a commanding lead during the tenure of his successor. It did this in part by enacting institutional reform that provided financial incentive for popular lecturing and put a premium on the ability to teach ethics, politics, and natural religion in a manner that was at once progressive and unthreatening, inspirational and conventional. In a sense Ferguson's appointment represented no sharp break with the past, for Edinburgh professors of moral philosophy had nearly always been practical moralists with strong Whig-Presbyterian affinities. What Ferguson and Stewart brought to their professorship were other attributes, including studied eloquence, pedagogical diligence, scholarly achievement, and international fame that helped to raise the Edinburgh chair to new heights of popularity and prestige. Far from being revolutionary, these and other attributes were largely borrowed from the father of eighteenth-century Scottish moral philosophy, Francis Hutcheson.

In a letter of 1761 about a proposed chair of political history at Edinburgh, Gilbert Elliot spoke for the consumers of Scottish education: "It is full time to endeavour to bring education hence to the real business and purposes of life; and to teach our sons when boys, what we desire they may retain and profit by when they become men."[103] He might as well have been talking about the chair of moral philosophy. An

---

[101] Henry Cockburn, *Memorials of his time*, ed. W. F. Gray (Edinburgh 1946), p. 21.

[102] The charge was made in the late 1820s by George Jardine of Glasgow University, as reported in G. E. Davie, *The democratic intellect* (Edinburgh 1961), p. 25. In his defence of Edinburgh University against Jardine's charge, Principal Lee stated that Edinburgh professors of moral philosophy had employed both examination hours (questioning of students about lectures and assigned readings) and exercises (essays) until Ferguson dropped the former and Stewart the latter. Both Jardine's charge and Lee's defence failed to notice that these pedagogical practices, particularly examination hours, were not well suited to large classes of the sort that Ferguson and especially Stewart taught.

[103] Elliot to William Robertson, 3 March 1761: NLS, MS. 3942, fols. 42–3.

Aberdonian professor of that subject, James Beattie, expressed a similar point of view towards the end of the century, in a letter explaining the purpose of his projected textbook *Elements of moral science*: "I wish rather to form the taste, improve the manners, and establish the principles, of young men, than to make them profound metaphysicians; I wish, in a word, not to make Humes of them, or Leibnitzes, but rather, if that were possible, Addisons."[104] In place of Beattie's hero Addison, other Scottish professors might have cited Cicero or Marcus Aurelius or Montesquieu, or even Hutcheson. But the thrust of Beattie's remarks would have been equally acceptable to nearly all his colleagues. If Hutcheson, Ferguson, Stewart, and Beattie could not compete with Hume as philosophers, it is difficult to imagine Hume equalling any of them as class-room moralists. For in the hands of these professors of virtue, *moral* philosophy earned its name.[105]

Department of Humanities
New Jersey Institute of Technology

[104] Beattie to William Creech, 28 March 1789: SRO, RH 4/26/1. Hume's own application of the same distinction to himself is to be found at E. 7.

[105] Research for this essay was supported by a summer stipend from the National Endowment for the Humanities and an "IPSE" fellowship at the Institute for Advanced Studies in the Humanities, University of Edinburgh. Portions of earlier drafts, under the title 'The road to Adam Ferguson', were presented to the American Society for Eighteenth-Century Studies in April 1979 and the Columbia University Seminar on Political and Social Thought in November 1980. I am grateful to the audiences at those sessions, and to Roger Emerson, Martin Fitzpatrick, Warren McDougall, James Moore, David Norton, Nicholas Phillipson, David Raynor, Christine Shepherd, Paul Wood, and especially M. A. Stewart, for criticism and references that were of great use in the preparation of the present version.

SCIENCE AND THE PURSUIT OF VIRTUE IN THE ABERDEEN ENLIGHTENMENT

P. B. WOOD

Responding in September 1739 to Francis Hutcheson's pointed criticism of the manuscript of Book III of *A treatise of human nature*, David Hume observed that "[t]here are different ways of examining the Mind as well as the Body. One may consider it either as an Anatomist or as a Painter; either to discover its most secret Springs & Principles or to describe the Grace & Beauty of its Actions. I imagine it impossible to conjoin these two views." (HL i. 32.) Although moralists like Hutcheson would not have recognized any incompatibility between the roles of the anatomist and the painter, with his customary acuity Hume here rightly identified a tension which lay at the heart of moral philosophy in the eighteenth century. For even though Hutcheson and his philosophical contemporaries in the Scottish universities typically combined the two roles, the imperatives of metaphysical inquiry did not always mesh comfortably with the demands of moral instruction and the pursuit of virtue. But despite the significance of this structural tension within moral philosophy which Hume so perceptively discerned, historians have, until very recently, paid little attention to the complex, and sometimes uneasy, relations between metaphysics and morals in the Scottish Enlightenment.

In the nineteenth century, the ambiguities of this relationship were effectively masked by the writings of James McCosh, who focused almost exclusively on the metaphysical achievements of the Scottish "school", and who defined the uniqueness of Scottish philosophy in terms of the application of the inductive method to the science of man.[1] In our own century, scholars have, on the whole, adopted the historiography of McCosh, and have similarly concentrated on Scottish metaphysics and celebrated the methodological innovations of thinkers

[1] James McCosh, *The Scottish philosophy* (London 1875), pp. 2–4. The concept of a Scottish "school" of philosophy in the eighteenth century was invented by Dugald Stewart; see his *Dissertation* in *The Encyclopaedia Britannica*, eighth edition, vol. 1 (repr., Farnborough 1970), pp. 204–26.

like Thomas Reid.[2] Consequently, eighteenth-century Scottish philosophy is generally seen as more of a unified intellectual structure than the evidence may warrant.

Within the past decade, two distinguished historians of the Scottish Enlightenment have challenged this scholarly consensus. In a series of highly original papers, Nicholas Phillipson has questioned traditional interpretations of eighteenth-century Scottish moral philosophy, and has argued that we should conceive of thinkers like Hume, Smith, and Stewart "as practical moralists who ... developed a formidable and complex casuistical armoury to instruct young men of middling rank in their duties as men and as citizens of a modern commercial polity". According to Phillipson, Scottish philosophers were far from being simply scientists or anatomists of the mind. On the contrary, Phillipson contends that the Scots "acquired a Shaftesburian distrust for those inquiries about the science of man that seemed to be irrelevant or positively harmful to the principles of practical morality", which in Hume's case meant that he renounced the metaphysical mode of the *Treatise* for the Addisonian moralizing style of the *Essays*.[3] Thus while he fully recognizes the revolutionary character of the reconceptualizations of human nature effected by Hume and his contemporaries, Phillipson seeks to redirect our attention to what he calls the "casuistical framework of Scottish philosophy", and to the efforts made by Scottish academic philosophers and men of letters to inculcate the principles of virtue in the citizens of North Britain.

Richard Sher has similarly stressed the importance of practical morality in his study of the chequered history of the Edinburgh Moral Philosophy Chair in the eighteenth century. Although Sher is much more sensitive than Phillipson to the differences between individual moralists and their institutional contexts, one of the major themes of his paper is that the rhetoric, pedagogical style, and content of Scottish moral philosophy in the second half of the century all bore the stamp of Francis Hutcheson, and consequently that the Edinburgh professors, along with their colleagues elsewhere, engaged in a form of moral preaching intended to instil "Whig-Presbyterian values" into the hearts and minds of their students. Like Phillipson, Sher portrays the majority

[2] See for example H. Laurie, *Scottish philosophy in its national development* (Glasgow 1902), pp. 4–7; G. Bryson, *Man and Society* (Princeton 1945); L. L. Laudan, 'Thomas Reid and the Newtonian turn of British methodological thought', in *The methodological heritage of Newton*, ed. R. E. Butts and J. W. Davis (Oxford 1970), 103–31.

[3] N. T. Phillipson, 'Hume as moralist: a social historian's perspective', in *Philosophers of the Enlightenment*, ed. S. C. Brown (Brighton 1979), 140–61; id., 'Adam Smith as civic moralist', in *Wealth and virtue*, ed. I. Hont and M. Ignatieff (Cambridge 1983), 179–202; id., 'The pursuit of virtue in Scottish university education: Dugald Stewart and Scottish moral philosophy in the Enlightenment', in *Universities, societies, and the future*, ed. Phillipson (Edinburgh 1983), 82–101.

of Scottish philosophers as artists skilled in delineating the lineaments of virtue rather than anatomists displaying the structure of the human mind.[4]

In this paper, I want to assess the cogency of the revisionist views of Phillipson and Sher by examining the teaching of moral philosophy in the Aberdeen Enlightenment. For while their work serves as a much-needed corrective to the traditional picture of Scottish philosophy in the eighteenth century, it is arguable that Phillipson particularly, and to a lesser extent Sher, have ignored significant dissimilarities between both individuals and institutions, and have simply turned accepted historiography on its head by emphasizing moral didacticism rather than metaphysical speculation. Taking Hume's comments quoted above as my text, I propose to look closely at the relationships between morals and metaphysics in the writings and lectures of the Aberdeen academic philosophers of the eighteenth century. Aberdeen provides a particularly instructive intellectual and institutional context, for, as I shall argue, the regents and professors teaching at Marischal and King's Colleges developed interestingly different pedagogical styles which reflected a genuine disagreement over the priority of morals as opposed to metaphysics in the curriculum. As we shall see, the regents at King's College in the second half of the century tended on the whole to stress the anatomy of the mind, following the example set by Reid during his stint as a regent at King's from 1751 to 1764, whereas the professors at Marischal, and in particular James Beattie, placed greater weight on moral exhortation and instruction. Furthermore, Aberdeen also repays close study because its two universities boasted a particularly strong indigenous philosophical tradition which historians have thus far largely ignored.[5] Although there is little question that the Aberdonians owed much to the writings of men such as Locke, Shaftesbury, and Hutcheson, figures like George Turnbull did much to fashion a distinctive style of philosophy in Aberdeen, and this style deserves wider historical recognition.

Finally, on the basis of the materials I have surveyed, I want to reflect on the question which gave rise to the title of my paper, namely, how much did moral philosophy owe to natural philosophy in the Aberdeen Enlightenment? Phillipson, at least, would have us believe that the

---

[4] R. B. Sher, 'Professors of virtue' (the preceding paper in this collection); and the same author's *Church and university in the Scottish Enlightenment* (Princeton 1985), pp. 166–74 (where Sher again discusses the distinction drawn by Hume between the anatomist of the mind and the moralist). I am grateful to Dr Sher for letting me see an advance copy of his paper.

[5] Honourable exceptions here are McCosh and John Veitch, who both paid careful attention to developments in Aberdeen, and attempted to rescue George Turnbull from historical oblivion; see McCosh, *Scottish philosophy*, esp. pp. 91–107, and J. Veitch, 'Philosophy in the Scottish universities', *Mind* 2 (1877), pp. 212–13, 214–16.

relationships between the two branches of philosophy were tenuous at best, and that scientism[6] played little part in the rise of Scottish moral philosophy. I shall argue on the contrary that there is considerable truth in the established view that Scottish moralists sought to effect a methodological reform of their subject, inspired by the perceived successes of the inductive method in the sciences of nature. However, the Aberdeen evidence also suggests that the established view must be seriously qualified, for there are signs that with the introduction of the professorial system at Marischal in 1753, the moral philosophers in that college were more concerned to assert their disciplinary independence and to underline the methodological and conceptual disparities between natural and moral philosophy than were their colleagues at King's.

I. 1715–1753

Although the teaching of moral philosophy at both King's and Marischal during the years following the curriculum reforms of 1753 can be fully documented, the evidence which survives for the period 1715 (when both colleges were temporarily closed by the authorities because of the Jacobite rising) to 1753 is extremely patchy, with virtually nothing remaining illustrating developments at King's. The records for Marischal are only marginally better, but there is a run of printed graduation theses covering roughly the first three decades of the century, and there are a few texts of actual lectures surviving, which need to be supplemented with printed sources. The extant theses show that the Marischal regents were introducing their students to the works of Descartes, Locke, Shaftesbury, More, Berkeley, Malebranche, and the expatriate Scottish physician George Cheyne.[7] Perhaps the most important theses historically are those penned by Turnbull in 1723 and 1726, for these reveal that some of the key ideas which Turnbull later elaborated in his published works were first expounded during his brief career as a Marischal regent from 1721 to 1727.

In both of his graduation theses, Turnbull proclaimed that natural and moral philosophy were intimately related, with the former serving as

---

[6] For a useful discussion of scientism see J. Ben-David, *The scientist's role in society* (Englewood-Cliffs 1971), pp. 78–87. The question of the role of scientism and the origins of the Scottish Enlightenment is sharply posed in R. L. Emerson, 'Natural philosophy and the problem of the Scottish Enlightenment', *Studies on Voltaire and the 18th century* 242 (1986), 243–91.

[7] See, for example, Patrick Hardie, *Dissertatio philosophica de immaterialitate animae* (Aberdeen 1719), pp. 5, 6–7; David Verner, *Dissertatio philosophica, de passionibus sive affectibus* (Aberdeen 1721), pp. 7, 11. See also C. M. Shepherd, *Philosophy and science in the arts curriculum of the Scottish universities in the seventeenth century* (Ph.D., University of Edinburgh 1975), pp. 135–41, 190–97, on the changing content of the curricula at Marischal and King's in the late seventeenth and early eighteenth centuries.

a foundation for the latter. He quoted approvingly Newton's statement about the method of analysis and synthesis in the 31st Query of the *Opticks*, that "if natural Philosophy in all its Parts, by pursuing this Method, shall at length be perfected, the Bounds of Moral Philosophy will be also enlarged", and Turnbull insisted that it was natural philosophy which demonstrated the central moral truths that immaterial beings exist, that there is one supreme Creator who rules His creation providentially, that nature is wisely and benevolently designed, and that evil is not an intrinsic characteristic of the natural order.[8]

Turnbull subsequently returned to the question of the structural connections between natural and moral philosophy in his *Principles of moral philosophy* and his *Observations upon liberal education*. In the *Principles*, Turnbull further urged the view that since both "physiology" and morals investigated final causes they formed one unified field of human knowledge, stating that "when natural philosophy is carried so far as to reduce phenomena to good general laws, it becomes moral philosophy; and when it stops short of this chief end of all enquiries into the sensible or material world ... it hardly deserves the name of philosophy in the sense of *Socrates*, *Plato*, Lord *Verulam*, *Boyle*, *Newton*, and the other best moral or natural philosophers".[9] Similarly, in the *Observations*, Turnbull repeatedly stressed the unity of natural and moral philosophy, and, in addition, sketched what he called a "tree" or "general map of the sciences", which he said was "of great use to open the minds of young people, to inflame their curiosity and desire of knowledge, and above all, to keep for ever in their eye the real unity of all the sciences, into whatever different tribes and classes they are divided". Turnbull briefly described his tree of the sciences as follows:

it is easy to conceive how such a tree may be delineated, since from natural experience, or knowledge of the laws of the material world, immediately and naturally sprout all the mechanical arts, and from moral experience as naturally and immediately sprout all the moral arts, among which the more considerable are politics, oratory and poetry, and all these have evidently a very close reciprocal connexion and dependence.[10]

[8] George Turnbull, *De scientiae naturalis cum philosophia morali conjunctione* (Aberdeen 1723), pp. 3–4; id., *De pulcherrima mundi cum materialis tum rationalis constitutione* (Aberdeen 1726), *passim*. For Newton's text see Isaac Newton, *Opticks*, fourth edn. (London 1730; New York 1952), p. 405. What ultimately became known as Query 31 was first published as Query 23 of the 1706 *Optice*. Turnbull's Marischal colleague Colin MacLaurin similarly believed that natural philosophy served as the basis for moral philosophy; see Colin MacLaurin, *An account of Sir Isaac Newton's philosophical discoveries* (London 1748), p. 3.

[9] George Turnbull, *The principles of moral and Christian philosophy*, vol. 1 (London 1740), pp. 8–9; compare his *Observations upon liberal education* (London 1742), pp. 209–10. Turnbull distinguished between moral and natural philosophy on the basis of the objects of study, namely mind and matter; see *Principles*, vol. 1, p. 2.

[10] *Observations*, pp. 430–31; for assertions of the unity of moral and natural philosophy see for example pp. 351–3.

This outline of Turnbull's map of knowledge is significant for a number of reasons. First, it helps to place in their proper historical context Hume's remarks on the relations between the sciences in the introduction to the *Treatise*, and suggests that Hume was not alone in contemplating cognitive structures or in seeing the science of human nature as the trunk of the tree of philosophy.[11] Secondly, it seems reasonable to assume that Turnbull discussed his conception of the tree of knowledge in his lectures at Marischal, and if he did indeed do so, it may well be that he was instrumental in shaping the attitudes of both his students and his colleagues towards the connections of the various branches of learning. This question is of some importance, since those responsible for reforming the curricula at both Marischal and King's in the early 1750s expressed views on the geography of knowledge which closely paralleled those stated by Turnbull. Consequently, it is arguable that the reforms of the 1750s were at least partly inspired by ideas initially formulated by Turnbull in the 1720s. Finally, Turnbull's comments on the map of the sciences imply that practical morality must be based on the empirical study of the powers of the human mind, and elsewhere in the *Observations* he asserts explicitly that "[a]n exact theory of human morals can only be formed from a full and accurate review of the various natural principles, or natural powers and dispositions of mankind, as these stand related to one another, and to surrounding objects".[12] For Turnbull, then, the moralist must also be, in the first instance, an accomplished anatomist of the mind. But while he was thus much closer to Hutcheson than to Hume in his analysis of the compatibility of the roles of the moralist and the metaphysician, it is arguable that Turnbull differed somewhat from Hutcheson too in so far as he placed much greater emphasis on the cataloguing of what he called the "furniture of the mind" than did the Glasgow professor. As we shall see, this stress on the anatomy of the mind became a characteristic feature of the Aberdonian philosophical tradition, and it would seem that here too Turnbull was a formative influence.[13]

[11] T. xv–xvi. Unlike Turnbull, Hume rests mathematics and natural philosophy on the science of man.

[12] *Observations*, p. 424; compare *Principles*, vol. 1, p. v, and *A methodical system of universal law*, vol. 1 (London 1763), Preface A2v.

[13] Although Hutcheson claimed that the moralist needed to study human nature, his analysis of the powers of the mind was largely superficial, and primarily restricted to what he called the "internal" or "reflex" senses. His rather cursory treatment of the structure of the mind reflected his antipathy towards purely metaphysical and speculative inquiries. Moreover, although William Leechman asserted that Hutcheson endeavoured to apply the experimental method to the study of morals, Hutcheson himself did not comment in any detail on methodological issues and did not indulge in the kind of scientist rhetoric employed by Turnbull. See Francis Hutcheson, *An inquiry into the original of our ideas of beauty and virtue* (London 1725), pp. iii–iv; id., *A short introduction to moral philosophy* (Glasgow 1747), pp. iv, 1–3; id., *A system of moral philosophy*, vol. 1 (Glasgow 1755), pp. xii–xv.

The scientistic belief in the application of the experimental or inductive method to morals is yet another feature of the Aberdeen philosophical tradition which can be attributed to Turnbull's influence. In his 1723 thesis, Turnbull only obliquely suggested that the methodology propounded by Bacon and practised by Newton be utilized in moral inquiries, but there is little doubt that in his Marischal lectures he urged the deployment of Newton's method of analysis and synthesis in the sciences of man. For Turnbull later remarked in the preface to the *Principles* that it was on the basis of a "hint" in the 31st Query of Newton's *Opticks* that he was "led long ago to apply myself to the study of the human mind in the same way as to that of the human body".[14] Turnbull also noted in his Preface that the text of the *Principles* was based on "the substance of several *pneumatological* discourses . . . read above a dozen years ago to students of *Moral Philosophy*", which means that his pupils at Marischal were bound to have been exposed to his scientistic methodological message. Writing in the *Principles*, Turnbull expressed the essence of this message thus:

But however philosophy may be divided; nothing can be more evident, than, that the study of nature, whether in the constitution and oeconomy of the sensible world, or in the frame and government of the moral, must set out from the same first principles, and be carried on in the same method of investigation, induction, and reasoning; since both are enquiries into facts or real constitutions. (Vol. 1, p. 2)

The details of what Turnbull took to be the correct scientific method need not detain us here. Suffice it to say that in all likelihood he based his exposition of the method of analysis and synthesis on passages in Newton's *Opticks* and Cotes's lengthy preface to the second edition of the *Principia*.[15] From the limited evidence available, it would seem that Turnbull was the first Aberdeen regent to announce the methodological reform of the moral sciences, and that it was Turnbull rather than his pupil Reid who initiated what Larry Laudan has called the "Newtonian turn of British methodological thought".[16]

If the contents of Turnbull's lectures were so innovatory, what can be said of his pedagogical style? Although there are apparently no surviving

[14] Turnbull, *De scientiae naturalis conjunctione*, p. 3; *Principles*, vol. 1, p. iii.

[15] Most of the methodological content of the *Principles* is taken up with analysis and synthesis, and Turnbull's debt to Newton and Cotes is clear from the text; see vol. 1, pp. 20–23.

[16] Laudan, 'Thomas Reid' p. 106. Turnbull may have derived his methodological ideas from Robert Steuart, the Edinburgh professor of Natural Philosophy with whom he studied. After the introduction of the professorial system in 1707, Steuart was nominally responsible for prelecting on both natural philosophy and ethics, and it may be that Steuart argued for the methodological unity of these two branches of learning. It is significant that Hume also studied with Steuart, and, like Turnbull, recommended the use of the experimental method in moral inquiries; see M. Barfoot, in the next paper in this volume.

accounts of his lecturing, circumstantial evidence suggests that his class-room delivery probably broke with established conventions. One *leitmotiv* of Turnbull's writings, including his correspondence during his period at Aberdeen with Lord Molesworth, is the love of liberty and virtue, and there is little doubt that Turnbull endeavoured to instil the appropriate moral principles in his young charges at Marischal. Indeed, Turnbull wrote to Molesworth in 1722 that "in my publick Profession", i.e. in his teaching, "I . . . shal always make it my business to promote the interests of Liberty and Vertue & to reform the taste of the Young Generation".[17] In order to reform the taste of his pupils, it may well be that Turnbull rejected certain aspects of traditional scholastic teaching methods, and that he adopted a more polite style, equally indebted to ancient models and to modern exemplars like Shaftesbury. Turnbull bitterly complained to Molesworth about the "Formal dogmatical spirit" and "Idle Pedantick Stuff" inflicted on university students, and he returned to this theme in his *Principles of moral philosophy*. Here he contrasted "that insipid, tedious ungainful manner" which he said had "prevailed in the schools" and brought philosophy into contempt and "as it were quite banished it from amongst the polite and fashionable part of the world", with "that free, elegant and pleasing way, which we may know from some few examples among the moderns, and from many among the ancients, not to be incompatible with the profoundest subjects in *Philosophy*".[18] Of course Turnbull himself was an exponent of the "free, elegant and pleasing way", both in his later published writings and to a lesser extent in his Marischal graduation theses. Given that these theses exhibit some of the stylistic mannerisms of Turnbull's subsequent works, it seems reasonable to assume that his lectures too shared something of this style. It is arguable therefore that in the class-room Turnbull adopted the guise of the Shaftesburian moralist, and indulged in the kind of florid rhetoric which he thought was appropriate to the communication of lofty sentiments concerning the moral economy of God's creation and of civil society. Furthermore, he was probably the first to lecture in this way, for although other Marischal regents were prelecting on Shaftesbury's ideas, it is unlikely that they cultivated the trappings of the role of the practical moralist as assiduously as Turnbull.[19]

If I am correct about Turnbull's stylistic innovations, then the development of Scottish moral philosophy in the first half of the eighteenth century begins to take on a pattern which differs significantly

[17] Quoted in M. A. Stewart, 'George Turnbull and educational reform', in *Aberdeen and the enlightenment*, ed. J. J. Carter and J. H. Pittock (Aberdeen 1987), p. 96.

[18] Stewart, ibid., p. 96; Turnbull, *Principles*, vol. 1, p. ii.

[19] Another Marischal regent who we know expounded some of the ideas of Shaftesbury was David Verner, who was a Crown appointment in 1717; see Verner, *De passionibus*, p. 11.

from that which has hitherto been widely thought to obtain. Beginning with Dugald Stewart, historians have often seen Hutcheson as the key figure in the formative years of the Scottish Enlightenment, and Sher has gone so far as to claim that Hutcheson was "the father of eighteenth-century Scottish moral philosophy" and that "[t]he grand 'farrago' of philosophical ideas and practical teachings that made up Hutcheson's so-called 'system' was the fountainhead of most Scottish academic moral philosophy during the second half of the eighteenth century".[20] In Sher's view Hutcheson's real achievement rested on his innovative pedagogical style, and his forging of an eclectic moral system which combined elements of Commonwealthman ideology with Presbyterian piety, and which was intended "not so much to produce expert philosophers as polite, virtuous, thoughtful, well-rounded, liberal Christian gentlemen". Yet it is striking that almost everything which Sher writes of Hutcheson could equally be said of Turnbull. Both men were staunch Whigs with Country leanings. Both were heavily indebted to Shaftesbury's ideas and rhetorical style. Both were innovative teachers, and concerned with practical morality, though as I have noted above Turnbull was arguably more interested than Hutcheson in the anatomy of the mind because of his Shaftesburian fascination with the analogies between the laws governing the mental and material realms of nature. Where they differed somewhat was over religion, for Turnbull privately proclaimed the virtues of free-thinking in religion, while maintaining a more orthodox public persona. None the less, despite their undoubted differences over the merits of presbyterianism, both men were warm Christians.[21] Hence Hutcheson was probably less original than Sher and others have claimed, and it would seem that we need to understand his Glasgow career within the context of a cultural formation which historians are only now beginning to explore in any detail. The recent work of M. A. Stewart is pertinent in this regard, for he has begun to reconstruct an important intellectual network which included Rankenians like Turnbull, student activists in Glasgow with whom Turnbull was in contact, and the milieu of the Irish presbyterians from which Hutcheson emerged.[22] Instead of focusing on single individuals,

---

[20] Dugald Stewart, *Dissertation*, p. 204; Sher, 'Professors of virtue', above; id., *Church and university*, p. 167. Although Sher recognizes that the Aberdeen tradition poses problems for his genealogy of Scottish philosophy, it is clear that he sees Hutcheson as the seminal figure in the development of moral philosophy in the Scottish Enlightenment. It is curious that he nowhere discusses in any detail the impact of Shaftesbury on Scottish moralists of the first half of the eighteenth century.

[21] For a characteristic expression of Turnbull's attitude towards the presbyterian clergy see M. A. Stewart, 'Turnbull and education', p. 96.

[22] Stewart, 'Turnbull and education'; id., 'Berkeley and the Rankenian club', in *George Berkeley: essays and replies*, ed. D. Berman (Dublin 1986), 25–45; id., 'John Smith and the Molesworth circle', *Eighteenth-century Ireland* 2 (1987), 89–102. On this cultural complex see also Peter Jones, 'The polite academy and the presbyterians, 1720–1770', in *New perspectives on*

we must scrutinize the workings of this network as a whole in order to understand fully the impetus behind the rise of Scottish philosophy in the eighteenth century.

The sole Aberdeen regent active prior to 1750 about whose teaching we otherwise have much concrete evidence is David Fordyce, who lectured at Marischal College from 1742 until his early death in 1751. As his published works indicate, Fordyce was, like Turnbull, something of a practical moralist in the Shaftesburian mode, and in his teaching he attempted to inspire "the minds of the Youth with just & manly Principles of Religion & Virtue".[23] Yet Fordyce was equally well versed in the science of the mind, and his correspondence with Doddridge reveals that by 1740 Fordyce had already penned an "Essay on Human Nature", of which he wrote to the English Dissenter:

> I believe you will find some of the passions considered in a light that is not quite so common, and some connexions in human nature seized that I have not seen traced elsewhere; some difficulties attempted to be explained, that have not before been . . . at all considered; an endeavour to distinguish some powers of the mind that have been confounded; and to explain some beautiful allegories and maxims of antiquity, particularly the grand rule of the heathen moralists, that of living according to nature.[24]

Fordyce's description of this early work suggests that he saw the roles of the moralist and the metaphysician as intimately related, and he later spelled out the relationship both in his lectures and in his *Elements of moral philosophy*.

When introducing his students to the "Nature, Origin, and Progress of Philosophy", Fordyce stressed that true philosophers deduce both moral and natural laws from facts and observations, and hence he defined ethics as the science that "Enquires into the active & moral part of Mans constitution, & thence deduces the Rule of Life & Conduct, & explains the several Offices or Duties to which he is obliged by the Laws

---

the politics and culture of early modern Scotland, ed. J. Dwyer and others (Edinburgh 1982), 156–78; id., 'The Scottish professoriate and the polite academy, 1720–46', in Hont and Ignatieff, *Wealth and virtue*, 89–117.

[23] Fordyce to Philip Doddridge, 6 June 1743: Doddridge Correspondence, New College London/Dr Williams's Library, MS LI/V, item 171, fol. 1v. Fordyce's Shaftesburian style is most marked in his *Dialogues concerning education* (London 1745). For practical advice in the class-room see 'A Few advices of the late Mr Da. Fordyce to his Scholars at the end of the Session Concerning Reading', appended to 'A brief Account of the Nature, *Origin*, and *Progress* of Philosophy delivered by the late Mr. David Fordyce P.P. Marish. Col: Abdn. to his Scholars, before they began their Philosophical course. Anno 1743/4', AUL, MS. M 184, fol. 28. Fordyce was familiar with Turnbull's *Principles*; see his positive remarks in a letter to Doddridge, 20 February 1740, in *The correspondence and diary of Philip Doddridge, D.D.*, ed. J. D. Humphreys, vol. 3 (London 1830), pp. 416–17.

[24] Fordyce to Doddridge, 10 April 1740, in *Correspondence*, vol. 3, p. 442.

of Nature".[25] Similarly, he stated in the *Elements* that "*Moral Philosophy* contemplates *Human Nature*, its *Moral Powers* and Connections; and from these deduces the Laws of Actions", and he here made explicit the methodological implications of the parallel he saw between the sciences of man and nature. Echoing other metaphysicians and moralists, Fordyce claimed that

> *Moral Philosophy* has this in common with *Natural Philosophy*, that it appeals to *Nature* or *Fact*; depends on Observation, and builds its Reasonings on plain uncontroverted Experiments, or upon the fullest Induction of Particulars of which the Subject will admit. We must observe, in both these Sciences, *Quid faciat & ferat Natura*; how Nature is affected, and what her Conduct is in such and such Circumstances. Or in other words, we must collect the *Phaenomena*, or *Appearances of Nature* in any given Instance; trace these to some *General Principles*, or *Laws of Operation*; and then apply these *Principles* or *Laws* to the explaining of other *Phaenomena*.[26]

Turnbull's methodological message was thus taken up at Marischal by Fordyce, though it should be noted that Fordyce seems to have been less inspired by the works of Newton than his predecessor, and much more indebted to the writings of Bacon.[27] None the less, it would seem that Fordyce urged the methodological unity of natural and moral philosophy in his lectures, and his conception of the cognitive structure of the sciences was akin to Turnbull's.[28] We see, therefore, that at Marischal at least, prior to the 1750s scientism played a significant role in the transformation of the curriculum which was gradually taking place, and that Turnbull and Fordyce were both practical moralists and anatomists of the mind who ostensibly founded their moral teachings on the science of human nature.

II. 1753–1800

Although the contents of the curriculum at Marischal and presumably at King's changed dramatically in the first half of the eighteenth century, its structure remained essentially the same as it had been in the sixteenth and seventeenth centuries. In the 1690s, for example, we find that

[25] 'A brief Account', fols. 2v, 27r.

[26] *The elements of moral philosophy* (London 1754), pp. 5, 7–8. Significantly, Fordyce also defined moral philosophy as the "*Science of* MANNERS *or* DUTY, which it traces from Man's Nature and Condition, and shews to terminate in his Happiness" (p. 5).

[27] Fordyce's preliminary lecture on the history of philosophy indicates that he placed greater importance on Bacon's role in the reformation of philosophy than did Turnbull, and his praise of Newton is less extreme than that of his predecessor; see 'A brief Account', fols. 22v–24v.

[28] See also 'A brief Account', fol. 27r, where Fordyce claims that both logic and politics rest on the study of human nature.

Marischal students followed a four-year course which began with the study of the languages of classical antiquity and the elements of arithmetic, and then progressed to logic and geometry in the second year; natural philosophy and ethics in the third year; and finally to metaphysics, astronomy, and what was known as "special physics", which encompassed the explanation of "all the particular phenomena of Nature".[29] By the 1740s a certain amount of reordering had occurred at Marischal, for it would seem that Fordyce taught the various branches of philosophy in the sequence logic, metaphysics, pneumatology and natural theology, ethics and politics, and lastly physics, which seems to have been the standard pattern in the college.[30] Evidence about the structure of the curriculum at King's is completely lacking, though it is unlikely that it differed significantly from that at Marischal since the reforms effected at King's in 1753 so closely paralleled those carried out at Marischal.

It is unclear what prompted the reforms of 1753, but after a relatively short period of discussion within the two colleges, new regulations governing the curriculum and other aspects of collegiate life were adopted at Marischal in January 1753 and at King's in August of that year.[31] Apart from the formal introduction of civil and natural history into the curricula, the most important alterations affected the order in which the philosophy course was taught. At both King's and Marischal, the course now began with civil and natural history, proceeded in the second year to natural philosophy, and then concluded with pneumatology and the other sciences of man. One notable feature of the reformed curricula is that they embody Turnbull's ideas regarding the tree of the sciences. At Turnbull's old college, Alexander Gerard and his colleagues stressed that ethics, logic, jurisprudence, and politics were all based on the science of the "constitution of man, and his several active powers", and the close relationship between natural and moral philosophy which Turnbull envisaged is reflected in their definition of pneumatology as being "the Natural Philosophy of Spirits". Furthermore, Turnbull's emphasis on the moral uses of natural knowledge is echoed in Gerard's proposal for a reformed science of metaphysics which would vindicate "the constitution of nature by pointing out the final causes of the general

---

[29] R. S. Rait, *The universities of Aberdeen: a history* (Aberdeen 1895), pp. 288–9; see also Shepherd, *Philosophy and science*, chap. 2, for a discussion of the curriculum in the Scottish universities during the seventeenth century.

[30] Fordyce, 'A brief Account', fol. 27r; see also the letter from Fordyce to Doddridge cited in footnote 23, fol. 1; and [Alexander Gerard], *Plan of education in the Marischal College and University of Aberdeen, with the reasons of it* (Aberdeen 1755), p. 3.

[31] On the curriculum reforms see P. B. Wood, *Thomas Reid, natural philosopher: a study of science and philosophy in the Scottish Enlightenment* (Ph.D., University of Leeds 1984), pp. 58–65.

laws to which beings are subjected".[32] Over in Old Aberdeen, we find King's College issuing one of the clearest expositions of the map of knowledge sketched by Turnbull. In their initial description of the newly adopted curriculum, Reid and his fellow reformers stated that in their third year the students would "be employed in the Philosophy of the Human Mind and the Sciences that depend upon it", and in response to requests for clarification of this statement, the faculty specified the topics covered in more detail:

By the *Philosophy of the Mind*, is understood, An Account of the Constitution of the human Mind, and of all its Powers and Faculties, whether Sensitive, Intellectual, or Moral; the Improvements these are capable of, and the Means of their Improvement; of the mutual Influences of Body and Mind on each other; and of the Knowledge we may acquire of other Minds, and particularly of the Supreme Mind. And the *Sciences depending on the Philosophy of the Mind*, are understood to be Logic, Rhetoric, the Laws of Nature and Nations, Politicks, Oeconomicks, the fine Arts and natural Religion.[33]

We see, then, that like their colleagues at Marischal, the King's men grounded the study of morals and related subjects on pneumatology, but this passage also shows that at King's greater stress was placed on the detailed anatomy of the mind than was the case at Marischal, and, as we shall see, this difference was to become more marked in the later decades of the century.

Regarding the method to be adopted in the study of pneumatology, the King's faculty were silent, but at Marischal Gerard and his associates were more forthcoming. Throughout his *Plan of education*, Gerard alluded to the fact that all philosophy had to be based on natural history, and pneumatology was no exception, for at one point he spoke of the necessity of a "natural history of the human understanding", and he indicated that history and the sciences themselves provided empirical materials for a "natural history of the human intellect". Moreover, he too proclaimed the methodological unity of natural and moral philosophy, writing that the "Philosophy of spirits, as well as that of bodies, is founded solely on experiments and observations" (pp. 5, 9, 18, 29, 31). The curriculum reforms of 1753 were thus informed by the ideology of scientism, as well as by the complex of ideas bequeathed by Turnbull

[32] [Gerard], *Plan*, pp. 23, 26–7, 33. Stewart, 'Turnbull and education', p. 101, suggests that Gerard's *Plan* "harks back not to Molesworth and Turnbull . . . but to the ancient Stoics and Bacon". Gerard was certainly indebted to the Stoics and Bacon, but, as I have indicated, there are a number of close parallels between Gerard's ideas and those of Turnbull. Gerard's proposals for a reformed science of metaphysics did not find favour at King's; see the criticisms in [James Dunbar], 'Institutes of Moral Philosophy': AUL, MS. 3107/5/2/6, fols. 2v–3r.

[33] *Abstract of some statutes and orders of King's College in Old Aberdeen* ([Aberdeen] 1754), pp. 13, 19. Reid, who had been a pupil of Turnbull, served on the committee which drafted these regulations; see Wood, *Thomas Reid*, pp. 60–61.

and his contemporaries. By ignoring the potency of this ideology, Phillipson has presented a highly partial and fundamentally misleading picture of eighteenth-century Scottish philosophy. For even if we admit that Scottish philosophers attempted to develop a "casuistical armoury" relevant to the concerns of a commercial society, the very logic of the moralists' position leads us back to the anatomy of the mind and the prescripts of the experimental method. According to the Aberdonian reformers, the practical moralist was necessarily a metaphysician as well, though it must be said that Hume's strictures on this combination of roles were soon to find support in Aberdeen from a most unexpected quarter.

Notwithstanding their agreement about the structure of the curriculum, the reformers at Marischal and King's differed over one central issue, namely the respective merits of the professorial and regenting systems. At Marischal, the faculty followed the example set by the other Scottish universities and introduced professorships, whereas King's resolved to retain the traditional teaching format, guided partly by the counsels of Thomas Reid.[34] One consequence of the introduction of the professorial system at Marischal was that the intimate relations between natural and moral philosophy which had hitherto existed were now somewhat weakened, as the professors sought to define the boundaries of their subjects. Gerard, the first professor of moral philosophy at Marischal, was, as his defence of the curriculum reforms demonstrates, deeply imbued with the ideas and ideals of men like Turnbull and Fordyce. Hence in his lectures he too said of the science of the mind, or what he termed "psychology", that "in a manner all our conclusions in it, as well as in Natural Philosophy must be founded on Experiments & observations", and, having paraphrased Newton's "Rules of Philosophizing" in the introductory prelection to his course, Gerard asserted that "[t]hese Rules are not only applicable to natural Philosophy but also to that of the human Mind".[35] But, like Hume, he recognized the difficulties inherent in the empirical study of human nature; and unlike his Aberdonian predecessors, Gerard told his students that there were important differences between the methods pursued in natural and moral philosophy. As one of his pupils recorded in 1759:

Tho' all Subjects of real Existence have this in Common, that they can be cultivated only by carefully reasoning from experience, or by Induction, yet they differ from one another in so many respects that the Induction that ought to

---

[34] For Reid's role in the retention of the regenting system see 'Statistical account of the University and King's College of Aberdeen', in *The statistical account of Scotland 1791–1799*, ed. Sir John Sinclair, vol. 1 (repr., Wakefield 1983), p. 280.

[35] [Alexander Gerard], Notes of lectures on Psychology, taken by Robert Morgan (1758–9), EUL, MS. Dc 5.61, pp. 6–7, 12.

be applied to them must admit of considerable varieties, & the methods of varying the Induction according to the nature of the Subject enquired into may no doubt be reduced to Rules. We shall only observe in general that the two great heads of Natural Knowledge are that of Matter & that of the Mind. & the method to be used in cultivating 'em will differ considerably; First in the manner of *making* Experiments. 2°. There will likewise be some difference in the *Nature* of the *reasoning* from Experiments arising from the difference of Ideas employed. 3°. There will be a variety also in the *Assistances* which the mind receives in its Enquiries on these different Subjects. The Subordinate Branches of each of these Sciences will also require some varieties in the methods of treating them, which may be deduced from the peculiarities of their Nature.[36]

Thus even though Gerard maintained that all branches of philosophy rested on natural history and employed empirical methods, he was more finely attuned to the distinctiveness of the methodological principles at work in the different subjects, and it may well be that his sensitivity in this regard was at least partly related to the fact that he needed to carve out an independent institutional niche for moral philosophy at Marischal after the introduction of the professorial system.[37]

Even if Gerard qualified the methodological assumptions of Turnbull and Fordyce in significant ways, he was in complete agreement with his predecessors regarding the relations between morals and metaphysics. He insisted in his lectures that our notions of moral duty must be deduced from our knowledge of human nature, and he argued that the concept of virtue could not be properly defined without reference to the science of the mind. In 1759 he put the point thus:

That which is the Business & Duty of Man, we call Virtue & if it be indeed his Business we may expect that it is the end of his constitution & the immediate result of that constitution when in its natural state. In order therefore to discover whither Virtue has any foundation in the nature of man, we must inquire what is the constitution & structure of human Nature . . . (Dc 5.62, p. 4)

For Gerard, then, the pursuit of virtue presupposed the detailed knowledge of human nature, and he envisaged no disjunction between practical morality and pneumatology or psychology. What is particularly interesting about his statement of this position is the Baconian rationale which he provided for the direct link between metaphysics and morals. When defining the "business of Philosophy", Gerard pointed out in true Baconian fashion that the conclusions reached in philosophy must be applied to practice, which for him meant that the knowledge attained in the science of the mind was to be used to improve our

---

[36] [Gerard], Notes on Logic: EUL, Dc 5.62, pp. 595–6; compare Hume, T. xviii–xix.

[37] Another indication of this may be Gerard's sharp distinction between anatomy and pneumatology; see Dc 5.61, pp. 56–7. The attitude expressed here differs greatly from that of a figure like Reid, who discussed anatomical detail in his lectures on perception.

cultivation of our intellectual and moral powers.[38] Gerard's Baconian equation of knowledge and control coupled with the demand for utility entailed, therefore, that the theoretical principles established in pneumatology were to be applied to the practical sciences of ethics and logic, which thus ruled out any Humean disjunction between metaphysics and morals.

A more decisive break with tradition was made by Gerard's pupil and successor, James Beattie. In certain respects, Beattie did not question the entrenched Marischal approach to moral philosophy. He accepted the view that pneumatology, ethics, and the other subjects covered in his course were all empirical sciences, though he did not elaborate on the precise methods to be pursued as did his predecessors. Furthermore, Beattie too held that ethical norms had to be deduced from our knowledge of human nature; yet his discussion of the anatomy of the mind differed radically from that of Gerard, for example, since Beattie provided only a perfunctory treatment of our external senses, and concentrated on the analysis of our faculties of taste (including the moral sense) and our active powers.[39] Moreover, he echoed Gerard's Baconian demand that knowledge be applied to practice, but he took the requirement of utility much further than his predecessor, and turned the utilitarian imperative into a crude weapon with which to attack heterodoxy.

In his lectures, Beattie emphasized that philosophy was to be valued chiefly because "it regulate[d] human practice", and he made it clear that in his view the pursuit of knowledge was subservient to the cultivation of virtue. Consequently, he condemned what he called the "restless Spirit in some Men which prompts them to be continually meddling with things that do not concern them", and he advised his students to "Restrain needless curiosity" and "enquire not into that Business or these Sentiments of other Men in which you have no concern; nor puzzle yourselves with intricate & unprofitable speculations or Enquiries".[40] Beattie also attacked those who published what he took to be subversive philosophical principles:

As to these authors who on the pretence of unfolding the Philosophy of Man have delivered to the world licentious Theories, & systems of Scepticism as *Hobbes, Hume, Helvetius* &c my advice is, that you should avoid them entirely.

[38] Dc 5.61, p. 6; see also Dc 5.62, p. 505, on logic.

[39] James Beattie, 'The Elements of Moral Philosophy' (Notes taken by Alexander Chalmers in 1777–78): EUL, Dc 2.64, pp. 3–4, 281; Dc 2.65, pp. 1–3. In the first of the volumes I have examined (Dc 2.64), the section devoted to the analysis of man's intellectual powers occupies pages 7–80, with a substantial portion of this (pp. 16–47) devoted to language. The section dealing with taste occupies pages 84–283, and the lectures on man's active powers take up pages 283–311.

[40] Dc 2.64, p. 307. I have expanded the contractions to be found in the notes.

They may do harm to weak minds, & they cannot possibly do good to any; Habits of wrangling & controversy are dangerous to the human understanding, & destructive of human happiness; & therefore though you should see & be able to confute the sophistries of these authors, I would not wish you to read them, because habits of doubting, & recollecting objections are very unfriendly both to the head, & to the heart, to the understanding & to the imagination. Read no bad books. In this country you have access to a greater number of good books than it will ever be possible for you to study with that attention which they deserve.[41]

This passage indicates that with Beattie the tension which Hume had discerned between the roles of the metaphysician and the moralist was now manifest in the Marischal class-rooms. Whereas a figure like Gerard maintained at least the pretence of dispassionate inquiry into the structure of the mind, in Beattie's lectures moral didacticism becomes the dominant mode, and there is no lack of warmth in the cause of virtue. Beattie's preoccupation with the inculcation of sound moral and religious values thus led him to renounce the anatomy of the mind for the graphic portrayal of virtue and piety.

Comments made by both Gerard and Beattie in their lectures further illustrate their different pedagogical styles. In his ethics prelections, Gerard distinguished between two methods of dealing with morals, the "abstract", and the "popular & sentimental". Regarding his own lectures, Gerard stated that he would treat the "Speculative part of Ethics . . . chiefly in the abstract manner tho' not without a mixture of the other", and that practical ethics would be treated "chiefly in the popular way, but rendred accurate by something of the Abstract attending it" (Dc 5.62, p. 3). Gerard therefore attempted to find a just balance between analytical rigour and moral inspiration, whereas Beattie's remarks on correct philosophical prose suggest that he did not.

According to Beattie, "nothing is more interesting to human creatures than that which immediately concerns human passions, feelings & sentiments. And therefore it is an authors fault & not the fault of the subject, if every part of Moral Philosophy be not made extremely entertaining." Consequently, he told his students that the phenomena of the mind should be illustrated by frequent examples drawn from history and everyday life, so that the "attention of the reader may be continually kept awake, & the abstract nature of the subject made level to the capacity of every person, who can observe what passes in his own mind, or in the world about him". As for those parts of the subject related to "our improvement in Virtue, & the regulation of the passions", Beattie said that they should be "not only entertaining but delivered with that

---

[41] Dc 2.65, pp. 251–2; see also p. 65. In a related vein, Beattie criticized in his lectures Hume's attack on the argument from design, without actually naming Hume as the target (Dc 2.65, p. 234).

simple & expressive eloquence which touches the heart, & disposes it to form good resolutions". Finally, Beattie asserted that in moral philosophy "the greatest exactness of method, accurracy of arrange-ment, & perspicuity of stile are indispensible", and that "particular care should be taken to avoid ambiguity of language" (Dc 2.64, pp. 281–3). By implication, then, Beattie's own pedagogical style can best be understood as an "entertaining" and "expressive" one, primarily designed to instil the principles of piety and virtue in the hearts of his pupils. Like Hume, Beattie believed that the roles of the metaphysician and the moralist were distinct, and *he* eagerly adopted the guise of the practical moralist.

At King's College, each regent active in the period 1753 to 1800 had a slightly different approach to teaching moral philosophy, but despite individual variations, certain common themes emerge in the lectures and related materials which survive. As I have already mentioned, the King's faculty endorsed Turnbull's view of the relations between metaphysics and morals in their published statements regarding the curriculum reform of 1753, and in their lectures the regents similarly insisted that moral precepts must be derived from the principles of pneumatology. Thomas Gordon, for example, pointed to the overriding importance of the anatomy of the mind for the practical moralist when he told his students that "the only way prior to revelation, by which we can discover the proper business or duty of man is to consider what is the real constitution of his nature; and from what it leads him to, to deduce what he was designed for", and most of his colleagues made similar claims in their prelections.[42] Outside of the class-room, Reid put the point most eloquently in the introduction to *An inquiry into the human mind, on the principles of common sense*:

In the arts and sciences which have least connection with the mind, its faculties are the engines which we must employ; and the better we understand their nature and use, their defects and disorders, the more skilfully we shall apply them, and with the greater success. But in the noblest arts, the mind is also the subject upon which we operate. The painter, the poet, the actor, the orator, the moralist, and the statesman, attempt to operate upon the mind in different ways, and for different ends; and they succeed, according as they touch properly the strings of the human frame. Nor can their several arts ever stand on a solid

---

[42] Thomas Gordon, 'A Manuscript of Moral Philosophy ... rewritten by Alexander Thomson. A.D. 1773–74': AUL, MS. K 166, p. 364; see also pp. 361, 362. Gordon also drew attention to the importance of applying knowledge about the constitution of the mind to practice; see pp. 2, 488. For comparable remarks on utility, see *Philosophical orations of Thomas Reid: delivered at graduation ceremonies in King's College Aberdeen, 1753, 1756, 1759, 1762*, ed. W. R. Humphries (Aberdeen 1937), pp. 19–23. On the relations between pneumatology and ethics see also Dunbar, 'Institutes', fol. 2v; [Roderick MacLeod], 'Moral Philosophy. Lectures from 1784': AUL, MS. K 171, p. 4.

foundation, or rise to the dignity of science, until they are built on the principles of the human constitution.[43]

Prior to his departure to the Glasgow chair of Moral Philosophy in 1764, Reid was also the most articulate spokesman at King's for the ideology of scientism, and his insistence on the use of the inductive method and on the elimination of speculative hypotheses in pneumatology found echoes in the lectures of Gordon, James Dunbar, and especially those of Robert Eden Scott, who claimed that "it is to a name of so late a date as that of our countryman Reid, that we are to consider [the science of the mind] as indebted for a firm foundation, & for having clearly pointed out the true mode in which alone it can be cultivated & established in a rank equally respectable with that of the other sciences".[44] Yet, on the whole, the King's men were also attuned to the methodological problems faced when studying human nature. Dunbar, for instance, warned that there were "difficulties of considerable magnitude" associated with the introspective method, and Scott likewise pointed to the problematic nature of introspection, as well as to the ambiguities of language and the extreme diversity of characteristics of the human mind produced by cultural variation.[45] By the second half of the eighteenth century, then, the initial enthusiasm of men like Turnbull for the application of the methods of the natural sciences to the sciences of man had been tempered somewhat by others, by the realization that the mind was apparently a more elusive object of inquiry than matter. Nevertheless, the brand of moral philosophy taught at King's following the 1753 reforms was, like that at Marischal, founded on the scientistic belief encapsulated in Pope's dictum, "Account for moral, as for nat'ral things".[46]

If the contents and structure of the King's moral philosophy prelections were comparable to those delivered by Gerard at Marischal, what can be said about pedagogical styles? Unfortunately we have no clues about William Ogilvie's classroom practice, which is particularly regrettable in so far as Ogilvie was one of the most innovative and interesting regents teaching at King's in this period.[47] Similarly, we

[43] Thomas Reid, *An inquiry into the human mind, on the principles of common sense* (Edinburgh 1764), pp. 2–3; compare Reid's statements in his Glasgow lectures, AUL, MS. 2131/4/I/13, fol. 1r; there is little doubt that Reid said essentially the same at King's College. See also Robert Eden Scott, 'Elements of Moral Philosophy for the Magistrand Class 1798': AUL, MS. K 190, pp. 1–2.

[44] Scott, 'Elements', p. 3; see also Gordon, 'Manuscript', p. 496; MacLeod, 'Moral Philosophy', pp. 1, 6, 35–36, 41; Dunbar, 'Institutes', fol. 3.

[45] Dunbar, 'Institutes', fol. 3r; Scott, 'Elements', pp. 3–6.

[46] Alexander Pope, 'An essay on man', in *Poetical Works*, ed. H. Davis (Oxford 1985), p. 245, line 162; see also Pope's interesting remarks on the anatomy of the mind, p. 239.

[47] Ogilvie was instrumental in the establishment of a natural history museum at King's, and among his other activities he initiated a subscription for a public library in Aberdeen; see

know next to nothing about James Dunbar's lecturing style, since his surviving lecture notes reveal little beyond the topics which he covered.[48] Of the older regents, Roderick MacLeod was an unreconstructed follower of Shaftesbury and Turnbull, and even in the 1780s his moral philosophy prelections amounted to little more than an epitome of Shaftesbury's *Characteristicks* and Turnbull's *Principles*; consequently, there is a great deal of extravagant rhetoric about virtue, but it must be said that there is little by way of practical advice. The other long-serving King's man, Thomas Gordon, was far more prosaic in his discussion of morals than MacLeod, and Gerard would no doubt have categorized Gordon's style as "abstract" rather than "popular & sentimental".

The most metaphysical of the King's moralists was unquestionably Reid. Having experienced Reid's lecturing in Glasgow at first hand, albeit at a later period, Dugald Stewart described his mentor's classroom manner thus:

The merits of Dr REID, as a public teacher, were derived chiefly from that rich fund of original and instructive philosophy which is to be found in his writings; and from his unwearied assiduity in inculcating principles which he conceived to be of essential importance to human happiness. In his elocution and mode of instruction, there was nothing peculiarly attractive. He seldom, if ever, indulged himself in the warmth of extempore discourse; nor was his manner of reading calculated to increase the effect of what he had committed to writing.[49]

The contrast between Reid's lecturing style, and that of Hutcheson, Ferguson, and Stewart himself, could not be more striking. Whereas the other academic moralists were, to use Sher's happy phrase, "philosophical preachers", Reid was the metaphysician *par excellence*, and Alexander Carlyle captured something of the differences between them when he said of Reid and Ferguson that they were the Aristotle and Plato of the Scotch philosophers.[50] Who but Reid would have delivered at the King's graduation ceremonies in 1759 and 1762 public orations devoted to the refutation of the theory of ideas?[51]

Francis Douglas, *A general description of the east coast of Scotland, from Edinburgh to Cullen. Including a brief account of the universities of Saint Andrews and Aberdeen* [etc.] (Paisley 1782), pp. 198–9, and [William Ogilvie], *Proposals for a publick library at Aberdeen* (Aberdeen 1764).

[48] The style in which the 'Institutes' are written indicates that Dunbar may have improvised his lectures on the basis of his general headings. If so, his lecturing style would have been similar to that of Adam Ferguson in this regard.

[49] Dugald Stewart, *Account of the life and writings of Thomas Reid, D.D. F.R.S.Edin.* (Edinburgh 1803), pp. 50–51; compare Ramsay of Ochtertyre's comments on Reid's pulpit style in *Scotland and Scotsmen in the eighteenth century*, ed. A. Allardyce, vol. 1 (Edinburgh 1888), p. 472. McCosh had a more evangelical view of Reid's pastoral style; see *Scottish philosophy*, p. 199.

[50] *Autobiography of the Rev. Dr. Alexander Carlyle minister of Inveresk*, ed. J. H. Burton (Edinburgh 1860), p. 549.

[51] *Philosophical orations*, pp. 27–47.

The conflict between Reid's approach to moral philosophy and that other member of the so-called "Common Sense school", James Beattie, is strikingly illustrated by remarks made by Beattie to Sir William Forbes in 1788. Having read Reid's *Essays on the active powers of man*, Beattie admired the work for its "perspicuity and acuteness", and said that it was "very interesting throughout" and occasionally even "very entertaining". Yet Beattie's praise was heavily qualified, for he noted that "I could have wished that Dr. Reid had given a fuller enumeration of the passions, and been a little more particular in illustrating the duties of morality". In addition, he expressed serious reservations about Reid's "abstract" style of philosophizing:

his manner is, in all his writings, more turned to speculation than to practical philosophy; which may be owing to his having employed himself so much in the study of Locke, Hume, Berkeley, and other theorists; and partly, no doubt, to the habits of study and modes of conversation which were fashionable in this country in his younger days. If I were not personally acquainted with the doctor, I should conclude, from his books, that he was rather too warm an admirer of Mr. Hume. He confutes, it is true, some of his opinions; but pays them much more respect than they are entitled to.[52]

As this passage reveals, Beattie the moralist had misgivings about the writings of Reid the metaphysician. Put simply, in Beattie's eyes, Reid did not display the requisite degree of warmth in the cause of virtue, and his style was all too reminiscent of the "theorists" and sceptics who threatened to undermine the principles of morality and religion. In Beattie's view, Reid was too much of a detached metaphysician, whereas it must be said that Hume, on the other hand, felt that Reid was occasionally too much of a moralist.[53]

At King's, therefore, the "popular & sentimental" style of philosophizing made little headway in the second half of the eighteenth century. Although not all of the regents were as metaphysically inclined as Reid, none of them so far as we know opted for the fervent moralizing of Beattie; and with the appointment of Robert Eden Scott in 1788 King's once again had a metaphysician in the Reidian mould.[54] Moreover, the

[52] Beattie to Forbes, 5 March 1788: *The letters of James Beattie, LL.D.*, vol. 2 (London 1820), p. 161. Although Beattie's view of the Hume-Reid relationship may seem odd, it is worth remembering that Reid did avow himself to be Hume's "Disciple in Metaphysicks"; see Reid to Hume, 18 March 1763: NLS, MS. 23157, letter 3, fol. 1r.

[53] For a pointed expression of Hume's annoyance, see P. B. Wood, 'David Hume on Thomas Reid's *An inquiry into the human mind, on the principles of common sense*: a new letter to Hugh Blair from July 1762', *Mind* 95 (1986), p. 416.

[54] Although Scott had serious literary interests, his lectures demonstrate that he was an anatomist of the mind like Reid, and his published works were highly "metaphysical"; see, for example, Robert Eden Scott, *Inquiry into the limits and peculiar objects of physical and metaphysical science* (Edinburgh 1810).

King's regents all believed that the roles of the metaphysician and the moralist were intimately related, and that the lineaments of virtue could only be drawn on the basis of sound anatomical knowledge of human nature.

III. CONCLUSION

The recent work by Phillipson and Sher on the moral didacticism of eighteenth-century Scottish philosophy has greatly increased our understanding of an important aspect of the Scottish Enlightenment largely ignored by McCosh and successive generations of historians influenced by him. However, we must guard against simply focusing on moral didacticism, as if this were the hitherto unrecognized key to the Scottish "school" of philosophy. Rather, we should follow up Hume's insight into the tensions between metaphysics and morals, and explore the various constitutive elements of academic moral philosophy in the Scottish Enlightenment. For Hume's distinction between these two philosophical styles provides us with a useful tool with which to probe the structure of Scottish philosophy, and to analyse the interplay of the various strands within it.

Utilizing Hume's distinction, I have argued that until the appointment of Beattie to the chair of moral philosophy at Marischal in 1760, Aberdonian philosophers typically combined the roles of metaphysician and moralist and firmly believed that ethical instruction had to be rooted in the anatomy of the mind. Opting exclusively for the public persona of the moralist, Beattie was an anomalous figure much closer in orientation to academic philosophers elsewhere than he was to his Aberdeen colleagues. By contrast, Reid and Scott perpetuated the indigenous Aberdonian tradition and continued to ground practical moralizing on metaphysical inquiry. With the exception of Beattie, then, the Aberdeen men adopted a mode of philosophizing which does not conform to the model sketched by Phillipson and Sher.

It should be stressed that the philosophical style of the Aberdonians was crucially dependent on the institutional structure of their universities. Sher has rightly emphasized the importance of institutional factors in the making of Scottish moral philosophy, and nowhere is this more apparent than in Aberdeen. For it was at Marischal and King's that the regenting system was retained years after the other universities had switched to fixed chairs in philosophy, and it was this system which nurtured the ideology of scientism and allowed for the kind of close conjunction between natural and moral philosophy envisaged by Turnbull and most of his successors. Whereas the professorial system promoted the establishment of cognitive boundaries between the various branches of philosophy and presupposed the existence of distinct sets of pedagogical competences, the regenting system can be seen to have encouraged a more unified view of human knowledge like that embodied in Turnbull's map of the sciences. Hence we can see that regents were more likely to have stressed the interrelations between natural and moral philosophy and the methodological unity of the philosophical enterprise than professors, and this pattern holds true in the case of Aberdeen. It is thus no accident that Beattie's philosophical style resembles that of Adam Ferguson more than that of Reid, since his brand of philosophical preaching was similarly the product of the professorial system, whereas Reid's metaphysical approach bears the unmistakable stamp of the regenting tradition.

What, finally, can be said of the role of science in the pursuit of virtue in the Aberdeen Enlightenment? This question should be sharply distinguished from that of whether the modes of investigation employed or the conclusions reached by the Aberdonian moralists were in any absolute sense "scientific". Generally speaking, the historian is more concerned with the self-perceptions and judgements of historical actors than with the criteria and categories which we currently accept. Consequently, we need to ask ourselves how the Aberdeen men regarded their philosophical enterprise, and the evidence surveyed above demonstrates that they viewed themselves as scientists of the mind, searching for the basis of virtue in human nature. Natural philosophy provided the moralists with the method which they thought would transform pneumatology from being a field riddled with fanciful hypotheses and empty conjectures into a true science which would furnish ethics with a firm empirical and theoretical foundation. Moreover, natural philosophy also supplied a fund of analogies and a terminology with which to describe the operations of the mind and the behaviour of man in society.[55] Scientism thus played a major part in the shaping of moral philosophy in Aberdeen, and, as we have seen, it was a driving force behind the curriculum reforms of 1753. Those who overlook the impetus given to moral philosophy by scientism in the Scottish Enlightenment do so at their peril.[56]

Department of History
Queen's University at Kingston

[55] Turnbull, *Principles*, vol. 1, pp. 190–93; vol. 2, pp. 179–80; Fordyce, *Elements*, pp. 23, 86–7.

[56] I wish to thank the Trustees of the National Library of Scotland, and the Librarians of Aberdeen University Library, Edinburgh University Library, and Dr. Williams's Library for permission to quote from manuscripts in their care; the Social Sciences and Humanities Research Council of Canada and the Advisory Research Committee of Queen's University for financial support; and Roger Emerson, Richard Sher, and M. A. Stewart for comments on an earlier draft.

HUME AND THE CULTURE OF SCIENCE IN THE EARLY EIGHTEENTH CENTURY

MICHAEL BARFOOT

I. THE PHYSIOLOGICAL LIBRARY

In 1724 Robert Steuart, professor of Natural Philosophy at Edinburgh, founded a class library. An early catalogue has survived, entitled *The Physiological Library. Begun by Mr. Steuart, and some of the students of natural philosophy in the University of Edinburgh, April 2. 1724: and augmented by some gentlemen; and the students of natural philosophy, December 1724.*[1] This was printed in 1725, by which time there were 149 members, or "Benefactors"—150 if we include Steuart himself. The catalogue provides a list of members, dividing them into three categories. Forty-nine natural philosophy students appear in the first category (p. 5); thirty-eight gentlemen in the second (pp. 6–7), plus five more who joined later and whose names are included at the end (p. 62). A further fifty-seven natural philosophy students who joined the Library in December are listed in the third category, and here the name 'David Hume' appears.

Hume's membership of the Physiological Library has been previously overlooked. From it we may now deduce that he attended Steuart's class during the 1724–25 session.[2] This information is crucial for understanding the general form his early scientific education took. Had a set of actual lecture notes for 1724–25 survived, it would be relatively easy to

---

[1] EUL, De 10.127, p. 1. All references to pages and the numbers of particular items listed in the catalogue are taken from this copy. See M. D. Bell, 'Faculty and class libraries', in *Edinburgh University Library 1580–1980*, ed. J. R. Guild and A. Law (Edinburgh 1982), at p. 164 and plates 10 and 11, where two introductory pages from the catalogue are reproduced.

[2] Although the name is printed and not a signature, the timing is precisely what we would expect, given Hume's matriculation date, and is consistent with "the ordinary Course of Education" at the university ('My own Life', HL i. 1). Hume matriculated as a member of the Greek class of William Scott in the session 1722–23 where he is clearly identified as being in his second year of studies (Matriculation register, 1704–62: EUL, MS. Da, p. 62). As Greek and natural philosophy correspond to the *second* and *fourth* years of the arts curriculum, it seems likely he attended the Logic and Metaphysics class of Colin Drummond for the intervening 1723–24 session.

reconstruct this, but since no complete set exists for any of the thirty-four years when Steuart was sole occupant of the chair, a more indirect approach is necessary.[3] This involves examining published descriptions of the course structure; analysing the contents of the Physiological Library and the role it played in Steuart's teaching; and, finally, relating the parts of Steuart's lectures which have survived to passages in Hume's works.

We can extrapolate from a later account of Steuart's syllabus in *The Scots magazine* of 1741:

He teaches, first, Dr John Keill's *Introductio ad veram Physicam*, and the Mechanics from several other authors. After that he teaches Hydrostatics and Pneumatics from a manuscript of his own writing. Then he teaches Dr David Gregory's *Optics*, with Sir Isaac Newton *of Colours*; describes the several parts of the Eye, and their uses, with the phaenomena of Vision; and describes all the different kinds of microscopes and telescopes. Then he teaches Astronomy, from Dr David Gregory's *Astronomy*, with some propositions of Sir Isaac Newton's *Principia*, and the Astronomical observations both ancient and modern. He likewise shews a set of Experiments, Mechanical, Hydrostatical, Pneumatical and Optical. He expects that before any student enter his class, he has read Geometry, &c. with Mr MacLaurin one year at least. (pp. 371-2)

There are several details here that are worthy of note. Firstly, Keill's work (originally published in 1702) was the introductory text in 1741. At some point it had supplanted Le Clerc's *Physica* (1696), which Steuart probably used as a regent.[4] At that time, he is said to have been a "Cartesian", but then adopted Newton's ideas later.[5] Steuart's reputed conversion is consistent with other information about the teaching of natural philosophy at Edinburgh in the late seventeenth and early eighteenth centuries. Although Newton's name appeared in dictates as early as the 1670s, he is cited as only one among British and Continental exponents of the new philosophy;[6] Robert Boyle is actually identified as

[3] Relatively little is known about Robert Steuart or Stewart (1675-1747). He was the son of Sir Thomas Steuart, first Baronet of Coltness. Robert inherited the title in 1737 but never assumed it. He was appointed regent in 1703, and became professor of Natural Philosophy in 1708 when the regenting system was abolished. He was educated at Edinburgh, Glasgow, and Utrecht, probably as a physician. He practised medicine in Geneva but not apparently in Edinburgh. He was elected to the Philosophical Society *c*.1738. See R. L. Emerson, 'The Philosophical Society of Edinburgh, 1737-47', *British journal for the history of science* 12 (1979), p. 187, n. 100.

[4] John Chamberlayne, *Magnae Britanniae notitia: or, The present state of Great Britain* (London 1708), p. 543. Subsequent editions included a sentence which acknowledged that regenting had been abolished at Edinburgh, but Chamberlayne never updated his account of the syllabus.

[5] A. Grant, *The story of the University of Edinburgh*, vol. 2 (London 1884), pp. 348-9.

[6] C. M. Shepherd, *Philosophy and science in the arts curriculum of the Scottish universities in the seventeenth century* (Ph.D., University of Edinburgh 1975), pp. 212-13. Newton's theory of light was the first part of his work to be assimilated.

its exemplary practitioner.[7] It was only in the early years of the eighteenth century that the regents began to teach Newton's views systematically. This does not mean that Newton dominated Steuart's course thereafter. Even as late as 1741, it can be seen that Newton's work played a more specialized role: Gregory's book on optics was preferred,[8] supplemented by Newton's paper on colours,[9] while only "some propositions" from the *Principia* were taught towards the end of the course. There was, then, a selective pedagogical assimilation of Newton into an existing heterogeneous body of natural knowledge.

Secondly, Steuart seems to have remained loyal to Keill and Gregory, two very early followers of Newton. Apparently, there was no move to adopt later authors, such as Pemberton, who wrote texts explicitly on Newton's natural philosophy.[10] While Newton's Scottish disciples of the 1690s and early eighteenth century included David, James, and Charles Gregory, James Stirling, George Cheyne, Thomas Bower, John and James Keill, John Craig, Archibald Pitcairne, and others, these men had not been constantly present in Edinburgh. David Gregory's role in the dissemination of Newton's ideas in Edinburgh is undergoing revision.[11] In his classes and those of his brother James, only advanced students studied parts of Newton's works. David Gregory's lectures on astronomy and optics had not embodied Newton's ideas to such a degree as to warrant labelling them "Newtonian". Thus a more careful distinction is required between the existence of a Scottish group of virtuosi who actively supported Newton's views in the early eighteenth century and the precise content of the selected texts which formed the basis for the routine transmission of natural philosophical ideas.

Thirdly, while the retention of Gregory and Keill in 1741 does not conclusively prove they were in use while Hume was a student, there is good evidence of a conservative attitude to pedagogical innovation in the experimental part of the course. The student lecture notes which have survived all refer to hydrostatics and pneumatics. Some are descriptions

[7] C. M. Shepherd, 'Newtonianism in the Scottish universities in the seventeenth century', in *The origins and nature of the Scottish Enlightenment*, ed. R. H. Campbell and A. S. Skinner (Edinburgh 1982), at pp. 69–70. Boyle was referred to by John Wishart as "the outstanding philosopher and theologian" of the seventeenth century.

[8] David Gregory's lectures, originally given while professor of Mathematics at Edinburgh University, were first published as *Catoptricae et dioptricae sphaericae elementa* (Oxford 1695). This was translated into English by W. Browne, as *Elements of catoptrics and dioptrics* (London 1715). It is not known which of these Steuart used.

[9] 'A letter of Mr. Isaac Newton . . . containing his new theory about light and colours', *Philosophical transactions* 6 (1672), 3075–9.

[10] Henry Pemberton, *A view of Sir Isaac Newton's philosophy* (London 1728). This was published after Hume left the university; however, Robert Steuart was a subscriber to it.

[11] C. M. Eagles, 'David Gregory and Newtonian science', *British journal for the history of science* 10 (1977), 216–25.

of the experiments only. Two others are copies of Steuart's lectures on the subject, which also contain accounts of the accompanying experiments. Collectively, they indicate that this part of the course changed very little from the early 1720s until the early 1740s. In 1709 the university had successfully applied to the Town Council for a grant of £50 sterling, "In order to the procureing Instruments and Machins necessary for confirming and Illustrating by experiments the truths advanced in the Mathematicks and Naturall Philosophy within the University of this Burgh".[12] In view of these circumstances, it is likely that Hume saw experiments performed in Steuart's course. However, the main argument for his familiarity with hydrostatics is reserved for the next section.

Fourthly and finally, whether the geometry requirement was in force during Hume's time cannot be answered with certainty. Mathematics was not yet a compulsory part of the arts curriculum, and there are no official records of attendance during the 1720s. However, the distinctive tradition of pedagogical interaction between mathematics and natural philosophy in the 18th- and early 19th-century curriculum at Edinburgh University is well known. Demonstrations using machines and experiments had an important role in mathematics as well as in natural philosophy classes.[13] Most students received an elementary, philosophically-based, mathematical education which tended to favour geometrical over algebraical approaches.[14] Only advanced students could expect to ascend to the heights of sophistication displayed in Newton's *Principia*, and be initiated in the mysteries of fluxions.[15]

Published summaries of Steuart's course provide limited detail about its contents. However, an analysis of the contents of the Physiological Library can provide more information. The foundation of the Library can be thought of as part of a wider movement to institutionalize and popularize natural knowledge in the Scottish universities and early

[12] Town Council minutes, 10 June 1709: City archives, Council records, vol. 39, p. 371. This feature of the course was first emphasized in the 1735 edition of Chamberlayne's *Present state of Great Britain*. It was part of a new description of Steuart's and other professors' teaching duties entitled 'An account of the University of Edinburgh', which was then reprinted in successive editions. Steuart taught the principles of natural philosophy together with "a Course of Mechanical, Statical, Hydrostatical, and Optical Experiments; for which purpose the University is provided with a very good Apparatus of Machines and Instruments" (pt. II, bk. III, p. 21).

[13] See, for example, 'A Collection from Mr McLaurens course of Experiments': EUL, MS. Dc 7.73. As well as experiments illustrating the principles of mechanics, MacLaurin included demonstrations of hydrostatics and pneumatics.

[14] R. Olson, *Scottish philosophy and British physics, 1750–1880* (Princeton 1975), pp. 26–54; id., 'Scottish philosophy and mathematics, 1750–1830', *Journal of the history of ideas* 32 (1971), 29–44.

[15] But see note 76 below, where new evidence is cited which suggests Hume was in this category.

scientific societies.[16] The actual selection of books, their classification, and relative weighting, reveal a great deal about how natural knowledge was perceived and what sorts of social values were attached to its pursuit in Edinburgh during the mid-1720s.

Practically everything we know about the nature, organization, and running of the Library comes from the brief introduction to the catalogue. It had six curators chosen by the students. Books donated were to be specially marked, and benefactors given special borrowing rights. The catalogue, or at least a list of accessions and donors, was to be published annually. (Whether this was in fact done is unknown.) Altogether there are 410 numbered items, but because an "item" often consists of more than one volume and sometimes more than one work, the actual number of books is greater than this. There is independent evidence that originally the collection was housed separately;[17] however, at some unspecified point, the Library was absorbed into the university stock.[18]

Some indication of the scope of the Physiological Library can be gained from the preface to the catalogue.[19] It was to contain:

the best Editions of Books, both ancient and modern; Of Natural History; Of Animals, Plants, Metals and Minerals: Of Anatomy, Botany and Chymie: Of Stones, Gems, Glass &c. Of Husbandry, Planting and Gardening: Of Natural and Experimental Philosophy; Of Astronomy; Of Opticks and Perspective; Of Acousticks and Musick; Of Mechanicks and Hydrostaticks: Of Geometry, Arithmetick, and Algebra: Of Book-keeping, Trade and Manufacture: Of Navigation, Geography, and Voyages: Of Architecture, Fortification and Gunery: Of the Power, Wisdom and Goodness of God manifested in the Works of Creation; Of the Truth of the Christian Religion. (p. 3)

On the whole, with only minor variations, the subsequent ordering of the books in the catalogue follows this description. A number of typographical devices are used to distinguish particular sections and individual works within them. A new section (such as 'Mechanicks and Hydrostaticks') is usually indicated by an over-sized first letter of the first

[16] R. L. Emerson, 'Natural philosophy and the problem of the Scottish Enlightenment', *Studies on Voltaire and the 18th century* 242 (1986), 243–91. Early in 1725, shortly after the Library was founded, two itinerant natural philosophy lecturers also visited Edinburgh to give experimental demonstrations. Their activities are reported in four letters from W. Adam to Sir J. Clerk: SRO, MS. GD18/4728/7–8 and 11–12.

[17] Chamberlayne, *Present state* (1735), pt. II, bk. III, p. 20, which distinguishes the University library from "two other Libraries, one Theological, the other Physiological".

[18] For example, the copy of Locke's *Essay* (no. 253) can be located in today's catalogue under the class mark N* 16.50. It has 'Liber Bibliothecae Physiologicae' written in ink on the title page, with the donor's name, James Wingate, one of the gentlemen members.

[19] Throughout the seventeenth century, 'physiological' usually referred to the study of nature in all its aspects. In the eighteenth, this usage persisted side by side with the more restricted sense of 'physiology' as the study of living systems. For a discussion, see J. Gascoigne, 'The universities and the Scientific Revolution', *History of science* 23 (1985), at p. 402.

author's name to be listed in it. Within each section, as well as the numbered items, there are often italicized references to authors elsewhere in the catalogue. This is supplemented by occasional comments added to a particular work. For example, beneath no. 144, *The great and new art of weighing vanity*, Steuart added, "This little Book was written against Mr. Sinclair by Mr. James Gregory, when he was Professor of Mathem. in St. Andrews; and Mr. William Sanders, who succeeded to that Profession when Mr. Gregory was translated to Edinburgh."

For convenience, the contents of the catalogue can be described in terms of what would be regarded today as the four major subject areas it covers: natural history, natural philosophy, mathematics, and religion. The last is represented in both its natural and revealed aspects (nos. 352–94, 409–10). Although it is the smallest, with only 45 numbered entries excluding cross-references, it is important not to underestimate the significance of theology to the public presentation of the Library as a whole. Clearly, "physiology" was a theologically useful subject, and this is reflected in the organization. After a short section on natural religion, there are expositions of Christian theology, defences against deism, and accounts of the evidences of revealed religion. The Boyle Lectures are well represented throughout (nos. 355–7; 360; and 388–392).

Natural history is the next smallest with 75 numbered entries. The Physiological Library was founded just before the Medical School and many years before there was a professorship of Natural History in the university. Thus it seems likely that aspects of the organization of living things originally fell within Steuart's province. The structure of this part of the catalogue is indicative of a more subtle ordering of books within each main subject area. First there are works which show the nature of natural history as an enterprise. Then there are those which illustrate the different kinds of natural object: animals, plants, metals, and minerals. The next group of works is organized into anatomy, botany, and chemistry—that is, the different ways in which the study of natural objects was arranged. Finally, it ends with works showing the usefulness of this knowledge when applied to stones, gems, glass, husbandry, planting, and gardening.

To a greater or lesser degree, this pattern of general works, special subjects, and their social utilities, can be found in the other subject areas too. Thus mathematics begins with geometry, arithmetic, and algebra, and proceeds to their various applications in book-keeping, trade, navigation, geography, architecture, and so on. Clearly, as well as presenting itself as theologically useful, the Physiological Library was also organized to manifest the social utility of its subject-matter. This is also evident in the natural philosophy subject area. It is first divided into natural and experimental philosophy. Then within a particular section each special subject is coupled with its particular application: optics and perspective; acoustics and music; mechanics and machines. It also displays other features which bear closer examination.

Natural philosophy begins with Lucretius' *De rerum natura*, followed by works of Seneca, Lipsius, Cardano, Scaliger, Baptista, and Digby (nos. 118–25). These are succeeded by several works of Descartes, including *Meditations*, *Principles*, and *Discourse on method*, as well as the writings of other "Cartesians"—Regius, Clauberg, Le Grand, Régis (nos. 126–32). The next authors include Gassendi, Du Hamel, Hobbes, Ward, Hale, Linus, Sinclair, culminating with the book already noted above, *The great art of weighing vanity* by James Gregory and Sanders (nos. 133–44). This represents a general, roughly chronological, introduction to natural philosophy presented as a review of rival systems of "physiology", particularly within the atomistic, corpuscularian, and mechanical traditions.

In the next subsection the same subject is approached in a less systematic, more specific way through the works of another series of authors. They include Du Hamel again, Mariotte, the Perraults, Huygens, James Gregory again, De la Hire, and Fairfax, as well as papers from the French Academy, Sprat's *History of the Royal Society*, and the sets of abridgements of the *Philosophical transactions*. Here the ordering is less easy to discern. However, the next section, experimental philosophy, is more easily interpreted. Authors cited include Welwood, Dobrzenski, Guericke, Sturm, Senguerdius, Dalencé, Wolff, Hauksbee, Desaguliers, 'sGravesande, and Worster, and the experiments of the Academia del Cimento (nos. 161–74). Once again the arrangement seems chronological and, significantly, it ends up with the work of virtuosi closely associated with either the Royal Society or private courses of experimental philosophy given in London.

Before the subsequent sections on astronomy, optics, microscopy, and perspective (nos. 184–213, 214–25, 226–8, 229–39), there is a small group of nine books which deal with the theory of the earth's creation. There are works by Ray, Burnet, Whiston, Keill, Woodward, and Harris (nos. 175–83). The discussion of the earth's origins was probably a means of involving students in natural and experimental philosophy by a specific example of its applications. They could see how different theories of the earth made use of principles such as pressure and specific gravity to explain how the earth was formed and evolved. Moreover, it was a topic which was perceived to have theological significance. Once again then, in cameo form, it is possible to discern a series of connections made between natural knowledge, its application to a problem of contemporary importance (some of the works were among the most recent acquisitions of the Library), and natural religion. This is particularly appropriate for a course which was part of the arts faculty, teaching youths many of whom had a limited mathematical and technical competence. Overall, these early sections reveal the limits of pedagogical innovation as well as the impact of comparatively new forms of natural knowledge. Examples like the arrangement of the natural history section, and placing the study of the earth midway between the natural and experimental philosophy of bodies generally and the study of heavenly bodies, are probably vestiges of older presentations found in regent dictates on general and special physics.

Works dealing with more technical aspects of mechanics and hydrostatics are listed towards the end of the natural philosophy section (nos. 245–51). They are followed by two further subsections which round off this subject area and pave the way for the next. The first is the nearest the catalogue comes to a metaphysical or logical subsection and deals with the epistemology of the new science. It includes Malebranche's *Recherche*; Locke's *Essay*; Tschirnhaus's *Medicina mentis*; Mariotte's *Essai de logique* and, finally, Watts's *Logic* (nos. 252–5); interestingly, none of Descartes' works listed earlier are cross-referenced to here. The next deals with mathematical natural philosophy. It begins with Newton's *Principia*, second edition (1713),[20] followed by a 1723 collection of his mathematical papers on fluxions (nos. 256–7). Thus whereas the *Opticks* had appeared in the earlier section on optics,[21] the *Principia* immediately preceded the mathematics section. Other works of mathematical natural philosophy by Ditton, Whiston, Hermann, and Huygens are also listed (nos. 258–60). Thus of the different kinds of natural philosophy on offer in the Library— mechanical, experimental, and mathematical—the last and most difficult was given a limited amount of space and reserved until the end.

The mathematics section itself contains 56 entries dealing with geometry, arithmetic, and algebra. Before moving on to applications such as book-keeping, it contains a very intriguing subsection of five books combining chronology with the progress of knowledge over time (nos. 318–22). They include two works by Glanvill (*Scepsis scientifica* and *Plus ultra*) and one by Wotton.[22] Among the books included in this subject area are classical authors such as Euclid, Apollonius, Archimedes; and "modern" writers such as Barrow, David Gregory, and John

---

[20] There is no mention of the first edition (1687), and the third (1726) appeared shortly after the catalogue was published.

[21] The Library held both Clarke's Latin translation of Newton's *Optice* (1706) and the recently published third edition of 1721 (nos. 221–2).

[22] Among the addenda listed at the end of the catalogue were eight by Bacon (nos. 395–402). *Silva silvarum* would presumably have been included in the natural history section, and *Historia naturalis et experimentalis de ventis* in the natural and experimental philosophy section. But his *Novum organum* and *De augmentis scientiarum* probably belong at the present point.

Harris. There are also a number of elementary textbooks, together with discussions of fluxions by Newton, Wolff, Nieuwentijt, de l'Hospital, Hays, Cheyne, Reyneaud, and Craig, as well as the recently published *Commercium epistolicum* of 1722 (nos. 303–14). These parts of the catalogue exemplify the close historical relationship between mathematics and natural philosophy referred to above.

These are some of the general ways in which certain forms of natural knowledge were presented and commended in the catalogue. It also employs three additional means of emphasizing particular authors of note. One is to capitalize the whole name of the author. Barrow's *Lectiones opticae geometricae* of 1674 is highlighted in this way, as is another of his mathematical works. Newton's *Universal arithmetic* is distinguished in a similar fashion, and there is a capitalized rather than an italicized cross-reference to two other mathematical works by him. Interestingly, the editions of the *Opticks* do not get this treatment. However, the second edition of the *Principia* is emphasized in a further way. Not only is the author capitalized throughout, but the initial 'I' is printed with an ornamental border. The only other book accorded comparable treatment is the *Novum testamentum Graecum* of 1703 edited by John Gregory. The third means of distinguishing authors is the most important of all and constitutes the most noticeable single feature of the catalogue as a whole. Up to this point, the categories of the Library have been analysed and described in terms of their pedagogical and broader social significance. However, one particular author is presented trans-categorically: Robert Boyle's writings actually precede the natural history section and constitute no fewer than the first 42 items of the catalogue, or just over one-tenth of the whole. The first 41 items are published books, and afterwards it is noted: "This is a complete Catalogue of the Honourable ROBERT BOYLE'S Works, but No. 7, 22 and 24 not yet in this Collection" (p. 15).[23] There then follows a separate and unnumbered section with a list of "Papers communicated by the Honourable ROBERT BOYLE to the Royal Society, and printed in the Philosophical Transactions". Finally, entry no. 43 is a Latin translation of fourteen books and two papers formerly listed in English. Boyle is also cross-referenced no less than six times to different sections of the catalogue, and his name appears in relation to the texts of five Boyle Lectures included in the religion section. On each occasion his name appears in capitals like some of the references to Barrow and Newton. Clearly, the works of Boyle were being canvassed and popularized in a

---

[23] Steuart's arrangement of Boyle's works seems to be a reordering of *A catalogue of the philosophical books and tracts written by the honourable Robert Boyle esq.* (London 1690).

mÁjor way.[24] Whereas the classification of texts was almost certainly Steuart's responsibility, it is impossible to know how much the decoration of a particular author's name was due to the printer's initiative. However, the typographical emphasis upon Boyle, Newton, Barrow, and the New Testament certainly seems to reflect the widely shared view that perfecting natural philosophy also implied enlarging the bounds of moral philosophy.

The catalogue of the Physiological Library is a complex document which requires further analysis. Although it was clearly designed as a map or plan for Steuart's students to find their way around "physiology", there is no direct way of knowing which books, if any, Hume himself borrowed or read. However, the principal features of the collection which Hume *could* have used to familiarize himself with the culture of science are clear enough. Firstly, the collection was European in outlook. Although Scots and English authors were well represented, other works were by no means excluded. Although modern texts predominated, a good selection of classical authors was also present. Secondly, mechanical and corpuscularian natural philosophy was very strongly represented, and the arrangements of particular sections appeared to favour the experimental tradition of the British Christian virtuosi of the seventeenth and early eighteenth centuries. Thirdly, within this tradition, Boyle was singled out above all others as a practising experimental mechanical philosopher and an exemplary exponent of the theological uses of this form of knowledge. Finally, Newton and Barrow were also distinguished from other authors although their works appeared in more specialized parts of the catalogue dealing with mathematics and mathematical natural philosophy. The additional information about the contents of Steuart's course provided by the catalogue can now be related to current assessments of the role science played in Hume's works.

II. BOYLE, HYDROSTATICS, AND THE EXPERIMENTAL METHOD

The textual evidence for Hume's so-called "Newtonianism" has recently been re-examined and found to be both limited and

---

[24] In her thesis on regent dictates, Shepherd notes that from the 1660s onwards, there was a general interest in experimental science. Boyle figured prominently, and his experiments were frequently referred to, especially those with the air pump; his works were bought extensively by the four university libraries (p. 82). Other English scientists who were mentioned, or whose experiments and observations were described in the dictates, are Ward, Wallis, Wren, Moxon, Flamsteed, Hooke, and Keill, most of them connected in some way with the Royal Society; again the Physiological Library lists reflect this interest.

ambiguous.[25] We can go further: if Hume's explicit statements about Newton and scientific procedure in *An enquiry concerning human understanding* are compared with the wider community of 18th-century texts which discussed such matters, it is clear that there is nothing unusual about them. In fact, it can be argued that his rather brief and undeveloped views were either commonplace or vicarious, and perhaps even inconsistent. Hume's insistence upon the role of empirical experience and facts in scientific discovery, together with the somewhat casual amalgamation of Newton's method with Bacon's, can be found in Pemberton and MacLaurin.[26] His appeal to the rules of reasoning in philosophy (E. 204) was also standard. Hume's related denial of men's perception of any necessary connection between physical phenomena was also widely accepted, alongside a more general nescience about the essence and process of nature.[27] A version of the well-known footnote about the ether (E. 73) can be found in Ramsay.[28] On the status of hypotheses, Hume displayed the same Janus-faced attitude evident in the period at large: he simultaneously endorsed their elimination from philosophy generally, while reserving a use for them in favoured instances.[29]

While it is right to revise the picture of Hume's "Newtonianism", this does not mean the wider culture of science was unimportant to him, or that he failed to incorporate features of it in a distinctive and innovative way. In fact the present focus on Newton and some of his followers has obscured other important uses of natural knowledge in Hume's writings.[30] When Hume was a natural philosophy student in the

[25] P. Jones, *Hume's sentiments* (Edinburgh 1982); J. P. Wright, *The sceptical realism of David Hume* (Manchester 1983).

[26] Pemberton, *View*, pp. 2–25; Colin MacLaurin, *An account of Sir Isaac Newton's philosophy* (Edinburgh 1748), pp. 56–63.

[27] See, for example, 'Lectures on medicine, taken by Robert Whytt': RCPE, MS. M 9.19, pp. 431–50; and 467–75. The lectures were originally given by George Young, a prominent extramural teacher of medicine in Edinburgh during the 1730s and a Rankenian. His discussion of the causal basis of muscular motion and sensation embodies several of the themes usually considered distinctive to Hume, which were actually widely taken for granted within the culture of 18th-century science. This point was well appreciated by Hume's later critics such as Thomas Reid, Dugald Stewart, James Gregory, and Thomas Brown.

[28] Andrew Michael Ramsay, *Philosophical principles of natural and revealed religion*, vol I (Glasgow 1748), p. 269.

[29] Although Hume made some changes to his footnote after the first edition, he still referred to the ether as an acceptable hypothesis, just as he had in *A letter from a gentleman to his friend in Edinburgh* (Edinburgh 1745), pp. 28–9. Compare this with a statement in the second *Enquiry*: "Men are now cured of their passion for hypotheses and systems in natural philosophy, and will hearken to no arguments but those which are derived from experience" (E. 174–5).

[30] It is remarkable how arbitrary and historiographically questionable the selection of comparative texts has been. Pemberton and MacLaurin are most frequently cited. Others such as J. T. Desaguliers' *Lectures of experimental philosophy* (London 1719); Benjamin Worster's *Compendious and methodical account of the principles of natural philosophy* (London 1722);

mid-1720s, Newton may have been at the height of his power and influence in the Royal Society, but his ideas were by no means fully institutionalized elsewhere in Britain, much less in Europe. This was a process brought about by Newton's disciples, who spread the word through a highly influential set of textbooks published in the first four decades of the century. During this period a Newton-inspired British natural philosophy emerged which gradually severed its connections with the European mechanical and experimental philosophy that had originally nourished it. Something of the time-scale of this process is suggested in one of Hume's own remarks. Even as late as 1742, he could write in his essay 'Of the rise and progress of the arts and sciences':

The severest Scrutiny, that *Newton's* Theory has undergone, proceeded not from his own Countrymen, but Foreigners; and if it can overcome the Obstacles it meets with at present in all Parts of *Europe*, it will probably go down triumphant to the latest Posterity.[31]

The reception of Boyle's work in the eighteenth century was deeply affected by Newton's ascendancy. There was widespread conflation of Boyle's views with Newton's own.[32] For example, in the preface to *Hydrostatical paradoxes* (1666), Boyle contended that his approach exemplified the operation of reason; that his experiments surprised because they proved unobvious truths; and that it had great utility. With claims of this nature, it is not surprising that experiments culled from Boyle's various notes and papers found their way into "Newtonian" textbooks, often without explicit acknowledgement. The process began as early as 1704 in John Harris's *Lexicon technicum* (s.v. 'Hydrostatics'), which reproduced Boyle's various hydrostatic paradoxes with a similar gloss to Boyle's own. A slightly different but related use can be found 44 years later in MacLaurin's *Account*. He stated that despite being useful, hydrostatics had been ill understood until Boyle "established its principles, and illustrated its paradoxes by a number of plain experiments, in a satisfactory manner" (pp. 61–2).

These historical orientations are important for the interpretation of a reference to Boyle in Hume's *History* which precedes the more famous passage on Newton:

Boyle improved the pneumatic engine invented by Otto Guericke, and was thereby enabled to make several new and curious experiments on the air, as well

---

William Whiston's *Praelectiones physico-mathematicae* (Cambridge 1710), and even W. J. 'sGravesande's *Mathematical elements of physics*, trans. Desaguliers (London 1720), are usually ignored. Despite the shared obeisance to Newton, these texts vary considerably from one another, especially on the respective provinces of experimental and mathematical evidence.

[31] Hume, *Essays moral and political*, 3rd edn. (London 1748), p. 169.
[32] M. B. Hall, *Robert Boyle on natural philosophy* (Bloomington 1965), p. 110.

as on other bodies: His chemistry is much admired by those who are acquainted with that art: His hydrostatics contain a greater mixture of reasoning and invention with experiment than any other of his works; but his reasoning is still remote from that boldness and temerity which has led astray so many philosophers.[33]

Note that Hume was quite specific here. He singled out Boyle's hydrostatics for special praise and stated that it contained "a greater mixture of reasoning and invention with experiment" than Boyle's other works. This succinct description captures a key feature of Boyle's programme for mechanical philosophy: neither blind empiricism nor abstract deduction, but a subtle, inventive use of both together.[34] By this time Hume could have taken his opinion about Boyle's hydrostatics from Harris or even MacLaurin. However, the special place given to Boyle and hydrostatics in Steuart's course now makes this unlikely.

Two surviving copies of Steuart's hydrostatics lectures show how thoroughly the subject was treated and how little the format seems to have changed during his tenure.[35] The actual lectures were given in Latin and organized in terms of definitions, scholia, propositions, and corollaries, although no advanced geometrical or mathematical demonstrations were actually used. The experimental part of the course was conducted in English, and the emphasis was upon hydrostatic and pneumatic experiments together with the practical calculation of specific gravities. Some separate descriptions of the experiments have also survived. One set was taken down by Alexander Cunningham (later Sir Alexander Dick);[36] he was in the first cohort of students to join the Library in April 1724 and attended Steuart's course a year before Hume. It is a very reasonable assumption that Hume witnessed the same or similar experiments.[37]

---

[33] Hume, *The history of Great Britain. Vol. II. Containing the Commonwealth, and the reigns of Charles II and James II* (London 1757), p. 451.

[34] My understanding of Boyle has benefited from S. Shapin and S. Schaffer, *Leviathan and the air pump* (Princeton 1985), which also contains an up-to-date bibliography of secondary works on Boyle.

[35] See 'Hydrostaticis compendium' (1723) and 'Hydrostaticae' (1740): AUL, MS. 2206(39) and (7). The former is a 1740 copy of lectures given in 1723. The latter seems to be a copy of Steuart's original hydrostatic and pneumatic "manuscript of his own writing" which he taught from. Both are very similar in form and content, with only slight variations in wording.

[36] 'Excerptions from Mr Stewart's college of experimental philosophy begun Febry. 6, 1724': GUL, MS. Murray 273.

[37] Although we do not know whether Hume actually took mathematics, the kinds of works available in the Library and the nature of the University course during the 1720s deserve further investigation. For example, see Cunningham's 'My algebraical studies anno. 1720': GUL, MS. Murray 273. This is the companion piece to his experimental lecture notes. *If* Hume attended the mathematics class, and *if* Gregory and his various deputies kept to the same syllabus, then it is possible that Hume, like Cunningham, learnt, for example, to represent algebraical equations geometrically as chords of a circle. Certainly, when Hume wrote about drawing lines on paper to produce the impression of a curve (T. 49), it is tempting to believe he spoke from first-hand experience of actual problem-solving. See also note 76 below.

Cunningham's 'Excerptions' deals first with hydrostatics, and then with pneumatics. Hydrostatics takes up twelve of the fifteen pages of notes and it records a series of eighteen experiments designed to prove ten propositions. In the pneumatics part, seven experiments are described which made use of an air pump. Experiments in the hydrostatic part were designed to prove propositions such as "Water weighs as much in water as it does in good Air"; or "The Upper parts of a fluid press upon the Lower" (p. 1). Those in the second part explained, for example, the phenomenon that "Air expands itself when an external pressure is taken of⟨f⟩" (p. 13). The experiments are not explicitly identified as Boyle's, although most if not all derive from his works. They are a systematized series of manipulations designed to introduce students to the principles of hydrostatics by experiment. The experiments were written up in a simple descriptive style, not that different from a modern school physics notebook.[38] All metaphysics has been eliminated. Thus the verb 'gravitate' is used freely as part of the vocabulary of mechanical causes, with no speculation about the "real" cause of gravity. Similarly in the pneumatics, the experiments are not designed to prove the existence of a vacuum rather than a plenum. Instead they simply assume that most if not all of the air is evacuated from the receiver as an accomplishment of the pump; this is then used as a resource or tool to investigate the nature of the pressure of the air, as shown, for example, by the behaviour of air-bladders within the exhausted receiver. So pneumatics is treated as a branch of hydrostatics, rather as Boyle insisted it should be in his later works. Throughout, weighing and measuring are emphasized, rather than mathematical demonstration.[39] The experiments exemplify the sensory, experience-based, largely non-mathematical approach to hydraulic phenomena which was associated with Boyle's version of the mechanical philosophy;[40] they were designed to be surprising, to be a public

[38] For example, under proposition 1: "We took a Glass Vial with a Valve"; under proposition 3: "He took a Glass tube open at both ends". The shift in pronouns is an interesting feature of the manuscript, but it is unlikely that it denotes actual student performances rather than professorial demonstrations.

[39] For example, proposition 5, experiment 1: "We weigh'd a cubical inch of Lead in Air & afterwards in Water & found that it weighed Less in Water than it did in Air, by the weight of a cubical inch of water" (p. 5). The actual weights were also carefully calculated as part of the experiment.

[40] Boyle was actually critical of demonstrative mathematical accounts of hydrostatics by authors such as Marinus, Stevin, and Wallis. In the preface to *Hydrostatical paradoxes*, he attacked their assumptions about the accuracy of the rectilinear figures made by the side of vessels and the surfaces of fluids from a point of view not unlike Hume's own criticisms of the foundations of geometry. Thus in the *Lexicon*, Harris was obliged to include a geometrical treatment of hydrostatics to balance Boyle's experimental piece. This aimed to satisfy more mathematically inclined readers. In Scotland, a version of Boyle's criticisms was repeated by George Sinclair in his *Hydrostatics* (Edinburgh 1672), subsequently reissued as *Natural*

spectacle, and to secure belief in the propositions of hydraulics by convincing the student's reason through his senses.[41]

Hume's familiarity with the experimental hydrostatics tradition, and Boyle's role within it, is suggestively echoed in Book Two of the *Treatise*. Consider the imagery throughout the discussion of the passions, especially where he likened imperfectly contrary passions towards the same object to oil and vinegar "which, however mingled, never perfectly unite and incorporate" (T. 433). Elsewhere he argued the passions could be treated as accurately as "the laws of motion, optics, hydrostatics or any part of natural philosophy".[42] A similar image involving flow and circulation can be found in the essay 'Of money' (published in the *Political Discourses* of 1752), with an identical commitment to discovering the underlying mechanisms of the phenomena in question. Steuart's interest in the specific gravity of different coins of the realm is evident in various copies of his lectures. Given this emphasis upon the utility of natural philosophy, it is likely that Hume witnessed the hydrostatic assay of different forms of money.[43]

The evidence presented here also suggests that Hume had more credentials to serve as one of the secretaries of the Edinburgh Philosophical Society than might appear. The sentiments expressed in the preface to the first volume of their *Essays and observations physical and literary* (1754) are consistent in both style and substance with views in Hume's writings. Thus he may have been responsible for it, rather than his co-editor, Monro *primus*. However, another extract in the second volume (1756) raises yet further suspicions that it may also have been his contribution. Article 36, 'Accounts of extraordinary motions of the waters in several places of North Britain, and of a shock of an earthquake felt at Dunbarton' (pp. 423–36), has an interesting preface which preceded the various eyewitness reports. This was probably added by one of the Society's officers. It began with a reference to the

---

philosophy improven by new experiments (Edinburgh 1683). The latter was attacked by Gregory and Sanders, who reasserted the supremacy of the mathematical tradition in hydrostatics. As noted above, this debate was specifically mentioned in the catalogue of the Library (nos. 142, 144) and may well have provided a precedent for Hume's own preference for the experimental over the mathematical method.

[41] On the public presentation of experimental philosophy, see S. Shapin, 'Pump and circumstance: Robert Boyle's literary technology', *Social studies of science* 14 (1984), 481–520; S. Schaffer, 'Natural philosophy as public spectacle', *History of science* 21 (1983), 1–43.

[42] 'Of the passions', in *Four dissertations* (London 1757), p. 181.

[43] GUL, MS. Murray 305, pp. 1–23, gives details of hydrostatic experiments attended by Robert Cay in 1718. Steuart's course laid considerable stress on specific gravity and its application to coinage. This could also be of use in teaching other subjects. See 'Excerpts from Mr Ro. Stuart's Mss of Weights & Measures': EUL, MS. Dc 5.24(2), pp. 1–7. This was copied by Charles Mackie, professor of Civil History, and contained a comparison of English, Scots, and Roman weights and capacities.

role of the Society as a repository of facts and phenomena which would lead to more accurate case histories. Similar points had been made in the original preface (vol. I, p. v). Then the writer noted:

That a tremor, which is hardly to be felt at land, or which may altogether escape notice there, may be very perceptible on the waters, will easily be believed; nor is it more incredible, that a small concussion given to a small body of water will produce a very remarkable agitation in the narrow creeks and shallows. And it is observable, that these commotions were most violent in the deepest lakes, particularly in *Loch-ness*; the extraordinary depth of which hath been sometimes assigned as a reason for its never freezing, the severest winters not being able to reduce it to the coldness of ice. (pp. 423–4)

Clearly, some independent corroboration of Hume's authorship would also be required, but such observations were certainly within the capacity of someone trained in hydrostatics by Robert Steuart. Be that as it may, the details of Hume's early scientific education certainly cast new light on his role as co-secretary and as arbitrator of a dispute between his own friend and the son of his original teacher (HL i. 185–8). Hume's agreement that Professor John Stewart had the better of the exchange with Lord Kames should no longer be so surprising.[44]

I have shown that Hume's experience of the culture of science was more complex than is usually acknowledged. He attended a course of lectures at Edinburgh University which included experimental demonstrations. By doing so, he was in the privileged vanguard of the expanding audience for 18th-century science, one who actually witnessed the practices of the new philosophy at first hand. He also had the opportunity to reinforce his knowledge of the subject through a range of books carefully organized and listed in the Physiological Library. Robert Steuart was a relatively early exponent of the experimentally-oriented teaching of natural philosophy, but by the late 1730s this approach could be spoken of in the following terms:

As to the method in general of teaching Philosophy by Courses of Experiments (that is, of drawing general truths and conclusions from a select number of simple experiments, first represented to our senses, and then explained to our understandings), it is now so much practised and approved of by the most eminent Professors all over Europe, and has so greatly contributed to the

---

[44] John Stewart was educated at Edinburgh High School and University and graduated M.D. at Rheims (1740). He was made joint professor with his father in 1742, succeeding him in 1747. He became a Licentiate and then a Fellow of the Royal College of Physicians of Edinburgh. He was succeeded by Adam Ferguson in 1759. See R. L. Emerson, 'The Philosophical Society of Edinburgh, 1748–68', *British journal for the history of science* 13 (1981), on pp. 157–9. For the dispute between Stewart and Kames, see M. Barfoot, *James Gregory (1753–1821) and Scottish scientific metaphysics, 1750–1800* (Ph.D., University of Edinburgh 1983), pp. 44–86.

propagation and increase of knowledge, in the little time it has been daily cultivated, that nothing more need be said to shew the usefulness and excellency of it.[45]

In the Introduction to the *Treatise*, the terms 'experiment' and 'experimental' appear no fewer than six times. However, by introducing the "experimental method of reasoning" into moral philosophy, Hume was doing more than simply jumping on a rhetorical bandwagon. He actually modelled his early work upon a prestigious form of natural knowledge which he encountered at the very beginning of his intellectual development while a student at the university. By "experimental philosophy", Hume understood a particular version of the mechanical philosophy, international in scope but exemplified in Britain by Boyle in the late seventeenth century.

The whole presentation presupposes a special relationship between the procedure of the science of man and the practice of experimental natural philosophy. Hume expected that the application of the latter to moral subjects would reveal new and surprising truths on a par with those discovered in hydrostatics. As long as the science of human nature based its experiments on what he described as "a cautious observation of human life" (T. xix), he anticipated it would be at least as certain as, and actually much more useful than, any other science. This was because it was presupposed in all other enquiries (T. xvi). His science of human nature incorporated all other disciplines. Mathematics, natural philosophy, and natural religion were "under the cognizance of men" and would be reformed if human understanding could be mastered: "'Tis impossible to tell what changes and improvements we might make in these sciences were we thoroughly acquainted with the extent and force of human understanding, and cou'd explain the nature of the ideas we employ, and of the operations we perform in our reasonings" (T. xv). Yet this does not mean Hume should be treated as a natural philosopher just because he applied the methodology of experimental philosophy to metaphysics. In statements about "the modern philosophy" elsewhere in the *Treatise*, he is critical of the ontological and epistemological positions routinely adopted by natural philosophers (T. 225–31). His reservations about "the imperfections of the mechanical philosophy" in the *History* are well known (1757, p. 452), as are his criticisms of

[45] Roger Cotes, *Hydrostatical and pneumatical lectures* [1738], ed. Robert Smith, 2nd edn. (Cambridge 1747), editor's preface (unpaginated). It is likely that this work, and copies of Boyle's *New experiments physico-mechanical* and *Certain physiological essays* which also appear in the catalogue of Baron Hume's library, were originally David Hume's own. A copy of the catalogue can be found in NLS, MS. 348. D. F. Norton, in 'New light on Hume's library', a paper presented to the Edinburgh Bibliographical Society, Nov. 23, 1986, has suggested various ways in which books belonging originally to the philosopher, and inherited by his nephew, can be distinguished from the rest of the collection.

mathematics.[46] Nevertheless there are occasions when Hume's familiarity with the culture of science informed the detailed expression of his philosophy. His views on the vacuum and infinite divisibility are cases in point.

III. HUME AND THE PALIMPSEST OF NATURAL KNOWLEDGE

Hume's treatment of space—and time—in *Treatise* I. ii is probably the least known and least understood part of his metaphysical writings. The discussion is puzzling in terms of the conceptual content of his position and the actual form of his account. Two of the major issues which concerned him were dealt with in the successive parts of his system. The first was whether extension and space, time and duration, matter and body, were finitely or infinitely divisible. The second was whether one can conceive of a vacuum or space without matter in it. In dealing with the former Hume criticized the foundations of arguments routinely used to defend the infinite divisibility of extension. In the latter he attacked arguments which supported the idea of a vacuum. Both topics are abstruse and the discussion proceeds by means of a bewildering array of examples. I shall argue that natural philosophy texts played an important role in the formulation of Hume's thinking on these topics: the organizational emphasis upon the twin themes of infinite divisibility and the vacuum can be related to the way these issues were discussed in the textbooks of the period. However, the manner in which Hume assimilated material from such works is not straightforward. Much of the opaqueness of his discussion of infinite divisibility can be located in a double obscurity. Firstly, he argued against a largely absent point of view; this has to be reconstructed from exemplary texts in the natural philosophical tradition in order to see the cogency of Hume's treatment. Secondly, he shaped his own reflections through Berkeley's account of metaphysical deficiencies perpetuated by that tradition. During the course of Hume's analysis, several of the arguments, illustrations, and examples used by Berkeley were reworked.[47]

[46] As late as 1755, Hume considered including "some Considerations previous to Geometry & Natural Philosophy" in his *Four dissertations* (HL i. 223). Although Hume restricted himself to a few brief comments in the first *Enquiry* (E. 31–2; 155–8), he remained very critical of mathematicians: "No priestly dogmas, invented on purpose to tame and subdue the rebellious reason of mankind, ever shocked common sense more than the doctrine of the infinite divisibility of extension, with its consequences; as they are pompously displayed by all geometricians and metaphysicians, with a kind of triumph and exultation" (E. 156). See also note 76 below.

[47] In order to develop the main argument about the palimpsest of natural knowledge underlying Hume's account, some of the important parallels between Hume and Berkeley's accounts of the vacuum and infinite divisibility are alluded to here but not treated in detail. Quotations are from George Berkeley, *Philosophical works*, ed. M. R. Ayers (London 1975).

Consider the following remark by Berkeley about optics in the *New theory of vision*:

There is at this day no one ignorant that the pictures of external objects are painted on the *retina*, or fund of the eye: that we can see nothing that is not so painted: and that according as the picture is more distinct or confused, so also is the perception we have of the object. (sec. 88)

Now here is Hume as he prepared to answer objections to his own argument that a vacuum is imperceptible without the existence of matter or the intrusion of tangible or visible objects within it:

'Tis commonly allow'd by philosophers, that all bodies, which discover themselves to the eye, appear as if painted on a plane surface, and that their different degrees of remoteness from ourselves are discover'd more by reason than by the senses. (T. 56)

Hume and Berkeley were both drawing upon a sub-domain of natural knowledge which dealt with optics and perspective. This was developed by 17th-century mechanical philosophers including Descartes, his followers, and other writers in Britain and Europe.

Berkeley's contribution was to question the "opinion of speculative men" who said distance could be calculated according to the angle made by the two optic axes when they met at an object: "these lines and angles, by means whereof some men pretend to explain the perception of distance, are themselves not at all perceived, nor are they in truth ever thought of by those unskilful in optics" (sec. 12). In most respects Hume sided with Berkeley in criticizing views of mathematicians and natural philosophers that were inadequately grounded in human understanding, and he also assimilated a great deal of Berkeley's vocabulary. However, in the particular case of the perception of distance, his text shows vestiges of the position Berkeley criticized. In his account of the "perceptions, from which we can judge of the distance" between two luminous objects, Hume listed the different means by which such perceptions could be produced. One way was by "the angles, which the rays of light flowing from [the objects] form with each other" (T. 58). In correcting this statement in the Appendix (T. 636), he showed that he had originally meant by it that the perceptions produced were the perceptions of the angles themselves. Yet the uncorrected view can be found elsewhere in Hume's illustrations of how men perceived visible objects. Within a few lines, Hume spoke of two visible objects affecting the senses in the same way precisely because they formed "the same angle by the rays, which flow from them" (T. 58). In another example of how, by association, the empty distance between two objects could be equated with another filled with visible bodies, this "conversion" of invisible to visible distance was said to occur "without any change on that angle, under which they appear to the senses" (T. 59).

This raises an interesting question about why Hume made the same "error" Berkeley had explicitly identified in Descartes and others. Did he lack a copy of the *New theory of vision* while writing the *Treatise* in France?[48] Whatever is the case, it should not be forgotten that Hume was taught the theory of vision by Steuart, a mechanical philosopher and probably a former "Cartesian" too. Furthermore, there were texts available in the Physiological Library which dealt with optics and perspective with which Hume may well have been familiar (nos. 214–25). Thus it is unlikely that he simply relied on Berkeley for his knowledge of optics, although a subsequent reading may have led him to make the correction in the Appendix. Both philosophers relied upon a prior discussion about vision and optics by natural philosophers and mathematicians. Although there was considerable controversy about the nature of light and its mode of propagation, there were probably very few significant differences between the mechanistic account of vision, found in "Cartesian" texts which deal with how the eye judged distance, and equivalent "Newtonian" passages. The whole psychophysiological model of how sense impressions were transmitted via the eye to the brain was a shared assumption of both camps until other forms of non-mechanical explanations emerged later in the eighteenth century. Nor were aspects of optics the only common ground.

The vacuum and infinite divisibility figure prominently on the agenda of many texts concerned with the role of matter theory in natural philosophy. A close study of Hume's approach to both these topics shows the important role natural philosophy texts had in the formulation of his views. It also clarifies many puzzling details of his response to problems about space (and time). In particular, it confirms Hume's allegiance to the experimental method in preference to the mathematical, which is also found in Berkeley. Hume shared Berkeley's concern to judge the truths of natural philosophy by appealing to human understanding and the evidence of the senses.

To show Hume's familiarity with the natural philosophy tradition in general, I consider two exemplary texts.[49] These are Samuel Clarke's

---

[48] R. Hall, 'Hume's actual use of Berkeley's *Principles*', *Philosophy* 43 (1968), 278–80, has argued that Hume's discussion of "outness" was modelled on Berkeley's *Principles*, not the *Theory of vision*.

[49] Other discussions of the vacuum and infinite divisibility can be found in Desaguliers, *Lectures*, pp. 7–12; id., *A course of experimental philosophy* [1734], 3rd edn., vol. 1 (London 1763), pp. 2–44; 'sGravesande, *Elements*, vol. 1, pp. 4–14; vol. 2, pp. 330–33; Worster, *Compendious account*, pp. 3–7. For slightly later treatments, see 'sGravesande, *An explanation of the Newtonian philosophy*, trans. E. Stone (London 1741), pp. 4–10; P. van Musschenbroek, *The elements of natural philosophy for the use of students in the universities*, trans. J. Colson, vol. 1 (London 1744), pp. 10–75.

edition of Rohault's *System of natural philosophy*, and Keill's *Introduction to natural philosophy*.[50] They have been chosen here because they were early models for subsequent natural philosophy texts, especially those British and Dutch works which became identified as "Newtonian" natural philosophy later in the century. Although neither is in the Physiological Library catalogue, Keill was Steuart's introductory text by 1741 at the latest, and could have been used by Hume much earlier. Rohault's *System* was arguably the best and most familiar natural philosophy textbook in the late seventeenth and early eighteenth centuries.[51] In 1697, Clarke added a series of critical notes to the Latin text of Rohault's book. This gave British readers an opportunity to compare "Cartesian" and "Newtonian" interpretations of nature; and as a result, the subsequent English translation, by Clarke's brother John, remained in use even as late as the early 1750s.[52] Keill's *Introduction* was also a popular work and went through many editions in both Latin and English.[53] It was originally based on a course of lectures given at Oxford in 1700, when he was deputy Sedleian professor of Natural Philosophy. Part of the course included experimental demonstrations, but by no means all of the subjects treated in his spoken lectures appeared in print. In fact, Keill's text reflects his tendency to prefer mathematical rather than experimental evidence in natural philosophy. Like most pedagogues with responsibilities for a course of lectures, Keill relied heavily on precedents for the structure of his course, if not always for the content. Particular lectures in the *Introduction* were probably modelled on various chapters in Rohault. This can be shown in the form of a table.

Rohault	*Keill*
Chs. 1–6 (dealing with aspects of method)	Lect. 1 'Of the method of philosophising'

---

[50] *Rohault's system of natural philosophy illustrated with Dr. Samuel Clarke's notes taken mostly from Sir Isaac Newton's philosophy done into English by John Clarke* [1723], 3rd edn. [1735], repr. with an Introd. by L. L. Laudan (New York 1969); John Keill, *An introduction to natural philosophy, or philosophical lectures read in the University of Oxford A.D. 1700* (London 1720). Rohault's text first appeared (unannotated) in French in 1671, Keill's in Latin in 1702.

[51] Other important though less influential European texts included Malebranche's *De la Recherche de la vérité* (1674–75), Régis's *Système de philosophie* (1690), Perrault's *Essais de physique* (1680), and Le Clerc's *Physica* (1696).

[52] On the different editions of Rohault's book, see M. A. Hoskin, ' "Mining all within": Clarke's notes to Rohault's *Traité de physique*', *Thomist* 24 (1961), 353–63.

[53] For a discussion of the changes Keill made to his text and the importance of his work in relation to the institutionalization of Newton's natural philosophical ideas, see R. E. Schofield, *Mechanism and materialism* (Princeton 1970), pp. 19–39; A. Thackray, *Atoms and powers* (Cambridge, Mass. 1970), pp. 43–73; and E. W. Strong, 'Newtonian explications of natural philosophy', *Journal of the history of ideas* 18 (1957), on pp. 55–65.

Rohault	*Keill*
Ch. 7 'Of matter'	Lect. 2 'Of the solidity and
Ch. 8 'Some corollaries of the	extension of bodies' (dealing with
foregoing notion' (dealing with the	the vacuum)
vacuum)	
Ch. 9 'Of the divisibility of matter'	Lect. 3 'Of the divisibility of
	magnitude' (dealing with the
	subtlety of matter)
	Lect. 4 'Wherein the objections
	brought against the divisibility of
	matter, are answered'
Ch. 21 'Of the elements of natural	Lect. 5 'Of the subtilty of matter'
things'	

Rohault's preface, his discussion of notions preceding the study of natural philosophy, the account of method, and the axioms and principles of the subject, all contain many positions similar to those found in Hume.[54] Keill's introductory lecture is equally informative in this respect. However, all such correspondences of method which stemmed from a shared familiarity with European mechanical philosophy will be taken for granted here, in order to concentrate the discussion on the vacuum and infinite divisibility.

IV. ROHAULT, KEILL, AND THE VACUUM

Following Descartes, Rohault identified extension as the essential quality of matter because others, such as impenetrability, figure, and divisibility, presupposed it. An immediate consequence of identifying extension and matter was *"that what Philosophers call a* Vacuum *cannot possibly be"* (*System*, vol. 1, p. 27). In effect, Rohault's argument in support of this was definitional: a vacuum implied space void of matter; but extension or space was synonymous with matter; therefore a vacuum was equivalent to matter without matter, which was contradictory. Rohault also employed an illustration to show that, however men tried, they could not arrive at the idea of a vacuum or space without some form of matter in it. Its purpose was to anticipate a problem about the logic of ideas. If the idea of a space without matter could be imagined, then that

---

[54] Rohault's discussion of optics in chapters 27–35 is particularly suggestive in view of various references to the subject in Berkeley and Hume. For example, the burning-coal illustration (T. 35), usually ascribed to Newton and Locke, also occurs there (p. 281). The seeing-double experiment (T. 210–11) is also discussed (p. 256). Rohault's description of how distance is judged according to angles (p. 252) is adopted without any critical annotations by Clarke, who only cited a further precedent for it in Malebranche.

space could possibly exist. But if it could be shown that we were unable to reason about the vacuum without contradiction, then it could have no real existence. Thus if asked

what *we conceive* would follow, if God should annihilate all the Air in a Room, and not suffer any other to enter in its Place? We should return for Answer, (not concerning our selves with what would come to pass without the Room,) that the Walls would approach one another so near, that there would remain no Space betwixt them. (p. 28)

In his extensive notes, Clarke put the alternative vacuist viewpoint. He maintained the "essence" of matter was "*solid Extension, impenetrable*, which is endued with *a Power of resisting*" (p. 24), and that the greater part of nature was a vacuum in which bodies moved. Clarke seemed to accept that those writers who affirmed the essence of matter was extension were consistent in denying a vacuum. Instead of making a case on logical grounds—by challenging Rohault's illustration, and showing that the idea of a vacuum was conceivable and therefore space without matter could possibly exist—he defended it experimentally. Phenomena such as the motion of comets in the heavens and the vibrations of pendula in exhausted receivers showed that there was little or no sensible resistance, and therefore no sensible matter was present in the respective spaces. The nature of gravity also implied the non-equivalence of matter and space. It always acted in proportion to the quantity of matter contained in a body; whereas, in a plenist universe, it would follow that all bodies were equally heavy, which contradicted our everyday experience of the world (vol. 2, p. 97).

Keill maintained the emphasis on solidity found in Clarke's notes. In his view, solidity was a better candidate for the "Essence and intimate Nature of Body" (*Introduction*, p. 15). He argued that whereas extension was also an attribute of things that were not body, the imagination could not separate the idea of solidity from body without destroying the idea of the latter. The "Cartesians" had used exactly the same logic to argue that the idea of space without matter was inconceivable and therefore nothing of the kind could be made to exist by any power. Keill sought to show that this was false by challenging the details of the illustration also found in Rohault:

Let us suppose then any Vessel, and let it first be filled with Air; then let the Air contained in this Vessel be exhausted, or, if you will, annihilated by a Divine Power, and let all other Bodies whatever be hindered from entring into its place: I would now ask, whether in this case there is not given a Space void of all Bodies? All that Body which was within the Vessel is destroyed, the Ingress of any other Body is prevented, and the Form of the Vessel is supposed to be preserved; it seems therefore to be necessary that a Vacuum, or a Space not replete with Body, is given. (p. 16)

Keill made it quite clear that this showed only that the vacuum was at least possible. Thus he rejected "Cartesian" claims that the sides would come together, principally on the grounds that they could not move themselves and that *ex hypothesi* there was no external body given in the example which could force them together. On the other hand, if air rushed into the vessel, a vacuum was presupposed in the space which it left.

Rohault and Keill appealed to the same illustration to support rival plenist and vacuist beliefs. One said that it showed the idea of a vacuum was inconceivable; the other that it could be imagined and therefore could possibly exist. The evidence it provided seemed to address the problem of whether the mind could form certain kinds of ideas. But at the same time, for Keill at least, the formulation of the example also implied empirical beliefs about the behaviour of physical bodies in certain specified conditions. Both sides agreed that the issue was whether a vacuum was conceivable, but what would happen inside the walls of the room/vessel was disputed. Rohault said that the walls must come together; Keill said this could not happen. Therefore the kind of evidence the example provided was as much at issue as the outcome itself; certainly, it was ambiguous enough to be claimed by both sides of the debate.

A version of the imaginary experiment found in Rohault and Keill was also used by Hume. After the deity had annihilated a part of matter while the others remained at rest, "what must we conceive to follow upon the annihilation of all the air and subtile matter in the chamber, supposing the walls to remain the same, without any motion or alteration?" (T. 54). Hume's 'chamber' follows Rohault's account (Keill referred to a "vessel"), but the general form of the illustration is the same for all three authors. Rohault and Keill were probably familiar with it in Descartes.[55] There are many obvious methodological allusions to the procedures of experimental natural philosophy throughout Hume's wider discussion, and these suggest he had a broad knowledge of the culture of science. Some aspects of the way he used this illustration imply a direct connection with presentations of the controversy in natural philosophy textbooks.

As one of the conditions of the illustration, Hume was careful to speak of excluding all "subtile matter" as well as air from the chamber. This qualification is not found in Rohault and Keill, and its significance can be seen by returning to Clarke's notes. Part of the defence of the vacuum entailed refuting the "Cartesian" use of "subtile matter". This helped to maintain the identification between space and body in explanations of

[55] René Descartes, *Principles of philosophy*, trans. V. R. and R. P. Miller (Dordrecht 1983), p. 48. Descartes referred to "vessels".

difficult physical phenomena, such as the rarefication of bodies, where it was proposed that the matter entered the pores of a body as it expanded in shape. Clarke's footnotes contain a sustained attack on this kind of "subtile matter". Yet because he employed an experimental defence of the vacuum, which only denied the existence in it of sensible matter, he also left open the possibility that a vacuum might still contain a form of insensible matter whose resistance was virtually nil. Despite his criticisms, Clarke simultaneously endorsed Newton's speculations about an analogous ether "which enters into the Pores of the rarefyed body" (vol. 1, p. 29). Once again, this shows that there were originally grounds for perceiving similarities between Descartes' and Newton's mechanically-inspired natural philosophies, despite Clarke's theocentric objection that plenism implied a view of nature as uncreated, infinite, and eternal.

In the context of this debate, Hume's exclusion of all "subtile matters", whether "Cartesian" or "Newtonian", is a significant pointer to the kind of solution that he sought to the dispute between vacuism and plenism. Various statements made in the course of Hume's discussion make it appear that he sided unequivocally with the plenists. For example, in the brief résumé of his "system", he stated that it was impossible to conceive of "a vacuum and extension without matter" (T. 40). Immediately prior to introducing the chamber illustration, he added that we could "form no idea of a vacuum, or space, where there is nothing visible or tangible" (T. 53).[56] Despite these programmatic statements, the actual details of the discussion suggest that he sought some kind of a synthesis between plenism and vacuism. Hume denied that the sides of the room would come together as Rohault, following Descartes, argued. But he also denied Keill's view that the resulting space between the walls gave men an idea of a vacuum or space without matter. Whereas Hume could have got only one side of the debate from Descartes, Clarke's edition of Rohault and successive British natural philosophy texts offered easy access to both. Yet Hume did not adopt any of the various solutions on offer there. He ruled out appeals to unperceivable entities whereby a vacuum might exist and yet still contain a form of undetectable matter. Nor did he show any apparent interest in straightforward claims about the physical necessity for a vacuum based on the requirements of motion or gravity. However there was a third kind of approach to the problem, which used mathematical demonstrations to show there was space without matter. Once again Hume rejected it, but he may also have adapted features of it to suit his own purposes.

---

[56] See Berkeley, *New theory of vision*, sec. 126, for a similar position.

Keill departed from Rohault and Clarke when he employed two related mathematical demonstrations which addressed the problem of the vacuum.[57] The first showed the possible existence of a space void of all bodies, and was based upon two "Axioms": (1) no body or portion of matter required another for its existence; (2) any body could preserve its figure if nothing external altered it. As in the previous illustration, it began with an act of God. This time, instead of evacuating a vessel, God collected all the matter in the universe into two spheres, represented by two circles with centres A and B (Fig. 1). Keill then reasoned in the following way. The spheres in question were either separated or contiguous. If the former, then it followed *ex hypothesi* that a space between them was given which was not body. On the other hand, if the latter was the case, then "by the Elements of Geometry", the spheres touched at one point only, C. Hence between other points of the spheres it followed there was some distance, or space, without matter (*Introduction*, pp. 17–18).

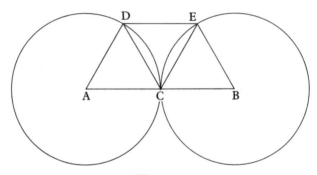

Figure 1

Whereas Keill's first illustration only sought to show the conceivability of a vacuum, his second advanced a much stronger claim. This was that "a space void of all Body" actually existed (pp. 18–19). The basic axioms and conditions of the former were maintained, except that the spheres were spoken of as equal as well as contiguous. Keill then spoke of allowing the straight lines CD and CE to be "accommodated" in the spheres, so that each was equal to their radius. Then when DE was joined, this straight line was exactly equal to the same radius. The proof

---

[57] Keill's mathematical approach to the vacuum, and several other features of Lecture 2, are similar to the account in Isaac Barrow, *The usefulness of mathematical learning explained and demonstrated*, trans. John Kirkby [1734] (London 1970), Lecture 10, 'Of space, and impenetrability', 163–85. However, unlike Hume, Barrow did not refer to the empty vessel or chamber in his account.

of this involved drawing more lines to make the equilateral triangles *ACD*, *CDE* and *BCE*, and then showing that their sides were all the same length.

Having established the length of *DE*, Keill argued that all the distances between other points of the spheres "out of contact *C*" were in a determinate ratio to the diameter of the sphere. Therefore there was always a determinate space without matter, into which a body agreeing with the distance in question could be admitted. But one of greater dimensions than the distance between two given points on the sphere could not "by any Power whatever be placed within that Space". He added:

Whence, since these Properties demonstratively agree with the Space here spoken of, and that Space may really exist, tho' no one should think at all, it evidently follows against the *Cartesians*, that the Idea we have of Space, is not chimerical or imaginary; for what is chimerical, can have no Existence out of the Intellect.

We conclude therefore, that there is in reality a Space distinct from all Body; which is as a universal Receptacle, wherein all Bodies are contained and moved. (p. 19)

As a mathematically-inclined natural philosopher, Keill used geometry not only to show the possible existence of a vacuum, but also to support the claim that it really existed. This begs many questions about his conception of geometry and how it applied to real bodies in nature. They can, however, be postponed until Hume's criticisms of mathematical demonstrations of infinite divisibility are discussed. For now, it is important to note that in conjunction with the empty-chamber illustration, Hume also used examples involving two bodies to address the problem of the vacuum. The approach he adopted provides a revealing contrast with the one found in Keill.

The first indication of Hume's willingness to adapt the two-bodies example to suit his own purposes is seen during a discussion of the mutual penetration of indivisibles, where he wrote: "Suppose two bodies containing no void within their circumference, to approach each other" (T. 41). (This occurred as part of a complex discussion of whether one indivisible point could penetrate another, which Hume referred to again in his discussion of the solidity of bodies (T. 229–30).) A more significant instance can be found as part of an investigation of whether the ideas of darkness and motion, in conjunction with men's experience of visible and tangible bodies, ever gave them the idea of a vacuum. Hume wrote that " 'tis evident, that when only two luminous bodies appear to the eye, we can perceive whether they be conjoin'd or separate" (T. 57). A similar presentation was offered for a man touching one object in utter darkness, and then, after an interval, feeling another. But instead of adopting the geometrical resolution of the relationship between two spherical bodies found in Keill, Hume transposed the example into a more general experiment about what people would experience when seeing and touching objects under various controlled conditions involving motion and darkness.[58] In all the cases he considered, Hume denied that they were ever sufficient to give us the idea of a vacuum.

Thus Hume thought and wrote about the vacuum in relation to two illustrations, differing versions of which can be found in the textbook tradition. However, his use of them was transformative and not a matter of simple borrowing. Impressions giving rise to the ideas of motion, darkness, annihilation, and rest were all re-examined to see if they could lead further to the idea of a vacuum. In fact, Hume appealed to his account of the derivation of ideas copied from antecedent impressions to argue that these candidate ideas were not a basis for the mind to arrive at the idea of space without matter. Nevertheless, they did often provide grounds for falsely imagining that one had the idea of a vacuum.

Hume continued to rely on features from both illustrations to formulate his own distinctive synthesis out of the competing claims of plenism and vacuism. After the contents of the chamber were annihilated, it was indeed impossible to believe that the walls would touch (T. 55). Rather, the chamber must be conceived of in much the same manner as it was before:

This annihilation leaves to the *eye*, that fictitious distance, which is discover'd by the different parts of the organ, that are affected, and by the degrees of light and shade; and to the *feeling*, that which consists in a sensation of motion in the hand, or other member of the body. (T. 62)

The hand's role here suggests a man touching one wall of the chamber and then, after an interval, touching the other, as in the example of feeling two tangible bodies in darkness. Situations like the chamber gave men the idea of "fictitious" or "invisible distance". It was this that was routinely mistaken for a vacuum.

Experience showed that invisible distance could easily be mistaken for its visible counterpart, not only in this case but in a variety of others. Hume explained why this occurred in terms of three relations between each kind of distance. His treatment of each is heavily indebted to concepts derived from natural philosophy. The whole discussion

---

[58] Cf. Berkeley, *De motu*, secs. 52–66, where versions of both the visual and tactile experiments can be found. Berkeley was himself reworking more technical illustrations found in Newton. See K. P. Winkler, 'Berkeley, Newton and the stars', *Studies in history and philosophy of science* 17 (1986), 23–42.

presupposes an underlying model of animal spirits and "traces" in the brain. This is much in evidence elsewhere in the *Treatise* and is part of the routine vocabulary used by mechanical philosophers when they describe the physiology of sensation. The justifications for the first two resemblances also draw upon arguments about distance judgements in optics, based upon angles made by rays of light flowing from objects, which I considered in the previous section. However, it is the grounds for the third resembling relation between invisible and visible distance which is the most revealing in this respect. Hume used an argument strongly associated with Keill:

For as all qualities, such as heat, cold, light, attraction, *&c.* diminish in proportion to the distance; there is but little difference observ'd, whether this distance be mark'd out by compounded and sensible objects, or be known only by the manner, in which the distant objects affect the senses. (T. 59)

In the opening few pages of the *Introduction*, Keill had offered a demonstration that "Every Quality or Virtue that is propagated every way in right Lines from a Centre is diminished in a duplicate Proportion of the Distance from that centre" (pp. 5–7). In fact this, and analogous demonstrations of the rarity of matter, became Keill's recognized trademark.[59]

Hume's final synthesis from plenism and vacuism was based upon considering a vacuum as the capacity of invisible and intangible distance to become visible, tangible distance (T. 64). He then claimed that a vacuum in this sense still existed, even though extension and matter were the same. Or even if this interpretation was rejected, motion was still possible in a plenum without impulse *in infinitum*, without returning in a circle, and without penetration.[60] Later in the Appendix, Hume equated the view that "bodies are said to be plac'd after such a manner, as to receive bodies betwixt them, without impulsion or penetration" with "*the Newtonian* philosophy" (T. 639). Thus it would appear to follow that this usage is not inconsistent with the notion of a plenum if it be "rightly understood".[61] However, Hume also added that if one went

[59] The same proposition can be found in Keill's teacher, David Gregory, *The elements of physical and geometrical astronomy* [1715], trans. Edmund Stone, 2nd edn., vol. 1 (London 1726), p. 102. Most commentators attribute the actual demonstration to Keill. This, or the Latin original, was also one of Steuart's set texts.

[60] Presumably, this was based upon the argument that because men could imagine the annihilation of a body interposed between two others on either side without disturbing them, they could also imagine it recreated on the same basis; and that this event is much the same thing as the motion of the body in question (T. 63). Furthermore, they found "*by experience*" that invisible distance was converted to its visible counterpart without impulse or penetration.

[61] Hume was phlegmatic about his paradoxical solution; he anticipated that his concern to explain the manner in which objects affected the senses, rather than the real nature and operations of bodies, would be considered unsatisfactory by others. Unfortunately, we do not have any response to this from a "Newtonian" natural philosopher. But see George Martine,

further, beyond "the appearances of objects to the senses", that is from the perception of objects to the objects themselves, then no decisive arguments existed on either side. At the same time, he seems also to have expressed a preference for the vacuist position because it was more consistent with common sense.

Some of the complexities of Hume's position on plenism versus vacuism can be unravelled by close attention to his treatment of illustrations and examples routinely used in the natural philosophy texts. They gave him access to a potentially damaging debate at the heart of natural philosophy which he could then attempt to resolve according to the tenets of the science of man. The key to Hume's solution lies in the role played by the imagination in his metaphysics. Whether men could or could not conceive of a vacuum as a space without matter was at issue; and it led on to a subsidiary question about how the mind falsely conceived it had this idea when it mistook invisible distance for a vacuum. At first sight, the two parts of Hume's discussion seem to refer to a priori and a posteriori aspects of the problem. In the first instance, "conceivability" addressed the problem of whether space without matter was contradictory and therefore could not possibly exist. In the second, it played a different role and helped to explain how men's experience gave them mistaken ideas about the nature of the vacuum. However, the actual use of the empty-chamber illustration in both the natural philosophy tradition and in Hume precludes any such clear-cut distinction.

Although Rohault, Keill, and Hume agreed that it was meant to address the conceivability or otherwise of a vacuum, they diverged over the interpretation of what would actually occur. The basis of their disagreement seems to have been different beliefs about what natural events would occur in the specified conditions. These undermined the purely formal or logical inferences which were supposed to follow from the illustration. Hence there was still widespread confusion about what kind of evidence bore upon the problem of whether men could conceive the idea of a vacuum. To the extent that Hume continued to use the same illustration, he perpetuated this confusion. At the same time, he was much clearer on the precise nature of what was seen and felt in the empty chamber, the nature of these impressions, and what ideas they could give

---

An examination of the Newtonian argument for the emptiness of space and of the resistance of subtile fluids (London 1740): this put forward criticisms of "Newtonian" arguments in favour of a vacuum based on the role given to the ether in Newton's later writing. Newton's private and public defences of the vacuum were themselves far from simple, and seem to have combined a posteriori and a priori justifications. See J. E. McGuire, 'Body and void and Newton's "De mundi systemate": some new sources', *Archive for history of exact sciences* 3 (1966), 206–48.

rise to in the imagination. Hume was also more circumspect on the debated issue of the relationship between the conceivability of a vacuum and its actual existence. He showed no inclination to rely solely upon arguments taken from natural philosophy to decide whether a vacuum was a physical necessity, as Clarke had implied. Nor did he rely upon mathematics to bridge the gap between conceivability and existence, as Keill certainly did. This rejection of mathematical evidence is more apparent in Hume's response to the problem of infinite divisibility, where geometry plays a much more direct role in the arguments rehearsed in natural philosophy texts. Notwithstanding this, there are many parallels between the structure of both debates, particularly with regard to the role played by the imagination.

V. ROHAULT, KEILL, AND INFINITE DIVISIBILITY

Rohault's discussion of infinite divisibility involved him in conceptual difficulties unlike anything connected with his denial of the vacuum. Throughout he strove to maintain a distinction between the concept of "indefinitely" divisible extension and the "real" division of matter, which always arose from motion. The former was performed in men's minds and did not affect the latter (*System*, vol. 1, p. 37). The problem was that inferences about divisibility which followed necessarily from the essence of matter as extension also implied claims which were inconceivable to the imagination. For example, Rohault argued that because matter was extended, it must have parts; and if the smallest part imaginable was placed on a plane surface, it must touch the surface at one part and not another. Thus this part must have parts (p. 23). Yet, *ex hypothesi*, these must be smaller than the smallest parts men could conceive; therefore men could not imagine them. A related train of reasoning produced similar difficulties. Rohault stated that the parts of matter existed independently of one another, and that whatever it was capable of in one part, so was it in all others. He added that, "As therefore we cannot doubt but that it is divisible in some Points, so also is it divisible in all the Points that can be assigned" (p. 32). A simple geometrical demonstration was then sufficient to show that the number of points that could be assigned to any definite quantity of matter was indefinite. Once again, the infinite divisibility of matter demanded the assent of reason but, strictly speaking, the imagination could not conceive how it could be the case.

Rohault went on to discuss objections to this and another mathematical demonstration of infinite divisibility which turned upon the inconsistency of incommensurable quantities with finite divisibility. He considered that the common basis for all the various difficulties raised was based on the premise *"That every thing is absurd, which our Imagination can't comprehend"* (p. 34); therefore he strove to refute it. One way would have been specifically to discuss the role of the imagination in mathematics, and so examine whether conceivability was a necessary condition for valid reasoning. Instead, Rohault argued on the much wider basis that "what exceeds our Imagination, is not therefore impossible" (p. 37). This involved an appeal to the subtlety of matter as a sort of a posteriori proof of infinite divisibility. He estimated how thinly gold could be beaten, and to what length it could be stretched by wire-drawers. The argument was that if this tenuity could be achieved by mere men, then it was likely nature could do much better.[62]

Rohault's approach involved appeals to different kinds of evidence for infinite or indefinite divisibility which was also a feature of the way the empty-room illustration was used. It is difficult to see how his a posteriori examples of the ductility of gold bear upon the problem of a priori mathematical divisibility, unless some correspondence between it and real divisibility is already presupposed. This seems implicit in Rohault's subsequent discussion of real divisibility in chapter 21, 'Of the elements of natural things'. There he returned to the theme that the evidence of microscopes led to the reasonable belief that there are parts of bodies which "escape all our Senses, all the Industry of Man, and exceed even our Imagination". This was evident from phenomena such as little eels in warm vinegar and mould on books. It was also evident "that a *Mite*, which is much less than a Grain of Sand, is an Animal, because we can see it move along":

Since a *Mite* walks along, it must have *Legs*, and these Legs must necessarily have *Joints*. In order to move the Joints, there must be *Muscles, Nerves* and *Tendons*, and in these Nerves *Fibres*, such as we see in those of larger Animals, or at least, something equivalent to them: And if we would carry this Consideration yet further, and speak of the *Heart, Blood, Brain, and Animal Spirits*, we shall be quite at a Loss, and forced to confess, that our Imagination is unable to comprehend or represent the extreme Smallness of the least Parts of which a Mite is composed. (p. 114)

Rohault's format of a priori demonstrations of infinite divisibility followed by a posteriori illustrations was a consistent feature of subsequent British and Dutch texts in experimental natural philosophy, including those which professed a "Newtonian" outlook.[63] Keill's

---

[62] Rohault also considered how silver wire covered with gold leaf could be drawn to immense lengths. See Thackray, *Atoms and powers*, pp. 176–9, for a discussion of such examples as part of the search for the smallest particle size by British mechanical philosophers like Boyle and Halley.

[63] In Rohault, infinite divisibility and the minuteness of nature were integrated into a plenist position and used to support the existence of different kinds of matter, especially the "subtile" kind closely implicated in the vortex theory of planetary motion (pp. 114–17). However, in the

Introduction reveals how elaborate this could become (*Introduction*, pp. 46–62). Besides expanding the variety of mathematical demonstrations, he also extended the range of a posteriori illustrations which displayed "the wonderful Subtility of Nature, and those minute Particles into which Matter is actually divided" (p. 46). As well as the ductility of gold, his examples included the minute particles of asafoetida and "Animalcules", or little organisms such as Rohault's mite:

Ten thousand two hundred and fifty six of the highest Mountains in the whole Earth do not contain as many Grains of Sand, as one Grain of Sand can of the Blood-Globules of these Animalcules. It is no wonder, if you here stand amazed, and being struck with so prodigious a thing, should call in question the infinite Divisibility of Matter, although it is supported by uncontroulable Demonstrations. (p. 59)

Moreover, there were even smaller particles which made the blood globules appear as mountains. Keill's descent into minutiae also culminated in the animal spirits which, once again, were said to exceed "all Calculation, and even the Force of the Imagination" (p. 62).

Hume referred to both the mite and the grain of sand as part of the process of establishing benchmarks for the limits of the imagination. However, as in his discussion of the evacuated room, Hume used them to give an original twist to appeals about these limits. He began with the consensus position that the capacity of the mind was limited, and therefore the imagination reached a minimum beyond which it could not go.[64] This was the case even though men used number to represent apparently smaller objects and spoke of "the thousandth and ten thousandth part" of a grain of sand: "The idea of a grain of sand is not distinguishable, nor separable into twenty, much less into a thousand, ten thousand, or an infinite number of different ideas" (T. 27).[65]

Despite agreeing about the limits of the mind, Hume went on to refute those who then concluded that " 'tis impossible for the imagination to

emerging alternative tradition, an identical set of arguments and illustrations was used to uphold a vacuist conception of nature. If it could be shown that particles of matter were much smaller, then it followed that there was less matter as a whole and therefore a lot more empty space. Thus both traditions were committed to defending infinite divisibility, albeit for different reasons. Also, despite apparent differences over the atomic structure of matter and the nature of space, "Cartesians" and "Newtonians" were united against defenders of finite divisibility, whom they criticized in the strongest terms. For a discussion of Newton's position, see J. E. McGuire, 'Space, infinity, and indivisibility: Newton on the creation of matter', in *Contemporary Newtonian research*, ed. Z. Bechler (Dordrecht 1982), 145–90.

[64] For the same argument against infinite divisibility based on the finite divisibility of men's ideas, see Berkeley, *Principles*, sec. 133.
[65] For a discussion of the sand metaphor, see G. N. Cantor, 'Weighing light: the role of metaphor in 18th-century optical discourse', in *The figural and the literal*, ed. A. Benjamin and others (Manchester 1987), at pp. 134–5. In Berkeley, *Principles*, sec. 101, it occurs as part of a wider discussion about scepticism based on the limits of the senses.

form an adequate idea, of what goes beyond a certain degree of minuteness as well as of greatness" (T. 28). He related the "error" about unimaginable minuteness to a defect in men's senses which was revealed, for example, by a microscope, when it showed that things previously considered uncompounded were composed of a number of parts.[66] In Hume's view, the evidence it provided did not allow us to conclude that there were other objects beyond the imagination. Microscopes merely "advanc[ed] to a *minimum*, what was formerly imperceptible". Rather, because men were able to form some ideas and images which were absolutely simple and indivisible, nothing could in fact be more minute than these. Therefore he concluded that "we can form ideas, which shall be no greater than the smallest atom of the animal spirits of an insect a thousand times less than a mite" (ibid.).

To Hume, the greater difficulty lay with the other aspect of the problem, or how men enlarged their conceptions. Although Rohault and Keill seemed to concern themselves only with minuteness, Clarke added a note to Rohault's discussion of the gold-beater in support of the existence of immense entities beyond the scope of the imagination:

Whence, by the way, it appears, how weakly they argue, who, because *Space* (and the same is true of *Duration*) may be divided into innumerable Parts which are unequal; and in *infinite Space* (or *Duration*) the Number of the greatest Parts is as much infinite as that of the least; which they think absurd, because they believe all Infinites to be equal in every respect; conclude from hence, that there can be no such Thing at all as Infinite *Space* (or *Duration*). (*System*, vol. 1, p. 34)

Thus in Rohault's text and Clarke's notes, as well as Keill's book, we find connections made among infinite divisibility, men's imagination, and the nature of space and duration. All of these are also found in the opening section of Hume's discussion where the same illustrations are used. Yet even here, where the evidence of a connection seems overwhelming, we must be cautious about arguing for too direct a relationship between Hume's text and these particular works, resting on the illustrations alone. Firstly, in the process of advancing a set of quite different arguments, the materials were transformed. Secondly, the images of the mite and the grain of sand were common features of other

[66] Hume's reference to the evidence of microscopes (and telescopes) clearly relates to passages in Rohault's *System*. However, it can also be related to Keill's discussion of "animalcules". Using a proposition taken from Gregory's work on optics (see note 8), Keill showed how it was possible to calculate the size of an object, such as an animalcule, whose parts appeared only as an indivisible point. This involved calculating the angle under which its parts could not be distinguished when viewed through a lens whose distance from the object was also known. The length of the object could then be deduced trigonometrically (*Introduction*, pp. 54–5).

natural philosophical texts.[67] Thirdly, the mite even occurs outside this context, for example in Pascal, where Hume could just as easily have encountered it.[68] Clearly, the mite was a sort of institution of discourse. It could do important theological work, for example, in Pascal, where it was used in a nescient but fideistic way to bring men to acknowledge God's supremacy in nature by a recognition of the limits of human understanding. Or it could be used by natural philosophers such as Rohault and Keill against sceptics who were disinclined to make inferences from the sensible to the insensible. A third and different use can be discerned in Hume, where the example of the mite's atom of animal spirit was a mark of the scope of men's imagination *and* a match for the minuteness or greatness of nature. In effect, Hume used it to justify the adequacy of human understanding.

Following the general trend of Clarke's notes, Keill's own display of a posteriori illustrations of the subtlety of matter was accompanied with copious calculations of the size of various minute particles. Given an evident predilection for mathematical reasoning which extended to demonstrations of the vacuum, it is not surprising that a priori treatments of infinite divisibility also received close attention in the *Introduction*.[69] Keill's volume presented a comprehensive review of mathematical and logical arguments for and against infinite divisibility.[70] Furthermore, given the likelihood that it served as the

[67] See Desaguliers, *Experimental philosophy*, vol. 1, p. 29; 'sGravesande, *An explanation of the Newtonian philosophy*, p. 10. Browne's introduction to his translation of Gregory (see note 8) is another possible source (pp. i–xv). After discussing the vastness of astronomical phenomena, Browne "descended" to the minuteness of some living organisms. He mentioned the mathematical estimation of microscopical distances given by "Dr. Keill in his *Physical lectures*" and emphasized how, for example, the microscopical study of animalcula would help eliminate medical conditions like the "itch".

[68] Blaise Pascal, *Pensées* [1670], trans. A. J. Krailsheimer (Harmondsworth 1966), 'Disproportion of man', pp. 89–90, where it was also used to show that nature exceeded man's imaginative capacity. Later works such as B. Nieuwentijdt, *The religious philosopher*, trans J. Chamberlayne [1717], 3rd edn., vol. 2 (London 1724), pp. 448–71, continued to make apologetic uses of this sort of material throughout the 18th century.

[69] The English editions of Keill's book introduced yet further material on the infinite divisibility of matter, in the form of two mathematical theorems at the end of Lecture 5, 'Of the subtility of matter' (pp. 63–7). For a discussion of their significance, see A. Thackray, '"Matter in a nut-shell": Newton's Opticks and 18th-century chemistry', *Ambix* 15 (1968), 29–53. Cf. Berkeley, *Philosophical commentaries*, Notebook B, no. 364: "Keils filling the world with a mite this follows from the Divisibility of extension ad infinitum."

[70] They included both Rohault's demonstrations and two others for good measure (pp. 26–30). He also refuted all the arguments conventionally cited by defenders of finite divisibility. Briefly, Keill's views were that any proposed distinction between the divisibility of mathematical body and the indivisibility of physical body was unfounded because both depended on "the Nature and Essence of Extension"; that indivisibility led to paradoxes about motion; that Epicurean claims about the absurdity of the finite containing an infinite number of parts merely begged the question; that parts whether finite or infinite always made a whole; that Atomist objections based upon paradoxes to show that the least quantity equalled the greatest were founded on the false hypothesis that all magnitudes were only to be measured by their

introductory text in Steuart's class, it was not only a convenient and available compendium on the subject, but also one which Hume may have encountered at an early stage in his development. In fact, arguments in the *Introduction* about the solidity and extension of bodies, and the divisibility of magnitude, seem to be very pertinent to sections of Hume's discussion of the foundations of geometry.

Once again, though, caution is required in making any claims about the evident correspondences between Keill and Hume. Firstly, Keill was probably drawing upon other sources besides Rohault for this part of his lectures. For example, there are similarities with Barrow's discussion of the divisibility of magnitude in the *Mathematical lectures*, a work also cited by Hume (T. 46).[71] Secondly, other natural philosophy books dealt with the topic.[72] Finally, there was a widespread dissemination of material dealing with infinite divisibility in many other mathematical and metaphysical texts. It is very unlikely that Keill's text, and others like it, were Hume's only sources for views on the foundations of mathematics. In spite of these qualifications, Hume's criticisms of geometry were certainly informed by applications of geometry found in Keill's *Introduction* and other mathematically-inclined works of natural philosophy.

Given the comprehensiveness of Keill's treatment, it is predictable that various details and arguments found there are also canvassed in Hume.[73] However, these are less important than uncovering the general view of geometry and its relationship to the world which underlies

number of parts; that the argument which said God, when dividing matter, would reach an ultimate part, was a conclusion repugnant to God's own "immutable Essence"; and finally, that arguments founded on a minimum part of extension, no longer capable of further division, were refuted by proofs of infinitesimals (pp. 30–45).

[71] Isaac Barrow, *Mathematical lectures*, Lecture 9, 'Of the termination, extension, composition, and divisibility of magnitudes', pp. 139–63. Keill himself referred to the endless space between the asymptote and an infinitely produced logarithmic curve which was nevertheless equal to a finite space "as is demonstrated by the great Dr Barrow in his Geometrical Lectures" (*Introduction*, p. 36). The role of this in proofs of infinite divisibility was also discussed in the *Mathematical lectures*, pp. 155–6.

[72] Of those already mentioned, 'sGravesande's *Mathematical elements* offered the most comprehensive discussion of the foundations of mathematics. He emphasized natural philosophy's place among those parts of mathematics whose object was quantity in general. 'sGravesande distinguished between pure and mixed mathematics, putting "physics" in the latter. He also discussed the relationship between demonstrative and sensory evidence and the respective forms of certainty appropriate to each (pp. i–ix). Later editions of his work included " 'An oration concerning evidence', spoken at Leyden the eighth of February, in the Year 1724, when the Author went out of his Rector's office". However, this appeared after the *Treatise* and it would be most helpful to know whether copies of it were available beforehand.

[73] For example, Keill discussed problems arising from the divisibility of finite extensions into infinite numbers of parts (pp. 33–4). Then he examined how an infinite series of diminishing fractions adds up to a finite unit (pp. 35–6). The same order of treatment is found at T. 29–31.

Keill's discussion. This provides a context for two central themes of Hume's criticisms: the attack on the intelligibility of the definitions presupposed in demonstrations of infinite divisibility; and the revision of the concept of equality implied in the measurement of minute quantities and by the construction of perfect figures.

In the preface of his work, Keill made it clear that geometry was the principal means of admittance to natural philosophy (p. x). Like most other exponents of infinite divisibility, he insisted that the understanding pay homage to a criterion of geometrical certainty. Thus he spoke of the power of demonstrations "to compel the Assent", even though it involved accepting things inconceivable to the imagination: "there is something in the Nature of Infinites, that seems not to be adequately comprehended by the human Intellect; and therefore it is no wonder, if some things follow from it, which the Mind of Man, involved in thick Darkness, is not able to conceive" (*Introduction*, p. 33). This was the theme of Keill's review of the various objections to infinite divisibility put forward by the "Atomical Philosophers". While they raised difficulties, nothing they said impeded the "Force" of demonstrations involving infinites. Hume clearly believed he had found a way round the thrust of this sort of position. He contended that the definitions presupposed in demonstrations of infinite divisibility were only conceivable in terms of finite divisibility:

A surface is *defin'd* to be length and breadth without depth: A line to be length without breadth or depth: A point to be what has neither length, breadth nor depth. 'Tis evident that all this is perfectly unintelligible upon any other supposition than that of the composition of extension by indivisible points or atoms. How else cou'd any thing exist without length, without breadth, or without depth? (T. 42)

Men could never conceive of the way points, lines, and surfaces terminate lines, surfaces, and solids respectively unless their ideas were indivisible. Conversely, if the terminations could not be conceived on the principle of infinite divisibility, then geometrical demonstrations which used terminations to prove infinite divisibility also collapsed. In fact, Hume seems to have considered that all forms of geometrical demonstration were impossible unless finite divisibility was accepted (T. 44).

Keill developed his general position on the relationship between mathematics and the world as part of a dialogue with philosophers who wanted to banish geometry from physics. One way of achieving this was to deny the existence of mathematical objects outside men's minds. Keill associated this view with du Hamel (*Introduction*, p. 22). A related criticism of "ungeometrical philosophers" was that the perfectly figured bodies, with perfect surfaces, lines, and points as conceived by geometry, could not be found in nature. Keill denied both of these. Once again, he appealed to a criterion of mathematical intelligibility to underwrite the reality of geometrical entities:

> So many beautiful Properties of those Figures discovered and demonstrated by the Geometers, evince their Possibility, for of an impossible thing there can be no real Property, no Demonstration. It remains therefore, that they acknowledge these Figures as possible; and if they are possible, it is in the power of God to form out of Matter, Bodies having such Surfaces. (p. 24)

Keill went on to show how lines could be generated by a spherical body moving across a planar body which it touched at one point only. However, as in his demonstration of the vacuum, he enlisted geometry to move from conceivability and possibility to actual existence. Keill further argued that if bodies existed, so did the real points, lines, and surfaces conceived by geometers. This was on the grounds that bodies must be terminated by surfaces with no depth; otherwise those surfaces would themselves be bodies, and this would lead to an absurd infinite regress. The same argument was applied to the termination of surfaces by lines and lines by points (p. 23). However, Keill's conception of "real" seems to have been that surfaces, lines, and points existed not as real matter but as "Modes, Terminations, or Accidents". This was analogous to the way that figure existed in a different way from the body figured (pp. 23–4). Whereas he started out with apparently clear distinctions between physical and mathematical divisibility, his view of geometry and its relation to the world blurred any remaining boundary between them.[74]

Interestingly, the positions canvassed by Keill were also discussed by Hume. He considered whether things without length, breadth, or depth might exist on other grounds besides the composition of extension by indivisible points. Thus he rejected the position that mathematical objects could not exist in nature, and for much the same reason as Keill: if one had a clear idea of a line, surface, or point, then this necessarily implied the possibility of its existence (T. 42). At the same time, he ruled out any process of abstraction which accounted for their "real" existence on the basis of the distinction between figure and the body figured, which Keill seemed to favour (T. 43). Hume also attacked those who,

---

[74] The key to this transformation was Keill's conception of magnitude. He argued that magnitude was a feature of extensionality common to space, physical bodies, mathematical solids, surfaces, and lines alike. Then, in so far as they all had magnitude, they were all infinitely divisible. How this affected his ontology of points is unclear. Although Keill emphasized that points had no magnitude and could therefore mutually penetrate one another, he also required them (as the terminations of lines) to be somehow "accommodated" in bodies (p. 18). This was necessary in order to demonstrate, for example, that there could be space without matter.

like Keill, used God to underwrite the exactness and real existence of mathematical objects:

In vain shou'd we have recourse to the common topic, and employ the supposition of a deity, whose omnipotence may enable him to form a perfect geometrical figure, and describe a right line without any curve or inflection. (T. 51)

However, his major criticism of arguments for the existence of perfect geometrical entities was reserved for the conception of equality used by geometricians. He argued that, whether geometry was founded on finite or infinite divisibility, it could not arrive at a precise standard of either a straight line or a plane surface. This was because the "ultimate standard of these figures is deriv'd from nothing but the senses and imagination" (T. 51), and these faculties are incapable of such precision. Therefore even if one allowed that terminations were conceivable without the idea of indivisible points which presupposed finite divisibility, demonstrations of infinite divisibility were still revealed as "magnificent pretentions". In Hume's view, writers who claimed, like Keill, to apply exact standards of equality in demonstrations involving infinite quantities, made imaginary measurements beyond the limits of men's ideas.[75] Like judgements about invisible distance, these were, strictly speaking, "useless as well as incomprehensible" (T. 48). In another sense, just as men routinely mistook experiences involving invisible distance for a vacuum, it was a perfectly natural procedure for the mind to imagine it possessed a more exact standard:

A musician finding his ear become every day more delicate, and correcting himself by reflection and attention, proceeds with the same act of the mind, even when the subject fails him, and entertains a notion of a compleat *tierce* or *octave*, without being able to tell whence he derives his standard. A painter forms the same fiction with regard to colours. A mechanic with regard to motion. To the one *light* and *shade*; to the other *swift* and *slow* are imagin'd to be capable of an exact comparison and equality beyond the judgments of the senses. (T. 48–9)

This essay has shown that Hume's debt to the culture of early 18th-century science was considerable. Understanding the palimpsest of natural knowledge beneath Hume's text enriches the interpretation of many otherwise puzzling features of *Treatise* I. ii. Aspects of the

---

75 Some of Keill's demonstrations of infinite divisibility involved appeals to the geometry of infinites. For example, he offered three proofs to show that, given quantities infinitely small, there were others infinitely less than these *in infinitum* (pp. 41–5). One in particular was taken from the concluding Scholium to bk. I, sec. i of the *Principia*, and involved a series of infinitely diminishing angles of contact between a curve and its tangent. They all involved conceptions of equality in their proofs and therefore fell within the terms of Hume's criticisms; furthermore, Hume specifically mentioned arguments for infinite divisibility derived from the "*point of contact*" (T. 53).

organization, structure, and content of his discussion can be closely related to treatments of the vacuum and infinite divisibility found in the natural philosophy tradition. However, the accompanying illustrations and examples were used to advance quite different arguments. Many of them have precedents in Berkeley and this invites further elaboration. The emphasis here has been restricted to some general features of the scientific texts which Hume had access to. In the future, it may be possible to be more precise about his early studies and identify more of the actual works he read and used. In particular, Hume's familiarity with mathematics and mathematical natural philosophy is now in urgent need of attention.[76] While science affords merely one of the intellectual cultures which impinged upon his development as a metaphysician, moralist, critic, and political theorist, its significance is more profound than most Hume scholars have previously recognized.[77]

Medical Archive Centre
Edinburgh University Library

[76] Hume's criticisms of mathematics were clearly relevant to the general debate about fluxions, but in an indirect way. His reluctance to deal with the nature of motion in *Treatise* I. ii means that he did not engage in the kind of technical discussion found, for example, in Berkeley's *Analyst* (1734). However, this does not mean that he was wholly incompetent to do so. This paper was in its final stages before a set of lecture notes copied down by Hume in 1726 and entitled 'A treatise of fluxions' appeared for sale at Sotheby's (see the editor's introduction to this volume). The lectures were given by George Campbell, an extramural mathematics teacher who subsequently engaged in a controversy with MacLaurin about the impossible roots of equations. On the basis of my brief examination of the manuscript, it seems likely that Hume was an advanced student of mathematics. The lectures provide an introduction to the subject and there is little evidence of the application of fluxions to natural philosophy as such. Nevertheless, Hume was exposed to Campbell's presentation of some of the sophisticated lemmas of bk. I, sec. i of the *Principia*, which lay the foundations for the mathematical method of the calculus. Given that Hume was prepared to pursue this sort of educational opportunity available to him in Edinburgh, it should not be surprising that he maintained an interest in the culture of mathematics later in life. See L. Gossman, 'Two unpublished essays on mathematics in the Hume papers', *Journal of the history of ideas* 21 (1960), 442–9.

[77] An early version of this paper was presented at the Institute Project on the Scottish Enlightenment at Edinburgh in June 1986, while I held a Wellcome research fellowship in the History of Medicine at Edinburgh University. I completed the penultimate draft while a General Council research fellow in the department of Anatomy—a location I shared with an imposing bust of Hume which, though not a life study, may be the only sculpture ever made of him. Many people have made helpful suggestions which I have incorporated, but I am particularly grateful to Roger Emerson, Mary and David Norton, and the editor of this volume for their assistance. Thanks also go to the Keepers of Manuscripts at the National Library of Scotland and the Scottish Record Office; to the staff of Edinburgh, Glasgow, and Aberdeen University Libraries; to the Librarian of the Royal College of Physicians of Edinburgh; and to the Edinburgh City Archivist, for permission to use unpublished materials.

HUME'S 'OF MIRACLES': PROBABILITY AND IRRELIGION

DAVID WOOTTON

David Hume wrote a philosophical essay on the subject of miracles at some time during the years 1735 to 1737 while he was living at La Flèche, where he made use of the Jesuits' library. It was intended for inclusion in *A treatise of human nature*, but the final work appeared "castrated" of this "nobler part". A discussion entitled 'Of miracles', possibly but not necessarily the one written at La Flèche, appeared however in 1748 with the publication of *Philosophical essays concerning human understanding*—the first *Enquiry*. 'Of miracles' provoked a debate which continues to this day; but scholars have been slow to explore a number of fundamental historical questions, which need to be studied if we are to understand both how Hume came to write this essay and—a matter of more directly philosophical interest—the significance of the argument in his own eyes.

In this article I want to propose answers to the following questions: What was the intended place of Hume's first discussion of miracles within the argument of the *Treatise*? How likely is it that the 'Of miracles' published in 1748 closely corresponds to the essay written at La Flèche? What reading influenced Hume's thinking on miracles? And how far was his discussion different in character from those of his predecessors?

The limited amount of evidence at our disposal makes these questions, so far as they refer to Hume's actions and intentions, uncommonly difficult to answer. Indeed we may well suspect that Hume intended that we should be unable to answer them, and that he was not above a certain amount of what he termed "innocent Dissimulation" in such matters (NHL 83). He appears to have suppressed publication of his original discussion for prudential reasons, so it is hardly surprising that it is hard to find out what its argument amounted to. In 'Of miracles' as it now stands, he follows the common practice of deistic writers in laying claim to a respectable ancestry for his arguments: in this case, Tillotson's discussion of transubstantiation. On other occasions—indeed in section XI of the *Enquiry*, immediately after 'Of miracles'—he adopts another common practice, that of resorting to dialogue form to avoid having to take full responsibility for irreligious arguments. We can well suspect that, when Hume discussed religious topics, he would have been inclined to conceal the extent to which he was indebted to irreligious authors.

One of my purposes in this article is to show that the anti-Christian literature Hume was in principle able to draw upon in first writing about miracles was more extensive than has been recognized, and that by the time 'Of miracles' was published there was a considerable literature attacking the Christian conception of miracles, much of it using arguments similar to those in Hume. I hope further to persuade you of the likelihood that Hume was familiar with some of this literature, and that it influenced his arguments.

It is not part of my purpose to prove that Hume was an unbeliever, or that 'Of miracles' is an attack upon Christianity. This is a subject on which there has been fairly general agreement. Nor do I think it necessary to refute in detail Selby-Bigge's notorious view that 'Of miracles' was "quite superfluous" to Hume's central philosophical purposes (E. viii). Hume's more astute readers have always felt that his philosophy as a whole was difficult to reconcile with Christianity. One of his first reviewers took the epigraph of the *Treatise*—"*Rara temporum felicitas, ubi sentire, quae velis; et quae sentias, dicere licet*" (so different from the traditional libertine adage, "*intus ut libet, foris ut moris est*")—as an open declaration of infidelity.[1] In fact it was only towards the end of his life—particularly on his death-bed—that Hume came close to such an open declaration; but the significance of the arguments of the *Treatise* for the critique of religion was scarcely concealed, and was in Hume's view central to the very purpose of a philosophical work of this sort. The *Enquiry* begins with the claim that one of the main purposes of true philosophy is to root out popular superstitions, which Hume remarks have a habit of taking refuge in metaphysics, as highway robbers take refuge in woods (E. 11). His own summary of his life's work is to be found in the statement that "he had been very busily employed in making his countrymen wiser and particularly in delivering them from the Christian superstition".[2] 'Of miracles' had a central part to play in the formulation of a philosophy incompatible with superstition.

The question of how far Hume had, and how far he was aware of having, precursors in this enterprise may appear to be tediously

---

[1] E. C. Mossner, *The life of David Hume*, 2nd edn. (Oxford 1980), p. 120; cf. also the attack on Hume cited in *A letter from a gentleman to his friend in Edinburgh* (Edinburgh 1745), p. 4. On the general libertine attitude, see D. Wootton, *Paolo Sarpi: between Renaissance and Enlightenment* (Cambridge 1983), pp. 16, 37, 150; T. Gregory, *Theophrastus redivivus: erudizione e ateismo nel seicento* (Naples 1979), pp. 30, 185; N. Fréret, *La Lettre de Thrasibule à Leucippe*, ed. S. Landucci (Florence 1986), pp. 76–7.

[2] William Cullen (1776), quoted in Mossner, p. 601.

empirical, but it is a useful way of approaching a more fundamental question: that of the intellectual preconditions for unbelief. It is generally agreed that Hume concealed the extent of his infidelity for prudential reasons. Such prudence was necessary both because there were legal sanctions against blasphemy and atheism, and because it was widely believed that unbelievers were necessarily of bad character. Since Bayle's *Pensées diverses sur la comète* (1682), this view had been under attack, and Hume's own moral philosophy was calculated to defend the position that atheists were capable of being good citizens.[3]

Was this the main barrier to unbelief? Certainly the period after the publication of Bayle's *Pensées* saw the composition of a growing number of attacks on religion, some published and others circulated in manuscript; and the principle of parsimony encourages us to conclude that the new arguments in defence, if not at first of the moral capacities of atheists, then at least of their capacity for enlightened self-interest, were a sufficient precondition both for a more extensive unbelief and for a more generalized defence of unbelief. One of the purposes of my argument, however, is to maintain that looking at 'Of miracles' in context helps to identify another crucial intellectual precondition for a systematic unbelief: one whose importance has hitherto been under-estimated. This precondition lay in the new concepts of evidence and probability, concepts which, as Ian Hacking has shown, stemmed in large part from the work of the philosophers of Port-Royal, and which made possible a new approach to problems of historical testimony, including those presented by the Gospel story.[4] The "emergence of probability" made it possible to ask, in place of "Can the truth of Christianity be demonstrated?", or "Is it supported by authority?", questions such as "Is it likely that the Gospel narrative is accurate?" and "How good is the evidence for God's existence?" Modern irreligion may be said to be born with these new questions.

I. THE INDIAN PRINCE

The problem Hume is concerned with in 'Of miracles' is that of whether one should believe reports of miracles offered by eyewitnesses and

[3] D. Wootton, 'The fear of God in early modern political theory', *Historical papers/Communications historiques* (1983), 56–80; D. F. Norton, 'Hume, atheism, and the autonomy of morals', in *Hume's philosophy of religion* (Winston-Salem 1986), 97–144.

[4] I. Hacking, *The emergence of probability* (Cambridge 1975). For further discussion of Hacking's thesis, see D. Wootton, 'Lucien Febvre and the problem of unbelief in the early modern period', *Journal of modern history* 60 (1988), 695–730; and, a work which appeared too late to be taken account of here, L. Daston's *Classical probability in the Enlightenment* (Princeton 1988).

historians.[5] Central to his discussion is the question of the reliability of testimony. Not all approaches to the problem of miracles proceeded in this fashion. Thus Bishop Sherlock's famous *Tryal of the witnesses* (1729) tried to escape from a narrow discussion of testimony, by considering a hypothetical case in which one was the immediate witness of a resurrection; and Annet, who set out to rebut Sherlock by systematically denying the possibility of miracles, felt consequently obliged to deny that one could trust one's senses in such a case.[6] Hume, however, never discusses this problem: an indication that he was not, as has been claimed, primarily concerned to refute Sherlock's arguments.

There is further evidence that Hume did not have Sherlock in mind. The passage in 'Of miracles' where Hume refers to the incredulity of an Indian prince when told of ice—which reads indeed like a rebuttal of Sherlock, who had claimed that this example was comparable to the case of people who adopted an irrational incredulity in the face of testimony in favour of miracles—was added in the second edition, apparently when the work was already in press.[7] It was not part of Hume's original text.

This passage deals with the issue of how one can distinguish that which lies outside one's own experience from that which is contrary to nature. The example Hume uses had previously been used more widely than has been recognized, but the most important instances are to be found in the writings of Locke, Sherlock, and Butler.[8] This would

---

[5] For an approach which takes this as its starting point, see A. G. N. Flew, *Hume's philosophy of belief* (London 1961); id., *David Hume, philosopher of moral science* (Oxford 1986).

[6] [P. Annet], *The resurrection of Jesus considered* (London [c.1740]), p. 89.

[7] R. M. Burns, *The great debate on miracles* (Lewisburg 1981), p. 284. For the main changes, compare [Hume], *Philosophical essays concerning human understanding*, first edn. (London 1748), pp. 179, 195, with second edn. (London 1750), pp. 179–80, 195–9, [260].

[8] John Locke, *An essay concerning humane understanding*, ed. P. H. Nidditch (Oxford 1975), IV. xv. 5; Thomas Sherlock, *The tryal of the witnesses* (London 1729), pp. 63–4, 99; Joseph Butler, *The analogy of religion* (London 1736), Introduction. It had however been used by Annet in his reply to Sherlock (*Resurrection considered*, p. 88), and in the ensuing debate between Annet and Jackson: J. Jackson, *An address to deists* (London 1744), pp. 20–21; Annet, *The resurrection of Jesus demonstrated to have no proof* (London [1744]), p. 51; [Annet], *Supernaturals examined* (London [c.1748]), pp. 177–9. It had also been used in an unpublished work by Bolingbroke ('The substance of some letters written originally in French, about the year 1720, to Mr. de Pouilly', in *Works*, vol. 3 (London 1754), at pp. 193–4), who had tried to blunt the force of Locke's argument by insisting that the Indian prince must have known of snow. Bolingbroke's argument was taken up by J. Levesque de Pouilly in 'Nouveaux essais de critique sur la fidélité de l'histoire', *L'Histoire et les mémoires de l'académie royale des inscriptions et belles lettres* 6 (1729), at pp. 72–3; but Bolingbroke's claim that the Indian prince could easily have argued from analogy was rejected by Pouilly, on the ground that if one were only to believe testimony when it could be supplemented by analogical arguments from experience one would have to abandon all faith in miracles. Gaskin, who was interested only in the use of the argument in Locke, Sherlock, and Butler, has maintained that Sherlock's use of it was different from that of Locke and Butler, in that he used it in support of belief in miracles (J. C. A. Gaskin, *Hume's philosophy of religion* (London 1978), p. 180; 2nd edn. (1988), p. 239), and that Hume's discussion of the question was thus a specific response to Sherlock. But even Pouilly had been able to see the evident relevance of the argument to the question of miracles.

suggest that Hume read or reread at least one of these authors shortly before the second edition went to press in 1750. It is not difficult to guess why. Early in 1749 he read in manuscript, for Millar the publisher, Philip Skelton's *Ophïomaches*.[9] There he would have found the original version of 'Of miracles' criticized for failing to take account of this argument, which, Skelton pointed out, appeared to establish that one could not rely upon arguments from the invariable course of nature in order to reject miracles as implausible. We can be fairly sure however that Hume did not rely upon Skelton alone; for in the published text (vol. 2, p. 23) Skelton, unlike Hume and everyone else, refers not to an Indian who is ignorant of ice, but to a Negro. From Skelton he must have turned to one of the authors who had used the argument—which was, as Skelton stressed, well known.

Hume had certainly read Locke before he wrote the *Treatise*, and Butler before the end of 1737, although in all probability he would not have read Butler before his return to England in that year.[10] But the changes made in the edition of 1750 suggest that Hume had not had them, or any of the other authors who had made use of the Indian prince argument, in the forefront of his mind when he had originally written 'Of miracles'. Indeed Hume's critics continued to complain even after 1750 that he had not paid sufficient attention to Butler's discussion of antecedently improbable events which have become matters of historical fact.[11]

The prominence of the Indian prince argument in the English literature makes Hume's original failure to take account of it strange. If he was not arguing against Locke, Sherlock, or Butler, whom was he arguing against? He would not of course have had Butler in mind if 'Of miracles' was substantially written at least a decade before it was published. But we need to place 'Of miracles' in an intellectual context where Locke would not have seemed to be an obvious and unavoidable reference point either. We need, I submit, to look to France to establish this context. This is, after all, where Hume first tackled the subject (the first formulation of the argument is described in HL i. 361). We have good grounds for suspecting that he did not systematically rethink his argument (whatever stylistic changes he may have made) after his return to Britain—until, that is, he happened to read Skelton's criticism.

---

[9] Philip Skelton, *Ophiomaches; or deism revealed* (London 1749). Cf. Mossner, *Life*, p. 232.
[10] Locke is cited in the *Treatise*; Butler dates his 'Advertisement' to May 1736. That Hume had been reading Butler on his return from France is an inference from HL i. 25; he indicates a respect for Butler's writing, and a need to remove (not change) passages in the *Treatise* which would offend him.
[11] E.g., George Campbell, *A dissertation on miracles* (London 1762), pp. 30–31; Richard Price, 'On the importance of Christianity, the nature of historical evidence, and miracles', in *Four dissertations* (London 1767), pp. 426–9.

'Of miracles', which was not originally intended as a reply to Locke, Sherlock, or Butler, by the second edition was meant to read like one.[12] Putting it back in its French context may help to explain some of the other puzzling characteristics of Hume's argument. Thus it has been said that he fails to deal, not only with the arguments of Locke and Butler, but also with those of other Christian philosophers such as Boyle and Glanvill.[13] But the omissions are not surprising, if his entry into the debate was not through the English literature, but through the French: in this context it is the extent to which he replies to the arguments of someone like Houtteville that is the best measure of his intelligence and intellectual integrity.[14]

If Hume first wrote 'Of miracles' without any of the key English authors in mind, does this help us understand why he assumed that the question of miracles could be narrowed down to a question of testimony? Others had approached the question in these narrow terms before, but the paradigmatic treatment from this point of view was still Arnauld and Nicole's *La logique, ou l'art de penser* (hereafter '*The art of thinking*'). With its appearance in 1662, the question of miracles had become not merely a question of the credibility of testimony, but one whose analysis was seen to involve balancing the inherent improbability of a miraculous event against the apparent reliability of human testimony.[15] *The art of thinking* ends with a series of chapters, almost certainly written by Arnauld, which represent, in Hacking's terms, the formulation of a new theory of probability and of non-deductive inference. But their first subject is the credibility of testimony regarding historical events, especially miracles. Arnauld's claim that "internal circumstances" (or evidence regarding the antecedent improbability of the event) could be overridden by "external circumstances" (or evidence regarding the reliability of the testimony) set the terms in which the problem of

---

[12] Hume also added in the second edition a long footnote extending his references to the miracles at the tomb of the abbé de Pâris, perhaps because reading Middleton had persuaded him of the topicality of the subject.

[13] Burns, *Great debate*, pp. 225, 228.

[14] C. F. Houtteville, *La religion chrétienne prouvée par les faits* (Paris 1722). There are other indications that the argument was not significantly changed in 1748. The terms in which Hume talks about both probabilities and proofs in the essay are closer to those employed in the *Treatise* than to those employed elsewhere in the first *Enquiry*, so that 'Of miracles' still has to be elucidated in the light of the *Treatise*: see L. Dorman, *David Hume and the miracles controversy, 1749–1800* (Ph.D., University of California, San Diego 1973), pp. 236–7; D. M. Ahern, 'Hume on the evidential impossibility of miracles', in *Studies in epistemology*, ed. N. Rescher (Oxford 1975), at p. 4. Against this it can be argued that the style of 'Of miracles' as we now have it is very different from that of the *Treatise*: however this was, by Hume's own account, already true of the "Reasonings concerning Miracles" which he described to Henry Home in 1737 (NHL 2).

[15] Hacking, *Emergence of probability*, pp. 78–9.

miracles was to be discussed for the next eighty years.[16] Hume's goal was simply to turn the argument of *The art of thinking* on its head: where Arnauld had argued that honest testimony could be accepted even for the most improbable of events, Hume argued that certain events were so improbable that no testimony could be strong enough to make them credible.[17]

Thus the question of miracles was tied by *The art of thinking* to problems of probability and history. It is in exactly this context that it was discussed by Locke in his *Essay*. Locke argued that there are certain observations which are based on constant experience and in which probability amounts to certainty. Yet,

> Though the common Experience, and the ordinary Course of Things have justly a mighty Influence on the Minds of Men, to make them give or refuse Credit to any thing proposed to their Belief; yet there is one Case, wherein the strangeness of the Fact lessens not the Assent to a fair Testimony given of it. . . . This is the proper Case of *Miracles*.[18]

Locke's arguments were derived from those of *The art of thinking*:[19] until he realized the force of the Indian prince argument in 1750, Hume probably felt no need to give Locke's treatment of the problem particular attention. Locke's motives, too, would have seemed indistinguishable

---

[16] Apart from Hacking, J. Noxon ('Hume's concern with religion', in *David Hume, many-sided genius*, ed. K. R. Merrill and R. W. Shahan (Norman 1976), at pp. 79–80) and P. Jones (*Hume's sentiments* (Edinburgh 1982), p. 48) have noticed the relevance of Arnauld's distinction to 'Of miracles'. For a general discussion of the influence of *The art of thinking* on Hume, see C. W. Hendel's foreword to the translation by J. Dickoff and P. James (New York 1964), pp. xvii–xxv. It is unfortunate that the three works devoted to discussions of probability and moral certainty in seventeenth- and eighteenth-century England ignore the English reception of this work: H. G. van Leeuwen, *The problem of certainty in English thought* (The Hague 1963); B. J. Shapiro, *Probability and certainty in seventeenth century England* (Princeton 1983); M. J. Ferreira, *Probability and reasonable doubt* (Oxford 1986).

[17] Putting 'Of miracles' in the context of probability theory helps to explain why Hume chose to give more space to miracles (which were central to probability theory as it then existed) than to prophecy. J. E. Force has argued that in the context of religious apologetics in England prophecy was the more important topic: 'Hume and Johnson on prophecy and miracles', *Journal of the history of ideas* 43 (1982), 463–75. But, firstly, authors such as A. A. Sykes (*The principles and connexion of natural and revealed religion* (London 1740)) and Conyers Middleton (*An examination of the Lord Bishop of London's Discourses* (London 1750)), who took the view that prophecies were more convincing than miracles, were severely criticized by more orthodox divines; and secondly, in probability theory prophecy was of peripheral interest.

[18] *Essay*, IV. xvi. 13. In recognizing only one such case Locke was going against Glanvill, who had argued in the case of witchcraft that the stranger the fact, the more credible the testimony (Dorman, p. 50). Annet in *Supernaturals examined* and Middleton in his *Free enquiry into the miraculous powers which are supposed to have subsisted in the Christian church* (London 1749), p. 22, both took advantage of the loss of belief in witchcraft to reverse Glanvill's argument: if witchcraft was no longer considered credible, despite all the testimony as to its efficacy, on the ground that it was contrary to the ordinary course of nature, then miracles must be as incredible as witchcraft.

[19] L. Obertello, *John Locke e Port-Royal: il problema della probabilità* (Trieste 1964).

from those of his predecessors, with the exception of his attack upon the authority of tradition (IV. xvi. 10), which was only to be expected in a Protestant reworking of a Catholic philosophy of history.[20] Where Aristotle and Descartes had both stressed the possibility of a deductive science of nature, Locke saw a need to open the way for a form of knowledge based upon experience and evidence, probabilistic forms of reasoning. But, remarkably, he did not approach the question of scientific knowledge from this standpoint. The main obstacle to scientific knowledge Locke saw not as lying in the problem of induction, but rather as being rooted in the difficulty of making the transition from the secondary qualities perceived by the senses to the primary ones which had to be hypothesized before causal relationships could be recognized and shown to be necessary. The place he gave to probability in the *Essay* was thus separated from his discussion of the logic of scientific enquiry, and instead reflected a purpose he shared with Arnauld and Nicole, that of defending the validity of historical testimony in face of the limited categories of knowledge recognized by Descartes, a defence which was necessary if the evidence for Christianity was to be found in the Gospels. Thus, in both *The art of thinking* and the *Essay*, the most important probabilistic arguments were those concerned with "degrees of assent", not statistical frequencies.

It is true that *The art of thinking* recognized the possibility of using probabilistic arguments to discuss chance events, and even presented a version of Pascal's wager which was in turn taken up by Locke; but nevertheless probability theory here represented little more than a supplement to a pre-existing corpus of philosophical knowledge. The chapters dealing with it seem to have been something of an afterthought.[21] Hume's *Treatise* was intended to change all this: indeed in the *Abstract* he explained that his primary purpose was to give probability the central place denied it by *The art of thinking* and the *Essay*.[22] Hume restricted demonstrative knowledge to the field of mathematics, and denied that causation could be demonstrated. As a result, the study of causes fell, in his view, entirely within the terrain of what had been traditionally regarded as probabilistic knowledge, and there was no clear distinction to be drawn between natural reasoning and moral reasoning, physical certainty and moral certainty. The absence of such a distinction was fundamental to Hume's attempt to ground all knowledge in psychology (E. 89–91).

[20] This passage is the source of Craig's argument, discussed below.

[21] Hacking, *Emergence of probability*, p. 74.

[22] [Hume], *An abstract of a book lately published* [1740], ed. J. M. Keynes and P. Sraffa (Cambridge 1938), p. 8. Locke and Hume are compared in J. P. Wright, 'Association, madness, and the measures of probability in Locke and Hume', in *Psychology and literature in the eighteenth century*, ed. C. M. Fox (New York 1987), 103–27.

Hume was unhappy with the relativistic implications of his attack on physical demonstration: he posed the problem of induction in order to distinguish demonstrative knowledge, inductive proof, and probability.[23] But he was quite clear that what he had done was greatly to reduce the scope for demonstrative knowledge and expand the area of what had previously been regarded as no more than probabilistic reasoning (T. 124). As a consequence, probability lay at the heart of the *Treatise*, occupying the whole of part III of Book One. There Hume discussed not only his new account of causation, but also the traditional topics of probability theory: chance, testimony, historical evidence. Missing only, in the published version, was a discussion of miracles, a topic which any philosophically educated person would have expected to see discussed in the same context. A clear indication that 'Of miracles' represents the missing discussion of miracles from the *Treatise* is the fact that its core arguments are presented in terms of probability theory.

We can now see that 'Of miracles' as published must originally have had a place in Hume's treatment of probability in the *Treatise*: indeed the last paragraphs of the chapter 'Of unphilosophical probability' seem to prepare the ground for the argument of 'Of miracles'.[24] Not only was the missing chapter necessary to a complete treatment of the subject as traditionally understood; but for Hume the subject of miracles was of additional importance, because it was relevant to his account of induction as providing the basis for an understanding of the concept of causation: miracles, after all, are singular incidents whose cause the faithful claim to be able to identify. Hume was seeking to transform a subject which had not only taxed minor thinkers like Woolston, Sherlock, and Annet, but major philosophers like Arnauld and Locke. But it was his own account of induction which had brought miracles (which had long been central both to Christian apologetics and, more

---

[23] David Norton has pointed out to me that a key source for the development of this distinction would appear to be Andrew Michael Ramsay, *Les voyages de Cyrus*, vol. 2 (Paris 1727), p. 43.

[24] This differs from the view of J. O. Nelson, 'The burial and resurrection of Hume's essay "Of miracles"', *Hume studies* 12 (1986), 57–76; but it may be remarked that Passmore, when he maintains that the argument of the *Treatise* is incomplete without 'Of miracles', takes it to be the argument of Book I, part III which needs to be completed (J. A. Passmore, *Hume's intentions*, 3rd edn. (London 1980), pp. 32–3). Despite 'Of miracles' being torn from its original context, some commentators have recognized that it is a study in probability theory. Clearest sighted of the contemporary critics were Richard Price, whose 'On the importance of . . . miracles' was received respectfully by Hume himself (NHL 233–4), and the anonymous correspondent whose views are discussed in John Leland, *A view of the principal deistical writers*, vol. 3 (London 1756), pp. 71–104. Exceptional amongst modern commentators in taking the same view have been C. S. Lewis, *Miracles: a preliminary study* (London 1947), pp. 121–30; and, more recently, J. H. Sobel, 'On the evidence of testimony for miracles', *Philosophical quarterly* 37 (1987), 166–86, and D. Owen, 'Hume versus Price on miracles', ibid., 187–202. David Norton has alerted me to a clear anticipation of the deleted section at T.120.

recently, to probability theory) from the periphery to the centre of the philosophical stage.

II. A CELEBRATED ARGUMENT

Placing 'Of miracles' in a tradition of sophisticated philosophy descending from *The art of thinking* and from Locke does not mean that Hume did not have other, humbler, sources in mind. Wollaston may have been one: he himself clearly refers to Wollaston elsewhere in the *Treatise* (T. 461), and Wollaston's discussion of testimony for events which lie outside the normal course of nature—his example is Herodotus's claim that the sun had been known in the distant past to rise in the west and set in the east—takes place within a discussion of probability. Wollaston's argument, like Hume's, is that the ordinary course of nature provides a better basis for trust than human testimony, which is often misconceived, self-interested, and perjured.[25] Hume must have read these pages of Wollaston with approval (despite his disapproval of the rest of the work), particularly because they tell so directly against the arguments of *The art of thinking* and Locke, and he may well have remembered them when he came to write about miracles.

There is, however, a further source which I believe must have confirmed Hume in his approach. The key to the identification of this source lies in Hume's chapter 'Of unphilosophical probability', where he refers to "a very celebrated argument against the *Christian Religion*" (T. 145). This argument, which Hume rejected, has long been recognized as derived from a book published in 1699 by Craig, whose starting point was an argument of Locke's (*Essay*, IV. xvi. 10) to the effect that testimony transmitted from one person to another becomes, as in a whispering game, progressively less reliable the more intermediaries it passes through.[26] Craig set out to calculate mathematically the declining plausibility of testimony over time, and to argue that the evidence for the Christian religion must thus become less convincing as one generation succeeds another, until at last it will cease to be probable. Before this happened, Craig argued, the millennium must occur, so that a mathematical calculation of the declining probability could give one a *terminus ante quem* for the end of the world. Craig may thus be said to

---

[25] William Wollaston, *The religion of nature delineated* (London 1724), pp. 54–9.

[26] John Craig, *Theologiae Christianae principia mathematica* (London 1699). Part of Craig's text is reprinted as Beiheft 4 of *History and theory* (1964). For discussion of Craig as the source of the argument referred to by Hume, see A. Leroy, *La critique et la religion chez David Hume* (Paris 1929), pp. 240–41; and, for Craig's influence elsewhere in the *Treatise*, D. R. Raynor, 'Hume's mistake—another guess', *Hume studies* 7 (1981), 164–6.

have calculated the "shelf-life" of the Gospels: on his argument, the end of the world had to occur within the following fifteen hundred years.[27] He was not arguing against the Christian religion, but rather applying mathematical probability theory to the dating of the millennium.

There are good reasons for thinking that Hume had not read Craig himself. He shows no knowledge of Craig's millenarian interests, or of his application, later in the same work, of his arguments to a version of Pascal's wager. Clearly there were others who made his argument both celebrated and anti-Christian. Our problem is one of identifying the commentaries upon Craig with which Hume was familiar. He would certainly have known of him from Bayle's appendix on Pyrrhonism in the *Dictionary*, a reference which would alone entitle the argument to be referred to as "celebrated", but which gave almost no information as to what Craig had actually said. It is not difficult, thanks in large part to the work of Carlo Borghero, to identify other references to Craig that Hume might in principle have encountered.[28] But only one source seems likely to have given rise to the precise version of Craig's argument that Hume gives in the *Treatise*: this is a work by an influential enemy of Christianity, the 'Réflexions sur l'étude des anciennes histoires et sur le degré de certitude de leurs preuves' of Nicholas Fréret.[29] This was an

---

[27] Hacking follows the established opinion amongst historians of probability in attributing to Craig the anonymous 'A calculation of the credibility of human testimony', *Philosophical transactions of the Royal Society of London* 21 (1699), 359–65 [irregular pagination]. But this essay implies very different conclusions as to the date when Christianity would cease to be credible, for on its argument this date could be pushed forward into the indefinite future. It would therefore appear to be by a critic of Craig, to whose work, however, it does not refer. Diderot, writing the article on probability in the *Encyclopédie*, seems to have believed that Halley was the author of 'A calculation', and this attribution should perhaps be restored. It would seem that the history of its reception can be separated from that of Craig's book. On the mid-eighteenth century debate in which it was invoked, see C. Borghero, *La certezza e la storia* (Milan 1983), pp. 211–16, and A. Prandi, *Cristianesimo offeso e difeso* (Bologna 1975), pp. 160–61.

[28] The following references to Craig (apart from those in Fréret and Hume) for the period 1699–1749 are known to me: P. Bayle, 'Eclaircissement sur les pyrrhoniens', in *Dictionnaire historique et critique*, vol. 4 (Rotterdam 1720), p. 3006; id., letter to M. Marais, 7 Sept. 1699, in *Lettres*, ed. P. Des Maizeaux (Amsterdam 1729), pp. 765–6; P. R. de Montmort, *Essay d'analyse sur les jeux de hazard* [1708], 2nd revised edn. (Paris 1713), pp. xxviii–xxxix; Houtteville, *La religion chrétienne*, pp. 333–9; W. Warburton, *The divine legation of Moses*, vol. 1 (London 1738), p. 2; A. Lemoine, *A treatise on miracles* (London 1747), pp. 352–5. I have not seen the work by Ernesti or the possibly fictitious work by Peterson discussed in Borghero, *La certezza e la storia*, pp. 201, 294. Craig is refuted without being named by H. Ditton, *A discourse concerning the resurrection of Jesus Christ* (London 1712), pp. 182–90 (with a French translation, Paris 1729); by Jackson, *An address to deists*, pp. 24–5; and by A. A. Sykes, *Natural and revealed religion*, pp. 207–8, 212–13; and defended, again without being named, in Trenchard's 'Of miracles' (below, n. 49).

[29] First published in *L'Histoire et les mémoires de l'académie royale des inscriptions et belles lettres* 6 (1729), 146–89. The work reappears in the various editions of Fréret's *Oeuvres*. Landucci has demonstrated that Fréret was the author of the *Lettre de Thrasibule à Leucippe*, an irreligious manuscript (above, n. 1).

important study of history as presenting problems of epistemological probability; it formed part of a wider debate on "historical pyrrhonism" as applied to the sources for our knowledge of Roman history, the contributions to which were of sufficient importance to continue to attract the attention of Voltaire and Gibbon in later decades.[30]

Fréret's subject was precisely Hume's at this point of the *Treatise*: that "there is no point of ancient history, of which we can have any assurance, but by passing thro' many millions of causes and effects", and yet there are facts of which we do have assurance (T. 145). Fréret, after briefly referring to Craig's millenarian interests, presents Craig's argument as one that delighted libertines and sceptics. Like Hume, he rejects the argument, stressing the importance of the difference between written evidence and oral tradition, and maintaining that we can have confidence in the fidelity of copyists and printers. He could thus be made use of in an apparent defence of orthodoxy against irreligion.

Fréret, however, had discussed not only testimony in general, but the testimony in support of prodigies and miracles in particular, thus dealing with the issues discussed by Hume in 'Of miracles'. This is not surprising, since he, like Hume, was dealing with a standard set of problems in the theory of "degrees of assent", a topic which he saw as an aspect of the theory of probability. (Indeed he was keen to show off his knowledge of the work of the Bernoullis and of other mathematical theorists of probability, while dismissing it as irrelevant to the immediate issue.) Fréret's argument is that we need to use the same standards in assessing historical as in assessing contemporary evidence, and he maintains, as Hume does in 'Of miracles', that there are certain categories of testimony that we can reject as unreliable no matter who the witnesses are or how their testimony reaches us: particularly, testimony regarding supposedly miraculous events, which we can dismiss as the product of a universal *amour du merveilleux*.[31]

Fréret had dealt with similar topics in an earlier work, his 'Réflexions sur les prodiges rapportés dans les anciens', published in 1723.[32] There he had set out to distinguish, as Hume was later to do in 'Of miracles', between natural prodigies (credible if well attested) and miracles (incredible because never sufficiently well attested). Fréret was willing to

---

[30] Borghero, *La certezza e la storia*, pp. 357–90.

[31] Annet and Middleton were both to argue, in the same vein, that one could discard fabulous events reported in ancient histories without undermining historical knowledge in general. Amongst those who held that even well attested miracles could be rejected unexamined were Trenchard, Sykes, and T. Chubb in *A discourse of miracles* (London 1741), and sec. VIII ('Concerning miracles') of 'The author's farewell', in *Posthumous works*, vol. 2 (London 1748), 177–249.

[32] N. Fréret, *Oeuvres*, vol. 1 (Paris 1796), pp. 157–214. First published in vol. 4 of *Les mémoires de l'académie royale des inscriptions*.

believe in rains of stones and the sun shining in the middle of the night, just as Hume was in principle willing to believe in a universal darkness; but he, like Hume, rejected all miracles which formed part of a system of religion, on the ground that they were the invention of the self-interested or the gullible.[33]

Fréret therefore provides a likely source for the treatment in 'Of unphilosophical probability' and 'Of miracles' of the problems of testimony and evidence. That Hume would have read Fréret when writing the *Treatise* is, I submit, more likely than that he would have read Sherlock. This is not simply because Fréret was probably available in the Jesuit library; for both Sherlock and Tillotson had been translated into French. Rather, it is because Fréret seems an indispensable source for Hume's knowledge of Craig, and for his treatment of the philosophy of history. As we shall see, there is in addition good reason for thinking that Hume would have known of Fréret and his work by the time he arrived at La Flèche.

Those who believe that Hume made a careful study of works of Christian apologetic such as Sherlock's, or even anti-Christian apologetic such as Woolston's, have an additional difficulty to overcome, for 'Of miracles' is itself designed to establish that there is no need to examine such works closely. As Hume wrote in reply to the criticisms of George Campbell, "Does a man of sense run after every silly tale of witches or hobgoblins or fairies, and canvass particularly the evidence? I never knew any one, that examined and deliberated about nonsense who did not believe it before the end of his inquiries." (HL i. 350)

III. THE ARGUMENT OF 'OF MIRACLES'

So far, then, the *Treatise*, the *Abstract*, and the 1748 edition of the first *Enquiry*, have enabled us to identify three likely sources for 'Of miracles' in Arnauld, Wollaston, and Fréret, and at the same time to discount the influence of Locke, Butler, and Sherlock. Sources such as these serve to confirm that Hume's purpose was to assess the probability that reported prodigies and miracles (that is, extraordinary events) had actually occurred. The standard approach had been to weigh the inherent unlikelihood of the event against the reliability of the testimony for it. This is precisely Hume's approach. He wants to argue that prodigies and

---

[33] Thomas Morgan, *The moral philosopher* (London 1737), made a rather different distinction, but one with similar consequences, when he argued that even if miracles could be authenticated, they would provide no proof of the truth of any system of religion, since it was impossible to establish what particular doctrine any miracle was intended to authenticate.

miracles are so inherently unlikely, when weighed against the infinite examples of nature pursuing a normal course, as to make testimony in favour of them incredible (assuming, as Arnauld and Locke had done, that credibility and likelihood are related concepts); and that the testimony in favour of miracles is, in particular, characteristically unreliable, so that even if it might be possible to find sufficiently good testimony to justify belief in a prodigy, it is impossible to find testimony good enough to justify belief in any miracle.[34] Part One of the essay is primarily directed at the first claim, Part Two at the second.

In disputing the reliability of most testimony for miracles, Hume was, of course, following in the footsteps of numerous Protestant theologians. Where Arnauld had argued that the eyewitness testimony of Augustine, for example, was unimpeachable, Protestants had demurred, arguing that miracles, frequent and well attested in the early Church, had ceased by Augustine's day. The quality of the testimony for miracles was thus central to the debate surrounding *The art of thinking*; and Hume could hardly proceed, unless he supplemented an argument for the incredibility of miracles derived from nature's uniformity, with an attack on the reliability of testimony, either in general or with relation to religion in particular.[35]

This two-pronged strategy did not require Hume to insist, as some think he should have and even suggest that he did, that miracles are "physically (and naturally) impossible", abandoning in the process his own attack on the idea of physical necessity and its corollary, physical impossibility.[36] It required him merely to argue from experience that miracles are antecedently improbable events, and to provide grounds for thinking that historical evidence is not sufficient to render events as improbable as these credible. Laws of nature are proofs against miracles, not because they show them to be impossible, nor even because they render all testimony for extraordinary events incredible, but because they show such events to be in the highest degree improbable.

The context I have identified also tells against the subtle argument that Hume, on the basis of his analysis of laws of nature as consisting in nothing but constant conjuncture, was intending to show that if miracles happened then no adequate concept of natural law could be preserved; while if the concept of natural law was abandoned, then miracles

---

[34] On credible hypothetical prodigies, see E. 127; HL i. 349–50.

[35] For a different view, see Burns (*Great debate*, pp. 142–71), where it is claimed that Hume originally intended to rely only on the first argument (christened, misleadingly, "the a priori epistemological argument"), and that the second part of the essay is a later addition.

[36] A. G. N. Flew, 'The impossibility of the miraculous', in *Hume's philosophy of religion* (Winston-Salem 1986), at p. 16.

themselves must cease to be identifiable.[37] Hume would surely have accepted this view. Indeed this may help to explain why he took the strange step of discussing belief in miracles as if it involved belief in only one single event contrary to any particular natural law, despite the fact that Christians believed, for example, in the resurrection of Lazarus as well as that of Jesus. A unique event represents a limit case which appears to leave natural laws almost intact.

However, the fact that Hume couched his argument in these terms suggests that he was seeking to minimize, not stress, the threat that belief in miracles posed to his concept of natural law; indeed, it would have been contrary to his avowed purposes to rely on an argument of this sort in 'Of miracles', for the precondition for its acceptance would have been adoption of his (or some other secular) account of natural law. His purpose was to provide a check to superstition, while an argument for the evidential incompatibility of miracles and natural laws could only convince those who were willing to abandon a theocentric viewpoint. Hume's critics consistently maintained that all events in nature, whether miraculous or not, equally reflected the will and omnipotence of God. If one assumed, as they did, that one could have knowledge of God through natural theology, then it was possible to argue that there was no ultimate incompatibility between natural laws and miracles.

Thus the a priori arguments attributed to Hume by some commentators could only convince those who were already unsuperstitious. In order to check superstition, by contrast, Hume needed an argument which would establish neither a priori limits on God's actions (as Spinoza, for example, had sought to do), nor logical restrictions on our capacity to experience miracles as exceptions to the laws of nature, but which would nevertheless in practice make it impossible to identify any particular event as a miracle. This was the exciting promise held out by an argument based upon the improbability of miracles (as opposed to their natural or evidential impossibility) and exploiting Arnauld's distinction between internal and external evidence.

As we shall see, a consideration of Hume's use of Tillotson's argument against transubstantiation reinforces the view that the case that Hume, following Fréret, wanted to make was that the quality of the external evidence for a miracle, if it consisted in the testimony of witnesses, simply never could be good enough. Hence it could be rejected unexamined. Others before Hume had glimpsed the possibilities that

---

[37] Ahern, 'Evidential impossibility'; D. F. Norton, *David Hume: common-sense moralist, sceptical metaphysician* (Princeton 1982), pp. 295–302; Flew, 'Impossibility of the miraculous', pp. 18–19. This certainly was one of the arguments put forward by Annet in his reply to Sherlock, and in his vindications of that reply, including *The resurrection reconsidered* (London 1744).

could be opened up by this line of argument, but Hume was the first to pursue it systematically and to concentrate all his attention upon intensifying the clash between internal and external evidence.

IV. TILLOTSON

At the heart of the argument of 'Of miracles' is the claim that there exists a uniform course of nature which entitles us to dismiss miracles as improbable or even impossible events. A strong version of the claim that there was an irreconcilable conflict between experience and one (though only one) alleged miracle lay at the heart of Tillotson's attack on transubstantiation. Even as the priest tells me that the bread and wine are the body and blood of Christ, my senses continue to tell me they are bread and wine.[38] Thus there can only be sensory evidence against, not in favour of, transubstantiation. To try to defend the doctrine is to place oneself in the position of Zeno, denying the possibility of movement while Diogenes walked in front of him. Even a miracle which could be perceived by the senses could not substantiate transubstantiation, for "then the argument for *Transubstantiation* and the Objection against it would just balance one another; and consequently *Transubstantiation* is not to be proved by a Miracle, because that would be, *to prove to a man by some thing that he sees, that he does not see what he sees.*"[39]

Tillotson thus thinks that in the particular case of transubstantiation a miracle in support of the doctrine would be flatly at odds with ordinary sensory experience, although he is careful to insist that testimony in favour of miracles can in other circumstances be good testimony. Indeed it is because the evidence for Christianity lies in the sensory experience of miracles that it is self-destructive for Catholicism to deny the validity of sensory evidence against transubstantiation. Hume's view is that in every case of a reported miracle a comparable conflict with sensory experience arises, and we must continue to prefer what we and others are agreed is the usual evidence of our senses to the claims made for exceptional experiences to the contrary.[40] Tillotson is clearly the model

[38] Flew objects that Catholics do not deny this (*Hume's philosophy of belief*, pp. 172–3). But Tillotson's point is that all our knowledge of religious truth comes at some stage through our senses. A religious doctrine which asserts the inadequacy of our senses is therefore self-destructive.

[39] [John Tillotson], *A discourse against transubstantiation* (London 1684), p. 39. Cf. Locke, *Essay*, IV. xx. 10. Tillotson's *Discourse* was readily available in all the posthumous editions of his works and is generally assumed to have been Hume's primary source. But W. R. Abbott, in an unpublished paper on 'Hume's Tillotson', has suggested that Hume's paraphrase is closer in wording to one of the sermons, 'The hazard of being saved in the Church of Rome'.

[40] Or, as Annet insisted, evidence that could in principle be that of our own senses: the king of Siam could experience ice if he chose to travel, but we cannot set out to experience a miracle.

for his claim that the evidence of our senses can provide proof against a miracle which outweighs any evidence in its support. The question is, how closely did Hume intend to follow his model?

If one accepts that Hume is concerned to identify a logical conflict between belief in miracles and belief in natural laws, one can point to Tillotson as demonstrating an evidential incompatibility between transubstantiation and sensory experience, an incompatibility in which questions of testimony are of secondary importance. But Hume gives only a careless account of Tillotson's argument, and in doing so stresses questions of testimony where Tillotson had stressed direct experience. Hume's own argument against miracles, unlike Tillotson's against transubstantiation, is couched in Arnauld's terms of a conflict between internal and external evidence, between ordinary experience of a series of events and testimony regarding a particular event outside our experience. Thus Hume's argument is essentially different in character from Tillotson's, although it is not hard to see why he should have wanted to appeal to the authority of an unimpeachable Protestant theologian engaged in attacking superstition, rather than that of a Catholic theologian such as Arnauld engaged in defending it. Where Tillotson's argument is primarily an epistemological defence of the primacy of sense experience, Hume's, like Arnauld's, is an argument about the conflict between our own experience of nature and the claims of other people.

V. HUME'S PRECURSORS

In taking a position of direct hostility to miracles, Hume was not without precursors. He himself refers to De Retz as refusing to give credence to miraculous stories, although De Retz had not done more than hint at the view that Hume attributes to him.[41] A strong appeal against miracles on the basis of the uniform course of nature had been made by Wollaston—although Wollaston would seem to have thought that miracles could be rejected as impossible where we have adequate demonstrative understanding of nature's working, but merely as highly improbable where we were relying on empirical induction, a distinction Hume would have been bound to reject. Both Sherlock and Butler had taken it for granted that an opponent of miracles would want to mount an argument of this sort, and there were a number of widely differing philosophical positions which, it was generally agreed, attributed an unvarying order to nature and made miracles impossible, from Aristotle as interpreted by

[41] Cardinal de Retz, *Oeuvres*, vol. 4 (Paris 1876), p. 550.

Averroes, through Epicurus, to Spinoza.[42] Blount had been able to compose a work denying the possibility of supernatural events—*Miracles no violation of the law of nature* (1683)—in which scarcely a word was his own, the whole thing being a compilation from the writings of Burnet, Hobbes, and Spinoza.[43]

Others before Hume, too, had sought to downgrade testimony to the point where it could never be strong enough to justify belief in a miracle, but leaving open whether one might not be obliged to believe the direct evidence of one's senses. Thus twenty years before, John Digby, in his notes on Lucretius, had adopted a determined scepticism with regard to testimony, giving several examples of natural prodigies which were apparently supported by unimpeachable testimony, but finally concluding, "Yet, after all, none but they who have been eye-witnesses of these things will readily give credit to them."[44]

It would thus be quite wrong to think that Hume's systematic hostility to miracles was without precedent. A number of authors have drawn attention to the similarity between 'Of miracles' and a passage in which Anthony Collins discusses some miracles related by Cicero:

> Hence we see what little Credit ought to be paid to Facts said to be done out of the ordinary Course of Nature. These Miracles are well attested. They were recorded in the Annals of a great People, believed by many learned and otherwise sagacious Persons, and received as religious Truths by the Populace; but the Testimonies of antient Records, the Credulity of some learned Men, and the implicit Faith of the Vulgar, can never prove That to have been, which is impossible in the Nature of Things ever to be.[45]

Collins died in 1729, but these words were not published until 1741, by which time Hume had already conceived the argument of 'Of miracles'. This would therefore appear to be a simple case of parallelism, to be explained in terms of the natural tendency of intelligent contemporaries to adopt similar arguments when they share similar purposes; but if it was intended to be the key argument of 'Of miracles' then the work was scarcely original.

Indeed it is not difficult to extend the number of such parallels. Shaftesbury had doubted whether anyone claiming to be a witness to a miracle could have been uncontaminated by the contagion of superstition, and attached "the specious Pretext of moral Certainty, and *Matter*

---

[42] Butler, *Analogy*, pp. 161–8; Sherlock, *Tryal*, pp. 58–9, 63–4, 99.

[43] U. Bonanate, *Charles Blount: libertinismo e deismo nel seicento inglese* (Florence 1972), pp. 47–54.

[44] T. Lucretius Carus, *Of the nature of things*, trans. T. Creech, vol. 1 (London 1715), p. 150. The identification of Digby as the annotator is made by C. A. Gordon, *Bibliography of Lucretius* (London 1962).

[45] Cicero, *Of the nature of the gods* [trans. Collins] (London 1741), p. 85. See D. Berman, 'Hume and Collins on miracles', *Hume studies* 6 (1980), 150–54.

of Fact" on which arguments in favour of miracles depended.[46] Bolingbroke, in a work written before 'Of miracles' was conceived, but published only afterwards, had given an almost perfect epitome of what was to become Hume's argument:

An historical fact, which contains nothing that contradicts general experience, and our own observation, has already the appearance of probability; and, if it be supported by the testimony of proper witnesses, it acquires all the appearances of truth; that is, it becomes really probable in the highest degree. A fact, on the other hand, which is repugnant to experience, shocks us from the first; and if we receive it afterwards for a true fact, we receive it on outward authority, not on inward conviction. Now to do so is extremely absurd; since the same experience that contradicts this particular fact, affirms this general fact, that men lie very often, and their authority alone is a very frail foundation of assent.[47]

And in 1746 Diderot provoked in France a controversy which paralleled that produced by 'Of miracles' in Britain, when he maintained that he would accept the testimony of a single honest man who reported that the king had won a battle, but he would reject that of all the inhabitants of Paris if they claimed to have witnessed a man resurrected from the dead.[48]

I do not think that there is any good reason to think that these authors, any more than Collins in his notes on Cicero, had a direct influence on Hume's essay. Shaftesbury's argument is different in structure from Hume's; Bolingbroke's, if it was known to him at all before the first drafting of the essay, would have been encountered only in a garbled form; while if Hume read Diderot, it was after his argument had taken shape. We could multiply the comparisons. Trenchard's essay on miracles, for example, which was composed before Hume's but published after it, parallels Hume's argument at a number of points. Trenchard even concludes by claiming that his argument against miracles is strictly parallel to Tillotson's against transubstantiation.[49] In dealing with Collins, Bolingbroke, and Trenchard, we are dealing, however, with a particular category of evidence: that of works which could have influenced Hume directly only if he read them in manuscript,

[46] Anthony, Earl of Shaftesbury, *Characteristicks of men, manners, opinions, times*, vol. 1 (London 1711), pp. 44–5.

[47] Bolingbroke, 'The substance of some letters', p. 191. Remarkably, Bolingbroke's purpose was to argue that in one case, and one case alone, the testimony for a miracle outweighed the inherent improbability of the event. That case was the creation of the world, an event recorded in the histories of all nations. Hume may well, of course, have read the paraphrase of this passage in Pouilly's 'Essais', where the argument is rejected; it is not impossible (although highly improbable) that Pouilly showed him the original.

[48] Denis Diderot, *Pensées philosophiques*, XLVI, in *Oeuvres complètes*, vol. 2 (Paris 1975), p. 42.

[49] The first essay in John Trenchard, *Essays on important subjects* (London 1755).

or saw them reflected in the works of others who had read them in manuscript. Can one establish at any point a firm link between Hume and any manuscript sources?

VI. THE CLANDESTINE FRENCH SOURCES

As early as 1912 Lanson pointed out the existence of a large number of irreligious manuscript treatises circulating in France in the period when Hume was writing the *Treatise*, and these sources have attracted a great deal of attention in recent years.[50] In view of this work, I do not need to detail here the evidence for the widespread diffusion of these attacks upon Christianity. In the light of this evidence we are bound, however, to ask whether Hume, a young *libertin érudit* in a country pullulating with libertine literature, could possibly have failed to hear of, seek out, and study at least some of this material. Moreover, it is not difficult to hypothesize a route by which he could have gained access to such material.

Hume's main contact when he first arrived in France was the Chevalier Ramsay. When, in *The natural history of religion*, Hume wanted to find a reasonably respectable source to quote in order to summarize what might be said against Christianity (and indeed precisely what had been said in the irreligious manuscript tradition in France), it is to Ramsay that he turned, quoting him at length.[51] Ramsay is also known to have had an interest in the writings of Spinoza.[52] More important still, for our purposes, is the fact that he was in direct contact with Fréret, of whose work (and of whose irreligious opinions) Hume would probably have learnt, either from Ramsay himself, or from Levesque de Pouilly, an opponent of Fréret's and friend of Bolingbroke's.[53] It seems likely then that Ramsay, or one of his circle, would have been in a position to gain access for Hume to clandestine irreligious writings—writings such as *La Moïsade*, which is typical of the sort of work which Hume appears to be summarizing when he asks whether the Old Testament narrative is

---

[50] M. Lanson, 'Questions diverses sur l'histoire de l'esprit philosophique en France avant 1750', *Revue d'histoire littéraire* 19 (1912), 1–29, 293–317; I. O. Wade, *The clandestine organization and diffusion of philosophic ideas in France from 1700 to 1750* (Princeton 1938); J. S. Spink, *French free-thought from Gassendi to Voltaire* (London 1960); C. J. Betts, *Early deism in France* (The Hague 1984).

[51] David Hume, *Philosophical works*, ed. T. H. Green and T. H. Grose, vol. 4 (repr., Aalen 1964), pp. 355–6.

[52] R. H. Popkin, 'Hume and Spinoza', *Hume studies* 5 (1979), at p. 66.

[53] See the 'Lettre de M. Fréret à l'auteur, sur la chronologie de son ouvrage', an appendix to Ramsay's *Voyages de Cyrus*. For the most recent discussion of the evidence that Ramsay introduced Hume to Pouilly, see J. S. Spink, 'Lévesque de Pouilly et David Hume', *Revue de littérature comparée* 56 (1982), 157–75.

convincing, and concludes that it is the product of "a barbarous and ignorant people" and full of "prodigies the most astonishing imaginable" (E. 130; cf. Fréret, *Oeuvres*, vol. 20, pp. 249–70).

Of course, Hume might have been influenced by any of the English deists to portray the Old Testament in such terms. It is often impossible in such cases to distinguish English from French influences, particularly as the English deists were widely read in France and circulated in clandestine translations. Indeed it is often impossible when dealing with the irreligious literature of this period to establish definitively which text was the source of a particular argument, for the same arguments, the same words, may have appeared in several different texts, any one of which may be the source on which an author has drawn. There are many clandestine works which are like Blount's *Miracles* in being no more than a compilation of the words and arguments of others.[54] This problem would bedevil anyone who tried to identify the sources which influenced Hume's 'Of the immortality of the soul'. Hume's arguments are to be found scattered throughout the French clandestine literature; many of them are also to be found in a sixteenth-century work which was known to Blount, and perhaps to Hume, Cardano's *De immortalitate animae*, which provides fifty-eight arguments against immortality; and many of them, of course, had been known in antiquity.[55] It would now, I think, be impossible to establish which particular sources Hume drew upon.

Fortunately 'Of miracles' uses arguments which are much more newly minted than those of 'Of the immortality of the soul'. It is hard to trace most of his key arguments back more than a few years before his arrival in La Flèche, for, as we have seen, the intellectual preconditions for a critique of miracles which appealed to a modern concept of evidence had not long been in existence. But we have also seen that it would be a mistake to think that Hume was an isolated figure, or that every case of similarity implies influence. Thus Hume stressed the difficulty of proving that a miracle had taken place, by claiming that it would take a miracle to make a rational person believe (E. 131). This argument is prefigured in the chapter on miracles of a widely circulated work, composed around 1715, *Doutes sur la religion*:

St Paul . . . étoit lui-même si peu convaincu des miracles de Jésus-Christ qu'il lui a fallu un miracle particulier pour le convertir; chacun de nous ne peut-il point en attendre autant?[56]

---

[54] See, for example, A. Niderst's commentary on his edition of *L'âme matérielle* (Rouen 1969).

[55] Hume, *Philosophical works*, vol. 4, pp. 399–406; C. Blount, *Anima mundi* (London 1679), pp. 69–72 (a work which is the nearest thing to a defence of "atheism" to appear before Bayle's *Pensées diverses*); G. Cardano, 'De immortalitate animae', in *Opera omnia*, vol. 2 (Lyons 1663), pp. 456–536.

[56] *Doutes sur la religion* (London 1767), p. 32.

However, it is possible that, if Hume had a clandestine source, it was not French but English: Trenchard's essay on miracles, for example. Or perhaps Hume's ending is a flourish added only in 1748, in which case he could have been influenced by either Annet or the younger Dodwell, both of whom had presented the same view: Henry Dodwell in particular, in *Christianity not founded on argument* (1741), had used it as Hume did to give his argument a veneer of orthodoxy. Once one begins to find a plethora of sources, as in this case, it is evident that the same argument may well have occurred independently to a number of authors.

Hume also insisted that, as a matter of fact, no miracle was sufficiently well attested for people in general to feel obliged to believe in it, an argument he presented by appealing to the miracles on the tomb of the abbé de Pâris, which were as well attested as any could be and yet most people were happy not to believe in them (E. 124–5, 344–6). The same argument had been employed in two manuscript works, both apparently written, like 'Of miracles', when the Pâris miracles were fresh in people's minds: *Recherches sur les miracles*, in particular, had a chapter closely paralleling Hume's treatment, entitled 'De la difficulté de constater les miracles'.[57] But it would be rash to conclude that Hume had read either of these works. After all, Sykes in 1742 also seized on the miracles of the tomb of the abbé de Pâris to show that even well-attested miracles might be rejected as incredible, and Middleton was soon, perhaps under Sykes's influence, to use the same example to make the same point.[58]

VII. THE CONTRARY MIRACLES ARGUMENT

Thus a number of works were to be found in manuscript in the period between 1735 and 1748, both in England and in France, which had purposes similar to, and arguments along the same lines as, those of 'Of miracles'. Despite the fact that the number of such works was smaller when Hume was at La Flèche than it had become by the time his essay was published, it is difficult to demonstrate that even these early works had a direct influence upon it. There is, however, one important exception to this generalization. The work is *Difficultés sur la religion proposées au Père Malebranche*, composed around 1711, and attributed by some to Robert Challe. It could have been seen by Hume only in manuscript, and it should be said that there is no independent evidence

---

[57] *Recherches sur les miracles* (London 1773), pp. 10–19; see also the anonymous 'Examen critique des apologistes de la religion chrétienne', in Fréret, *Oeuvres*, vol. 19, p. 124.

[58] A. A. Sykes, *A brief discourse concerning the credibility of miracles and revelation* (London 1742), pp. 52–73; Middleton, *Free enquiry*, pp. 223–6. On the miracles themselves, see B. R. Kreiser, *Miracles, convulsions, and ecclesiastical politics in early eighteenth-century Paris* (Princeton 1978).

that he did have access to a manuscript of this work.[59] Nevertheless, the internal evidence is, I believe, in this case unusually strong: strong enough—and here of course we are dealing with problems of historical methodology of the sort that Hume himself set out to analyse in 'Of miracles'—to justify what would otherwise seem an improbable conclusion.

The key evidence for believing that the *Difficultés* influenced Hume derives from one particular detail in his general attack on miracles, the "contrary miracles" argument (E. 121–2).[60] Various versions of the contrary miracles argument are widespread in the English and French literature of the early eighteenth century. Thus, in France, it is found in numerous clandestine manuscripts: not only in the *Difficultés*, but in earlier works such as *De tribus impostoribus*, and in other works which almost certainly pre-date 'Of miracles', such as *Doutes sur les religions* (c.1715), Fréret's *Lettre de Thrasibule à Leucippe* (1722?), and *Les Sentiments des philosophes sur la nature de l'âme* (first published in 1743).

According to this argument, Christian miracles are adduced to prove the truth of Christianity as compared with other religions. But if they do so, it can only be because God alone creates miracles, and he does so only for the true religion. Therefore all the miracles claimed for other religions must be false. However, the evidence for these other miracles is no different in kind from that for Christianity—except often better. In support of this claim, Hume introduces a number of examples from classical literature which were commonplace amongst both the English deists and the French clandestine authors—"that false prophet Alexander", the emperor Vespasian—to which he added, as we have seen, the miracles on the tomb of the abbé de Pâris (E. 121–5).

It follows from the well-attested miracles argument that the evidence for Christianity is no better than that for the truth of other religions. Christianity, however, unlike polytheistic religions, claims to be exclusively true. Since the evidence runs counter to this claim to exclusive truth, this central claim is almost certainly false. The argument from contrary miracles is thus an argument against the different monotheistic religions which claim a monopoly of religious truth, but it is not an argument against polytheism, for a polytheist could admit that there was truth in the miracles of other religions. This was probably

[59] For a recent discussion of this text, see Betts. If, as I suggest below, the argument of the *Difficultés* derives at one point from Blount, at another from clandestine tracts such as the infamous *De tribus impostoribus* (c.1660), then its author's claim not to have read any deists was deliberately misleading. Small deceptions of this sort may well explain the minor discrepancies between the biography of Challe and the supposed autobiography of the author of the *Difficultés*.

[60] On this argument see J. C. A. Gaskin, 'Contrary miracles concluded', *Hume studies*, tenth anniv. supplement (1985), 1–14.

apparent to the author of *De tribus impostoribus,* who directed the argument against Judaism, Christianity, and Islam, and has since been remarked on by Hume's critics; but it seems to have escaped Hume himself, for in 'Of miracles' he treats it as an argument equally threatening to the religions of Rome, Turkey, Siam, and China (E. 121).[61]

How to explain such a mistake? The explanation is simply that Hume was adopting the argument wholesale from the *Difficultés*; had he thought it out from scratch for himself he would probably have recognized its limitations. The *Difficultés* presents the problem of the conflict between religions in terms of a series of trials where each religion (including polytheistic ones) is in turn the defendant and all the others are witnesses for the prosecution. Although each religion may appear not to refer to the others, each, in testifying to its own truth, is testifying to the falsehood of the others. Given that there are many religions, each religion is faced with numerous witnesses to its own falsehood.[62]

In support of the claim that Hume took his version of the contrary miracles argument from the *Difficultés*, one may note not merely the error they share in common, but the language with which Hume illustrates the argument. In Hume, as in the *Difficultés*, we encounter witnesses at a trial who give conflicting evidence: although Hume, having started off writing of an "infinite number of witnesses" (E. 121), tries, in a somewhat confused way, to come closer to the real circumstances of a trial by then talking of two equally balanced sets of witnesses for the defence and the prosecution, thereby obscuring the preponderance of evidence which tells against rather than for any religion. This imagery of a trial with witnesses against the truth of a religion is not, as far as I know, to be found elsewhere: not even, strangely enough, in Sherlock's *Tryal of the witnesses*, where the witnesses are the witnesses for Christianity who are being tried *in absentia*, and only prosecution, defence, judge, and jury speak. (As Annet complains, this is scarcely a satisfactory trial.) Finally, it is in effect the same witnesses to whom appeal is made in Hume as in the *Difficultés*: the miracles of Turkey and Siam. Unless the coupling of these countries together in such a context can be shown to have been a commonplace, this constitutes further evidence of influence rather than mere similarity.

---

[61] Hume's error was pointed out by George Campbell, *A dissertation on miracles* (Edinburgh 1762), pp. 168–81. It is hard not to read Locke's 'Discourse of miracles', in *Posthumous works* (London 1706), 219–25, as a criticism of some earlier version of the contrary miracles argument which made the same error as Hume's: but there are no reasons to think that Locke's source employed the same language as Hume.

[62] R. Challe, *Difficultés sur la religion proposées au père Malebranche*, ed. M. Deloffre and M. Manemencioghu (Oxford 1982), pp. 84, 218.

VIII. A VOICE IN THE CLOUDS

Once this tell-tale similarity between the *Difficultés* and the argument of 'Of miracles' has caught our attention, the grounds for thinking that the one influenced the other become stronger as the extent and character of the similarities between the two become apparent. Like Fréret, Wollaston, Collins, Bolingbroke, Trenchard, and Hume, the author of the *Difficultés* argues that historical testimony is only to be trusted when it reports events which fall within the ordinary course of nature. D'Holbach's paraphrase of the argument (which employs the term 'laws of nature' which is not to be found in the manuscripts, but which is otherwise faithful to the sense of the original) can be translated as follows. Such reports

as soon as they concern events which do not conform to the ordinary course of human affairs, then they are termed fables or stories, and they are rejected without further examination. But what are the books of factitious religions full of? Marvellous events which are beyond the capacity of nature, which are contrary to her invariable laws, and which are equally repugnant both to the wisdom and justice of God, and to reason and truth. Consequently these are no more than fables or stories.[63]

Our author goes on to argue that he would not believe that the Louvre had been built in an hour, if assured as much by a hundred thousand people and a hundred million books, because it would be more probable that they should all be mistaken than that a natural impossibility should come about, just as Hume insists that he would never believe that Queen Elizabeth had been resurrected from the dead, no matter how extensive the testimony in support of such a claim (E. 128).

The *Difficultés* also contains an argument which is reminiscent not only of 'Of miracles', but also of Hume's *Dialogues*. Its author maintains that he would only begin to believe that the Pyrenees had been transported to Japan if a voice from the heavens announced the fact, and he would believe indeed if the stars rearranged themselves to spell out the news, for *"la preuve seroit alors aussi étrange que le fait et seroit en proportion avec lui"*. Thus a miracle is the only possible evidence sufficient to support belief in a miracle. His conclusion is that the Christian revelation would only be plausible if it was authenticated by a continuing series of miracles which formed part of the immediate experience of every believer. Now this, of course, is the argument of 'Of miracles', that one should proportion one's belief to the evidence, that

[63] Chapter 10 of the "London" edition (1770), entitled *Le militaire philosophe*. See Challe, pp. 65, 86–9.

the evidence for an extraordinary event needs to be stronger than for an ordinary one, and that the Christian religion, based as it is upon belief in miracles, cannot even now be believed by any reasonable person without a miracle (E. 110, 115–16, 131). The principle that one should proportion one's belief to the evidence is found in Locke (Locke's own index to the *Essay*, under *Assent*, is clearer here than the text), as is the principle that strange facts require proportionately stronger evidence than common ones: but the author of the *Difficultés* (who seems to be familiar with the philosophical literature on testimony) is, as far as I know, the first—although not, as we have seen, the last—to draw this particular conclusion from these principles.

One of the problems about reading 'Of miracles' is that Hume never gives an example of an event that would meet his criterion for a demonstrable miracle.[64] It has been claimed that his suggestion that miraculous events are improbable and insufficiently proven, but not impossible, is merely ironic—so impossible would it seem to be to convince him that a miracle had taken place.[65] The author of the *Difficultés*, however (although like Hume he generally treats miracles as effectively impossible), does give a hypothetical example of an incontestable miracle; and it is important to note that Hume on his own criterion would have been able to accept that if the stars themselves bore testimony to a miracle, then a miracle had indeed taken place. In this case (barring the hypothesis of lunacy) the falsehood of the testimony would be more miraculous than the miracle it relates.

Indeed Hume discusses this kind of possibility at the beginning of Part Three of the *Dialogues*, where Cleanthes asks us to "suppose . . . that an articulate voice were heard in the clouds, much louder and more melodious than any which human art could ever reach". His point is that there are some conceivable experiences which would incontestably be experiences of divine power. He proceeds from the example of the voice in the clouds to the possibility of a "vegetating library", from which he attempts to conclude that our experience of nature itself is an experience of this sort. The evidence, he thinks, for design in the universe is so strong that we can have no doubt of the designer's existence. It is highly unlikely that Hume accepted Cleanthes' conclusion; but it is striking that his model of unimpeachable evidence for the activity of a supernatural power was so similar to that of the *Difficultés*.[66]

If Hume's argument was indeed constructed on the basis established by the *Difficultés*, then this supports an interpretation of 'Of miracles' as

---

[64] I discuss in the next section his remarks on universal testimony to a prodigy at E. 127.

[65] Burns, *Great debate*, pp. 142–58.

[66] So much so that P. L. Heath, in order to expound Hume, reinvents the argument of the *Difficultés* ('The incredulous Hume', *American philosophical quarterly* 13 (1976), at pp. 162–3).

being concerned, not to deny the possibility of miracles, but to establish stringent criteria which effectively exclude belief in them. In confining himself to a discussion of the second-hand testimony, Hume was following in the path of all previous philosophical discussions of probability and evidence, none of which dealt with the question of direct sensory experience of a miracle. But in the standards he set for proving a miracle, he was implicitly identifying himself with the small group of those who did not argue that miracles were a priori impossible (and therefore the seemingly miraculous must in fact be natural), but rather maintained that the only adequate evidence for a miracle would be immediate sensory experience of an event which was clearly contrary to the order of nature and could not be falsified, and that no second-hand testimony could be adequate. Hume's position is thus much closer to that of the *Difficultés* than it is to Blount, Collins and (broadly speaking) Wollaston, who were willing to deny the possibility of such events on a priori grounds.

IX. PRIESTCRAFT

Craig's account of the decay of evidence over time, Locke's story of the Indian prince, and the version of the contrary miracles argument to be found in the *Difficultés*, are all sufficiently idiosyncratic for us to be able to identify them even in authors who paraphrase and distort them. All three deal with the problem of testimony. There is, I believe, a further argument regarding testimony which is in principle sufficiently distinctive to be readily identifiable, although unfortunately Hume presents it in a form where its distinctive qualities have been obliterated.

It was crucial to Hume's thesis that one could discount testimony in favour of miracles, because the temptation to pose as a prophet or apostle could adequately explain why some would make false claims to miraculous powers, while the passion for the wonderful could explain why others would believe them (E. 125, 117–19). The *Difficultés sur la religion*, just as it discusses the evidence which would be needed to substantiate a miracle, filling in a gap left by Hume in the argument of 'Of miracles', also develops an argument which is crucial to Hume's case, but is so understated by him that it often escapes notice. Hume maintains that he might believe in a natural prodigy supported by universal testimony, such as darkness covering the face of the earth, but nothing would make him believe in the resurrection of a dead monarch, no matter what the evidence (E. 127–8). And what is more, he would be even less willing, if that were possible, to believe in such an event if it were adduced in support of a system of religion (E. 129). Now Hume's critics often treat this pair of arguments (which Fréret, as we have seen, had also sketched out) as if they rested upon an irrational prejudice against religion, maintaining that Hume is concerned at all costs to deny the possibility of Christ's resurrection.[67] It is important to note therefore that Hume appeals in the first place to a key difference between the resurrection of a dead person and darkness at noon: in the first case there is scope for the knavery and folly of men; in the second there is not. In the one case some sort of fraud is conceivable, in the other not.

But why go on to make a specific exception for religious miracles? Challe (if he was indeed the author of the *Difficultés*) was well aware that it would be dangerous to reject all accounts of the prodigious. He remarks, for example, that because the Indians of South America did not understand the natural properties of gunpowder, they had mistakenly thought that the *conquistadores* had magical powers (*Difficultés*, p. 221). And although he does not explicitly deal with the question of belief in prodigies, he does provide an argument to justify singling out religious miracles. This argument, which Hume seems largely to have taken for granted, had earlier appeared in Blount's *Diana of the Ephesians*.[68] It is presented in a developed form in the *Difficultés sur la religion*, and goes as follows (p. 89): My son is at the wars. If a messenger arrives and reports his death, I am likely to believe him. But if a messenger arrives, reports his death, and reports also that with his dying breath my son bequeathed to this messenger all his worldly goods, I am likely to reject his testimony as fraudulent because self-interested. But this is the case with testimony for miracles. It comes from those who will benefit through the furtherance of their faith, and (if they are priests or religious leaders) of their careers if their story is accepted. A contemporary version of this might be termed the "used-car salesman" argument. If you tell me your car is ten years old, has never had any mechanical problems, and has only done 50,000 kilometres, I believe you. But if you are a used-car salesman and I am thinking of buying a car, I cease to believe your words, and trust only the evidence of my own senses. In the view of the unbelievers of Hume's day, the testimony of apostles and priests was similarly suspect.

Given his sceptical principles, Hume could not maintain that testimony in favour of miracles must be dismissed on the ground that the idea of an event contrary to the ordinary course of nature, even of a specifically supernatural event, is inherently unreasonable. Testimony in favour of miracles, Hume needs to maintain, is a very particular type of testimony, in that it is self-interested, not disinterested; and it is on these grounds, and not merely on the ground that some events are more

[67] Burns, pp. 227–8, 238–41; A. E. Taylor, *David Hume and the miraculous* (Cambridge 1927), pp. 16–18.

[68] [Charles Blount], *Great is Diana of the Ephesians* (London 1680), Preface.

susceptible to fraudulent misrepresentation than others, that one is justified in applying much more rigorous criteria to evidence for miracles than to evidence for natural prodigies. Instead of developing a theoretical justification of this sort (and he may have thought it unnecessary, given how extensive was the literature attacking priest-craft), Hume provides little more than an empirical fact, that "the violations of truth are more common in the testimony concerning religious miracles than in that concerning any other matter of fact", on the basis of which he concludes that "this must diminish very much the authority of the former testimony" (E. 129).[69]

The *Difficultés sur la religion* thus both clarifies and supplements Hume's 'Of miracles' when it comes to Hume's discussion of the evidence that would lead a reasonable person to believe in a miracle. The *Difficultés* is one of very few works, written before he arrived at La Flèche, which clearly presents the case that the evidence in support of a miracle needs itself to amount to a miracle if belief is to be proportionate to the evidence, and it does so by developing arguments which are either explicit in 'Of miracles' (the contrary miracles argument), or implicit (the voice in the clouds argument and the used-car salesman argument). Like Hume, its author thought it was reasonable not merely to place the witnesses in favour of miracles on trial, but to condemn them without even pausing to give them a hearing; and like Hume he reached this conclusion without relying on a priori arguments.

X. CHRISTIAN SCEPTICISM

My main concern up to this point has been to establish how far arguments similar to those of 'Of miracles' had been put forward before 1748, and to try to establish how far Hume was aware of his predecessors. Another method of assessing the significance of Hume's argument is, of course, to look at the response it evoked amongst those who first read it. As Hume complained, however, the publication of his own work was overshadowed by that of Middleton's *Free enquiry* (HL i. 3). The latter claimed to accept the truth of the Gospel miracles, but argued that, when one considered all other miracles, if one balanced the improbability of the events reported against the strength of the testimony of the witnesses for them, one was obliged to conclude that the evidence of testimony was insufficient, no matter how strong it might at first appear. As one critic paraphrased Middleton's argument, it was "that the Evidence of the

---

[69] But see also E. 125: it might be maintained that Hume had here made clear how this fact was to be explained. If so, commentators, both sympathetic and hostile, have given less weight to his explanation than its role in his argument requires.

known Course of Nature was stronger than any Evidence could be of the ·
Reversal of it; which amounts to a Denial of all supernatural Works".[70]
Now this was almost exactly Hume's argument: would Hume have felt
that there was anything of substance in his essay that was not in
Middleton's *Free enquiry*—or vice versa?

Unfortunately we cannot be sure of the answer to this. Middleton did
not review Hume's "trial of the witnesses", nor Hume Middleton's.
There is however one author who had independently arrived at a
position which would seem to be very close to Hume's, whom we can
watch responding to Hume's essay. In 1740 A. A. Sykes, a prolific and
unorthodox apologist for a rationalist Protestant Christianity and a
member of the Hoadly circle, had published *The principles and connexion
of natural and revealed religion*. In it he had, at least for the sake of
argument, admitted the inadequacy of miracles as proofs of the Christian
revelation:

> So much Fiction has obtained in the World, partly through Superstition and
> Folly, and partly through pious Frauds, that it is very hard to produce evidence
> for *real* Miracles, which will not be baffled and confounded by counter Evidence
> that may be produced for *fictitious* ones. The Miracles done by St. *Antony,
> Hilarion, Martin*, and others of old; and the later ones of *Ignatius* told by his
> great Admirers, and those of *Abbé Paris*; and Ten Thousand others at Home as
> well as Abroad, are gravely and seriously related, and with such Circumstances,
> that it will be very hard to distinguish betwixt the Evidence for Miracles really
> and truly done, and those pretended to be done by these sanctified Cheats.
> (pp. 204–5)[71]

What was needed was extraordinary evidence if extraordinary events
were to be rendered credible. But historical evidence was by its very
nature incapable of providing evidence strong enough to render
miraculous events indubitable. This did not unduly worry Sykes, for he
maintained, as Pascal had done before him, that prophecies were
different in character from miracles. We could, once the authenticity of
the prophetic texts had been established, judge for ourselves whether
prophecies had been fulfilled or not, and thus did not have to rely upon
the testimony of others as to the extraordinary nature of the events in
question; and as prophecies continued to come true, the evidence for
Christianity from prophecies grew over time, while the evidence from
miracles might be thought to diminish as we become ever further
separated in time from the original eyewitnesses.

Sykes was thus well placed to respond favourably to Middleton's *Free*

---

[70] William Dodwell, *A free answer to Dr. Middleton's Free enquiry* (London 1749), p. 6.

[71] Sykes had found such a distinction easier to make in an earlier work, *An essay upon the
truth of the Christian religion* (London 1725), pp. 136–45, 159–70, where he had discussed the
evidence in favour of the Gospel miracles.

enquiry, a work that will always be famous because it led the young Gibbon to conclude that he must either abandon belief in miracles, or accept contemporary miracles and become a Catholic. He opted, at first, for Catholicism. In 1750 Sykes published *Two questions previous to Dr. Middleton's Free enquiry*, a work directed at what was to be Gibbon's dilemma. Despite a few reservations and expressions of caution, his conclusion was that miracles in general were incredible; for nothing was credible that was improbable; miracles were highly improbable by virtue of being contrary to common experience; and such massive improbability could not be adequately counterbalanced by the credit of witnesses, even of good character. Only the evidence of prophecy could tilt the scales towards faith, and such a faith must necessarily be Protestant in character.[72]

Two years later Sykes published Part Two of this work, by which date he felt obliged to distance himself from "Some who imagine that no Evidence can be produced, sufficient to establish the Credibility of Any Miracles at all". Such a one was Mr David Hume, who had written on miracles under the guise of being a Christian, but "Such a Mask, such a Disguise is so very thin, that every one may see the Features of the Man through the Veil he has put on" (pp. vii-viii). Sykes's objection was that Hume was no Christian, for he regarded Christianity as irrational. He did not present any refutation of Hume's actual argument against miracles; indeed it is hard to see how he could have, other than by appealing to the evidence (discounted by Hume) of prophecies, which entitled one, Sykes held, to believe that Christ had supernatural powers.

The claim that Sykes could not have found much to object to in Hume's analysis of miracles is not founded merely upon conjecture, for if we read on we discover that he has been sufficiently impressed by Hume's argument to restate his own case in terms that he had evidently derived from Hume's essay:

Let us suppose a Man from *China* or *Japan*, or nearer Home, to tell us, that He saw another raise a Dead Man to Life by a mere Word . . . one may consider which, in general, is most *probable*, Whether that God has reversed the Course of Nature, or that the Man who reports what he affirms he has seen, reports a *Falshood*. The *Probabilities* certainly lie strong against the Man; and the point is only, how we can be assured of the *Truth* of the *Fact* reported. . . . We see and know that the Alteration, or Reversal, of the course of Nature is not very *probable*; and though it *may* happen, and has happened, yet upon all Schemes it does happen *very rarely*: Whereas the Numbers of Lyars and Impostors are very *common*, and the Produce of almost every Day. The *Probability* of the One, is in Proportion to the *Fewness* of Instances in which God has been pleased to exert

---

[72] Sykes's view was criticized in the lengthy preface to Wm. Dodwell's *A full and final reply to Mr. Toll's defence* (London 1751).

such Acts of extraordinary Power: the *Probability* of the Other, is in Proportion to the Frequency and Commonness of the Lyes and Deceits of Men. . . . Nor have we any surer Test of the Truth of any Fact, than by *trying* it by the stated Course of Things. The *Credibility* therefore of any Fact does not depend upon the mere *Possibility* of it; nor does the *Incredibility* of it depend upon its *Impossibility*. . . . but upon its *Probability* or *Improbability*. . . . When such stories as these are reported . . . the *Improbabilities* of them outweigh the *Assurance* that we have, that the Facts were really done, as they are reported. (pp. 169–73)

Sykes had argued in terms of probabilities before. What was new here was the statement of the case in terms of two sets of aleatory probabilities which could in principle be compared in mathematical terms. It would seem almost certain that Hume was the inspiration for his decision to present his argument in this way, although he had to modify Hume's account in terms of conflicting proofs in order to allow for the presumed truth of the Gospel. Thus Sykes did not entirely agree with Hume. He seems to have thought that a miracle done in public and before hostile witnesses might in principle be sufficiently well attested for it to command belief. If testimony might under favourable circumstances amount to proof, the case against a miracle, on the other hand, could never pass beyond a high level of probability. But the thrust of his argument was in the same direction as Hume's, just as it was in the same direction as Middleton's. Sykes was exceptional in being willing as a theist to adopt arguments that others saw as directly hostile to Christianity, but then these two authors were arguing cases similar to the one he had advanced a dozen years before. The difference between his own view of arguments from testimony, and the views of Middleton and Hume, was that Sykes alone went on to recognize in prophecy an adequate criterion by which to distinguish true miracles from false ones. He may be said to have abandoned arguments from miracles in 1740, long before Middleton mounted his learned assault upon them, and to have sought a way of evading Hume's philosophical critique of miracles a full decade before he came to read it.

XI. PRELIMINARY CONCLUSIONS

If these three authors, along with so many others, could advance closely comparable arguments against miracles, it was, I submit, for a simple reason: their arguments were easy to derive from those of *The art of thinking* and *An essay concerning humane understanding*, even if Arnauld and Locke had wanted to uphold rather than undermine belief. Le Clerc's *Art of reasoning*, for example, which had sought to employ Arnauld's reasoning to undermine belief in Catholic miracles, had already travelled a considerable distance towards systematically casting doubt on testimony for improbable events.[73] Indeed, it is now clear that it is harder to identify what is original in Hume's essay than it is to find sources for, and parallels to, his argument. Before turning to this final problem, however, let me state in summary form a number of conclusions which I think the evidence we have looked at so far justifies our reaching:

1. 'Of miracles' should be seen as being one of numerous discussions of miracles in the context of probability theory; setting it in this context serves to establish both that the structure of Hume's argument was largely dictated by those of his predecessors, and that the details of his argument had already been anticipated in a number of important respects.

2. Its proper place was in the *Treatise*, alongside the other discussions of probability to be found there. Why then was it separated from the discussion of probability when it was published in the first *Enquiry*? Partly because probability itself is downplayed there. Hume drops the section 'Of unphilosophical probability' which had appeared in the *Treatise*, which dealt with subject-matter which had traditionally been inseparable from the question of miracles, and avoids subordinating his discussion of causation to the topic of probability; rather he sees problems of probability as arising where one is ignorant of causes. Hume was thus no longer willing to present his work in terms of the expansion of probable knowledge at the expense of certain knowledge; this meant that the framework laid down by *The art of thinking* no longer governed the exposition of his views, and 'Of miracles' was free to be uprooted and reattached to a discussion of one of the other key questions for unbelievers in this period, the question of providence. When Hume first sent a copy of his "Reasonings concerning Miracles" to Henry Home in 1737, he expressed concern that, isolated from its original context in the *Treatise*, it would be harder to understand (NHL 2): conversely, restoring it to that context is an important first step in clarifying its meaning.

3. A number of sources can be identified as having influenced Hume in writing 'Of miracles' at La Flèche, other than those he explicitly refers to; some with virtual certainty (*The art of thinking*), others with a high level of probability (Fréret, the *Difficultés*). 'Of miracles' was then perhaps only superficially revised for the first edition of the *Enquiry*. This is the best available explanation for the fact that Hume was obliged to modify its argument significantly in 1750, in order to take account of an English tradition represented by Locke, Sherlock, and Butler.

4. These sources suggest that the intellectual context in which 'Of

[73] Jean Le Clerc, *Logica: sive ars ratiocinandi* (London 1692).

miracles' was originally written was at least as much French as English, and consisted at least as much of attacks on Christianity as of defences of it.

5. Many of Hume's arguments were far from original. Indeed the close correspondence with the works of his contemporaries is extremely surprising, once account is taken of the fact that many of these works were apparently written entirely independently of 'Of miracles'. Collins, Bolingbroke, and Diderot provide epitomes of Hume's argument; Trenchard turns to Tillotson's argument against transubstantiation as a model for an argument against superstition; Sykes and Middleton appeal to the miracles at the tomb of the abbé de Pâris as well-attested miracles that are properly rejected as incredible. Here we are faced in practice with precisely the methodological problem that Hume was addressing in 'Of miracles', that of explaining the improbable in history.[74] Are these merely coincidences, or was Hume linked to other irreligious writers by a network of clandestine manuscripts and oral debate? In only one case (that of the *Difficultés*) have I concluded that the evidence justifies the view that Hume was directly influenced by a work he must have read in manuscript. In other cases it seems reasonable to presume that Hume and his contemporaries were applying similar resources to similar problems.

If such similarities exist between 'Of miracles' and works Hume is unlikely to have read, we must be all the more cautious before we conclude that he had read a published work simply because its argument seems relevant. We cannot assume that Hume had read Sherlock because his arguments seem to be a reply to Sherlock's, or Annet because Annet's arguments parallel Hume's. Collins's short work, *An essay concerning the use of reason in propositions, the evidence whereof depends upon human testimony*, published in 1707, follows *The art of thinking* (although without referring to it). Collins holds that testimony can convince one of the reality of miracles, however improbable they may seem, but, he continues, no testimony can justify belief in a meaningless proposition. For Collins such meaningless propositions include the doctrines of transubstantiation and the Trinity. Was Hume aware of this previous attempt to blunt the arguments linking history to faith? Did he set out to write a parallel "Essay concerning the use of reason in events, the evidence whereof depends upon human testimony"? We cannot tell; but it is useful to know that the argument of *The art of thinking* was an obvious reference point for opponents of Christianity, but one which, at the beginning of the century, still looked like a stronghold to be circumvented, not directly assaulted.

[74] For an example of Hume applying the principles of 'Of miracles' to such a problem see the letter on Ossian, HL i. 398–401.

Recognizing the commonplace nature of the intellectual resources Hume put to use in 'Of miracles' brings home the fact that what is remarkable about his essay is not so much his sceptical attitude to miracles as his intention to publish a direct attack on them. The arguments of Bolingbroke and Trenchard were published posthumously. Dodwell and Middleton made a pretence of orthodoxy. Others, such as Wollaston and Fréret, had confined themselves to a discussion of pagan miracles, avoiding direct reference to the New Testament (which Hume likewise refers to only implicitly) or the Old (which he refers to explicitly). Hume would have known that Woolston, who had directly attacked the miracles of the New Testament, had been tried and convicted; in 1746 Diderot was imprisoned for publishing *Pensées philosophiques*; in 1762, well after the publication of 'Of miracles', Annet was to be placed in the pillory and sentenced to a year's hard labour for attacking the Pentateuch. There is no reason to doubt that Hume had adequate prudential motives for postponing publication. What is surprising is that 'Of miracles' was not, like the *Dialogues*, saved for posthumous publication. One may hypothesize that he was encouraged by Annet's escape from prosecution for his reply to Sherlock (and defence of Woolston), published in 1744; but Hume can have been under no illusion that publication was potentially dangerous.

6. From 1660 on, probability theory provided one of the crucial contexts within which Christianity defended itself. There were, I would suggest, three key arguments that were needed to refute theism and Christianity in the context of the intellectual life of the early eighteenth century: an argument to show that atheists could be good citizens (pioneered by Bayle and refined by Hume); an argument against the testimony of the apostles as defended by *The art of thinking* (pioneered by Wollaston, Fréret and the author of the *Difficultés*, and developed by Hume); and a refutation of the argument from design as developed in the Newtonianism of the Boyle lectures. This last argument Hume tried to pioneer, above all in the *Dialogues*, but it was scarcely adequately developed until Darwin. As Hume himself admitted, the "religious hypothesis", in the narrow sense of the argument from design, remained hard to dispute, even if one could show that the arguments fell far short of intellectual proof. (This is perhaps one reason why Hume saved the *Dialogues* for posthumous publication, while insisting on going ahead with the publication of the "decisive" argument of 'Of miracles'.)

XII. HUME'S ORIGINALITY

These conclusions, stated here in no more than summary form, leave us with a central problem which any contextual account of Hume's essay is obliged to solve. Why, if his argument was in so many respects no different from that of his predecessors, did he present it as a *discovery*? Where is the original element in 'Of miracles'? This, I think, is a genuine problem for the history of philosophy, but one to which I think it is possible to propose a tentative answer.

First, unlike Tillotson, who had maintained that our senses assure us the bread is bread, the wine wine during the Mass, Hume was concerned not with one sensory experience but many. Unlike most of those before him who had appealed to the invariable course of nature, he did not present the law-governed nature of the universe as an a priori certainty, but as the experience of statistical regularity:

A wise man, therefore, proportions his belief to the evidence. . . . He weighs the opposite experiments: He considers which side is supported by the greater number of experiments: to that side he inclines, with doubt and hesitation; and when at last he fixes his judgement, the evidence exceeds not what we properly call *probability*. All probability, then, supposes an opposition of experiments and observations, where the one side is found to overbalance the other, and to produce a degree of evidence, proportioned to the superiority. (E. 110–11)

His claim was that where there is no counterbalancing instance one has proof; where (as in the case of a miracle) one has one instance overbalanced by an almost infinite number of contrary instances, one has a moral certainty (effectively a proof) that the miracle report is false.

Hume may well have believed that, in treating the question of miracles in this way as a question of statistical incidence, he was breaking fresh ground. If so, the ground was not hard to break. Locke had acknowledged that an event which corresponded with common experience was probable, and that an event which was contrary to common experience was inherently improbable. Wollaston, in his somewhat muddled argument, had shifted between cases which he felt he could declare to be in the highest degree improbable because they were contrary to the law of nature (the sun rising in the west), and those which he could declare improbable only because they were contrary to perceived statistical regularity (the sun not rising in the morning). Hume had only two things to do. First, in the light of his treatment of causation, he had to abandon Wollaston's first argument (which in fact amounted to the claim that it was a priori impossible for anything to happen contrary to the laws of nature, but that we could not be certain in any particular case that we had understood those laws correctly, an argument from epistemological probability), and develop the second, an argument from aleatory probability. Hume's denial that we are able to recognize necessary connections in nature obliged him to treat epistemological probability as a branch of aleatory probability, an obligation which he turned to his advantage in his account of the improbability of miracles. Secondly, he had to think of the reliability of testimony also in terms of aleatory probability, rather than in terms of "degrees of assent", so that, in balancing the possibility of false testimony against the improbability of the event, he would be comparing mathematical ratios. Here Craig's mathematical treatment of testimony was perhaps a helpful precedent. The clarity with which he focused upon this strategy of comparing aleatory probabilities was admirable—we have seen that Sykes was only able to take this step once he had Hume's example to follow—but it does not in itself justify, I think, Hume's pride in his achievement.

Had he then merely provided a brilliant exposition of a fairly obvious argument? One might suspect that this was a case where Hume was claiming originality because he had devised a new tune for the drums and trumpets of his philosophical army, rather than because he had brought new troops into the field (T. xiv). However we need not, I think, adopt a conclusion which attributes either ignorance or cynicism to Hume. The problem he had to solve was that of the circumstances under which belief in a miracle would be rational. Given that solution, he could then test actual claims to miraculous events. Others had said they would only believe what they had seen for themselves, or that it would take a miracle to convince them of a miracle. Hume said something different, and in doing so made clear, I think, that it was here that his claim to originality lay:

The plain consequence is (and it is a general maxim worthy of our attention), "That no testimony is sufficient to establish a miracle, unless the testimony be of such a kind, that its falsehood would be more miraculous, than the fact, which it endeavours to establish . . ." When anyone tells me, that he saw a dead man restored to life, I immediately consider with myself, whether it be more probable, that this person should either deceive or be deceived, or that the fact, which he relates, should really have happened. . . . If the falsehood of his testimony would be more miraculous, than the event which he relates; then, and not till then, can he pretend to command my belief or opinion. (E. 115–16)

With this formulation, which concludes Part One of 'Of miracles', Hume had established a clear procedure for making a decision. One should only believe in an improbable event if the alternative was to believe in an even less probable event. The systematic application of this principle to the question of miracles was new, although there was nothing particularly problematic about the principle itself. Wollaston, for example, had argued that it was more likely that Herodotus had been misled by a taste for teratical stories than that the sun had indeed risen in the west. Hume's originality lay in formulating the principle so that it could be applied not only to poorly attested miracles, like the prodigies of

Herodotus, but even to well-attested ones. It was this characteristic, of his "general maxim" which made it a "decisive argument . . . which, if just, will, with the wise and learned, be an everlasting check to all kinds of superstitious delusion, and consequently, will be useful as long as the world endures" (E. 110). This was the argument that met with the protest—when Hume first presented it to a young Jesuit of La Flèche as an argument against the miracles of contemporary Catholicism—that it told directly against the miracles of the Gospel (HL i. 361). For the application of this principle decisively tipped the balance away from an emphasis on the quality of the testimony for the resurrection of Jesus (of the sort that had impressed the authors of *The art of thinking* and Locke), to an emphasis on the inherent improbability of the event. Through this argument, Hume could explain what for the author of the *Recherches sur les miracles* was merely an empirical fact: that even well-attested miracles were widely felt to be incredible. Others—Trenchard, Middleton, Sykes—had independently demonstrated a fairly clear grasp of the principle, but none of them had dared to conclude from it that belief even in the miracles of the Gospel was irrational.

Putting Hume back in the context of the literature on miracles, which we have seen to be more extensive than has been generally recognized, may at first sight seem to undermine his claim to originality. Plenty of others, after all, had expressed incredulity. But this was not where he claimed to be original. His claim rested on a precise and novel application of probability theory to the question of miracles. Even in 1750, by which date it was clear that others were arguing from similar principles, Hume could still have claimed to be the first to have focused on this one principle and applied it unhesitatingly to each and every miracle. With hindsight it seems straightforward, but hindsight surely misleads us here. The argument was not only "concise and elegant", but, in Hume's view, both original and decisive. Putting Hume back in context helps us to see what the argument consisted in, how far it was original, and why, in the end, it was decisive.

Hume was not, as one of his critics claimed, the first who ever denied "that events contrary to firm and constant experience, may become credible by human testimony . . . giving us his reason for doing so".[75] Apart from the fact that this interpretation, like many more recent commentaries, ignored Hume's willingness to be persuaded of natural prodigies, and thus the extent to which his insistence that all miracles were inherently incredible depended on what I have termed the used-car salesman argument, it overstated Hume's originality. Yet he was the first to formulate his reason for refusing to believe in miracles with

---

[75] [J. Douglas], *The criterion, or miracles examined* (London 1754), p. 36.

philosophical precision. Because of this, 'Of miracles' has survived where its precursors and critics have been forgotten. The price of its survival has been isolation from its original context, its meaning obscured, its purpose disputed. But the passage of two hundred years is only partly to blame for this state of affairs. Putting 'Of miracles' back in context means, first and foremost, replacing it in the *Treatise*, and reading it alongside the *Abstract*. In 1750, 'Of miracles' was read by its critics as an inadequate reply to Butler;[76] in 1737, Hume must surely have seen it as a decisive reply to Arnauld.

Far from being prophetically ahead of its time, 'Of miracles' was, like Collins's notes on Cicero, Bolingbroke's letter to Pouilly, and Trenchard's essay on miracles, outdated by the time it was published, in that it, like them, had not taken account of Butler's discussion of testimony for antecedently improbable events. But this was no posthumous work; it had already been remodelled for the second edition, so that it could nearly pass as contemporary. Already the books which had dominated Hume's thinking at La Flèche seemed irrelevant: not one of Hume's critics bothered to mention *The art of thinking*, a work which had still been an indispensable reference point for Annet in his attack on Sherlock. Those who read Hume had not read Fréret or the *Difficultés*; but many of them had already read Middleton. This English context was the one in which Hume was, and has continued to be, read. Thus the past was lost, almost as decisively as if one was dealing not with a printed work but with an oral tradition. In such circumstances, reconstructing the history of Hume's thinking on miracles is fraught with difficulty, but the sources available to us are far richer now than they would have been to a disinterested critic in 1750. If we are content to deal with probabilities, not certainties, we can make some progress, for history is not subject, as Craig believed, to an inflexible law of diminishing returns. We can hope to conjure up a picture, as our predecessors could not, of *le bon David* at work in La Flèche, volume six of *Les mémoires de l'académie royale des inscriptions* open on his desk, and a copy of the *Difficultés* concealed in a drawer.[77]

Department of History
University of Victoria

[76] Skelton seems to have been almost the only critic who read the first edition. Warburton also planned a riposte, but never completed it (Mossner, *Life*, p. 289).

[77] I would like to thank D. Berman, R. M. Burns, J. M. Dunn, J. C. A. Gaskin, D. F. Norton, and M. A. Stewart, for comments on an earlier version of this paper.

HUME AND BERKELEY'S *THREE DIALOGUES*

DAVID RAYNOR

There is no doubt that Hume was acquainted with Berkeley's philosophical writings. External evidence that Hume read *A treatise concerning the principles of human knowledge* is to be found in a letter of 1737 to Michael Ramsay, a boyhood friend:

I shall submit all my Performances to your Examination, & to make you enter into them more easily, I desire of you, if you have Leizure, to read once over la Recherche de la Verité of Pere Malebranche, the Principles of Human Knowledge by Dr. Berkeley, some of the more metaphysical Articles of Bailes Dictionary. . . . Des-Cartes Meditations woud also be useful. . . . These Books will make you easily comprehend the metaphysical Parts of my Reasoning. . . .[1]

Before this letter was discovered, Richard Popkin argued that in the *Treatise* Book I Part IV "Berkeley is not mentioned, nor are his striking and startling theories ever stated, alluded to, or rejected".[2] After it was discovered, Popkin still urged that "No doctrine of Berkeley's is used by Hume to establish any of his own views, and where Hume and Berkeley come closest to discussing the same subject or holding the same view, Hume neither uses Berkeley's terms nor refers to him."[3] This bold claim was refuted by Roland Hall, who showed that a sentence in the *Treatise* was directly derived from Section 43 of Berkeley's *Principles*, and noted that "many more" of Hume's borrowings from Berkeley "remain to be discovered".[4] I myself have argued elsewhere that Hume adopts, but transforms, Berkeley's doctrine of *minima sensibilia*.[5] Here I shall argue that in the *Treatise* Book I Part IV Hume both alludes to and rejects Berkeley's favourite argument for immaterialism. As Berkeley expressed it in *Three dialogues*: "if my notions are once thoroughly understood,

---

© David R. Raynor 1989

[1] Hume to Michael Ramsay, 31 August 1737: *Archiwum historii filozofii i mysli spolecznej* 9 (1963), p. 133.

[2] R. H. Popkin, 'Did Hume ever read Berkeley?', *Journal of philosophy* 56 (1959), p. 541.

[3] R. H. Popkin, 'So, Hume did read Berkeley', *Journal of philosophy* 61 (1964), p. 778.

[4] R. Hall, 'Hume's actual use of Berkeley's *Principles*', *Philosophy* 43 (1968), pp. 278ff.

[5] D. R. Raynor, '"*Minima sensibilia*" in Berkeley and Hume', *Dialogue* 19 (1980), 196–9. Cf. M. R. Ayers, 'Berkeley and Hume: a question of influence', in *Philosophy in history*, ed. R. Rorty and others (Cambridge 1984), pp. 306ff.

that which is most singular in them, will in effect be found to amount to no more than this: that it is absolutely impossible, and a plain contradiction to suppose, any unthinking being should exist without being perceived by a mind" (p. 244).[6] I shall show that Hume read and was influenced by this work. I shall argue first that, in a famous acknowledgement to Berkeley, Hume was referring to the *Dialogues*. Secondly and more importantly, I shall discuss those passages in the *Dialogues* which appear to have influenced, and therefore illuminate, central doctrines in Hume's *Treatise*.

This exegesis is intended to buttress the interpretation of Hume as a realist about the external world, and to place in a new light his views on the self. Early in this century it was suggested that Hume was a realist *manqué*; Passmore later characterized him as an "anti-phenomenalist" who "is much closer to Locke than he is to Berkeley"; and recently Wright has more thoroughly explored this interpretation.[7] Of course, Hume shares some of Berkeley's doubts about the intelligibility of the concept of insensible matter; so, in this respect, Hume is unlike Locke. Yet both Hume and Locke are realists and dualists in that they both contrast mental entities with a mind-independent world; they differ chiefly as to the conception and knowability of that reality. This interpretation of Hume is opposed to the still prevalent "neutral monist" view that Hume dissolves both the mental and physical worlds into a homogeneous heap of perceptions.

Though our concern is with *Treatise* Book I Part IV, it will be best to look first at its recasting in the first *Enquiry*, where Hume distinguishes *two* philosophical objections against the belief in external existences: first, we instinctively believe in a mind-independent reality and take "the very images, presented by the senses, to be the external objects"; but this belief is destroyed by reason, which informs us that our immediate objects are "nothing but perceptions in the mind, and fleeting copies or representations of other existences, which remain uniform and independent" (E. 151f.). This short recapitulation of the main plot of 'Of scepticism with regard to the senses' entirely neglects the Berkeleyan scenes, and instead evokes Hobbes, who emphasized "the *great deception of sense*, which also is to be by sense *corrected*".[8]

---

[6] Page references to Berkeley's *Three dialogues between Hylas and Philonous* (hereafter *DHP*) are to *The works of George Berkeley*, ed. A. A. Luce and T. E. Jessop, vol. 2 (Edinburgh 1949).

[7] W. P. Montague, 'A neglected point in Hume's philosophy', *Journal of philosophy* 14 (1905), 30–39; J. Passmore, *Hume's intentions* (London 1968), p. 90; J. P. Wright, *The sceptical realism of David Hume* (Manchester 1983), pp. 86ff.

[8] *Human nature* [1650] in *The English works of Thomas Hobbes*, ed. W. Molesworth, vol. 4 (London 1840), pp. 8f. When Hume (T. 210f.) requires an argument to take us from what Hobbes called "the *great deception of sense*", he adapts that of Hobbes in chapter 2 of *Human nature*: "that divers times men see directly the *same* object double, as *two candles for one*"; but

Unlike Hobbes, however, Hume observes that it is *reason* which corrects the deception, and he also draws the sceptical conclusion that reason "can never find any convincing argument from experience to prove, that the perceptions are connected with any external objects" (E. 154). The belief in external existence is either a delusion or unjustifiable. In 1784 Thomas Reid remarked on the unBerkeleian nature of the first horn of this sceptical dilemma. "In this acknowledgement," he wrote, "Mr Hume indeed seems to me more generous, and even more ingenuous than Bishop Berkeley, who would persuade us that his opinion does not oppose the vulgar opinion, but only that of the philosophers; and that the external existence of a material world is a philosophical hypothesis, and not the natural dictate of our natural powers."[9] In Hume's *Enquiry* Berkeley comes on stage only with the restatement of 'Of the modern philosophy' as the *second* philosophical objection against the belief in external objects. This objection "goes farther" than the first by representing our belief "as contrary to reason: at least, if it be a principle of reason, that all sensible qualities are in the mind, not in the object" (E. 155). *If* secondary qualities exist only in the mind, and primary qualities cannot be abstracted from secondary qualities, then "external" objects exist only in the mind.

In an important footnote Hume credits this objection against external objects to his Irish predecessor:

> This argument is drawn from Dr. Berkeley; and indeed most of the writings of that very ingenious author form the best lessons of scepticism, which are to be found either among the ancient or modern philosophers, Bayle not excepted. He professes, however, in his title-page (and undoubtedly with great truth) to have composed his book against the sceptics as well as against the atheists and free-thinkers. But that all his arguments, though otherwise intended, are, in reality, merely sceptical, appears from this, *that they admit of no answer and produce no conviction.* Their only effect is to cause that momentary amazement and irresolution and confusion, which is the result of scepticism. (E. 155)

It is sometimes assumed that Hume is here referring to Berkeley's *Principles*. This assumption seems reasonable in light of Hume's letter to Ramsay. But the titles which match Hume's description are those of the three editions of the *Dialogues*. The *Principles* is announced only as an "inquiry" into the "grounds" of scepticism and atheism; but the *Dialogues* is explicitly proclaimed to be written "in opposition to sceptics and atheists".

"the thing seen cannot be in *two places. One* of these images therefore is *not inherent* in the object: but seeing the organs of the sight are then in equal temper or distemper, the *one* of them is no more inherent than the *other*; and consequently *neither* of them both are in the object."

---

[9] Thomas Reid, *Essays on the intellectual powers of man* (London 1784). Essay 2, chapter 14.

Those who belittle the extent of Hume's indebtedness to Berkeley overlook or downplay this footnote. Popkin misrepresents it as "a footnote to a brief summary against abstract ideas".[10] H. M. Bracken, in a paper almost entirely devoted to an examination of Hume's supposed debt to Berkeley, does not mention this note, and suggests that Hume's discussion of primary and secondary qualities—"a topic this putative follower of Berkeley almost never mentions"—may have been independently derived from Bayle.[11] But in 'Of the modern philosophy', and in the first *Enquiry*, Hume invokes Berkeley's novel argument that bodies are *inconceivable* without secondary qualities: primary qualities cannot be abstracted from secondary qualities. *This* argument is not to be found in Bayle, however much his writings may have suggested it to Berkeley. And if Bayle's writings had independently suggested it to Hume, why should he have acknowledged Berkeley?

In the first dialogue Hylas and Philonous agree that the real sceptic is one who denies the reality of sensible things. After Philonous claims to have proved that it is not himself but rather Hylas who is "a downright sceptic", Hylas protests that he is for the moment "if not entirely convinced, at least silenced", and that he is "at present so amazed" that he needs time to "recollect" himself. Another round of dialectic makes Hylas confess to Philonous: "your arguments seem in themselves unanswerable, but they have not so great an effect on me as to produce an entire conviction" (*DHP*, pp. 206f., 223). Hume's famous claim that Berkeley's arguments are unanswerable but unbelievable, and that their effect is to produce a "momentary amazement and irresolution and confusion", thus reproduces Hylas's sentiments about his intellectual wrestling match with Philonous. Hume even characterizes Berkeley as "a real Sceptic" in the Index that he prepared for the first *Enquiry*, thereby turning the tables on Philonous.[12] If several hints for Hume's *tour de force*, and even some of its phraseology, are present in the *Dialogues*, then we have some reason to explore the possibility that Hume's views of the self and the identity of sensible objects were derived from Berkeley's *Dialogues* and were intended as a response to immaterialism.

On two occasions in the *Dialogues* Hylas attempts to turn the tables on Philonous by urging objections against spiritual substance which appear to be similar to the objections that Philonous raised against material substance. Hylas at first does not question the intelligibility of the

[10] Popkin, 'Did Hume ever read Berkeley?', p. 541.

[11] H. M. Bracken, 'Bayle, Berkeley, and Hume', *Eighteenth-century studies* 11 (1977–8), p. 229. Cf. also 'On some points in Bayle, Berkeley, and Hume', *History of philosophy quarterly* 4 (1987), 435–46.

[12] See Hume's index to his *Essays and treatises on several subjects* (London 1758), p. 538.

concept of immaterial substance; rather, he challenges Philonous to explain the relation of extended ideas to an unextended mind: "Can extended things be contained in that which is unextended? Or are we to imagine impressions made on a thing void of all solidity? You cannot say objects are in your mind, as books in your study: or that things are imprinted on it, as the figure of a seal upon wax. In what sense therefore are we to understand those expressions?" (pp. 249f.). In the *Principles* Berkeley met this objection by insisting that objects are not literally in the mind, but are "in" the mind only "by way of *idea*". Philonous offers the same answer: "when I speak of objects as existing in the mind or imprinted on the senses; I would not be understood in the gross literal sense, as when bodies are said to exist in a place, or a seal to make an impression upon wax. My meaning is only that the mind comprehends or perceives them; and that it is affected from without, or by some being distinct from itself." (p. 250)

This defence invokes Berkeley's strategic principle that "that which bears equally hard on two contradictory opinions, can be proof against neither": if a difficulty cannot be solved by the materialist, "it is plain it can be no objection against *immaterialism*" (pp. 259f.). But Berkeley himself never satisfactorily explains the relation between extended ideas and unextended minds. He says again and again that a mind *perceives* ideas; but what does this mean? It appears to be a primitive element of his system. Berkeley's non-explanation may be an effective *tu quoque* in so far as there is a problem here for all who subscribe to a simple unextended mind whether they be materialists or immaterialists; but if immaterialism is no worse off than materialism on this issue, it is also no better off than the latter. Hume evidently saw this embarrassment and capitalized on it in 'Of personal identity': "what must become of our particular ideas upon this hypothesis?", he asks. "After what manner . . . do they belong to self; and how are they connected with it?" (T. 252). These problems, he thought, are dissolved with the rejection of a substantial unextended self. We have no idea of substance. We have no idea of inherence. The self "as far as we can conceive it" (T. 657) is nothing but a bundle of self-subsistent perceptions.

Berkeley had ignored the bundle theory in the *Principles* and the first two editions of the *Dialogues*, presumably because he believed that he had shown that a spirit is "the only substance or support, wherein the unthinking beings or ideas can exist: but that this *substance* which supports or perceives ideas should itself be an *idea* or like an *idea*, is evidently absurd" (*Principles*, 135). But a theory along Hume's lines had been enunciated by Berkeley's Hylas in passages which appear only in the revised 1734 version of the *Dialogues*. It is invoked as a *reductio* of immaterialism:

you acknowledge you have, properly speaking, no idea of your own soul. You even affirm that spirits are a sort of beings altogether different from ideas. Consequently that no idea can be like a spirit. We have therefore no idea of any spirit. You admit nevertheless that there is spiritual substance, although you have no idea of it; while you deny there can be such a thing as material substance, because you have no notion or idea of it. Is this fair dealing? To act consistently, you must either admit matter or reject spirit. (*DHP*, p. 232)

This objection, unlike the previous one, is directed at the *meaningfulness* of the concept of spiritual substance, and is original with Berkeley, who himself once flirted with a bundle theory of the mind.[13] Philonous concedes that we have no *idea* of spiritual substance, but insists that this is not damaging to immaterialism. An unsatisfied Hylas presses the objection: "in consequence of your own principles, it should follow that you are only a system of floating ideas, without any substance to support them. Words are not to be used without a meaning. And as there is no more meaning in spiritual substance than in material substance, the one is to be exploded as well as the other." (p. 233). Philonous replies that there is "no parity of case between spirit and matter": we have a *notion* of spiritual substance.

These passages suggest that Berkeley, if he had been a consistent concept empiricist, would have "exploded" immaterial substance as well as material substance. It is not difficult to discern in them the inspiration of Hume's bundle theory of the self. In the Appendix to the *Treatise* Hume modestly suggests that he is simply extending to the self what is already accepted concerning matter: "Philosophers begin to be reconcil'd to the principle, *that we have no idea of external substance, distinct from the ideas of particular qualities*. This must pave the way for a like principle with regard to the mind, *that we have no notion of it, distinct from the particular perceptions*." (T. 635). In *A letter from a gentleman* (1745) Hume distinguishes the vulgar and the philosophical conceptions of the self, and mentions Berkeley. Hume asserts that he has never "denied the Immateriality of the Soul in the common Sense of the Word" but merely contended "That that Question did not admit of any distinct Meaning; because we had no distinct Idea of Substance. This

---

[13] *Works*, ed. Luce and Jessop, vol. 1, p. 72 (entries 577–81). H. M. Bracken has argued that Berkeley's argument against material substance had already been turned against spiritual substance by the anonymous reviewer of the *Principles* for the *Journal litéraire* in 1713 and by Andrew Baxter in *An enquiry into the nature of the human soul* in 1733. See *The early reception of Berkeley's immaterialism*, 2nd edn. (The Hague 1965), pp. 43, 46, 65f., 83. They argued that if the attributes of bodies are not in them, then bodies do not exist; so, if the attributes of souls are not in them, then souls do not exist. However, this point is far from Hylas's conceptual point that 'immaterial substance' is meaningless because we cannot have any idea corresponding to it.

Opinion may be found everywhere in Mr. *Lock*, as well as in Bishop *Berkley*."[14]

The bundle theory of the self was being debated before Berkeley developed his theocentric metaphysical system. Ralph Cudworth, for example, maintained that since it is inconceivable "how that whole *Heap* or Bundle of things, should be *One Thinker*", the self must be "one *Single Substance*, and not a *Heap* of *Substances*".[15] Something like the bundle theory was advocated by Anthony Collins and satirized by Berkeley's friends the Tory wits who composed *The memoirs of Martinus Scriblerus*.[16] And (as I shall show below) Pierre Bayle dangled it in front of Leibniz as a necessary but unpalatable option. But only Berkeley presents the bundle theory as the supposed consequence of a consistent meaning empiricism. Moreover, Hume first invokes the bundle theory of the self in the course of what appears to be a response to Berkeley's immaterialism. It is unlikely that Hume did not realize that he was adopting what Berkeley had shied away from accepting.

A decade before Berkeley penned the above-quoted addition to *Three dialogues*, Francis Hutcheson had considered the bundle theory of the self but had rejected it. He had done so in a letter of 1727 to a friend in London, in which he also anticipated Hume in associating Berkeley and scepticism:

> I was well apprized of the scheme of thinking you are fallen into, not only by our Dr. Berkly's books, and by some of the old academics, but by frequent conversation with some few speculative friends in Dublin. As to your notion of our mind as only a system of perceptions, I imagine you'll find that every one has an immediate simple perception of *self*; to which all his other perceptions are some way connected, otherwise I cannot conceive how I could be anyway affected with pleasure or pain from any past action, affection, or perception; or how there could be any unity of person, or any desire of future happiness or aversion to misery. My past perceptions or future ones are not my present, but would be as distinct as your perceptions are from mine: that it is otherwise I believe everyone is conscious. As to material *substrata*, I own I am a sceptic; all the phenomena might be as they are, were there nothing but perceptions, for the phenomena are perceptions. And yet, were there external objects, I cannot imagine how we could be better informed of them than we are. I own I cannot see the force of the arguments against external objects, *i.e.* something like or

---

[14] *A letter from a gentleman to his friend in Edinburgh* (1745), pp. 30f. Note how Hume at T. 635 observes the verbal distinction so dear to Berkeley and Peter Browne of referring to *ideas* of material substances and *notions* of minds. That this is a *merely* verbal distinction was argued in the long review of Browne's works in *Bibliothèque britannique* 3 (Avril-Juin 1734), pp. 50f.

[15] Ralph Cudworth, *The true intellectual system of the universe* (London 1678), p. 830.

[16] *Memoirs of the extraordinary life, works, and discoveries of Martinus Scriblerus* [1728], ed. C. Kerby-Miller (New Haven 1950), pp. 138ff. Cf. Anthony Collins, *An answer to Mr. Clark's third defence of his letter to Mr. Dodwell*, 2nd edn. (London 1711), pp. 43, 44, 56, 59–63. This tract is the chief butt of Butler's essay 'Of personal identity'.

proportional, to our concomitant ideas, as I call extension, figure, motion, rest, solidity.[17]

Soon after the first two volumes of the *Treatise* were published, Hume's friend, Henry Home, sent copies to Hutcheson. After reading these, Hutcheson wrote that he "was every where Surprized with a great acuteness of thought and reasoning in a mind wholly disengaged from the prejudices of the Learned as well as those of the Vulgar".[18] He expressed a desire to meet Hume, and they met that winter. Hume responded to some of Hutcheson's objections in a letter to him and in the Appendix to the *Treatise*. "I shall consider more carefully all the particulars you mention to me," Hume wrote, "tho' with regard to *abstract Ideas*, tis with Difficulty I can entertain a Doubt on that head, notwithstanding your Authority. Our conversation together has furnish'd me a hint, with which I shall augment the 2d Edition."[19] Hutcheson's opposition to Hume's reliance upon Berkeley's account of abstract ideas thus failed of its intended effect, and instead furnished Hume with a new argument to bolster what he had characterized as "one of the greatest and most valuable discoveries that has been made of late years in the republic of letters" (T. 17). Given Hutcheson's views on personal identity, it is probable that he voiced objections to the *Treatise* on that score too; and, if so, Hume's famous second thoughts about the self may have been occasioned by Hutcheson's *viva voce*. However that may be, in 1727 Hutcheson, who was not committed to deriving all ideas from experience, and who was also inclined to side with the vulgar against the philosophers, could not "see the force of [Berkeley's] arguments against external objects". Not seeing the force of Berkeley's argument, he saw no need to adopt the bundle theory in order to meet it. And if reading the *Treatise* suggested that immaterialism could be avoided by adopting the bundle theory, he likely would have resisted this way out. For in the above-quoted letter Hutcheson tacitly drew the distinction that Hume makes explicitly, "betwixt personal identity, as it regards our thought or imagination, and as it regards our passions or the concern we take in ourselves" (T. 253). And Hutcheson took the latter to *refute* any bundle theory of the former. Hume, on the other hand, inverts this reasoning, and argues that "our identity with regard to the passions serves to corroborate that with regard to the imagination, by the making

---

[17] Hutcheson to William Mace, 6 Sept. 1727: *European magazine* (1788), p. 258. Hume may not have known Hutcheson's response to the Molyneux problem, but likely knew the similar response of Père Percheron's 'Dissertation métaphysique au sujet d'un problème proposé par M. Molineux, & communiqué à M. Locke', *Journal de Trévoux* (Novembre 1730), 1974–94.

[18] SRO, GD 24/1/553, fol. 158. See I. S. Ross, 'Hutcheson on Hume's *Treatise*: an unnoticed letter', *Journal of the history of philosophy* 4 (1966), 69–72.

[19] HL i. 39. Hume developed this "hint" in the Appendix (T. 637).

our distant perceptions influence each other, and by giving us a present concern for our past or future pains or pleasures" (T. 261). Evidently Hutcheson was not convinced, for in his last work he again rejected the bundle theory, citing against it arguments of Aristotle, Baxter, and Clarke.[20]

Hutcheson's reasons for refusing to extend the attack on material substance to immaterial substance differ somewhat from those which Berkeley puts into Philonous's mouth. Besides thinking that the bundle theory is wrong-headed, Hutcheson in the same letter argues that Molyneux, Locke, and Berkeley are mistaken about the abilities of a man born blind and suddenly made to see, because "concomitant ideas" provide us with ideas common to sight and touch. But this is cutting the knot rather than untying it. Hume would have sided with the modern philosophers and have regarded Hutcheson's solution to the Molyneux problem as an unnecessary retreat to innatism, for a sufficiently sophisticated theory can explain how we fashion ideas common to sight and touch. For Berkeley, visible extension and tangible extension are heterogeneous, so that 'triangle' is equivocal when predicated of something touched and of something seen; and Berkeley used this conclusion to support immaterialism. Unlike Berkeley, however, Hume sees that a visible triangle can represent a tangible triangle because the *relations* can be abstracted from the related parts by a *distinction of reason*. Moreover, Hume deliberately invokes Berkeley's account of generality in order to deny this paradoxical Berkeleian doctrine:

Suppose that in the extended object, or composition of colour'd points, from which we first receiv'd the idea of extension, the points were of a purple colour; it follows, that in every repetition of that idea we wou'd not only place the points in the same order with respect to each other, but also bestow on them that precise colour, with which alone we are acquainted. But afterwards having experience of the other colours of violet, green, red, white, black, and of all the different compositions of these, and finding a resemblance in the disposition of colour'd points, of which they are compos'd, we omit the peculiarities of colour, as far as possible, and found an abstract idea merely on that disposition of points, or manner of appearance, in which they agree. Nay even when the resemblance is carry'd beyond the objects of one sense, and the impressions of touch are found to be similar to those of sight in the disposition of their parts; this does not hinder the abstract idea from representing both, upon account of their resemblance. (T. 34)

Michael Ayers[21] takes Hume to be implying here that "Berkeley need not have bothered to deny" the existence of ideas of two senses. It may be that here too Hume was taking his cues from *Three dialogues*, for it is only

---

[20] *A system of moral philosophy*, vol. 1 (Glasgow 1755), p. 200.
[21] Ayers, 'Berkeley and Hume' (n. 5 above), p. 311.

in this work that Berkeley concedes that immaterialism is independent of his theory of vision. Near the end of the first dialogue Philonous states: "But allowing that distance was truly and immediately perceived by the mind, yet it would not thence follow it existed out of the mind. For whatever is immediately perceived is an idea: and can any *idea* exist out of the mind?" (*DHP*, p. 202). Reflection on this concession, with its implicit distinction between spatial externality and mind-independence, was probably responsible for Hume's crucial observation "that when we talk of real distinct existences, we have commonly more in our eye their independency than external situation in place" (T. 191).

In the *Principles* Berkeley acknowledges that immaterialism is contrary to common prejudices; but in the *Dialogues* he makes some attempt to reconcile his system with ordinary beliefs. In the first dialogue Philonous invokes the contrast between variable ideas and unchanging objects in order to persuade Hylas that our ideas cannot be like, and hence cannot even represent, external objects, even if we could conceive of such objects. After Hylas concedes that external things as he understands them have "a stable and permanent nature independent of our senses", Philonous quickly silences him with the following challenge: "How then is it possible, that things perpetually fleeting and variable as our ideas, should be copies or images of any thing fixed and constant?" Again, "how can any determinate material objects be properly represented or painted forth by several distinct things, each of which is so different from and unlike the rest?" (*DHP*, pp. 205f.). This Malebranche-like challenge is assumed by Berkeley to be unanswerable; but it must be answered by anyone who wishes to explain the origin of the vulgar belief in external objects. Berkeley is concerned to explain away these prejudices, for he is aware that his system is not really compatible with ordinary beliefs such as the belief that we see the same object as we touch. He explains this vulgar "fiction" as follows:

But in case every variation was thought sufficient to constitute a new kind or individual, the endless number or confusion of names would render language impracticable. Therefore to avoid this as well as other inconveniencies . . . men combine together several ideas, apprehended by divers senses, or by the same senses at different times . . . all which they refer to one name, and consider as one thing. Hence it follows that when I examine by my other senses a thing I have seen, it is not in order to understand better the same object which I had perceived by sight. . . .

Berkeley adds that the variability of our ideas is consistent with the deliverances of the senses, but inconsistent with the common man's

preconceived notion of (I know not what) one single, unchanged, unperceivable, real nature, marked by each name: which prejudice seems to have taken its rise from not rightly understanding the common language of men speaking of several distinct ideas, as united into one thing by the mind. And indeed there is cause to suspect several erroneous conceits of the philosophers are owing to the same original: while they began to build their schemes, not so much on notions as words, which were framed by the vulgar. . . . (*DHP*, pp. 245f.)

Berkeley is somewhat ambivalent about the vulgar belief in external objects: he hovers between saying that it is an impossible belief which we therefore do not have, and that it is a false belief which we have only because it is so convenient. It is clear that he favours the former interpretation, for in *Principles*, 4, he writes: "It is indeed an opinion strangely prevailing amongst men, that houses, mountains, rivers, and in a word all sensible objects have an existence natural or real, distinct from their being perceived by the understanding. But with how great an assurance and acquiescence soever this principle may be entertained in the world; yet whoever shall find in his heart to call it in question, may, if I mistake not, perceive it to involve a manifest contradiction." In 'Of scepticism with regard to the senses' Hume evidently favoured the latter interpretation and therefore devotes many pages to the mind's activity in forming beliefs about external existences. We may discern Hume's reaction to *Principles*, 4, in the otherwise dissimilar reaction of Henry Home, who protested that even "supposing mankind to be under so strange and unaccountable a delusion, as to mistake their ideas for men, houses, mountains, *&c.* it will not follow, that there is in this, any manifest contradiction, or any contradiction at all. For deception is a very different thing from contradiction."[22] In the *Principles* Berkeley had explained the vulgar belief in body by invoking the *involuntariness*[23] of some perceptions: "this made them maintain, those ideas or objects of perception had an existence independent of, and without the mind, *without ever dreaming that a contradiction was involved in those words*" (*Principles*, 56; italics added). But it is a *contradiction* only if one subscribes to a conception of the self as a simple and unextended

[22] Henry Home, *Essays on the principles of morality and natural religion* (Edinburgh 1751), p. 256.

[23] Another novel and important feature of Hume's explanation of the vulgar belief is that the *involuntariness* of perceptions is at best a necessary, and not a sufficient, condition of our belief in mind-independent objects. It has been conjectured by Ayers that this innovation may have been suggested by a passage in the *Dialogues* (p. 235); but as it might equally well have been suggested by a passage in Descartes' third Meditation or in Cudworth, I shall not insist on this. According to Cudworth: "Neither doth every Involuntary Phantasm, or such as the Soul is not Conscious to itself to have purposely excited or raised up within itself, seem to be a Sensation or Perception of a thing, as existing without us; for there may be Straggling Phantasms, which come into the Mind we know not how; and bubble up to themselves, which yet the Soul may distinguish from Sensations or Perceptions of things, as existing really without it; because of some other Phantasms at the same time in the Soul, whose Vigours and Lustre do cloud and eclipse them." (*A treatise concerning eternal and immutable morality* (London 1731), p. 119).

substance which supports necessarily dependent ideas. Hume asks: "How can we satisfy ourselves in supposing a perception to be absent from the mind without being annihilated?" He answers: "what we call a *mind*, is nothing but a heap or collection of different perceptions", from which "it evidently follows that there is no absurdity in separating any particular perception from the mind; that is, in breaking off all its relations, with that connected mass of perceptions, which constitute a thinking being" (T. 207).

Hume's strategy is latent in Berkeley's response to the objection that "it sounds very harsh to say we eat and drink ideas, and are clothed with ideas" (*Principles*, 38). This phrase would not sound paradoxical if 'idea' and 'thing' really were synonymous terms. Berkeley may have the assent of the vulgar when he claims that this harsh-sounding phrase merely means that we are fed and clothed with what we perceive by our senses; but he cannot plausibly claim their assent when he maintains that it *also* means that "we eat and drink, and are clad with, the immediate objects of sense which cannot exist unperceived or without the mind". When he joins forces with the vulgar against the materialists he treats 'idea' and 'thing' as synonymous terms; but when he develops his immaterialism, 'idea' clearly means 'sensation'. If 'idea' and 'thing' really were synonymous, there would be no grounds for preferring one over the other. But Berkeley carefully explains his preference: "the term *thing* in contradistinction to *idea* is generally supposed to denote something existing without the mind", but sensible objects "exist only in the mind", therefore he "chose to mark them by the word *idea* which implies those properties" (*Principles*, 39f.; cf. *DPH*, pp. 235f.). The air of paradox arises because 'idea' and 'thing' are *not* synonymous terms. When it suits Berkeley's purpose he stipulates that they are; yet by acknowledging that they imply different properties, he betrays the fact that his system merely appears to satisfy both the vulgar and the philosophers. Berkeley's avowed preference for 'idea' over 'thing' has its counterpart in Hume's studied avoidance of any such preference. Indeed, it may be argued that on this matter Hume is simply holding Berkeley to his word. If we stipulate that 'idea' and 'thing', or 'perception' and 'object', are synonymous terms, then they must not imply different properties. Their ordinary meanings must be disallowed or cancelled if we are to explain the sophisticated theory which they embody. Since Hume's readers would have believed that 'unperceived perception' is a contradiction, he had to show that, while it is a contradiction from a Berkeleian standpoint, it is not so from a pre-theoretical one. The philosophical term 'perception' is theory-laden; but if we entirely abstract from the theory we will see that the *term* cannot make the separation of a perception from a mind absurd.

Towards the end of the third dialogue Berkeley sets out the strategy which he has implicitly followed in this work:

I do not pretend to be a setter-up of *new notions*. My endeavours tend only to unite and place in a clearer light that truth, which was before shared between the vulgar and the philosophers: the former being of opinion, that *those things they immediately perceive are the real things*; and the latter, that *the things immediately perceived, are ideas which exist only in the mind*. Which two notions put together, do in effect constitute the substance of what I advance. (*DHP*, p. 262)

Hume appears to accept this strategy, but draws a different conclusion from it:

When I view this table and that chimney, nothing is present to me but particular perceptions, which are of a like nature with all the other perceptions. This is the doctrine of the philosophers. But this table, which is present to me, and that chimney, may and do exist separately. This is the doctrine of the vulgar, and implies no contradiction. There is no contradiction, therefore, in extending the same doctrine to all the perceptions. (T. 634)

Hence Hume does lend a hand to Hylas: the bundle theory of the self is a necessary condition of having the conception of external existences. The imagination completes the story, and is what has to be added to sensation in order to make us take our perceptions to be external objects. Like Berkeley, Hume insists that the senses alone cannot yield a belief in the continued and distinct existence of objects. As Berkeley puts this point: the senses "make no inferences" (*DHP*, p. 175). Berkeley himself goes some way towards reintroducing the intentionality or directedness of perception after banishing it from sensation. Two people, similarly affected by the senses, may yet perceive things differently, because they have had different past experiences (p. 204). But Berkeley stops short of realizing that objectivity and reidentification are intimately linked. Jonathan Bennett has praised Hume for seeing "that there is a deep and intimate connexion between identity and objectivity", but has criticized him for failing to see "that the worst possible route into objectivity is through identity".[24] But for Hume it was the only possible route. Given that *all* perceptions are logically distinct from minds; and that we believe that some are contingently dependent on minds, while others are not; the presence of identity in the latter, but not the former, class is of obvious importance.

The third dialogue contains Berkeley's only published discussion of the concept of identity, and there can be little doubt that it was one of several contemporary discussions which influenced Hume's treatment

[24] J. F. Bennett, *Locke, Berkeley, Hume: central themes* (Oxford 1971), p. 342.

of identity in Part IV of the first book of the *Treatise*.[25] Berkeley is content to accept that, strictly speaking, we never see the same object as we touch, and that we never see the same thing on successive occasions. But he appears to be less willing to accept that, strictly speaking, no two people ever see the same thing at any one time. At least he tries to diminish the absurdity involved in denying that two or more people can see the numerically same thing. In response to Hylas's objection Philonous maintains that two people, similarly affected by their senses, may nevertheless be said to be seeing the same thing: "some regarding the uniformness of what was perceived, might call it the *same* thing: others especially regarding the diversity of persons who perceived, might choose the denomination of different things. But who sees not that all the dispute is about a word?" (*DHP*, pp. 247f.). Hume took up just this challenge. He writes: "Thus the controversy concerning identity is *not* merely a dispute of words. For when we attribute identity . . . to variable or interrupted objects, our mistake is not confin'd to the expression, but is commonly attended with a fiction . . ." (T. 255, emphasis added). In other words, identity is an essential ingredient in Hume's explanation of the origin of the "fiction" of continued and hence mind-independent objects.

I hope that enough has been said to show that Hume wrote 'Of scepticism with regard to the senses' with Berkeley in mind: not only the *Principles* but the *Dialogues* as well. Even the dialectical structure of Hume's difficult section owes something to the *Dialogues*: for Hume may reasonably be regarded as transforming Berkeley's critique of Malebranche's non-causal representative theory of perception into a criticism of *all* representative theories. In the second dialogue Philonous charges that Malebranche's theory "is liable to all the absurdities of the common hypothesis, in making a created world exist otherwise than in the mind of a spirit. Besides all which it hath this peculiar to itself; that it makes that material world serve to no purpose." (*DHP*, p. 214). According to Hume, the philosophers' representative theory "contains all the difficulties of the vulgar system, with some others, that are peculiar to itself". The vulgar system involves the "gross illusion" that our perceptions continue to exist unperceived, and the philosophical system

---

[25] That Hume wrote about identity with Locke's *Essay* in his eye has been convincingly argued by Roland Hall. See his 'Hume's use of Locke on identity', *Locke Newsletter* 5 (1974), 56–75. Hume appears to have had an eye on Shaftesbury's *Moralists* too, for the wording of the following bears a close similarity to a segment of Hume's text: "What you Philosophers are, reply'd I, may be hard perhaps to determine: But for the rest of Mankind, I dare affirm, that few are so long themselves as *half* seven Years. 'Tis good fortune if a Man be *one and the same* only for a day or two." (*Characteristicks*, vol. 3 (London 1723), p. 351.) Compare Hume: "setting aside some metaphysicans of this kind, I may venture to affirm of the rest of mankind, that they are nothing but a bundle or collection of different perceptions" (T. 252).

is "liable to the same difficulties; and is over-and-above loaded with this absurdity, that it at once denies and establishes the vulgar supposition" (T. 211, 217). Thus the evidence suggests that, in spite of telling Michael Ramsay to read the *Principles*, Hume was using the 1734 London edition which includes *Three dialogues*, without bothering to distinguish between the two works.

Hume's explanation of the intentionality of perception takes place in a wider context than Berkeley's works, so it is appropriate here to give a thumbnail sketch of that context. In *De la Recherche de la vérité* Malebranche marshalled many arguments against the view that the mind alone can conceive of, and *a fortiori* can perceive, the external world. Hence we see all things in God. Arnauld and Bayle[26] easily pointed out the flaws in Malebranche's theory; but Arnauld never saw, or made little or no attempt to surmount, the various difficulties which Malebranche had urged against the view that the mind alone can represent the external world. Hume no doubt agreed with Berkeley's assessment that Malebranche's vision in God is "incomprehensible" (*Principles*, 48); yet Hume, unlike Arnauld, was not content simply to assert that our ideas of external existences are innate and *essentially* represent their objects. Nor was Hume willing to settle for Berkeley's immaterialism. Hume's very detailed explanation of how the mind forms its ideas of external objects meets Malebranche's strictures, and also explains the individuation of objects; so that Hume at once attempts to solve a problem from which Arnauld and Locke turned away, and offers an original solution to one of the problems which had shipwrecked Malebranche's system.

In the first *Enquiry* our beliefs in external objects are said to be due to a "blind" instinct, whereas in the *Treatise* Hume shows in great detail how they are acquired. In the *Treatise* he is untying rather than cutting the knot bequeathed by his predecessors. Malebranche and Berkeley had challenged anyone to show *how* mind-dependent perceptions can represent mind-independent objects. I believe that Hume accepted this challenge, and attempted an answer. In other words, he accepted some of Malebranche's arguments about perception, without of course accepting his bizarre theory that we see all things in God; just as he accepted some of the latter's negative arguments on causation, without adopting the view that God is the only true cause. Malebranche's critical point that *"un homme ne peut pas former l'idée d'un objet s'il ne le connaît auparavant, c'est-à-dire s'il n'en a déjà l'idée"* had effectively proscribed Locke's view that our complex ideas of substances are made "in reference to" external

---

[26] See esp. Pierre Bayle, *Oeuvres diverses*, vol. 1 (The Hague 1727), pp. 26 and 282f. Bayle thought Malebranche was closer to the truth than Arnauld, but characteristically concluded that their dispute shows that *how* we know objects is "inexplicable".

objects which they are "intended" to represent.[27] Hume had to show how the mind, without design, creates its ideas of external things, and does so by attributing to its perceptions "different relations, connexions and durations" (T. 68). While other countrymen sought to reconcile the physics of Descartes and Newton, Hume sought to reconcile the metaphysics of Locke and Malebranche (T. 648).[28] To supply what Norris had called "the great omission" in Locke's *Essay* required the rejection of Berkeley's "most singular" notion.

It should not be an objection against what I have tried to prove if I mention two controversies which probably also caught Hume's attention, thereby over-determining his adoption of the bundle theory of the self.

In a series of searching criticisms of Leibniz's new system of pre-established harmony, Pierre Bayle argued that it is impossible to understand how a multitude of perceptions can exist in an indivisible substance: Leibniz's theory "would be less incomprehensible if it were supposed that the soul of man is not one spirit but rather a multitude of spirits", he argued. "But then the soul of man would be no longer a single substance but an *ens per aggregationem*, a collection and heap of substances just like all material beings."[29] Leibniz at first avoided the issue, stating that the soul is *essentially* representative and a kind of "immaterial automaton": "the soul, however simple it may be, always has a sentiment composed of many perceptions at once, a fact which serves our purpose as if it were composed of parts like a machine".[30] In a

---

[27] Nicolas Malebranche, *De la Recherche de la vérité*, III. ii. 3; John Locke, *An essay concerning humane understanding*, II. xxx. 5. Malebranche's disciple John Norris believed that his master's arguments were "sufficient to shew [Locke's] new Account of Humane Understanding to be as false as any of the rest, which resolves our Ideas into the supposed *essentially Representative* Modalities of our own Souls". Consequently, Norris recapitulated Malebranche's arguments, insisting that Locke had neither obviated them nor explained the nature of our ideas. "I would not be thought to slight or undervalue the performance of this ingenious Author, which I allow to be very valuable and considerable in many respects. . . . But as to the Account which he has given us of *Ideas* (which ought to have been the great Subject of his undertaking, in an *Essay of Humane Understanding*) that, I think, is as Lame and Defective as any thing can well be. . . . If this Censure be thought too severe, I should be glad to be shewn how to mollifie it. In the mean time, as to the present Account, that which is the great omission in Mr. *Lock*'s is sufficiently supplied here, by that special Enquiry which we have made into the Nature of those Ideas whereby we understand." (Norris, *An essay towards the theory of the ideal or intelligible world*, Part II (London 1704), pp. 406, 517f.)

[28] Hume's sometime mentor, Chevalier Andrew Michael Ramsay, suggested that Newton's "milieu Etheréen, son esprit subtil, & son principe d'attraction peuvent être conciliés avec la doctrine de Descartes. La vraye Physique résulte de la combinaison de ces deux systèmes. Les Géomètres Ecossois y travaillent. La Nature semble avoir réservé à ces Insulaires la gloire de terminer les discordes Philosophiques entre les Français et les Anglais, comme autrefois les guerres sanglantes entre ces deux Nations." ('Le Psychomètre, ou, Réflexions sur les différents caractères de l'esprit', *Journal de trévoux* 35 (Avril 1735), p. 701.)

[29] Article 'Rorarius' in his *Dictionary*; quoted in Leibniz's *Theodicy* [1710], ed. A. Farrer (London, 1951), pp. 43f. Hume alludes to the *Theodicy* in the *Abstract*.

[30] *Leibniz: Philosophical papers and letters*, trans. L. E. Loemker, 2nd edn. (Dordrecht 1969), p. 496.

later exchange Leibniz insisted that he could not understand the difficulty which Bayle had raised, because "*everyone* who recognizes immaterial and indivisible substances also attributes to them a multitude of simultaneous perceptions"; and he added, for good measure, that "It is no proof of the impossibility of a matter merely to say that one cannot understand this thing or that. . . ."³¹ Similarly, in a controversy with Norris, Locke retorted that he should not be expected to be able to explain what alteration of the mind perception consists in "because no man can give any account of any alteration made in any simple substance whatsoever; all the alteration we can conceive, being only of the alteration of compounded substances; and that only by a transposition of parts".³² With so many confessions of ignorance and mystery it is not surprising to find Hume untying the knot by explaining how perception is possible without a simple subject: "External objects are seen, and felt, and become present to the mind; that is, they acquire such a relation to a connected heap of perceptions, as to influence them very considerably. . . ." (T. 207). Thus to have a physical object "present to the mind" does not require that it be literally a perception which becomes *part* of the mind, as the "neutral monist" interpretation would have it. Like Locke, but unlike Berkeley, Hume is able to hold that what we perceive causes our perception of it. His analysis of causation undercuts the usual motives for neutral monism. And the misinterpretation has been fostered by the failure of many commentators to see that at this point in the *Treatise* Hume is explaining how, on his principles, the vulgar belief that there is an "immediate intercourse between the mind and the object" (E. 152) is conceivable, but in fact false.

I shall conclude with a speculation. When Hume recast the *Treatise* he considerably reduced the sections on scepticism about the external world. He shortened and simplified his account of causation in the *Enquiry* as he had done in the *Abstract*. But in the *Abstract* he at least mentions his view that "when we believe any thing of *external* existence, or suppose an object to exist a moment after it is no longer perceived", this belief is nothing but a "peculiar sentiment, or lively conception" *produced by habit* (T. 657). He also there singles out as "peculiar to himself" the opinion that the self is "nothing but a system or train of different perceptions" (T. 657). But in the *Enquiry* the bundle theory of the self is not mentioned and our belief in external reality is no longer held to be produced by habit but is left unexplained. Why are these two features of the *Treatise*, which are singled out in the *Abstract*, absent from the *Enquiry*? The answer may be simply that Hume wished to

---

³¹ ibid., pp. 580f.; italics added.
³² 'Remarks upon some of Mr. Norris's books, wherein he asserts P. Malebranche's opinion of seeing all things in God' [1720], in *Works of John Locke*, vol. 10 (London 1823), p. 250.

shorten and simplify his system. But perhaps he deleted them because they had been misunderstood and unappreciated by earlier readers.

To make this speculation plausible let us briefly consider the review of *Treatise* I and II in the *Bibliothèque raisonnée* for 1740. Of the early reviews of the *Treatise* it is the only favourable one. It has recently been noticed that this review is mostly a French translation of Hume's *Abstract*.[33] It is striking that the reviewer avoided translating the passage of the *Abstract* which mentions external existence, and translated but mocked the passage concerning the self. His comment on the latter is blunt: "*ainsi* LOCKE *n'est pas moins absurde que* DESCARTES, *selon les principes de l'Auteur*".[34] The reviewer added that it was an opinion that Hume "*paraît spécialement affectionner*" and that he "*entasse paradoxes sur paradoxes à cet égard*". Thus the reviewer ignored one, and criticized the other, of two juxtaposed passages in the *Abstract*. Since Hume regarded his analysis of the self as required by his doctrine of external existences, he must have been annoyed that the connexion had been entirely missed. An examination of Reid and Beattie's works would reveal that they too missed the connexion between these two Humean doctrines, and that they therefore conflated Hume's views on the external world with Berkeley's immaterialism.

We have seen that the real interest of Hume's explanation of our belief in mind-independent entities lies in showing exactly how we fall into that "nicer strain of abstraction" of which Berkeley (*Principles*, 5) thought we were incapable. That Reid misunderstood Hume's project is evident from his counter-position that sensations are "natural signs" of external objects. After observing that Berkeley and Hume proved that we cannot infer the existence of external objects from our sensations alone, Reid concluded "that this connexion between our sensations and the conception and belief of external existences cannot be produced by habit, experience, or any principle of human nature that hath been admitted by philosophers".[35] Thus Reid shows no sign that he was aware that in the *Treatise* Hume was engaged in showing *how* the successful

---

[33] *Bibliothèque raisonnée* (Avril-Juin 1740), p. 349. See J. W. Yolton, 'Hume's *Abstract* in the *Bibliothèque raisonnée*', *Journal of the history of ideas* 40 (1979), 157–8. Hutcheson may have arranged this review. His "ancien & intime Ami" William Smith was one of the publishers of the *Bibliothèque raisonnée*. See Avril-Juin 1735, p. 476. Copies of the *Treatise*, a manuscript copy of the *Abstract*, and a letter from Hutcheson, were sent to a "Mr Smith" in early 1740: HL i. 37.

[34] *Bibliothèque raisonnée*, pp. 353f. Another reviewer excused himself from any consideration of Hume's explanation as to why we believe in external objects: "elle est traitée d'une manière si abstraite, qu'il faudrait copier la Section II en entier pour se faire entendre; & peut-être même encore n'y comprendrait-on pas grand'chose, tant les idées de l'anonyme sont singulières, & tant il fait donner un air de singularité aux idées les plus communes." (*Nouvelle bibliothèque, ou histoire littéraire* (Septembre 1740), p. 59.)

[35] Thomas Reid, *An inquiry into the human mind* (London 1764), chapter 5, section 3.

connexion between sensations and our belief in external objects is the product of experience and habit. Hume for his part charged that Reid's doctrine "leads us back to innate Ideas".[36] But neither Reid nor Beattie ignored Hume's doctrine of the self-subsistence of perceptions, which they ridiculed and suggested was but the logical conclusion of Berkeley's attack on material substance. Their misrepresentations of Hume's views are fairly well known. What is not so well known is that the conflation of Hume's views with Berkeley's immaterialism began very soon after the *Treatise* was published and well before Reid and Beattie flourished. There is evidence in the form of a student essay that as early as 1740 "Hume was being read in Edinburgh as a Berkeleyan"; and a few years later another Edinburgh critic pointed out that Hume's theory of the self was inconsistent with, and hence undermined, his supposed Berkeleyan immaterialism.[37] But the *Treatise* did not suffer only from critics. Even some of Hume's defenders missed the serious purpose of the section on scepticism about the external world. As a friend of Hume wrote:

Locke had admitted matter, spirit, and ideas. By many passages, one would be apt to think that he saw no absurdity in *material spirit*, or in *spiritual matter*. Berkeley comes, sees the difficulty and strikes out matter. Then comes a *Parisian Egoist*, who strikes out all spirit but his own. And, lastly, our friend Hume, strikes out even his own spirit, and leaves nothing but Ideas! This, in Mr. Hume, I looked upon as a mere philosophical amusement, and not ill adapted to turn all those doctrines into ridicule. . . .[38]

Around the time that Hume disavowed the *Treatise* he also would have had the mortification of reading, in an anonymous review in a major periodical, that "this very extraordinary notion of the continued existence of ideas . . . is a greater innovation of the established doctrine of ideas as laid down by Mr. Locke, and all other modern philosophers, foreign as well as British, than any with which the three Scotch doctors [Beattie, Reid, and Oswald] have ever been charged".[39] Given this

---

[36] P. B. Wood, 'David Hume on Thomas Reid's *Inquiry into the human mind*: a new letter to Hugh Blair from July 1762', *Mind* 95 (1986), p. 416. For Reid's reply to this letter see D. F. Norton, 'Reid's abstract of the *Inquiry into the human mind*', in *Thomas Reid: critical interpretations*, ed. S. F. Barker and T. L. Beauchamp (Philadelphia 1976), 125–32.

[37] M. A. Stewart, 'Berkeley and the Rankenian club', in *George Berkeley: essays and replies*, ed. D. Berman (Dublin 1986), pp. 40ff., citing John Carre (1740) and George Wallace (1760).

[38] George L. Scott to Lord Monboddo, 3 April 1773, in William Knight, *Lord Monboddo and some of his contemporaries* (London 1900, pp. 77f.). For the identity of the "Parisian Egoist" see Lewis Robinson, 'Un solipsiste au XVIIᵉ siècle', *L'année philosophique* 24 (1913), 15–30. Hume may have been partly responsible for Scott's misunderstanding, for in *A letter from a gentleman* he asserts "that so extravagant a Doubt as that which Scepticism may seem to recommend, by destroying *every* *Thing*, really affects *nothing*, and was never intended to be understood *seriously*, but was meant as a *mere* Philosophical Amusement, or Trial of *Wit* and *Subtilty*".

[39] Review of Joseph Priestley's *Hartley's theory of the human mind*, in *Monthly review* 53 (1775), 380–90; 54 (1776), 41–7. The quotation is from p. 383 and was almost certainly penned

history of misinterpretation, from the early reviews up to 1775, and from friends as well as foes, Hume must have despaired that this part of the *Treatise* would ever be understood and appreciated. But if the first *Enquiry*, with its footnote on Berkeley, was intended to separate Hume's views on external objects from those of his predecessor—and we have seen that it had this effect on Reid—then it is more understandable why Hume could in 1775 repudiate the *Treatise* and characterize his action as "a compleat Answer to Dr Reid and to that bigotted silly Fellow, Beattie".[40]

Department of Philosophy
University of Ottawa

by Hume's friend William Rose, to whom the entire review has traditionally been attributed (B. Nangle, *The monthly review, first series 1749–1789 : Indexes of contributors and articles* (Oxford 1934)). However, most of the review was in fact written by Reid: see 'Miscelaneous reflections on Priestly's account of Hartley's theory of the human mind': AUL, MS. 3061/9. Reid ridicules Priestley's account of identity, which is quite similar to that found in Hume's *Treatise*. I am indebted to Paul Wood for this information. The attribution of part of the review to Reid is due to Ian Douglas of the University of Leeds.

[40] Hume to William Strahan, 26 October 1775: HL ii. 301.

METAPHYSICS AND PHYSIOLOGY: MIND, BODY, AND THE ANIMAL ECONOMY IN EIGHTEENTH-CENTURY SCOTLAND

JOHN P. WRIGHT

I. INTRODUCTION

At the beginning of his *Institutions of medicine* William Cullen defined "PHYSIOLOGY, or the Doctrine of the Animal Oeconomy" as "the doctrine which explains the conditions of the body and of the mind necessary to life and health".[1] Commenting on the same definition in his Edinburgh medical lectures in 1770, he noted that while physiologists normally discussed mental conditions it was not usual to include the mind in the definition of physiology. Some people had criticized him for introducing *metaphysics* into medicine. In response, Cullen employed a distinction which was also made by his friend David Hume, between two meanings of 'metaphysics'. It can mean "subtile Disquisitions": like Hume, he wanted to avoid metaphysics in this sense. However,

if by Metaphysics we understand as I think we should the Operations of the human Mind in thinking, that is, the History of the human Mind, then I say Metaphysics are unavoidable not only in Physick, but perhaps in every Science if a man goes deep.

True metaphysics for both thinkers was concerned with "the Mind and its Operations". Cullen saw this as a particularly important study in medicine because "it is not less certain that the Conditions of the Mind do mutually affect the Body" than that "the Conditions of the Body do affect the Mind".[2]

In proposition 31 of the *Institutions* Cullen adopted the view that there

---

© John P. Wright 1989

[1] William Cullen, *Institutions of medicine. Part I, Physiology* [1772], 3rd edn. (Edinburgh 1785), prop. 4.

[2] 'Lectures on the institutes of medicine by Dr Cullen, 1770–71': NLS, MS. 3535 (hereafter, 'NLS Cullen'), fols. 25–6. This manuscript appears to be in Cullen's own hand. On "metaphysics", cf. Hume, E. 12–13. For the friendship between Cullen and Hume, see HL i. 163, ii. 449–50.

is an immaterial mind in a living man and that all thinking is a property of this alone. However, he also insisted that this soul or mind (he used the terms interchangeably) is closely connected with "the material and corporeal part" of man, in particular with the nervous system. While he accepted this connection as a fact, "the mode of it we do not understand, nor pretend to explain". He would probably have included questions about *how* mind and body are interconnected among the false metaphysics which he rejected. At the end of his 1770–71 lecture on this proposition Cullen mentioned three philosophico-theological hypotheses about the nature of this connection—the ancient theory of "Physical Influx", the doctrine of "occasional Causes" which he ascribed to Descartes, and the "pre-established Harmonies" theory of Leibniz. However, he said no more about these except that there are "Difficulties" with each (NLS Cullen, fols. 78–9). In his final course of lectures he stressed that none of these systems "have the least effect or influence in explaining anything. They do not either admit of any application in Physic, or in any part of science that I see." The adoption of one or the other only affects "the business of religion".[3]

Cullen had a very different attitude to the questions concerning the relation of mind and body raised by eighteenth-century physiologists, and discussed these at length in his lectures. They concerned the "degree and extent" of the mutual influence of soul and body, no matter what the soul may be. He noted that his predecessor Robert Whytt had "with great strength of argument shown that the Phenomena even of the body itself, cannot be explained, but upon the supposition of a Soul as . . . a sensible principle" (NLM, II, fols. 25–7). Whytt had maintained that all life functions require a soul or mind. In *An essay on the vital and other involuntary motions of animals* he had formulated the issues of physiological metaphysics of his day rather succinctly. He could not

conceive the reason why Physicians have laboured so long in accounting for the action of the heart and other vital motions of animals, from the powers and properties of body independent of the mind: if it be not, that in some, the leaven of Cartesianism still continues to work; in others a too great fondness for mechanical reasoning in Physiological matters; and in both, a contempt of the extravagant flights of *Stahl* and his followers, with regard to the manner in which the mind regulates all the actions of the body.[4]

Whytt was opposed to the Cartesian principles that the vital functions take place independently of the mind, that the essence of the mind is to

---

[3] 'The institutes of medicine by Dr Cullen Oct. 28, 1772' (5 vols.): National Library of Medicine, Bethesda, Md., MS. B4 (hereafter 'NLM'), vol. II, fol. 25.

[4] Robert Whytt, *An essay on the vital and other involuntary motions of animals* (Edinburgh 1751), p. 277. Subsequent quotations are from this first edition except where otherwise indicated.

be conscious, and that the body operates through the same mechanical laws which govern inanimate nature. But he was also opposed to the main alternative—the so-called Stahlian theory, which maintained that the mind controls the body by acting as a "rational" principle (*Essay*, p. 289). Both the Cartesian view and the Stahlian theory were espoused by Whytt's Scottish contemporaries.

In this paper I shall explain the issues concerning the mutual interaction of mind and body which were debated by eighteenth-century Scottish physiologists. Their debates must be understood against the background of a dualism between mental and vital *functions*. This dualism, which we may call *function dualism*, had been clearly set out in Cartesian writings such as the *Description of the human body*, where Descartes rejected the view that the soul or mind is responsible for life processes, and where he limited its functions to those accompanied by self-conscious thought.[5] Such a position was adopted by Hermann Boerhaave, whose thought played an important role in eighteenth-century Scottish physiology. The essential problems posed by the writers we shall look at concern the extent to which the vital processes affect the mind, and the extent to which and manner whereby mental processes, however they arise, affect those vital processes. These problems, though independent, are closely related to the question whether the vital processes can be explained mechanically. But I shall argue that physiologists such as Whytt and Porterfield, who maintained that the life functions require mind or soul, went beyond a bare rejection of mechanism. They conceived of mind and its basic functions of sensation and volition in very different ways from those who subscribed to the basic principles of Cartesian metaphysics, as well as in very different ways from one another.

It may be cause for surprise that major issues in what we should now call philosophy of mind were discussed by medical writers of whom few present-day philosophers have heard. However, I hope to show that our lack of acquaintance may not indicate any lack of profundity in their thought or in the problems they debated. Traditional history of philosophy in addressing the philosophy of mind has perhaps concentrated too narrowly on theological issues which arise from a *substance* dualism. This dualism was also given a seventeenth-century philosophical formulation by Descartes, in his conceptual distinction between two different natures, a thinking and an extended one. But it needs to be

---

[5] *The philosophical writings of Descartes* (hereafter '*PWD*'), trans. J. G. Cottingham and others, vol. 1 (Cambridge 1985), pp. 314–15. Cf. *Passions of the soul*, arts. 4–5 (*PWD*, vol. 1, p. 329). On the Cartesian programme in physiology see T. S. Hall, *History of general physiology*, vol. 1 (Chicago 1975), esp. pp. 256–7, and his translation of René Descartes, *Treatise of man* (Cambridge, Mass. 1972).

carefully distinguished from what I have called *function* dualism. Many who adopted substance dualism (Boerhaave and Haller are obvious examples) hold that there is a one-to-one correspondence between mental events and brain events, however it is to be explained. Nevertheless, the central issues of mid-eighteenth-century philosophy of mind lie elsewhere—in the problems raised by function dualism. Both a more accurate history, and (in so far as our present-day concepts have their roots in that history) a more fruitful philosophy, will result from taking such problems seriously.

By the time Cullen was giving his lectures in the early 1770s, the Edinburgh Medical School was among the most renowned in Europe. He himself had been a student in its early years in the mid to late 1730s. In his clinical lectures of 1785–86 he commented that during his studies he had "learned the system of Boerhaave" and was taught to think that that medical system was "very perfect, complete and sufficient". When he had returned to Edinburgh some twenty years later he "still found the system of Boerhaave prevailing as much as ever".[6] Cullen claimed to reject important parts of Boerhaave's system—for example, the view of the body as a hydraulic machine.[7] He stressed the centrality of the central nervous system in the production of life processes,[8] and tended to think of it as operating on principles analogous to those of static electricity (*Institutions*, props. 125, 130). However, in section V of this paper I shall argue that Cullen adopted a Cartesian conception of mind which was closer to that of Boerhaave than to that of his own immediate predecessors. It is Cullen's analyses of "sensation" and "volition" which provided his solution to the problem of mind-body interaction posed by them.

Although there are good grounds to question Cullen's retrospective claim about the monolithic teaching of physiology among his predecessors, there is no doubt that Boerhaave's doctrines were very important in the Edinburgh curriculum until about 1760. For this reason I begin in the next section with a study of the central principles of Boerhaave's physiological system. In section III, I examine the metaphysical physiology of William Porterfield and its seventeenth-century anti-Cartesian origins. The fourth section is devoted to the ideas of Robert

---

[6] John Thomson, *An account of the life, lectures, and writings of William Cullen, M.D.*, vol. 1 (Edinburgh 1859), pp. 118–19.

[7] NLM, II, fol. 1. Cullen purported to adopt the system of Friedrich Hoffmann, whose *Fundamenta medicinae* was published in 1695. But Cullen exaggerated the extent to which Boerhaave disregarded the nervous system. Indeed, Haller took issue with Boerhaave because he attributed *too much* influence to the nervous power (sect. IV below).

[8] In commenting on proposition 97 of his *Institutions* in 1772, Cullen spoke of the animal power seated in the brain as "the fundamental part of the System without which the Functions cannot long remain". This power was either "a Sentient principle or a Mechanical Energy" (NLM, II, fols. 195–6).

Whytt, the undoubted genius of eighteenth-century Scottish physiology, whose metaphysical ideas are rooted in a very different medical and philosophical tradition from that of Boerhaave. In the final section I examine the synthesis of earlier ideas which was effected by Cullen.

II. BOERHAAVIAN PHYSIOLOGY AT EDINBURGH

While there had been earlier attempts to found a medical school in Edinburgh, it has been traditional to date its beginning from the appointment of four new professors in 1726. Porterfield had been appointed to the first chair in the Institutes and Practice of Medicine in 1724; but while he continued to be an active member of the Royal College of Physicians of Edinburgh, and the Edinburgh Society for the Improvement of Medical Knowledge, there is no evidence that he ever lectured or played any further role in the Medical School. Another earlier appointment was that of Alexander Monro (*primus*) who, as professor of Anatomy, played a fundamental role in the foundation of the faculty.[9] All of these men, including Porterfield, had matriculated in medicine at the University of Leiden between 1718 and 1720, and probably attended the lectures of Boerhaave while they were there.[10] Boerhaave's texts were certainly assigned in Edinburgh in the early 1740s. An advertisement for medical lectures in 1741 announced that Dr Andrew St Clair, professor of the Theory of Physic, would teach "by explaining the *Institutiones medicae* composed by Dr Herman Boerhaave".[11] St Clair had been one of the first professors, so it is possible that Cullen had attended earlier lectures by him, as well as those of the other teachers in the new School.

The topics which interest us are outlined in various propositions of Boerhaave's *Institutiones medicae*. This work underwent a number of editions, beginning in 1708. The numbered propositions often served as little more than a succinct statement of the doctrines developed in Boerhaave's actual lectures. A student's transcription of St Clair's Latin lectures on this work has been preserved and I shall refer to this after examining Boerhaave's own doctrines. These were readily available to students after 1739 with Haller's publication of Boerhaave's lectures.[12] A somewhat free English translation appeared a few years later under the

[9] A. Grant, *The story of the University of Edinburgh*, vol. 1 (London 1884), pp. 298–315, 217–29.
[10] E. A. Underwood, *Boerhaave's men* (Edinburgh 1977), esp. pp. 102ff.
[11] *Scots magazine* 3 (1741), p. 371.
[12] Hermann Boerhaave, *Praelectiones academicae in proprias institutiones rei medicae*, edited with notes by A. von Haller [1739–44], 2nd edn., 6 vols. (Venice 1743–45). Hereafter, '*Praelectiones*': I shall refer to this by volume and page number.

title *Dr. Boerhaave's academical lectures on the theory of physic;*[13] in the following account I shall generally quote from this, supplementing or replacing it where necessary.

Boerhaave's commitment to mechanism in medicine was announced in his *Oratio de usu ratiocinii mechanici in medicina,*[14] delivered in Leiden in 1703, in the third year after his appointment to a lectureship in medicine. He compared the human body to a clock which anyone can see to be faulty, but which can only be corrected by the expert who "from his knowledge of the correct structure, discerns the defects of the parts and the ways and means of repairing them" (*Orations*, p. 111). To the objection that "life, diseases and health derive from non-mechanical principles", since the mind has power over the body, Boerhaave replied that "as soon as the capacity of thinking influences our body, every effect it brings about therein is wholly corporeal, and so subject to mechanical laws". Even if the prime cause were incorporeal, still the physician need only concern himself with corporeal conditions in medicine (p. 114).[15]

The clock image appeared again in Boerhaave's discussion of the natural sources of medical knowledge at the beginning of the *Academical lectures*. He noted that the human body can act as an automaton, and gave a watch as the example of the latter. An automaton is a "Machine that performs various Motions without any other Cause than the Mechanism of its own Parts within itself; which, when once put in Motion, continues so, from the same Cause". The analogy is used to support a view of the animal body as a machine which can operate completely independently, without any cause but the necessary motion of its own inner mechanism. The mainspring in the body is the heart, "which continues its alternate Contractions and Dilations so long as the Animal lives". Boerhaave noted that such motions are independent of the mind: they can be neither produced nor destroyed "by the influence of the Mind or Will" (*Lectures*, 4.1).

The examples of automatic motions which he went on to give indicate that he had in mind a far more complex machine than a clock. In proposition 4 he was primarily concerned with the automatic responses of the body for preserving health and warding off disease. He gave a number of examples of automatic defence mechanisms of the body—which he identified with the Hippocratic *healing power of Nature*.

---

[13] *Dr. Boerhaave's academical lectures on the theory of physic, being ... a translation of his Institutes and explanatory comment*, 5 vols. (London 1752–56). Hereafter, '*Lectures*': propositions themselves will appear as a number alone or with a section number in parentheses (e.g. 401(2)); numbered lecture notes will follow a decimal point.

[14] Translated in *Boerhaave's orations*, trans. E. Kegel-Brinkgreve and A. M. Luyendijk-Elshout (Leiden 1983), 85–120.

[15] Cf. Descartes' *Description of the human body* (*PWD*, vol. 1, p. 315).

When Poison, has been taken, the Animal must inevitably perish, if its Force gets into the Blood ... ; but provident Nature, or this automatic Motion generally does, what every expert Physician ought first to do, i.e. ejects it by Vomit.

Another example used to stress the independence of these defensive motions from the mind is of particular interest. The mind is not

able to suppress these automatic Endeavours of our Machines for Self-preservation. Suppose one Friend tells another that he is only going to threaten him with a Blow upon the Eye, and therefore bids him endeavour not to shut it at the Offer: The Mind is at that Time secure from Danger; but the specious Offer is no sooner made than the Lids of that tender Organ are closed; notwithstanding all the Reasons and Reluctancy of the Mind to the contrary. (*Lectures*, 4.1)

This example had been employed by Descartes in his *Passions of the soul* (sec. 13). It appears that for both thinkers the action of the mind is identified with our conscious effort to keep our eyes open; the action which occurs in spite of our conscious effort is ascribed to the mechanism of the body. Boerhaave stressed that the automatic defence motions of the body are made without any consciousness of the mind (*sine ulla mentis conscientia fiunt*: *Praelectiones*, I, p. 5).

The purely automatic and unconscious action of the body of proposition 4 of the *Institutes* is contrasted in proposition 5 with those actions which arise from an "uneasy Sensation" (*molesta perceptio*) in the mind. Boerhaave stressed that this latter is a principle "quite distinct from that of the automatic Motions of the Body", and that "these Endeavours" to remove a painful sensation "belong to the Mind". But he carefully distinguished these "Endeavours of the Mind for Ease" into two kinds—those which are quite spontaneous, and those which arise from reason and observation. In the first category he places actions such as the rubbing of one's eye to get rid of an itching or the attempt to relieve a muscular pain by trying out different positions of one's body. The second involves a rational observation which determines which of these spontaneous remedies really work. This is regarded as an important source of the art of medicine (*Lectures*, 5.1).

The Cartesian doctrine of soul or mind as essentially conscious—like that of the automatism in a living body—is central to Boerhaave's *Academical lectures*. In proposition 27 of his *Institutes* he asserted that "Man is composed of a Body and Mind, united to each other". He also noted that mind and body have distinct natures. In his lecture he explained that "the essential Nature of the Mind is to be conscious, or to think".[16] For Boerhaave, no less than Descartes, this disjunction does

[16] "*Mentis est, esse conscium sive cogitare*" (*Praelectiones*, I, p. 41). Boerhaave was awarded a doctorate in philosophy for a thesis *De distinctione mentis a corpore* (Leiden 1690). He argued

not indicate a mere tautology. Thought is inherently reflexive: we are not merely aware, but are aware of ourselves as being aware.

Boerhaave wrote that volition (*voluntas*) "is the action of the mind" (*Lectures* 27.6; cf. Descartes, *Passions*, secs. 13, 17). We have already seen that conscious effort played a fundamental role for him in distinguishing the action of the mind from the automatic motions of the body machine. He included volition, along with perception and judgement, as one of the three functions of the mind which constitute its "life", and noted that the life of the mind is nothing but "to be conscious". Later, he describes a voluntary movement (*motus voluntarius*) as one which results from a definition or determination of the mind (*a mente definiente*). He illustrates this by a situation where he has decided to move a limb when the hands of a clock reach a certain position ten minutes hence; this is "certainly a Foresight of something not yet existing: The inclination comes to me (*accedit voluntas*), I will (*volo*), and I define the time". Voluntary action, at least in this case, clearly arises from a conscious effort of the will (*Lectures*, 695.13; *Praelectiones*, VI, pp. 1, 6–7). But while everyone is acquainted with volition, it is what "no one can explain" (*Lectures*, 27.6).

While Boerhaave conceived of the conscious will as a source of motions in the human body, he also thought that the will itself arises from mechanical actions in that body, in particular those arising from changes in the nervous system. He describes the way that external objects, after causing motions in the nerves, transfer those motions to the common sensory in the brain. There they form an idea of the object:

generally this Idea or Representation of the Object excites something more than the bare Representation, which is not a simple Idea or Perception, but a Determination of the Will with respect to the Idea. (*Lectures*, 572.1)

It is in the "sensorium" in the brain where all the nerves terminate that the impressions of external objects "determine the will either to love or hatred" (574.2). Even when we recall a certain idea in obedience to the will, this results from "nothing more than a *mechanical* Disposition or Change" in the common sensory (581; cf. 580 for the context). The only

---

that the mind "excludes the body" on the ground that mind is "conscious to itself of its own thought" and that as such it turns back on itself without being divided; this is impossible in an extended thing (chap. 3). He appealed here to the authority of Gerard de Vries, who had argued against Dutch Cartesians that belief in innate ideas is irreconcilable with the principle that all thought must be conscious (G. Lewis, *Le Problème de l'inconscient et le Cartésianisme* (Paris 1950), pp. 140–41, 170). Boerhaave was closely connected with the Cartesian de Volder (G. A. Lindeboom, *Hermann Boerhaave, the man and his work* (London 1968), p. 24), who held that the mind apprehends itself directly in being conscious (Lewis, pp. 117–18). On Descartes' own view see R. McRae, 'Descartes' definition of thought', in *Cartesian studies*, ed. R. J. Butler (Oxford 1972), 55–70; Lewis, pp. 37–103.

hint of an exception to the complete mechanical determination of our perceptions, judgements, and volitions came when Boerhaave suggested that the thinking of a person engrossed in abstract thought, who becomes totally impervious to the state of his body, gives us some evidence that the mind "may live hereafter without any Commerce with its Body" (27.4). But in general, as Cullen later told his students, the stress throughout Boerhaave's discussion was on the dependence of mental processes, including volition, upon the mechanical changes in the body. Boerhaave insisted that there is "such a reciprocal Connection and Consent between the particular Thoughts and Affections of the Mind and the Body, that a Change in one always produces a Change in the other, and the reverse" (27(4)). In fact, at least from the point of view of medicine, he thought that mechanical changes in the nervous system had priority over changes in the mind. He insisted that the physician did not need to concern himself with the condition of mind of his patient, even in mental disorders, since if the body "is set to rights" the mind "will quickly return to its Office" (27.8).

Given his apparent mechanical determinism, we may well ask about the significance of dualism in Boerhaave's lectures, for, as we have seen, he asserted unequivocally that mind and body are of different natures. In fact, he stressed the difference between sensations on the one hand, and the mechanical changes in the brain and the object which cause the sensation on the other:

The Idea of Pain which we perceive, neither expresses the Burning nor the Dissolution of the Nerve; for there is only one Intelligence given to the Mind of a present Evil, agreeable to the good Will of the Creator. Sensation therefore is nothing either in the Object, or the Nerve affected; but a certain Idea which God had determined or assigned to each particular Change in the corporeal Sensory. (570.7)

It is the fact that these processes are of such a different nature which requires that they be connected by a law established by the Deity. Like Cullen later, Boerhaave briefly outlined the three philosophical theories of the connection of mind and body; but unlike Cullen he opted for one of them, namely the Leibnizian. It is likely, he told his students, that there is "a Harmony establish'd by God, taking it for an infallible Rule, that determinate actions of the Mind must be necessarily attended with corresponding Motions in the Body, and the contrary". But he added that the occasionalist theory was also possible.

However, there is a more important dualism implicit in Boerhaave's lectures which is quite different from his distinction between immediate objects of awareness and the related mechanical changes in the body. This is a dualism between those (brain) processes on which our mental functions depend and those processes on which life itself depends. At the beginning of his section on pathology Boerhaave made a distinction between "animal" or mind-related functions of the body on the one hand, and "vital" and "natural" ones on the other. An animal function is defined as one which has the power of directly changing thoughts or ideas in the mind or being directly changed by the mind. A vital function is one on which life immediately depends: the beating of the heart is the standard example. The natural functions, like digestion and excretion, are required to maintain the body in a continuous state of health. The animal functions have no direct effect on the vital and natural ones, nor do these directly affect the animal ones:

> The vital Actions do not change the Thoughts or Ideas of the Mind; nor, on the other Hand, are those Actions dependent on, or determined by, the Mind: For the Heart continues to act, whether I am sleeping or waking. Nor are the Ideas of the Mind changed from the Exercise of the natural Faculties by which the Aliments are formed into Chyle. . . . (695.11)

Thus we have no sensation of the operation of the muscles involved in our vital and digestive processes,[17] and these neither directly affect, nor can be affected by, the thoughts of the mind.

This dualism of functions depends on the independence of the organs on which the functions depend. In his discussion of the "Action of Muscles" he noted that when the brain is damaged "in such a Manner as to let the Injury extend to the Medulla" then "the actions of all the voluntary Muscles cease instantly, together with all the Senses and Memory". In spite of this, the "spontaneous Motions of the involuntary Muscles" continue in all the "vital Parts". However, these too are destroyed along with the animal functions, when the cerebellum alone is destroyed. Boerhaave stressed that the nerves to the heart arise only from the cerebellum, not from the higher brain (401(2–3), 401.7). He also distinguished the voluntary muscles from the involuntary ones, even those involved in respiration.[18] Indeed, in his discussion of sleep, Boerhaave went so far as to speak of two distinct machines in the bodies of men and animals. One of these "is dead" through much of our lives (that is, whenever we are in a dreamless sleep), while the other continues to function throughout. He stressed the independent operation of these machines, though he also clearly acknowledged the dependence of the former on the latter (590.1).

---

[17] Boerhaave did hold (*Lectures*, 301.6) that when the heart and other visceral muscles become inflamed we feel pain. However, he denied that distinct muscles of the heart were sensible.

[18] Boerhaave distinguished the vital from the voluntary causes of respiration and maintained that the former can override the latter. Two distinct sets of muscles are controlled by two different parts of the brain (*Lectures*, 601ff.).

Boerhaave's separation of animal and vital functions is closely connected with his rejection of the notion of a life soul. In his discussion of pathology he identified the soul or *psyche* as that part of us which thinks (*Praelectiones*, VI, p. 5). He opposed those who have taken into account an "animating Principle" in medicine. In particular, there is no evidence for the existence of an "Archeus" or "cogitative Principle". Thus he sets himself clearly against the immaterial physiological and pathological principles of two earlier medical writers, Jean-Baptiste van Helmont and Georg Stahl (*Lectures*, 697, 697.2).

But at least one phenomenon lay, as it were, in the gap between the two functions which Boerhaave tried to hold separate. We have seen that, for Boerhaave, an essential feature of animal functions is that they take place with consciousness. This was clearly true of voluntary actions, which he located in the brain itself and in certain muscles. But in his *Institutes*, when dealing with muscular action, Boerhaave had written that "while the Will remains undetermined" there is no movement of nervous fluid toward the voluntary muscles, and thus they remain at rest (*Lectures*, 40(14); *Praelectiones*, III, p. 202). He noted that in sleep "none of the voluntary muscles will . . . be brought into action" (*Lectures*, 401.23). However, he also felt compelled to note an anomalous phenomenon which does not easily fit his account. Some actions which originally had their source in the will come to be performed by custom without consciousness. We often walk without thinking about what we are doing; and after we wake up in the morning, we sit up and in doing so place our limbs in that position "to which they have been accustomed through the whole Course of Life, without giving them any sensible Command of the Will". The English translation has Boerhaave claiming that in such cases we operate "from Custom *by the Influence of the Mind*, of which by continued Use we are insensible" (401.24, italics mine); but Boerhaave himself did not say that *the mind* acts insensibly.[19] The translation clearly conflicts with what he says elsewhere. Nevertheless, Boerhaave does seem to have a problem, given his insistence that voluntary muscles operate only under the influence of the will. If the mind must operate in order to effect the motion of voluntary muscles, why not say that in the problematic cases it acts unconsciously? This is what certain of Boerhaave's Scottish critics were quite prepared to say.

I have called Boerhaave's distinction between mental and vital functions "Cartesian". He rejects any vital soul and identifies soul with that part of us which is conscious. This is clearly in accord with the conceptual revolution which Descartes proposed at the beginning of his

---

[19] "*Sunt omnino in corpore musculi voluntarii, qui ex sola consuetudine, injussi & nobis non consciis operantur*", i.e. the voluntary muscles "operate solely from habit, unbidden, and without our consciousness of it" (*Praelectiones*, III, p. 218).

Description of the human body and elsewhere. Boerhaave went on, in accord with the physiological programme which Descartes laid out, to describe bodily processes such as the motion of the heart, as resulting from the mechanism of the parts and as being entirely automatic. Yet it would be wrong simply to call Boerhaave a Cartesian, for his conception of the mind and body differ in certain key respects from that of Descartes. The difference between their theories of mind is not relevant to our present concerns,[20] but it is important for our subsequent discussion to consider briefly Boerhaave's general conception of the body and how it differs from the Cartesian one.

Like Descartes, Boerhaave held that the basic principles operating in the human body were the same as those operative throughout the universe. But Descartes had held that body could be completely characterized by the attribute of extension, and its processes by the mechanical transfer of motion from part to part. In his lecture on *Institutes* prop. 27, Boerhaave adopted the conception of body—then accepted by Locke and Newton, as well as Leibniz—as that which is *impenetrable*, as well as *extended*. Moreover, while he held that the "action" of a body consists in the transfer of motion to another body, he also spoke of all bodies as having a "life". Among those things which constitute the life of bodies he included the force of attraction between the constituent parts. It is commonly said that Boerhaave thought of the body merely as a hydraulic machine; but it is more accurate to say he conceived of the body machine as involving an interaction between the solid elastic vessels and the fluids which were forced through them. The force of elasticity played an important role in his conception of the generation of motion in the living body. Boerhaave described the body as "an Assemblage of small elastic Solids, by whose conjoined and regular Actions, Life and Health are produced". Later he identified elasticity with a "Resistance or Re-action common to all Bodies" (695.2). This force of elasticity is a "universal Principle of Nature", and like the power of gravitation by which planets are attracted towards each other it is not innate in matter itself. It is "to be ascribed only to the Creator of the Universe, who has determined this as a Principle uniting the Parts of Bodies". Boerhaave was clearly drawing on a set of concepts which were richer than those allowed by Cartesian physics.

Boerhaave defined "mechanics" very broadly as the study which teaches one "to apply the general Laws of Motion to all kinds of Bodies" (29.3). The fact that he was willing to allow principles such as elasticity and attraction did not for him constitute any limitation to mechanism.

---

[20] Against Descartes, Boerhaave held that there is *no more* to mind itself than the thought of the present moment (*Lectures*, 581.1); he also rejected Descartes' view that judgement is a function of *will* (586.14).

However, other writers more firmly planted in the Newtonian tradition were concerned to show that the existence of such "active" principles did indicate the limits of mechanism in nature itself.[21]

By Boerhaave's time most writers on the animal economy expressed reservations about the universal application of mechanical principles. However, it is important to consider carefully the exact nature of the limitations which any given author imposed. Boerhaave commented that "they who think that all physical Appearances are to be explained mechanically, are in my Opinion misled" (19.7). When examined in context, this will be seen to be a comment on the limits of our knowledge, not a remark to indicate that other principles operate in things besides mechanical ones. In his lecture on proposition 40 Boerhaave told his students that "there are many, and considerable Motions performed in Nature, of whose Causes we are ignorant; but the Motions themselves are always subject to those universal Laws which appear true in all sensible Bodies" (40.20). He was particularly critical of attempts to apply geometrical principles taken from "Bodies of particular Dispositions" to the explanation of complex organic processes (19.7).

It is, however, misleading to take Boerhaave's declarations of epistemological scepticism too seriously. He did not hesitate to put forward mechanical hypotheses to support his own mechanical view of the operations of the human body. Throughout his lectures he described how the elastic solids which constitute the "vessels" of the body react to the "dilatation" or expansion caused by the fluids which flow into them. This interaction was employed in his explanation of the operation of the heart. Boerhaave thought that all muscular motion results from the motion of a "nervous liquor" or "spirit" which flows from the brain via the nerves, so that it "*dilates*, fills and alters the Membranes of the Fibres [of the muscles], as to reduce them from an *oblong* to a rounder Figure, increasing their smaller Diameter, and diminishing their larger, so as to bring Tendons nearer to each other" (402(7)). Boerhaave thought that there is a constant pressure of nervous fluid in all the muscles of the body keeping them in a constant state of contraction. However, when the muscle of the heart contracts, the flow of blood into the auricles makes them expand and cut off the flow of fluid from the cardiac nerves "which pass into the Heart by the Side of the Aorta and pulmonary Artery". This makes the muscles of the ventricles "paralytic", allowing them to relax and fill up with blood from the auricles. This releases the pressure on the cardiac nerves and allows nervous fluid to flow into the muscles of the ventricles again, causing them to contract and start the process again. The whole system operates in a purely automatic way, depending only

[21] J. P. Wright, 'Matter, mind and active principles in mid eighteenth-century British physiology', *Man and nature* 4 (Edmonton 1985), 17–27.

on a continuous pressure of nervous fluid through the nerves and a constant supply of blood from the vena cava and pulmonary veins (409). We shall see that Robert Whytt presented convincing arguments to show that this mechanism of the operation of the heart muscles will not work.

It is difficult to draw firm conclusions about the teaching of these doctrines in Edinburgh. It would, of course, be wrong to conclude that just because Boerhaave's *Institutes* was used as a text his views were always taught uncritically. Nevertheless there is some reason to think, both from the statements of Cullen and from the rough set of student notes surviving from St Clair's lectures in 1740,[22] that some version of these doctrines was presented in the 1730s and early 1740s. Like Boerhaave, St Clair held that the only explanatory principles for life phenomena are mechanical ones; however, he showed, if anything, more scepticism about our ability to fathom what these are. Part of the note on proposition 4 reads:

The greatest mistake is of those who wish nothing to be considered in medicine except what can be explained mechanically. Nothing indeed should be explained except mechanically, but many things may be considered for which no mechanical explanation can be given and for which we can give no a priori cause. (St Clair, I, pp. 15–16)

This scepticism appears to continue in the lecture on proposition 27, where, instead of giving the essence of body and mind as Boerhaave had done, the view is expressed that "the cleverest philosopher does not know the intimate nature of anything" (p. 79). Nevertheless, though in a rather confused way, Boerhaave's central teaching on these topics emerges in the course of the lecture.

What appears to be a more substantial difference occurs at the beginning of the lecture on proposition 27. At first sight St Clair appears totally opposed to Boerhaave's own central doctrine on the independence of cognitive and vital functions. The manuscript reads: "Mind is part of man himself. If the soul is destroyed, this makes the body lifeless and rigid" (p. 79). It would seem that life processes are being ascribed to some sort of vital soul! However, what follows is a Boerhaavian account which clearly separates the mind from any vital functions:

Let me first overturn the objections of those who argue that the human body without the prop of mind is lifeless and useless. . . . Let such a philosopher order if he can his own heart to move slower or faster. Can he determine the blood through his own body by the power of mind . . . ? From these and many others it is clear that most activities obey the power of mind not at all. (p. 80)

Like Boerhaave, St Clair claimed that "to think is to be conscious" and

[22] 'Praelectiones in Institutiones Boerhavii a Andreo St. Claire M.D.', 3 vols. (1740): RCPE, MS. M9.35–7.

that "thought comes from the mind alone" (p. 81). Earlier he asserted the existence of animal automatism: "Our body can move of its own without the help of mind" (p. 16). He gave a number of examples of automatic defence mechanisms in the body which were supposed to arise merely from the structure of the parts. Hence, the views expressed in these passages are opposed to the remark at the beginning of the lecture on proposition 27. It seems likely that that remark was based on a confusion on the part of the student taking down the note.

But whatever the confusions in the student's notes, the central doctrines of Boerhaave *were* clearly stated—for example, in the *rejection* of the view that the body requires the mind in order to move. It is particularly interesting to find St Clair suggesting that his students should challenge any philosopher who holds this view, to "order, if he can, his own heart to move slower and faster". For, as we shall now see, there was a leading member of the Edinburgh medical community who would have taken such a challenge seriously.

III. PORTERFIELD'S THEORY OF THE PHYSIOLOGICAL MIND

While Boerhaave's theories of mind and body were taught in some form in the Medical School in Edinburgh from the mid-1730s to the early 1740s, it appears that quite a different theory was prevalent in the wider medical community. In his lectures, Cullen referred to Porterfield as the major Scottish proponent of the Stahlian system.[23] Porterfield, who became president of the Royal College of Physicians of Edinburgh in 1748, had been, like many of the professors of the medical faculty, an active participant in the Society for the Improvement of Medical Knowledge which was founded in 1731.[24] Five volumes of papers were promoted by the society between 1733 and 1744. In volumes 3 and 4, Porterfield published his 'Essay concerning the motions of our eyes',[25] which aroused considerable interest both in Scotland and abroad. His theories underwent further refinement in his later *Treatise on the eye*.[26]

[23] "It has crept into France, maintained by Mr Perrault: in England, by Dr Nichols who infected his worthy Father-in Law, Dr Mead with it: into Scotland, by Dr Porterfield, & besides, is tacitly received by many others, many of whom admit it, & at the same time do not know it." (NLS Cullen, fol. 167).

[24] For the history of this society, see R. L. Emerson, 'The Philosophical Society of Edinburgh . . .', *British journal for the history of science* 12 (1979), esp. p. 155; ibid. 14 (1981), esp. pp. 134–5; also S. Shapin, 'Property, patronage, and the politics of science', ibid. 7 (1974), esp. pp. 6–7.

[25] Part I, 'Of their external motions', appeared in *Medical essays and observations*, vol. 3 (Edinburgh 1735), 160–261; Part II, 'Of their internal motions', in vol. 4 (1737), 124–294.

[26] William Porterfield, *A treatise on the eye, the manner and phaenomena of vision*, 2 vols. (London 1759).

Porterfield's comments on the operations of the mind in the body first appeared towards the end of the initial part of the article, in the course of his discussion of the cause of the fact that our two eyes—unlike those of chameleons and other animals—operate together ('Motions of our eyes', I, pp. 163ff.). He began with an account of what he called "the final Cause of this uniform Motion", or, in other words, the ways in which it is advantageous to us. The first advantage is that it results in a stronger, more lively, and perfect image of the object (p. 184). He also argued that uniform motion is *not* necessary to see a single object with two eyes (pp. 192–252).[27] He rejected Berkeley's theory of vision (which relies on an experienced correlation of sight with touch), arguing that we have a kind of immediate knowledge of externality through sight (pp. 229ff.). Nevertheless, his own account of vision is not purely innatist and, like that of Berkeley, takes account of the role of experience.

The most important advantage of the uniform motion of our eyes, according to Porterfield, is in enabling us "to judge with more Certainty of the Distance of Objects" (p. 187). The most common and reliable method of judging distance is by our knowledge of the angle made by the axis of each of our eyes when they focus together on an object in front of us: the smaller the angle made at the convergence of the lines from each eye at the object, the more distant the object. The judgement is made on the basis of our feeling or sensation of the motion of each eye as it focuses inward on the object (p. 189). His account here closely follows that of Malebranche.[28] Like Malebranche, he held that this sensation incorporates a kind of natural judgement of distance.[29] This depends on an innate principle that "Every Point of an Object appears and is seen without the Eye nearly in a straight Line, drawn perpendicularly to the *Retina*, from that Point of it where its Image falls" (p. 208). Porterfield seems to think that it is by employing this principle that we are naturally able to judge the distance of objects by the uniform motions of our eyes. Malebranche had called such judgements "natural" because they are formed "in ourselves, independently of ourselves, and even in spite of ourselves".[30] He ascribed such judgements to God, who makes them just as we would do if we knew all the laws of optics and geometry as well as everything

[27] He argued that this is effected in cross-eyed people in spite of the fact that their two eyes do not focus together. Porterfield correctly opposes Claude Perrault on this.

[28] Nicolas Malebranche, *The search after truth*, trans. T. M. Lennon and P. J. Olscamp (Columbus 1980), pp. 737–8.

[29] "The Judgment we form of the Situation and Distance of visual Objects, depends not on Custom and Experience, but on an original connate and immutable Law, to which our Minds have been subjected from the Time they were first united to our Bodies." (p. 214)

[30] Malebranche, *De la Recherche de la vérité*, ed. G. Rodis-Lewis, in *Oeuvres complètes de Malebranche*, vol. I (Paris 1958), p. 119; cf. p. 99. My translation. For an account of Malebranche's theory of vision see J. P. Wright, *The sceptical realism of David Hume* (Manchester 1983), pp. 66–7, 225.

that was happening in our eyes and brains. Porterfield, on the other hand, does not claim that the natural judgement takes place entirely independently of our will. What I have called his innate principle is not in itself sufficient to allow us to judge the distance of objects. Indeed our judgement of distance by means of the innate principle depends on a voluntary and rational decision to use our eyes together.

This becomes clear when Porterfield turns to "the efficient Cause" of the uniform motion of our eyes at the end of the first part of the essay (pp. 253ff.). "By what Necessity", he asks, does it happen that "both Eyes are always turned the same way, so that none of us are able at pleasure to give them different Directions?" He rejects the ancient theory which attempted to account for this by the union of the two optic nerves, pointing out that these nerves have no connection with the muscles of the eye which are responsible for this motion. The true cause turns out to be nothing but "Custom and Habit", which operate under the direction of the mind. Whatever necessity there is in the action results from the mind itself. For "it is not to be doubted but these Motions are voluntary, and depending upon our Mind, which being a wise Agent, wills them to move uniformly" (p. 255).

There are really two closely related features of this action which lead Porterfield to ascribe it to the mind—that it is learned and that it is useful to us. Like chameleons, human infants "for some Time after Birth, can look different Ways with their Eyes". Moreover, they continue to do so until "discovering the Advantage of directing them the same way, they come to move them always uniformly" (p. 259). Here experience plays a role: infants make a voluntary decision to employ their eyes together after discovering that this results in the ability to determine the distance of objects. In this also, we see the importance of Porterfield's earlier discussion of the "final cause" of the uniform motion of our two eyes; he clearly regarded the action of moving both together as an intentional action adopted for its utility. The infant acts both freely and with some kind of foresight, based on the experienced result of employing both eyes together.

It is due to the repetition of this action that, after a time, most human beings and other animals cannot move their eyes independently: "This uniform Motion by Use and Habit at last becomes so necessary, that the Eyes cannot be moved differently" (p. 259). That there is no "intrinsical Necessity" in this is clear from cross-eyed children who move their eyes separately. The necessity experienced by most of us arises from the fact that "the Mind has imposed upon itself that Law founded upon the Utility and Advantage that arises from this sort of Motion" (pp. 255–6). Later, in *A treatise on the eye*, Porterfield will refer to this as a "moral necessity" (*Treatise*, vol. 2, p. 154).

In the second part of the original essay Porterfield extended this analysis to motions of the body which most would consider to be quite involuntary. Indeed he includes among them one which, as we have seen, Boerhaave and Descartes considered to be directly contrary to the action of the mind.

If a Body be hastily moved towards our Eyes, they will shut without our being conscious thereof; neither is it in our Power to do otherwise, because we have accustomed ourselves to do so on the like Occasions; for such is the Power of Custom and Habit, that many Actions which are no doubt voluntary, and proceed from our Mind, are in certain Circumstances rendered so necessary, as to appear altogether mechanical and independent on our Wills. ('Motions of our eyes', II, pp. 213–14)

Unlike Boerhaave, Porterfield did not think that this action actually *is* mechanical and independent of our wills. He asserts that it is voluntary and directed by the mind. Indeed, Porterfield did not identify voluntary with conscious action. For he acknowledges that we are not conscious of the motions of our eyelids. It is clear that we do not have any consciousness even of an effort of the mind in producing those motions: indeed, what I am conscious of is the contrary effort to keep my eyes open. But Porterfield did not think that my current consciousness of an inability to keep my eyes open shows that the action is not performed by my mind. He thinks that the true action of my mind is the one which results in the closing of my eyelids. This arises from a law which I impose on myself through custom and habit.

The most obvious objection to Porterfield's claim that the closing of the eyelids is voluntary is that we cannot do otherwise. However, he thinks that there is an important sense in which this is just false. There are people "who can keep them open, though the Organs subservient to their Motions are the same as in other Men". He appeals to the case cited in Plempius of Roman gladiators, who, through "uncommon Fortitude and Courage, had not accustomed themselves on every trifling Occasion to shut their Eye-lids for the Defence of their Eyes" (p. 215). This and other examples show that the shutting of the lids is preventable even for the rest of us. In his *Treatise* Porterfield held that in "philosophical Strictness of Speech" a "moral Impossibility" such as that which we find in the case of the closing of our eyelids "is indeed no Necessity or Impossibility at all". Custom still "leaves the Mind at absolute Liberty to do as it pleases". One might as well deny the freedom of an honest man who, having formed a "fixt and determined Resolution of acting always agreeably to what he sees to be fit and right", finds it impossible to "do a dishonest Thing". The impossibility is merely that "it is absurd, mischievous and morally impossible for it to chuse to act . . . foolishly and unreasonably" (*Treatise*, vol. 2, pp. 154–5). Like Boerhaave and the Cartesians, Porterfield thought the shutting of our eyelids contributes to our self-preservation, but he rejected the view of these thinkers that it is automatic—performed by the body without the mind ('Motions of our eyes', II, p. 215). The goal of self-preservation is that of the individual mind itself which freely adopts this way of acting.

It is surprising to discover Porterfield does not even consider the possibility that what is performed through custom and habit is performed mechanically. Descartes, Malebranche, and even Locke, had presented mechanical hypotheses—based on the creation of pathways in the brain—to account for the formation of mental and physical habits. While Boerhaave was troubled by the fact that voluntary muscles can move habitually without the action of the will, he accounted for the associations of ideas on which such habits depend by postulating mechanical connections in the common sensory (*Lectures*, 580.1). Thus he had the basis for the mechanical account of habit developed by his predecessors.

The chief function of custom and habit in Porterfield's explanation of actions such as the uniform motions of our eyes and the shutting of our eyelids was, it seems, that of making them unconscious, and so giving them the appearance of necessity. He wrote that "the Mind, which at first always acted from a Principle of Interest, comes at length to be determined by Habit and Custom, without examining how far such motions may be profitable or hurtful to us, or at least *without being sensible* of any such Examination; and this is the only Reason can be given, why none of us are now able to move our Eyes differently" (pp. 214–15, italics mine). This suggests that even after such actions are performed insensibly they may still involve a rational examination of what is the best motion. Perhaps Porterfield thought that when a hand is thrust in my eyes I make a very quick inference that closing them is the most useful action! In any case, he seems to have recognized that in allowing that the mind could act insensibly he was stepping into philosophically dangerous waters. He knew that "it has been alledged by *Locke* and others, that all the Thoughts and Operations of the Mind, must necessarily be attended with Consciousness", and that this would be thought to tell against his claim that the actions he was describing were performed by the mind. In the article Porterfield did not want to get involved in the "metaphysical Question" of the extent that "Thoughts and Operations of the Mind, may or may not imply Consciousness" (p. 216); though in his later book, he rejected Locke's appeal to direct experience to show that there are times in sleep when the mind is neither "sensible nor active". Porterfield claimed that, while direct experience could not decide the question, there were arguments to show that animals "are always both percipient and active" when asleep.[31] In the essay he limited himself to the claim that "there are Motions unquestionably voluntary and depending on the Mind, which by Custom and Habit have become so easy as to be performed without our Knowledge or Attention" (II, p. 217). While he drew back from his earlier statement that such actions are performed "without our being conscious thereof" (p. 213), it is difficult not to conclude that he is saying the same in different words.[32]

These views about the unconscious operation of the mind are important when, in the second part of the essay, Porterfield spelled out an earlier suggestion that the mind itself is the efficient cause of the vital and natural operations of the body. He argued that, if the mind can think and be "very little conscious" of it as the Cartesians claimed, "I see not why it may not also be allowed to exert its active Power in the Government of the *vital and natural Motions*, without our Knowledge and Attention". When children first learn to walk, "the whole Mind is employed in conducting the Motions necessary for their Progression", so that if they cease to attend to the activity, they will soon fall down. But when these motions come to be performed easily through custom and habit, "they need but little Attention, and allow the Mind to employ its most serious and anxious Thoughts about other Matters" (pp. 226–7). By parity of reasoning, when a baby is born, its soul is totally involved "in regulating and governing the internal Motions, which are yet difficult, by reason it has not yet been much accustomed to them". But when the soul or mind becomes accustomed to performing vital actions such as the beating of the heart, and natural actions such as the digestion of food, it is progressively able to attend to "external Objects". Thus the baby comes to appear "less and less sleepy and unactive". But what is really happening is that the mind, while it continues to perform them, is able to direct its attention away from the vital and natural operations of its own body (pp. 225–6). Thus Porterfield is suggesting that, just as in the case of the habitual actions which were discussed earlier, these latter continue to be produced voluntarily but without any self-conscious awareness.

What Porterfield has noted is a common process by which actions which are self-consciously chosen come to be performed without our conscious control. Such actions, for example of the muscles in walking,

---

[31] *Treatise on the eye*, vol. 2, pp. 156–9. Porterfield argues that it is especially clear that birds, which have to grip branches in the wind, perceive and put forth some active power. While Borelli, in *De motu animalium*, had argued convincingly that the "mechanical Disposition of the Muscles" is used to help them "grasp the Branch more forcibly", it is clear, thinks Porterfield, that these muscles alone are not sufficient to account for the phenomena.

[32] Porterfield confuses the issue in his book by claiming that the mind is conscious while asleep. Robert Whytt had no such hesitancy in admitting that the mind acts unconsciously.

come through custom and habit to be performed without knowledge and attention. His suggestion about the control of the vital and natural operations of the body is based on an extrapolation of the common process to explain a phenomenon to which we do not ordinarily think it applies. The legitimacy of this extrapolation was challenged by later Scottish thinkers.

In support of his hypothesis that the vital operations of the body are voluntary, Porterfield also cited evidence which had been presented a few years earlier in George Cheyne's popular study, *The English malady*. Cheyne had described the case of a Colonel Townshend who had summoned him a few days before death to show that he "could at pleasure suppress all the vital Motions, so as in all Respects to appear dead, and yet by an Effort, or some how, he could come to Life again, and restore these Motions" ('Motions of our eyes', II, p. 222). Cheyne had reported that he and two other physicians, while doubtful that any such thing was possible "as it was not to be accounted for from now *common Principles*", agreed to witness the experiment. After a half hour or so the man's pulse was no longer detectable and they assumed he had carried the experiment too far. However, the pulse did finally become detectable again and the man did regain full consciousness. Cheyne "went away fully satisfy'd as to all the Particulars of this Fact, but confounded and puzled, and not able to form any rational *Scheme* that might account for it".[33] In reporting the case, Porterfield wrote that it is "not at all to be accounted for, without allowing the Mind to preside over the vital Motions" (p. 222). He appears to have considered this case parallel to that of the gladiators who can prevent themselves from closing their eyelids when a hand is thrust in their faces. The unusual case supports the hypothesis that even ordinary heart motion is voluntary.

Porterfield and Cheyne seem to have believed that the Townshend case provided a kind of crucial experiment which challenged the claim of Boerhaave and his followers that the mind cannot affect the vital and natural motions of the body. However, as we have seen from St Clair's lectures, the whole medical establishment was not immediately won over. St Clair challenged physicians like Porterfield and Cheyne to show that they could voluntarily control the beating of their own hearts. They seem never to have taken up the challenge!

Our authors also appealed to the evidence that the vital motions of the body are influenced by the passions of fear, grief, joy, rage, etc. ('Motions of our eyes', II, p. 222; *English malady*, p. 68). Boerhaave had

---

[33] George Cheyne, *The English malady* (London 1733), pp. 307–11. Cheyne was a Scot from Aberdeenshire who had studied medicine in Edinburgh with Archibald Pitcairne, one of the leading figures of European iatro-mechanism. Cheyne went to London in 1702, where, as well as setting up a medical practice, he became a member of the Royal Society.

considered love and hatred to arise in a kind of automatic way from the effect of objects on us. In his pathology he explicitly identified the passions with mechanical changes in the common sensory (*Lectures*, 744.4). This was in accord with the general conception of the passions espoused by Descartes, who regarded the mental aspect of the passion, that is the feeling, as a kind of epiphenomenon.[34] But writers at this time challenged this account and argued that the influence of the passions indicated the effect of the mind on the body.[35]

Porterfield and Cheyne regarded themselves as breaking with the dominant physiological tradition when they presented their accounts of both the nature and extent of the mind's control over the body. At the same time, both writers accepted current mechanical accounts of the bodily processes themselves. Porterfield wrote that "we all know there is nothing in the animal Machine but an Infinity of branching and winding Canals, filled with Liquors of different Natures, going the same perpetual Round" ('Motions of our eyes', II, p. 219). He was repeating the image set out in the introduction of Cheyne's *English malady*. Cheyne told his readers that to understand what he had to say about nervous diseases, they

need only suppose, that the Human Body is a Machin of an infinite Number and Variety of different Channels and Pipes, filled with various and different Liquors and Fluids, perpetually running, glideing, or creeping forward, or returning backward in a constant *Circle*, and sending out little Branches and Outlets, to moisten, nourish, and repair the Experience of living.

Cheyne had even sought to give some satisfaction to "those acquainted with first Philosophy, Natural History, the Laws constantly observed by Bodies in their actions on one another, and the established Relations of Things" (*English malady*, pp. 4ff.). Clearly, like Boerhaave, Cheyne and Porterfield thought that the general laws of mechanics were applicable to organic processes; neither thought that any other laws were required. In order to understand how these writers conceived of the limits of mechanism in explaining organic processes, it is useful to examine how they related their own views to those of two of the most important philosophical systems of the seventeenth and eighteenth centuries, namely Cartesianism and Newtonianism.

Porterfield's clear rejection of Cartesianism emerged through his criticism of Descartes' attempt to give a purely mechanical account of animal reproduction from the mixture of fluids of the male and female of each species. In the formation of an animal, Porterfield wrote, "there is a

---

[34] See *Passions of the soul*, arts. 27, 29 (*PWD*, vol. 1, pp. 338–9).

[35] See the interesting argument in Nicholas Robinson, *A new system of the spleen, vapours, and hypochondriack melancholy* (London 1729), pp. 85–6. This originates with Claude Perrault.

necessity that the Head, Heart, Nerves, Veins and Arteries, should be formed at the same time", not successively, since none of these organs can operate without the others. But this is impossible, "for no Motion of any Fluid or Fluids, howsoever disposed, can ever form all these at the same instant". Porterfield also implicitly criticized the pre-formationist theory which was accepted by most contemporary physiologists.[36] Since, as these thinkers admitted, some "active immaterial Cause" is necessary in the first formation of animals, it is puzzling that "after that, so great Concern should be shewn to reduce all to mere Mechanism". Why not agree that the operations of the living body continue to have "Need of new Impressions from some such vital Principle as first set them a-going" ('Motions of our eyes', II, pp. 219–21)?

Through the use of the expression 'active immaterial Cause' Porterfield placed his own claim that the vital and natural motions of an animal body cannot be explained entirely mechanically in the context of the Newtonian philosophy of his day. He cited (p. 219) a note in *Rohault's System of natural philosophy, illustrated with Dr. Clarke's notes taken mostly out of Sir Isaac Newton's philosophy* (1723), in which Samuel Clarke stated that perpetual motion on purely mechanical principles is impossible. Porterfield argued that there can be no perpetual motion machine, because "there is no avoiding a greater or lesser Degree of Friction, though the Machine be form'd according to the exactest Principles of Geometry and Mechanicks" (p. 218). In making such an appeal he could also have turned directly to the authority of Newton. Newton had claimed in his *Opticks* that the mechanical motion in the universe is "always upon the Decay" owing to the "Tenacity of Fluids, and Attrition of their Parts, and the Weakness of Elasticity in Solids". He concluded that, since

the variety of Motion which we find in the World is always decreasing, there is a necessity of conserving and recruiting it by active Principles, such as are the Cause of Gravity, by which Planets and Comets keep their Motions in the Orbs, and Bodies acquire great Motion in falling; and the cause of Fermentation, by which the Heart and Blood of Animals are kept in perpetual Motion and Heat.

There are "active Principles" in the universe which are required to recruit the constant loss of motion; these principles are identified as being like those which cause perpetual motion in animal bodies.[37] Even more explicitly, in his famous dispute with Leibniz, Newton's spokesman Clarke stated that any sort of increase in motion in nature must arise from "a principle of life and activity".[38] In insisting on the importance of

---

[36] Among them, Boerhaave. See S. A. Roe, *Matter, life and generation* (Cambridge 1981), esp. pp. 1–9.

[37] Sir Isaac Newton, *Opticks* (London 1931), pp. 398–9.

[38] *The Leibniz-Clarke correspondence*, ed. H. G. Alexander (Manchester 1956), p. 112.

non-mechanical active principles in animal bodies, Porterfield was appealing to a doctrine at the heart of Newtonian natural philosophy.

But Porterfield also distanced himself from the form of the Newtonian philosophy which we have seen reflected in Boerhaave. According to this the motions of an animate body depend on the same active principles, for example elasticity, as other inanimate bodies in the universe. Porterfield wrote that

> If it should be said, that these Motions do not depend on Mechanism alone, but on Mechanism join'd with certain active Powers or Forces, imprinted by the Author of Nature upon all the Bodies of this Universe, such as are the Powers of Attraction and Repulsion, by which the greatest Phaenomena of Nature are unquestionably produced; it is incumbent on those who entertain this Opinion, to explain particularly how these Motions are thus continued by these active Principles, before they can expect that we should believe them. (pp. 221–2)

In his later *Treatise*, he took issue with what appears to be a variant of this theory which he ascribed to his great Swiss contemporary, Haller. According to Porterfield, Haller held that the irritability which he had discovered to exist in muscle fibres even after they were cut out of the body, like Newtonian gravitation, results from the stimulus acting as a mere occasional cause of the muscular motion. But Porterfield himself held that "transient and short-lived Motions", such as those excited by stimuli applied to muscles when they are cut out, can be explained purely mechanically (*Treatise*, vol. 2, esp. p. 167). It is only the continued operation of these and other motions *in vivo* which requires the existence of an active principle.

The principle postulated by Porterfield is neither the Deity nor some special active material principle under the Deity: it is the individual mind of the organism which acts continually to keep it going throughout life, and even perhaps, as Cheyne had suggested, was responsible for the first formation of the animal's body. Porterfield presents a specific account of the limits of mechanism. Nothing in his account requires any other physical laws besides mechanical ones. However, he clearly rejected the view, supported by Boerhaave as well as Descartes, that the animal body is an automaton. The processes of that body are not self-maintaining: they require the intervention of an active principle peculiar to it, which, as we have seen earlier, possesses both intelligence and will.

The account of this principle places us in the centre of Porterfield's physiological psychology. For, as we shall see in the next section, the Newtonian ideas about the limits of mechanism and about the necessity for active powers which he adopted could be given an entirely different physiological interpretation. What is central in Porterfield's discussion is his anti-Cartesian view that there is a continuous transition from actions which are consciously chosen to those which are done necessarily and without consciousness. On the Cartesian account such actions were interpreted as undergoing a radical transition from being activities of mind to being purely physical operations of the body machine. For Porterfield, they are considered to have their source in a single principle, the mind itself. Such actions are considered voluntary because they are chosen, at least initially, for their usefulness. We cease to be aware of them because they are performed under the influence of custom and habit. On Porterfield's account, the criteria that an action is under the control of the mind are that it is learned, and that it is originally chosen because of its usefulness.

The anti-Cartesian nature of Porterfield's central ideas is clear from an examination of their roots. Cullen identified Porterfield as a Stahlian, but I have found no evidence in Porterfield's writing of any influence of Stahl himself. On the other hand, some of Porterfield's main ideas are clearly taken directly from an earlier writer, the French physician Claude Perrault.[39] Perrault's ideas, developed in the 1670s, were certainly written against the backdrop of Cartesianism. The close parallel between their arguments reveals that the same concerns which led Perrault to attack Cartesianism in France in the 1670s were still very much alive in Scotland in the 1730s, though in the latter case the philosophical views opposed probably appeared largely within the context of Boerhaave's physiology. Put generally, these include the view that the mind only acts consciously, that the body machine is an automaton, and that the actions of the mind cannot affect the vital and natural operations of the human body. Porterfield, no less than Perrault, directs his theory against these doctrines.[40]

One central doctrine of Perrault does not appear to have been adopted by Porterfield, namely the anti-Cartesian position that the soul is not only located in the brain but is literally spread throughout the nervous system. Indeed, on this issue, Porterfield does adopt the generally accepted view rather than that of Perrault.[41] However, a version of Perrault's position was central in the work of Robert Whytt, to whom I shall now turn. It emerges naturally from his metaphysical commitments and experimental work with animals.

---

[39] Many authors, including Haller, have considered Perrault to be a forerunner of Stahl (W. Hermann, *The theory of Claude Perrault* (London 1973), p. 196).

[40] See my account of Perrault in 'The embodied soul in seventeenth-century French physiology', forthcoming.

[41] For Perrault's view see 'Du toucher', in Claude and Pierre Perrault, *Oeuvres diverses de physique et de mechanique*, vol. 2 (Leiden 1721), pp. 529ff. Stahl apparently located the soul in the brain. His view is contrasted with that of Perrault in Haller's notes to Boerhaave. See *Praelectiones*, III, p. 228, note 3.

IV. WHYTT AND THE SENTIENT PRINCIPLE

Whytt appears to have entered the University of Edinburgh in 1728 (matriculating Feb. 1729) and to have been a student in the fledgling Medical School in the early 1730s. Some of his student notes have survived and show that at least one teacher associated with medical education at that time was critical of Boerhaave's medical philosophy. Part of Whytt's notebook is based on his studies with Dr George Young, an adjunct teacher who practised as a surgeon in the city. Dr John Boswell, who obtained the notebook after Whytt's death, wrote in the front that he and Whytt were fellow students under Young in 1730–31. According to Boswell, Young was "a great Sceptick in medicine (& empirick) as well as in every other thing", and "confin[ed] himself to good evident common sense". But the notes show that Young went beyond scepticism to suggest that there are absolute limits to the application of mechanical laws in the human body, limits which made the sorts of mechanisms postulated by Boerhaave—or Porterfield— quite superfluous. Moreover, his "common sense" appears to have led him to suggest that there are special laws which apply to animal bodies as a result of their being animated by a spiritual being.[42]

Of particular interest for our present purposes are notes entitled 'Of muscular motion' (pp. 431ff.) and 'Of Sensation' (pp. 467ff.). Whytt headed the first 'An Enquiry into the Cause of muscular Motion, from Mr Youngs papers', and it is a reasonable assumption that, since the second note continues many of the same themes and is written in the same style, it too is from Young's papers.

In the first note Young was concerned with the cause of the motion of voluntary muscles. Writers on this agreed that the "free Influx" of appropriate fluids from the arteries and nerves was a necessary condition for this motion (since when they are tied it cannot occur) and that the "voluntary motion of the act of the will is the ultimate cause". They also assume that the will must use "some Instrument to Dilate the muscle", and only disagree as to "what is the Instrument or Instruments" by which this is effected (pp. 431–2). Young runs through the various mechanical and chemical hypotheses of late 17th- and early 18th-century writers, pointing out that none of them could be supported by any evidence of the senses: "the great Boerhaave himself never saw his greater Influx of the animal Spirits by which he accounts for muscular motion" (pp. 434–5).

[42] RCPE, MS. M9.19. George Young (1692–1757) was a member of an important intellectual society in eighteenth-century Edinburgh called the Rankenian club. See M. A. Stewart, 'Berkeley and the Rankenian club', in *George Berkeley: essays and replies*, ed. D. Berman (Dublin 1986), esp. pp. 36–7.

Young did not reject the existence of all mechanisms which cannot be directly perceived by the senses, but he argued that the only basis for postulating such a mechanism is that it is found together with some other phenomenon which we have discovered to be inseparably connected with it in our experience. Thus he considered the objection that his rejection of unobservables would lead to the denial that the blood circulates, since "we cannot trace it through its smallest vessels". Moreover, "how shall we know that the sun shall rise to morrow or any thing e⟨ls⟩e that is future since they are not yet the objects of our senses? are not these sensible things that are Discoverable by our Reason?" (p. 436). His answer was that the existence of these items can be legitimately inferred, only because the relevant "Phaenomena of Bodys are so Inseparably connected that we never see" one without the other (p. 438). Such inferences are not only sufficient "to Direct our Conduct throughout our Life" (p. 439), but for science as well. Thus the reason we know that the blood circulates through the invisible tubes is that "we perceive it to be a piece of the same order which we have formerly seen, where the whole order was perceivable by our senses" (p. 441). This is like the case of tomorrow's sunrise, only more complex. Since we have observed closed systems wherein fluid circulates, we can conclude that without such intermediate vessels the blood which flows to the extremities "could not flow in such a proportion and not return". Unless there were such vessels we would observe the blood "Springing out of the Extremitys" (p. 444). The evidence of our senses allows us to postulate the mechanism. But there is no such evidence where mechanisms are postulated to account for the motion of the muscles.

Young's conclusion is not merely that we don't *know* what the mechanism is to account for the dilation of the fleshy part of the muscle when we exert our wills, but rather that there might very well *be* no hidden mechanism—that is, any phenomenon which is in principle capable of being sensed. He thought that the search for mechanical causes here is like the case where someone who has traced out the mechanical connections of the parts of a watch finally ends up enquiring into the cause of the elasticity of the mainspring. He might form a hypothesis about the general cause of elasticity and "foolishly conclude" that no other is possible (p. 442). The postulation of a cause in this case would be arbitrary, since the phenomenon has no relation to any known thing. But, more importantly, we need to stop our enquiries somewhere and, if we don't stop at the connections we can observe, we shall end up pursuing the "Invisible mechanism In Infinitum" (p. 443). He asked how we know in the case of the spring "that there is some mechanism in it beyond what we see". He agreed that there is some cause of the elasticity, but "how Do we know its a mechanical cause"? Perhaps it is nothing but the "will of God" (p. 445). In the case of the muscle, there is a dilation of the "fleshy Belly" of the muscle which follows on the act of the will. Here he is willing to allow that "there must be something which Dilates the Muscle", but "whether this something be a Phaenomenon that would be perceivable by our senses if more acute or if it be only the act of the will is what we know nothing about. i,e, we know not if there be any mechanicall cause of the Dilatation of the muscle" (p. 447). Those who consider that any observable mechanical cause we give is insufficient, and who always seek another, are really demanding a "mechanicall connection betwixt the Soul (or if you please the will) & a Living body". They are really leading us "to the mechanicall operation of the Spirit of man" (p. 449).

In 'Of Sensation' Young made clear his belief that the scientific demand for causal mechanisms is really no more than the demand that a given correlation be subsumed under a more general law: "To Explain the mechanism of any particular Phaenomenon is to reduce it to some common General Law of Bodies own'd to be such By every Body" (p. 470). Young asked why there need be mechanisms in this sense for all phenomena, for there may be a particular order "only agreeing to two or 3 bodies". The particular laws of nervous action may constitute such an order. We know that when a certain nerve is stimulated in a healthy person such and such a sensation follows. But no one has been able to formulate a more general law of nervous action of which these laws of specific nerves can be seen as an instance, and therefore "it would not be absurd to say that perhaps there is no other mechanism in our sensations". It may be "a particular Law which only agrees to animal bodies while connected with a Spirit" (pp. 467–71).

Hence Young combined a rejection of mechanical explanation with a belief that special laws apply to bodies in virtue of their being animated by an immaterial spirit. These philosophical ideas found fertile soil in the mind of Whytt. But there were, no doubt, other important formative influences on Whytt. He subsequently studied in London, Paris, Leiden (where he is said to have heard the lectures of the then aged Boerhaave), finally receiving his doctorate in Medicine at Rheims in 1736. He returned to Edinburgh, where he began a private practice in 1737.[43]

Whytt seems to have begun lecturing on the institutes of medicine in the mid-1740s after St Clair took ill; he was appointed professor in 1747. It is commonly accepted that he used Boerhaave's *Institutes* as a textbook,[44] but he must have treated central Boerhaavian doctrines in

[43] W. Seller, 'Memoir of the life and writings of Robert Whytt, M.D.', *Transactions of the Royal Society of Edinburgh* 23 (1862); R. K. French, *Robert Whytt, the soul and medicine* (London 1969), chap. 1.
[44] French, *Robert Whytt*, pp. 6–9.

a very critical way. Whytt's *Essay*, published in 1751, contained refutations of many of these doctrines, including Boerhaave's accounts of the automatic operations of the heart and lungs. In the Advertisement there was an extended attack on "the hypothetical method of philosophizing" where "causes are usually assigned, which not only cannot be proved to exist, but which are frequently more intricate and complex than even the effects to be explained from them" (*Essay*, p. vi). It seems likely that many readers would have seen this as a challenge to much of the contemporary physiology, pre-eminently that of Boerhaave. Whytt called Boerhaave's explanation of the mechanical operation of the heart a *"hypothesis"* which, "however ingenious", was quite inadequate (p. 28). He presented a series of arguments to show its inadequacy. We have seen how Boerhaave accounted for the diastolic motion of the heart by supposing that the nervous fluids were cut off by the expansion of the auricles at the end of systole. But Whytt pointed out that not *all* the cardiac nerves do pass between the auricles and arteries as Boerhaave supposed, and therefore the nervous impulse to the heart could not be completely cut off. Even if all the nerves did take that route, the external coats of the auricles and arteries are soft and fleshy, and it is not plausible that the nerves would be compressed to such an extent as to cut off their impulse to the heart. There are no other examples in the body of the kind of temporary paralysis of muscles which Boerhaave postulated and, when nerves are cut off by being tied, their effect returns only gradually—not suddenly, as required by Boerhaave's mechanism for the heart. Whytt gave eight arguments based on anatomical and physiological evidence to show that Boerhaave's hypothesis for the mechanical and automatic operation of the heart just won't work.

On the other hand, in the first edition of his *Essay*, Whytt commended the a priori arguments "proposed with great strength and perspicuity by my ingenious friend Dr. *Porterfield*" to show "that the motion of the heart and circulation of the blood, are altogether inexplicable upon principles purely mechanical" (p. 267). Whytt seems to have been referring to those general arguments based on the impossibility of a perpetual motion machine which Porterfield had borrowed from Clarke and Newton. But, since he claimed to have a general distrust of a priori arguments, Whytt added "a variety of arguments *à posteriori*, chiefly of the analogical kind", which not only show the impossibility of purely mechanical explanations of the vital operations, but also that they are due to "the immediate energy of the mind or sentient principle" (p. 268).

To support the view that there can be no perpetual motion in animal bodies, Whytt first appealed to the experiments of Stephen Hales, indicating that "in every circulation, the blood loses 9/10 of the *momentum* communicated to it by the left ventricle of the heart". From this Whytt inferred the need for some "cause generating motion" within the animal body: "matter, in its own nature inert, is incapable of this". He also appealed to observations of hibernating animals, which "lie in a dead inactive state in the winter" but can be revived again at any time with a slight stimulus of heat which slowly "excites the heart into action". To support the conclusion that this action cannot be explained mechanically, Whytt appealed to the principle that a cause cannot produce an effect greater than itself. There is "some living principle" in these animals, which is capable of generating motion when certain parts of the body, such as the heart, are aroused by some slight stimulus (pp. 268–9).

While Whytt appealed to experience to show that animals generate motion, he also seems to rely on an a priori principle in drawing the conclusion that such motion cannot derive from the body itself. He assumed with Newton, Clarke, and others that all increase of motion must come from *mind*, and that matter itself is inert and passive. There is no doubt that this is a central thesis of Whytt's book. It begins with a motto from Cicero's *Tusculan disputations* which, according to Whytt, shows that some of the ancients believed that all animal motions derive from "the energy of a living principle wholly distinct from the body".[45] In Section XI of Whytt's book there is a passage which suggests that he had been following the recent controversy in Europe surrounding La Mettrie's infamous *L'Homme machine*. Whytt sees a natural progression from the mechanistic principles of Descartes concerning the motions of animals to the dangerous doctrines of La Mettrie concerning man as a machine (pp. 291–2). The latter had been a student of Boerhaave and had produced the French translation of *Praelectiones academicae*.[46] Whytt piously closed his own book with the hope that, by showing that the motions of our bodies "are all to be referred to the active power of an *immaterial* principle", he will have shown how "unjustly the study of Medicine has been accused of leading men into Scepticism and irreligion" (p. 391). Should we not read Whytt's claim that self-movement of animals is due to an immaterial principle as a mere a priori assumption employed to keep medicine theologically respectable?

However, if we do not go beyond this conclusion, we shall miss what is most distinctive in Whytt's physiological metaphysics. When he ascribed self-motion as well as other specific properties of animate nature to the mind, he was giving a positive account of the phenomena he was trying to explain, based on a careful reading of the physiological

---

[45] See *Essay*, p. 266, and Cicero, *Tusculan disputations*, trans. J. E. King (London 1966), pp. 64, 70.

[46] A. Vartanian, *La Mettrie's L'Homme machine* (Princeton 1960), pp. 75ff.

evidence. The key to his analysis of the involuntary motions of animals lies in his claim that they depend upon the mind acting as "a sentient principle" (p. 271 *et passim*). We may question the analogies which he used to draw his conclusion that the mind is involved in the involuntary motions of the body, but in order to understand his theory we need to consider with some care the arguments he employed. The core of his belief that the vital and other involuntary motions of a living body cannot be explained mechanically lay in his observation that such motions rely on the reaction of muscles to a *stimulus*. Whytt held that muscular motion was caused either by the will *or* by a stimulus, and that it is the latter which causes all the involuntary motions.

In Section X Whytt carefully examined the current theories of muscular contraction—those based on the elasticity of the muscle fibres themselves, on the elasticity of the unobservable parts of a nervous fluid, on chemical explosions, on electricity, etc.—and pointed out that the actual reaction of the fibres of living tissue to stimuli is quite different from what such theories would lead one to expect (pp. 229ff.). For example, the alleged spring-like properties of the parts of the muscle or the nervous fluid do not explain why the muscle reacts in so much more violent a way when it is lightly touched with a needle than when it is struck much harder with a blunt object. Why should a spring react in a violent way to acids "any more than the mildest milk, or oil of almonds" (p. 231)? We observe no such reaction in springs large enough for us to see. To those who held that muscular contraction results from a chemical explosion or perhaps from "the peculiar energy of some very subtile ethereal or electrical matter residing in the nerves", Whytt replied that none of these hypotheses explains why the muscles react to certain stimuli and not others. Gunpowder requires fire and "electrical *effluvia*" require a charged object: but neither is necessary for the stimulation of a muscle. It makes no difference "whether the stimulating substances be electrics *per se*, or *non*-electrics" (p. 236). Whytt went on, in the first edition, to attack the view of Haller (as expressed in his notes to Boerhaave) that the spontaneous motion of muscles is due to some latent power in the muscles themselves. In this opening shot in his important dispute with Haller about the cause of muscular movement, Whytt calls this postulation of a latent power "a refuge of ignorance" (p. 239). He clearly thought, at least initially, that his own explanation, unlike that of Haller, was based on a principle of which we all have direct knowledge. Finally, Whytt considered the general view of those who say that the "AUTHOR of nature" has endowed the muscle fibres with some matter superior to ordinary matter. Here alone, Whytt's reply seems to be based purely on a priori considerations, when he argues that to claim that matter "can, of itself, by any modification of its parts, be rendered capable of sensation, or of generating motion, is equally absurd, as to ascribe to it a power of thinking" (pp. 241–2).

Whytt thought that any particular response could be explained by ascribing it to "an active sentient PRINCIPLE animating these fibres". Whytt's sentient principle must be understood as the source of an inherent sensibility in the nerves of the muscles which causes them to react in determinate ways to the stimuli which are applied to them. Whytt thought that this could explain why the application of a stimulus to a bare muscle produces "instead of only one contraction lasting for a considerable time, several contractions and relaxations alternately succeeding each other, which become gradually weaker, and are repeated after longer intervals, as the force of the irritating cause is diminished". When first stimulated, the sentient principle "determines the influence of the nerves" into the muscle fibres "more strongly than usual", in order to remove the pain. However, as the feeling of pain diminishes, the muscle reacts less often; indeed "if by one or two contractions the irritating cause be thrown off, and, together with it, the disagreeable sensation removed, the muscle will return to its former state of rest" (pp. 242–3). Such contractions are not like those of a vibrating body which "performs its vibrations in equal times, whether it be acted upon by a stronger or a weaker force" (p. 247). Thus the particular nature of the response in removing the irritating cause indicates that what is operating is a sensible principle.

In ascribing the response to a sentient principle, Whytt was not merely making the point that the response is generally the most useful one under the circumstances. This was also a common observation among the mechanist writers whom he opposed, and like those writers he held that the involuntary motions of the body could under certain circumstances turn out to be quite harmful (pp. 289–90). Rather, his central point is that the particular nature of the observed response becomes intelligible when it is seen as a reaction to a pain or uneasiness. For example, "if *stimuli* excite the muscles of animals into contraction by acting upon them, rather as sentient than mere mechanical or material organs, it is easy to see, why the mildest aliment is apt to excite vomiting when the coats of the stomach are inflamed" (p. 256). Here the sensibility of the stomach due to the inflammation explains its violent response to the mild food. The muscle reacts in direct response to the feeling. Similarly, the response of a muscle is very different when the feeling is constant from what it is where the contraction of the muscle gives some degree of relief. Thus "the causes which produce the erection of the *penis*, though they be generally excited into action by the *stimulus* of the seed, yet do not act by alternate fits, because the erection has no effect to lessen the stimulating cause". On the other hand, *musculi ejaculatoris seminis* act through alternate contractions and relaxations because through such actions the irritation is gradually relieved. These muscles relax for a moment because each contraction briefly lessens the uneasy sensation of the stimulus (p. 261). In general, we can understand the nature of muscular action if we consider the muscles to be "endued with feeling, and animated by a sentient principle" (p. 369).

Whytt's sentient principle explains animal motions as a direct response to the degree of pain that is felt. His most important contribution to physiology is generally considered to be his work on reflex action. Through careful experimentation he identified the spinal cord as the locus of the reflex in the limbs of the frog, and discovered that there is a period of inhibition after the frog has been decapitated in which this reflex is delayed. But his explanation of this phenomenon may seem to be more remarkable than the phenomenon itself. In his *Physiological essays* (1755) Whytt wrote that "the great pain occasioned by cutting off the head rendered the animal for some time insensible when its toes were wounded". Thus the frog's mind is too preoccupied with the loss of its head to react to the relatively minor pain of its toes being pinched! In support, Whytt appealed to Hippocrates' principle that "a greater pain destroys, in a considerable degree, the feeling of a lesser one".[47]

Whytt collapsed the distinction which Boerhaave had made between the purely automatic motions of the body and those which arise from some "uneasy sensation". For Whytt, *all* muscular motion must be seen as an attempt to get rid of some "pain or uneasy sensation".[48] This was

[47] Whytt, *Physiological essays*, third edn. (Edinburgh 1766), p. 98. See F. Fearing, *Reflex action* (Cambridge, Mass. 1930), pp. 74–83; G. Canguilhem, *La Formation du concept de réflexe aux XVIIe et XVIIIe siècles* (Paris 1977), pp. 101–7 *et passim*.

[48] *Essay*, p. 243. Cf. pp. 288–9, where Whytt also writes of "a disagreeable perception", and likens the sentient principle to the *moral sense* "whence we approve of some actions, and disapprove of others, almost instantly, and without any previous reasoning about their fitness or unfitness". In *Medicine as culture: Edinburgh and the Scottish Enlightenment* (Ph.D., University of London 1984), Christopher Lawrence concludes from this that Whytt "was drawing on the moral philosophy of Hutcheson or his followers to develop a new conception of the body" (p. 232). Lawrence has misunderstood the significance and context of the parallel which Whytt drew. He bases his interpretation on Hutcheson's assertion that desires arise in us to obtain an agreeable sensation when we apprehend a good object, or "to prevent the uneasy Sensation when it is evil" (Francis Hutcheson, *An essay on the nature and conduct of the passions and affections* (London 1728), p. 7). But there is nothing uniquely Hutchesonian about the concept of *uneasy sensation*. We have already seen the basic idea present in Boerhaave under the heading '*molesta perceptio*' (rendered as 'uneasy sensation' in the English translation of the early 1740s). It was Locke who suggested that "the chief if not only spur to Humane Industry and Action is uneasiness" (*Essay*, II. xx. 6). Indeed, Hutcheson was probably criticizing Locke when he wrote *against* those who held that desire is "*Uneasy Sensation upon the Absence of any Good*". According to Hutcheson, "Desire is . . . distinct from *Uneasiness*" (see D. F. Norton, 'Hutcheson's moral realism', *Journal of the history of philosophy* 23 (1985), at p. 401). The same criticism was levelled explicitly against Locke in Carmichael's dictates on pneumatology at Glasgow *c.*1711–12 (see C. M. Shepherd, *Philosophy and science in the arts curriculum of the Scottish universities in the seventeenth century* (Ph.D., University of Edinburgh 1975), p. 134).

The significance of the parallel which Whytt draws between the operation of his own sentient principle and the moral sense lies in the claim that both operate without reason and reflection. The passage occurs in a context where Whytt is rejecting the Stahlian system which maintains

the principle operating when, under normal conditions, the heart contracts in reaction to the stimulus of the returning blood from the veins: the motions of the heart result from the fact that the nerves of the heart muscles are "highly sensible, and the *stimulus* is immediately applied to them" (*Essay*, p. 311). Boerhaave had rejected just this explanation by denying that there is a distinct sensation in the muscles of the heart; he had noted that if the distinct motions of the muscles were accompanied by sensation we would be in constant pain from their continuous operation. There is, in fact, only a general feeling of pain when the tissues of the heart muscle become inflamed (*Lectures*, 301.6). As we have seen, Boerhaave tried to explain the motion of the heart according to purely mechanical principles which operate independently of the mind.

Whytt argued that his own account of these phenomena was superior to that of the mechanists for two reasons: it avoided multiplying causes unnecessarily, and it explained the phenomena in terms of a principle the properties of which are directly experienced. According to Whytt, the mechanists explained the reaction of different organs of the body to stimuli by means of different mechanisms. Thus on grounds of simplicity alone his explanation of all these motions as resulting from variations in the degree of feeling was superior (*Essay*, p. 265; cf. p. 4). Perhaps even more importantly, while the mechanists and materialists ascribed the movement of muscles from a stimulus to a "hidden property of their fibres . . . or other unknown cause", he claimed to show how these movements are "easily and naturally accounted for, from the power and energy of a known sentient PRINCIPLE" (p. 265). While we may lack theoretical knowledge of how the mind affects the body, "we know from experience, that it feels, is endued with sensation, and has a power of moving the body" (p. 276).

Unlike Young, Whytt did not deny that there was some "material cause in the brain, nerves, and muscular fibres" which the mind uses "as its instrument" for putting the muscles in motion. But he did argue that such speculations were unnecessary, in "a science already labouring under too many *hypotheses*" (pp. 325–6).

There was an obvious objection, at least from the point of view of Boerhaavian physiology, to Whytt's claim that sentience is the principle operating in vital and other involuntary motions. For we are commonly *not conscious* either of the stimulus or the "exertion of the mind's power"

that everything occurs in the body through a rational principle. Like the mechanists, Whytt is concerned to establish that basic life processes occur spontaneously. Elsewhere he stressed that moral *actions* must be accompanied with a consciousness of freedom, and that in this respect they are entirely different from the actions from an uneasy sensation which control our vital functions. See p. 287 below.

in producing the response (p. 299). In breathing, for example, we are not ordinarily conscious of the stimulus, though we are sometimes conscious of an effort of the mind in producing the action. (Indeed this action is clearly sometimes voluntary.) In other cases, such as the widening of the pupil of the eye, we can be conscious of the stimulus—the increase in the intensity of the light—but not the effort of the mind in moving the relevant muscles. In the case of the heart, we are not normally conscious of *either* the stimulus *or* the supposed action of the mind in producing the contraction of the muscles. Is not our lack of consciousness a clear indication that these actions are *not* performed by the mind? Whytt tried to answer this in Section X of his *Essay*.

He suggested that our unconsciousness of the stimuli of our vital motions may be due to the fact that we have become habituated to them and that they are relatively gentle (p. 292). Just as we cease to be aware of the impressions of external objects when they become familiar to us, so we become unconscious of those internal stimuli which have affected us since birth. We always have before us a large number of impressions, though most are so lost among stronger and more novel ones "as to escape our attention and memory" (p. 294n.). But we do become conscious of them when they affect us with greater strength than usual. For example, "the sensation arising from the impetuous course of the blood through the pulmonary vessels" (p. 294)—which is, according to Whytt, the stimulus for the motion of the lungs—is normally "very slight as not to be felt or attended to". But it becomes "very perceptible" to a person suffering from an asthmatic attack, when it is "accompanied with the most painful anxiety" (pp. 295–6).

Similarly, Whytt denied that our lack of consciousness of any effort in the production of the action is proof that it is not produced by the mind. He assumed that anyone would agree that a motion which arises from an *idea* must be produced by the mind, and went on to note that such actions are often performed without any consciousness: "As the erection of the *penis* often proceeds from lascivious thoughts, it must be ascribed, in these cases at least, to the mind, notwithstanding our being equally unconscious of her influence exerted here, as in producing the contraction of the heart" (p. 301). Here one is aware of the idea (memory, etc.) which produces the effort of the mind, but not of the effort itself. Whytt also pointed out that the heartbeat can be increased by certain ideas (e.g. a frightening thought). In such a case the mind influences the motion of the heart, but we are not "sensible of its power being directed to that end" (p. 303). Even voluntary motions "are many times performed, when we are insensible of the power of the will exerted in their production"—for example, when one walks while deep in thought, or while talking to another person.

Whytt's claim that the vital motions are performed by an unconscious action of the mind might make one think that he would be quite open to Porterfield's suggestion that these actions are voluntary. In fact, quite the opposite. While, in the first edition of his *Essay* in 1751, Whytt's remarks on Porterfield's theory were all commendatory, he distanced his views from those of Porterfield in the second edition in 1763. One factor may have been Porterfield's own criticism of Whytt in his *Treatise on the eye* in 1759. In 1763 Whytt in turn criticized Porterfield, "a subtile defender of the Stahlian doctrine".[49]

In his first edition Whytt had criticized the view of the Stahlians that the mind acts as "a rational agent" in bringing about the vital and other involuntary motions:

We think it a very clear point, that the mind does not, as Dr. *Stahl* and others would persuade us, preside over, regulate, and continue the vital motions, or, upon extraordinary occasions, exert its power in redoubling them, from any rational views, or from a consciousness that the body's welfare demands her care in these particulars.

He denied that the mind can *rationally* control the heartbeat "when life is endangered by the too violent circulation of the blood". Rational action must take place with consciousness, and, since we have no consciousness of bringing about the vital motions, they cannot be performed with reason. According to Whytt, when one acts rationally one compares different alternatives, and "in consequence of this comparison" makes a certain choice. But the comparison of alternatives is a comparison of *ideas*, and "we cannot but be sensible of the ideas formed within us by the internal operations of our minds". Unlike sensations, ideas exist only as long as we are conscious of them (pp. 285–7).

In his first edition Whytt had briefly dismissed the view that our inability to control the muscles of the heart was due to their having become, like the motion of the eyes, "in a manner necessary through long habit" (p. 286). In the second edition he specifically identified this argument as that of Porterfield.[50] Whytt argued for an essential difference between muscles like those which control the movements of our eyes and those like the heart:

But although custom may enable us to perform some actions with surprising facility and little or no attention, yet it will not render the motions of muscles absolutely involuntary, which were originally voluntary.—There is no instance in the human body of any muscle, whose motion can be fairly proved to have

[49] Whytt, *An essay on the vital and other involuntary motions of animals*, 2nd edn. (Edinburgh 1763), p. 343n.

[50] *Essay* (1763), p. 341, paraphrasing from *Treatise on the eye*, vol. 2, p. 149.

been voluntary in the beginning of life, that has by custom or habit become so far independent on the will, as to be in *no degree* under its immediate controul. (*Essay* (1763), p. 341)

Thus, while I cannot help but move my two eyes together, I still can decide the speed at which to move them, and the direction. I have no such control over the motions of my heart, or the peristaltic motion of my stomach and guts. Thus there is no reason to think that the actions of *these* muscles were originally voluntary.

Whytt also took issue with Porterfield's claim that while there was no physical necessity involved in actions performed by custom and habit, there is a "moral necessity". According to Whytt, morally necessary actions must be sufficiently voluntary to allow one to praise or blame the agent, and in order for this to be legitimate they "must be attended with a consciousness of liberty". This consciousness is lacking in the case of our heartbeat, or the peristaltic motions of our stomach or guts. In his Pathological Lectures Whytt told his students that Porterfield's argument that the mind is not conscious of its volitions in producing such motions was based on a "metaphysical Subterfuge".[51]

But Whytt's chief objection to Porterfield's explanation of our lack of control over the vital motions was based on the fact that there is a much more plausible explanation. Even voluntary muscles come to move involuntarily when their "fibres or nerves are irritated" (*Essay* (1763), p. 342). We find throughout the animal body that stimuli produce involuntary motion through an irritation of their sensitive parts. This is clearly the explanation for the fact that the vital and natural motions of our visceral organs are carried out without any sort of voluntary control.

While Porterfield and Whytt both rejected the Boerhaavian or Cartesian theory which denied that the mind operates in governing the vital and natural operations of the body, their positive accounts are very different. Whytt's view is that the mind

in producing the vital and other involuntary motions, does not act as a rational, but as a sentient principle; which, without reasoning upon the matter, is as necessarily determined by an ungrateful sensation or *stimulus* affecting the organs, to exert its power, in bringing about these motions, as is a balance, while, from mechanical laws, it preponderates to that side where the greatest weight prevails. (*Essay*, p. 289)

Like the mechanists, Whytt held that those motions which take place independently of the conscious will take place necessarily. They follow as a "necessary and immediate consequence of the disagreeable

[51] EUL, MS. Gen. 745D, fol. 4. The lecture notes are bound with notes in the same hand as notes from the midwifery lectures of Thomas Young. The attribution to Whytt is made in the manuscript catalogue, and given the contents this seems to me probable.

perception". Neither the means nor the goal of such actions is chosen by the mind which performs them. Rather, the Deity has so formed the mind-body connection that "in consequence of a *stimulus* affecting any organ, or of an uneasy perception in it" our minds "immediately excite such motions . . . as may be most proper to remove the irritating cause" (p. 288).

Porterfield questioned the significance of ascribing body motions to the "Energy and active Power of the Mind" if those motions occur necessarily.[52] He noted that according to Whytt the vital and natural motions of the body are "altogether involuntary" and are "not subjected to the Will"; that in performing these supposed actions the mind "has no Views, . . . proposes no End, . . . acts without Choice" and "without Preference or Election". Porterfield argued that there is no point in saying that such motions are "*caused by the Mind*" if, in spite of the addition of sentience, they come about "*by a Law* established by the All-wise Creator" (*Treatise*, vol. 2, p. 162).

It is tempting, when one thinks about Porterfield's criticism of Whytt, to conclude that, because he held that the vital motions occur necessarily, there is essentially no difference between his physiological views and those of Boerhaave. In fact, in *a certain respect* Porterfield's physiology is far closer to that of Boerhaave than that of Whytt. As we have seen, Porterfield no less than Boerhaave described the body itself as a hydraulic machine. Whytt, on the other hand, held that one "must not consider the body as an inanimate hydraulic Machine which stops when one pipe is obstructed, but as composed of exquisitely *sensible* tubes".[53] Unlike Porterfield and Boerhaave, Whytt held that the basic principle of animal motion is *feeling*.

The difference between Porterfield's and Whytt's explanations of the motions of animal bodies comes out clearly in their differing accounts of the motions of muscles separated from the brain. In the last section of his *Essay* Whytt had presented a remarkable range of cases describing "the motions observed in the muscles of animals after death, or their separation from the body". He realized that some would think that such phenomena show that muscles operate independently of the soul or sentient principle, but he argued that this is not the case. Since muscles separated from the rest of the body continue to operate in the same way that they do in the body, they "bespeak a feeling, and cannot be explained without it". Unless we assert that feeling is a property of matter we must admit that the sentient principle continues to operate in them (*Essay*, pp. 389–90). Whytt claimed that this is a conclusion supported "by the strongest analogy" (p. 388). But Porterfield argued

---

[52] *Treatise on the eye*, vol. 2, p. 162; cf. Whytt, *Essay*, p. 302.
[53] 'Whytt's clinical lectures 1762–1764': RCPE, MS. Whytt 2, fol. 2. Italics are mine.

that Whytt's account of such motions was less plausible than that of Albrecht von Haller (*Treatise*, vol. 2, pp. 165–6). Indeed, as we have seen, Porterfield himself argued that such transient and short-lived motions could be explained in a purely mechanical way. In the second edition of his *Essay* Whytt responded by pointing out that some of these motions were hardly ephemeral:

> if the motions of a viper's heart for three days after its head has been cut off, and those of the heart of a tortoise for six months after the loss of its brain, may be owing to a mechanical power resulting from their particular structure, why may not the motions of the heart in these as well as all other animals, from the beginning to the end of life, be owing to mechanism *alone*? (*Essay* (1763), p. 431n.)

Whytt argued that there is an inherent inconsistency in a view which demands the voluntary control of vital actions during the lifetime of the organism, but is willing to allow that they can take place purely mechanically after destruction of the brain.

However, as Whytt himself recognized, his own view that the motions of separated muscles are under the control of the sentient principle was not itself without problems. In Section XI he had favoured the hypothesis that "the involuntary motions in man are not owing to a principle distinct from the rational mind", on two grounds—that the motions of voluntary muscles can themselves become involuntary, and that in man it is clearly the same principle which is conscious of thinking and of feeling (pp. 282–5). In general, Whytt favoured the view that the soul is a unity. But, as we have just seen, he also maintained that the soul or living principle does not leave the body immediately after the brain is destroyed and conscious function ceases. Does this not show the independence of the thinking and sentient principles? Moreover, in holding that the soul is responsible for the motions of separated muscles, Whytt implied that it continues to act in spatially discrete nerves. Should he not have concluded that there were different souls in the discrete parts? But Whytt argued that experiments with hibernating animals showed that the soul acts independently in different parts, even though the brain itself is dormant. Moreover, anyone who examines the structure and function of the brain will find implausible the view that the mind occupies a single indivisible point. Whytt cited an impressive list of authorities—including Gassendi, Newton, and Clarke—who held that a single unified soul can exist in extended parts. Just as the Deity can act independently in different parts of space without in any way losing unity or indivisibility, so there can be independent operation of the same unified soul in the scattered parts of animals after death. Any residual problems with this idea he put down to our ignorance of "the nature of an immaterial substance, its manner of existing, and way of acting upon, or being present with the body" (pp. 377–84).

Whytt's view that the motions of separate muscles must be due to a soul or sentient principle took on a special significance in the dispute with Haller, which broke out after the publication of Whytt's *Essay*. Haller supported an even more radical form of automatism than his teacher Boerhaave. In the notes to his edition of Boerhaave, Haller had asserted in opposition to his teacher that "the heart is moved by some unknown cause, which neither depends upon the brain nor the arteries, but lays concealed in the very structure of the heart itself".[54] Like Whytt, Haller held that the motion of the heart was due to the irritability of the heart muscle in response to the return of venous blood.[55] But Haller claimed that irritability is due to a "physical cause which depends upon the arrangement of the ultimate particles" of the animal gluten of the muscles—though he maintained that, like gravity, the actual cause of the motion is not perceivable ('Sensible and irritable parts', p. 692). Like Boerhaave, Haller asserted that there is a mechanical cause of the motion of the heart, though he refused to speculate on its exact nature. He also maintained that there can be no feeling without consciousness (pp. 677–8). But he went further than Boerhaave in maintaining that the basic motion of the heart and other such organs is not only independent of the mind, but also independent of the whole nervous system. Taken in this context, Whytt's view that the vital and other involuntary motions of animals are caused by the sentient principle came to have a twofold significance. On the one hand, it signified the dependence of all motions of muscles on feeling; on the other, it signified the general dependence of such motions on the nervous system. Whytt's dispute with Haller touched on both issues.[56]

Much of the argument on both sides turned on the question of the correct explanation of the motions of muscles which were cut off from the influence of the brain. Haller argued that these depended on the irritability of the muscle fibres due to their own *vis insita*, while Whytt argued that irritability depended on the nervous power which remained in their nerves. Each brought an impressive array of experiments to support his view. Whytt distinguished the metaphysical issues involved from the issue concerning the anatomical source of the living principle.

[54] Albrecht von Haller, 'A dissertation on the sensible and irritable parts of animals', with introduction by Owsei Temkin, *Bulletin of the history of medicine* 4 (1936), at p. 694. This is a reprint of the anonymous English 1755 translation of Haller's *De partibus corporis humani sensilibus et irritabilibus*; the Latin original was published in Gottingen in 1753.

[55] Haller, *First lines of physiology* [1786], reprinted with an introduction by L. King (New York 1955), sec. 103.

[56] For a good recent account of this dispute see F. Duchesneau, *La physiologie des lumières* (The Hague 1982), chap. 6; also French, *Robert Whytt*, chap. 6.

The latter issue can be decided entirely on the basis of experiment. In the last edition of his *Physiological essays* in 1766, Whytt noted that even someone who held that the powers of the nerves are "owing to the particular disposition and arrangement of the matter of which they are composed" could adopt his view on the relation of irritability to sensibility (pp. 244–5). He thought that a good portion of his dispute with Haller could be settled by an agreement that life is due to a single nervous power which can be retained for a limited time in the nerves of the muscles after they are separated from the rest of the body.

Nevertheless it is also true that much of the dispute hung on the differing conceptions of mind adopted by Whytt and Haller. Haller's most important metaphysical challenge to Whytt's view was clearly stated in his 1753 paper *De partibus corporis humani sensilibus et irritabilibus*. He noted that Whytt had "found himself obliged to admit the divisibility of the soul, which he believes to be separable into as many parts as the body". Haller observed that when the intestines were quickly removed from a small animal and cut into four or eight pieces, all moved separately and responded individually to an irritation. He did not think it made sense to maintain, with Whytt, that the soul continues to operate in all of them independently. In general,

The soul is a being which is conscious of itself, represents to itself the body to which it belongs, and by means of that body the whole universe. I am myself, and not another, because that which is called I, is changed by every thing that happens to my body and the parts belonging to it. . . . But a finger cut off from my hand, or a bit of flesh from my leg, has no connexion with me. I am not sensible of any of its changes, they can neither communicate to me idea nor sensation; wherefore it is not inhabited by my soul nor by any part of it; if it was, I should certainly be sensible of its changes. ('Sensible and irritable parts', pp. 677–8)

In this discussion Haller identified self and soul, and denied that there can be activity of soul without consciousness. The soul cannot be operating in the separated muscles of the body as Whytt claimed, for it does not feel the irritation of those muscles.

In response to the first part of Haller's criticism, Whytt repeated his claim that the soul need not be divisible, even though it continues to exist in the scattered parts: an "immaterial substance cannot, like the body, be divided by the anatomical knife, and . . . the indivisibility of the soul does not depend on the unity of that body which it animates, but on its own particular nature" (*Physiological essays*, p. 242). Unfortunately Whytt never really explains the significance of this unity of the soul itself after all conscious functions cease, beyond what he had already set forth in his *Essay*.

In response to the second part of Haller's objection, Whytt made an important distinction between the nature of feeling as it exists in the periphery of the nervous system and as it exists in the brain. He held that it is probable that, even in living animals, the soul is "present every where in the body", and that "there may be some kind of feeling or sensation excited in the nerve itself" which causes the response to a stimulus (p. 155n.). Whytt carefully distinguished the location of "simple sensation" from that of sensation accompanied with consciousness. Thus the soul "can only taste in the tongue, smell in the nose, see in the eyes, hear in the ears, and feel hunger in the stomach". On the other hand, it exercises the power of "reflex consciousness and reason" only in the brain. Consciousness is due to a "reflex act, by which a person knows his thoughts or sensations to be his own". When communication with the brain is cut off, the part of the body can still retain its power of sensation through the peripheral nerves and so react for a time to stimuli. But it is no longer able to communicate that sensation to the brain where it can become conscious (pp. 155–8). In a footnote to the final edition of his *Essay* Whytt referred to the sensation which is retained in the parts of muscles separated from the rest of the nervous system as "*some kind* of feeling or *simple* sensation (such as oysters or other animals of the lowest class, who have no brain are endued with)" (*Essay* (1763), p. 433n.).

The metaphysical issue between Whytt and Haller turns largely on their different conceptions of the soul. For Haller, like Boerhaave, the essence of the soul is to be conscious. For Whytt, the soul is essentially that which gives life to the body and which is only conscious in so far as it performs its operations in the brain. As we have seen, Whytt thought that his contemporaries rejected his view of the soul partly because they still retained Cartesian principles, and partly because they had become too enamoured of mechanical reasoning in physiology. Perhaps Haller's unwillingness actually to give a mechanical account of the *vis insita* blunted the force of the second part of this criticism, but the first remained entirely relevant to their dispute. Whytt rejected that form of Cartesian dualism which maintained that the vital and other involuntary motions of animals are independent of the thinking principle—the view which was most forcefully set out by Haller. In his account of the soul or mind Whytt reaffirmed its essence as the principle of life and maintained the centrality of feeling as the root of all life processes.

V. CULLEN'S GEOGRAPHY OF THE MIND

In 1766, after Whytt's early death, William Cullen resigned his position as professor of Chemistry at the University of Edinburgh, and was appointed professor of the Theory of Medicine. Over the next seven years he gave five year-long courses of lectures on physiology.[57] In 1772 he published his *Institutions of Medicine,* containing only short propositions, which were discussed at length in his lectures. In the latter, Cullen considered the physiological views of a number of his contemporaries, especially Whytt, Haller, and Jerome Gaub. His own views are not always easy to discover, because he employed a sceptical style of reasoning, balancing one contemporary doctrine against another. But, like Hume, Cullen was an *academic* sceptic who used this type of reasoning to reach conclusions which he thought highly *probable.*[58] He provided a dialectical synthesis of his predecessors' views by applying what Hume had called "mental geography" (E. 13)—that is, through a careful analysis of the powers of the mind. It was through such an analysis of sensation and volition, albeit one which rested partly on Cartesian principles, that Cullen showed the extent and nature of the interaction between mind and body.

As I indicated in section I, Cullen regarded this mutual interaction as of major concern to physiology. In what appears to be a supplementary private note on his lectures from the mid-1760s, he wrote that the problem of the action of the mind on the body reduces to the problem "how one State of the body or of one part can affect another part of it". He identified the mental states or faculties as "thought, Intellect & will". The reason they had been generally ascribed to "a Substance very different from our bodies" is that the mechanism by which they are produced "is not ⟨at⟩ all obvious". Nevertheless, he pointed out that they are clearly "inseparable from some conditions in the body". Cullen adopted the doctrine of two substances and their connection espoused by Boerhaave and Haller, who had never been "Suspected of irreligion", but this dualism and the problems connected with it were of little intellectual concern to him. The important problem concerning the influence of mind on body was a problem of how certain states of the brain—namely mental ones—affect those of other organs such as the heart: "This is a problem to the Solution of which we may hope to attain."[59]

Whytt and Porterfield had opposed Boerhaave's view that the essence of mind or soul is to be conscious. It is therefore striking to discover that, in spite of his alleged opposition to the system of Boerhaave, Cullen

[57] Thomson, *Life of Cullen* (note 6 above), vol. 1, p. 458.
[58] On Cullen's recommendation of "the slow consenting Academic Doubt", see J. R. R. Christie, 'Ether and the science of chemistry', in *Conceptions of ether,* ed. G. N. Cantor and M. J. S. Hodge (Cambridge 1981), esp. p. 92. Christie ties this academic scepticism with that of Hume, stressing the importance of a cautious acceptance of hypotheses—especially that of the aether—for both thinkers.
[59] 'Lectures on physiology': RCPE, MS. Cullen 16(1), preliminary folios.

followed him in holding that consciousness characterizes what is mental. This is clear from his analysis of the concept of *sensation*. In his lectures in the fall of 1770, Cullen said he followed Hume in distinguishing sensations from *ideas*—that is, from the thought of "an Object absent arising from Reminiscence". A sensation is a thought which arises directly from an "external Impression or certain other Changes in the Body". Cullen went beyond Hume (and Whytt) in carefully distinguishing sensations from impressions—that is, from the motions in the body which are their causes.[60] Cullen defined "sensation" in general as "the Mind's being *conscious* of any changes in the State of the body, or more nearly of the Nervous System" (fols. 89–90, my italics). In proposition 49 of his *Institutions* he asserted (with Haller) that the mind can have or attend to only one sensation at a time, thus rejecting Whytt's suggestion that the mind can have a number of unconscious sensations at any given moment. Finally, in his 1770 lecture on proposition 122, he stated plainly that "to say there is Sensation without Consciousness is to me almost a Contradiction in Terms" (fol. 160).

Unlike Whytt, Cullen held that processes of the body can take place purely automatically—that is, without being accompanied by any mental state. Herein we see the significance of his distinction between sensations and impressions. In proposition 80 he asserted that "certain impressions and certain states of the body . . . may . . . act on the nervous system without producing any sensation"; and in proposition 122, that "many impressions have their affects without sensation and volition". Indeed he held that fundamentally our vital and natural motions are of this nature. In proposition 119 he maintained that "the motions of the heart and arteries, of the organs of respiration, of the stomach, intestines and perhaps other parts" are caused by "certain internal impressions . . . which produce no sensation, nor motions of which we are conscious except when exercised in an unusual manner".[61] Cullen did accept Whytt's view (opposed to Haller) that the motions of muscles are always

---

[60] After distinguishing sensations from ideas, Cullen wrote: "In this point I follow David Hume; he indeed uses the Term *Impression* instead of *Sensation*, but I employ *Impression* in another place I think more properly, nor would Impression convey the whole meaning of Sensation, but only as far as it arises from the body." (NLS Cullen, fol. 80). On Whytt's interchangeable use of 'impression' and 'sensation' see sect. IV above.

[61] In an article which is widely referred to ('The nervous system and society in the Scottish Enlightenment', in *Natural order: historical studies of scientific culture*, ed. B. Barnes and S. Shapin (Beverly Hills 1979), 19–40), C. Lawrence cites this passage to support the conclusion that Cullen "retained all the characteristics of Whytt's sentient principle—purposeful action, coordinating ability, and, *most importantly, unconscious feeling*—without introducing second substances into physiology" (p. 26, my italics). I can see how this passage could be read as Lawrence reads it when taken out of the context of the rest of the *Institutions*, but I cannot see how it can be so read in the context of propositions 80, 122, and numerous comments in the lecture notes. For reasons set out in the last section I also consider quite misleading Lawrence's view that *Whytt* thought the vital motions are carried out through any "purposeful action".

due to some form of nervous power, and he stressed that in the living body they require a constant energy from the brain (props. 96, 97).[62] However, he drew an entirely different metaphysical conclusion from Whytt's. For Cullen, the fact that "some of the Functions of our System can be performed without Sensation or Volition" gives "a strong Proof of the Brain's being a Mechanical Organ" (NLS Cullen, fol. 146; cf. *Institutions*, prop. 116).

In proposition 122 Cullen balanced this against the claim that the mechanism of the brain is insufficient "without being united with a sentient principle or mind that is constantly present in the living System". He argued for this partly on epistemological grounds, because "the mechanism of the brain suited to its several functions is not at all perceived". Unlike Boerhaave, Cullen did not think that mental states are, for practical purposes, reducible to their mechanical causes. But he also gave a more positive reason: very few of the functions of the brain are "carried out without sensation and volition" (prop. 122). Here he appears to agree with Whytt's claim that the sentient principle operates throughout the body. We need to consider how this is reconcilable with Cullen's assertions about vital and natural motions which we considered in the last paragraph.

While Cullen appealed to the authority of Whytt in support of a sentient principle, he took issue with Whytt's view that sensation takes place in the peripheral nervous system, apart from the brain itself (NLM, II, fol. 243). But their different accounts of the operation of the sentient principle go deeper than that. Since Cullen identified mental functions with conscious ones, he held that basic life functions can go on independently of the mind. At the same time he criticized Whytt for holding with Boerhaave that our visceral functions are carried on with an absolute necessity,[63] without any kind of influence by the conscious mind. For Cullen, the sentient principle influences our basic life functions, but as an independently identifiable principle whose effects on those functions can be determined by experience. While he began from a basic acceptance of what I earlier called function dualism, Cullen asked himself just how those states of the nervous system which are mental interact with those on which our basic life functions depend.

Cullen regularly returned to what he called the "Stahlian contro-

---

[62] Cullen seems to adopt the position suggested by Whytt in the last edition of the *Physiological essays*, discussed in section IV above.

[63] "But to understand Boerhave you must observe this Application of these Doctrines to his System in his Definition of Disease, where he says the Consideration of the Mind is to be neglected. . . . He explains this still more particularly . . . where he expressly says Omne hoc pendet &c.——mechanica dispositio. . . . I join with Boerhave, Dr Whytt, who after taking much pains in his Vital Functions, to prove the Existence of a Sentient Principle . . . thinks that all our Motions are directed by a Physical Necessity." (NLS Cullen, fol. 76).

versy"—the question whether the mind voluntarily directs the vital and natural motions of the body. At the beginning of his lectures on the nervous system, he said he was following Gaub in subscribing to a compromise between the view of Boerhaave and Whytt on the one hand and that of the Stahlians on the other.[64] To understand this we must examine his mental geography of volition—that is, his account of the extent and manner in which the mind can be said to have control over our bodies.

In proposition 119, Cullen listed seven causes of the action of the brain in bringing about changes in the body, five of which are said to be "modes of volition" (NLM, III, fol. 49). These include the operation of the will in performing voluntary actions, the passions, imitation, appetites directed to external objects, and propensities to remove an uneasy sensation. In arguing that "some Volition is concerned" in the last of these, Cullen gave an idea of just what he meant by 'volition'. A typical case of a propensity which arises from an "uneasy sensation" is the voiding of urine and faeces. In such cases the relevant motions "can often be prevented by another volition presenting itself", and we can put forward greater or less effort in exercising them (*Institutions*, 119.5).

The Excretion of Urine is often very urgent, yet a Lady in company with men will restrain this Propensity; neither will a well bred Man expel wind by the Anus in company with Ladies; he can restrain it. . . . [A] Man in going to Stool . . . in pressing out Faeces . . . holds his Breath in order to give a greater Effort, & if it is still more difficult, he grins most horridly. (NLS Cullen, fol. 152)

The number of muscles which come into play is determined by the degree of effort which is put forth (NLM, II, fols. 271–2). While Cullen did not deny that motions from an uneasy sensation are sometimes caused without any volition—that is, without the ability to do otherwise or to put out greater or less effort—the paradigm is those in which some volition is involved. In contrast, we should remember that Whytt postulated a sentient principle to explain those involuntary motions of the body which, according to him, were necessarily determined by the uneasy sensation.

Volitions, in Cullen's wide sense, constantly affect our vital functions. While the basic motions of my heart and lungs are carried out purely mechanically, they are constantly affected by my passions, i.e. "more general and vehement volitions" (*Institutions*, 119.2). There is "nothing more evident than that the passions of the mind affect the motion of the

---

[64] NLS Cullen, fols. 76–7. For Gaub's views on mind and body see L. J. Rather, *Mind and body in eighteenth-century medicine* (Berkeley 1965). Rather stresses the difference between Gaub's view of the passions and that of Descartes. For Gaub, like Porterfield and Cheyne, they are actions of the mind. This view seems to be shared by Cullen.

heart"—for example, anger will produce a violent beating of the heart and grief will slow it down (NLM, II, fol. 274). Though Cullen considered the passions to be "modifications of the will", he noted that they are generally instinctive in so far as they arise directly in response to a certain sensation. When we are angry, even the outward motions of our bodies often arise without our having much awareness of them. However, Cullen also stressed that when our passions are not too violent we have some degree of conscious control over the relevant motions.

But it is not only those volitions which are essentially instinctive which affect our vital motions; some are also constantly affected by what are clearly voluntary actions. Cullen wrote that "there is no proof of any one muscle of the body being more under the power of the will, than the action of respiration" (NLM, II, fol. 273). The rate and manner of my breathing is affected by a number of my voluntary actions, including talking. Does this not mean that Cullen followed Porterfield and the Stahlians in holding that we have voluntary control over the vital and natural motions of our bodies?

Cullen's mental geography of the will consisted of two elements, both basically Cartesian. First, he held that the will is a mode of thought and that what we will is only that which we are immediately conscious of willing.[65] In bodily motions subjected to the will "the Mind only wills an End. . . . We know nothing of the particular muscles put in action. When I bend my arm, I commonly only attend to the contraction of the Biceps, but Winslow has shewn that many other Muscles partake in that Action" (NLS Cullen, fol. 161: cf. *Institutions*, prop. 119.1). Cullen denies that we have anything but a very limited and general consciousness of the parts of our bodies moved, and draws the conclusion that we will only the general movements of a limb or muscle.

Related to this is his second Cartesian principle, that "in the moral Administration of the System only a general end or purpose is in view, & *the Almighty Creator has connected certain Motions with the Volition of these Ends*" (NLS Cullen, fol. 161; my italics). Thus there are certain motions of our body naturally or originally connected with the willing of certain general goals or purposes. To take Descartes' own example, "if we want to adjust our eyes to look at a far-distant object, this volition causes the pupils to grow larger" (*PWD*, vol. 1, p. 344). I cannot directly will the bodily motions, but only certain general conscious aims to which they are *naturally joined*. Both Descartes and Cullen held that through custom and habit these original connections of ideas and bodily motions

[65] For Descartes' view see *PWD*, vol. 2, p. 113, Def. 1. This new translation of Descartes' works unhelpfully translates the Latin *'immediate conscii sumus'* by 'we are immediately aware'. As McRae and Rodis-Lewis (note 16 above) show, Descartes was using *'conscii'* in a new and important way which became fundamental in modern philosophy.

could be changed so that the willing of a quite different idea could bring about the relevant bodily change.

From these two principles Cullen concluded that, while my passions or even my voluntary actions affect the vital motions, it is not in the way that the Stahlians thought. In general, we do not directly will the motions of individual muscles, nor do we have any distinct consciousness of bodily sensations. While he accepted Porterfield's and Perrault's claim that the uniform motion of our eyes was originally voluntary (NLM, II, fols. 101–11; cf. *Institutions*, prop. 55), he did not accept that certain motions of muscles were chosen over others in order to achieve the goal of forming a distinct image of the object. Rather, it was merely by willing the general end of seeing objects distinctly that the motions of the muscles became uniform. Moreover, most of us have, through custom and habit, come to perform this action completely without consciousness, and hence the mind is no longer involved in it (NLS Cullen, fol. 153).

Cullen held that many motions which we may consider to be involuntary, including vital and natural ones, are not entirely so. But he showed exactly how such motions can be a matter of voluntary and rational choice. In his 1772 lecture on proposition 119, Cullen told his students that he differed from other physiologists with regard to "the extent of the powers of the mind or with regard to the manner of acting". He distinguished the question whether the visceral motions are affected by the mind from the question whether they are "directed" by the mind. Consideration of the passions and unintended effects of voluntary actions shows that the motions of our internal organs are constantly affected by the mind. However, like Porterfield and Cheyne, Cullen held that vital motions such as those of the heart can be "directed by the mind", though for him it is only *"in one limited sense"* (NLM, II, fol. 287). The mind controls the body through conscious rational choice. The question is how, through conscious choice of a certain means to end relation, we might be able to control the motion of our heart and other internal organs.

Cullen maintained that when we are calm we have some control over our passions through imagination, and that in so far as the passions are voluntary both these and the internal motions of our bodies are also under our control. Clearly, we can under certain circumstances control our passions by directing our thoughts in a certain way—that is, by choosing to think of certain objects with which our passions are naturally joined. We have "a power whereby we can recall these objects that give us anger or fear". Cullen recalled that

There is a famous instance of Colonel Townshend by Dr. Cheyne who stopped his heart at pleasure and died when he thot proper. I can explain it. . . . By recollecting an object of fear we can diminish its action, and [by some such way as this] Colonel Townshend had power over his heart. So have no doubt that we can by recalling one or other of these passions make it voluntary, and if you will a certain end, it has the power of exciting a variety of actions and combining these together, at the same time the heart.

Thus the mind *can* control the motion of the heart. Cullen's idea is that Townshend was able to do it, not by directly desiring that his heartbeat should decrease in frequency, but rather by calling up certain thoughts which have that result. He suggested that perhaps "that power might have been greater and ⟨been⟩ destroyed by repetition". Apparently he thought that many of us have lost the power of controlling our passions and the related motions of our bodies by calling up certain ideas. He concluded that "the heart itself is not clearly separated by the voluntary motions in a certain view of it" (NLM, II, fols. 273–5).

This clearly does not mean that Cullen sided with Porterfield and the Stahlians on either the manner or the extent of the mind's control over the body. He limited such control to our conscious choice, and while, apart from such choice, the motions of the body are affected by the mind, they are not voluntary. Earlier Cullen did consider the possibility that all actions of our internal organs may originally have been voluntary like the motions of our eyes, and only became automatic through custom and habit; but he argued that this is improbable, given that in adults an internal organ can react to new stimuli without their being in any way conscious of it or requiring any process of habituation. Moreover, the kind of control which Cullen envisioned over our internal organs is only of the most general kind—not involving a choice of the operation of specific muscles. This is essentially what was proposed in section 45 of Descartes' *Passions of the Soul*:

Our passions, too, cannot be directly aroused or suppressed by the action of our will, but only indirectly through the representation of things which are usually joined with the passions we wish to have and opposed to the passions we wish to reject. For example, in order to arouse boldness and suppress fear in ourselves, it is not sufficient to have the volition to do so. We must apply ourselves to consider the reasons, objects, or precedents which persuade us that the danger is not great. (*PWD*, vol. 1, p. 345)

Descartes himself had recognized the importance of such control of our passions for health and disease in his correspondence with Princess Elizabeth.[66] But both Cullen and Descartes, because they limit the

[66] Descartes to Elizabeth, May or June 1645, *Oeuvres de Descartes*, vol. 4, pp. 218–22. Theodore Brown, in 'Descartes, dualism, and psychosomatic medicine' (in *The anatomy of madness*, ed. W. F. Bynum and others, vol. 1 (London 1985), at p. 52), implies that Descartes cannot consistently hold that the mind can affect the passions. Brown is certainly correct that Descartes considered the passions themselves to arise directly from somatic states, but it is also consistent with the central principles of his philosophy that Descartes gives the mind an *indirect* control over the passions.

mind's operations to those of which we are conscious, have a more limited conception of the mind's control over the body than did Porterfield, Perrault, and the Stahlians.[67]

Still, we may want to ask whether, in admitting that the mind can act independently of sensation in voluntary action (NLS Cullen, fol. 78), Cullen was not allowing with Porterfield and Whytt that it has special *active powers* not possessed by inanimate matter. Indeed, at the beginning of his 1772–73 lectures Cullen said that he did not want to deny that "the soul has a power of beginning motion" (NLM, II, fol. 35). He later noted that "Causes that in no part of nature have any tendency to excite motion—but rather diminish it . . . are frequent Causes of it in animal bodies" (fol. 280). (He claimed that when a depressant drug such as opium is given, sometimes the brain is excited instead of relaxed by it.) He regarded the healing power of nature itself as a kind of active power in the animal economy (fol. 276–80). Nevertheless, there are good indications that Cullen thought that such properties resulted from a certain kind of matter, not from a substance entirely immaterial.[68] While he was very cautious in putting forward a theory of animal electricity, he admitted that his important neurophysiological concepts of "excitement and collapse" first occurred to him when he was formulating a "Theory" from "an Analogy I observed in the Phaenomena of electricity" (NLS Cullen, fol. 185). There is reason to think that, like Hume, Cullen asked himself whether "it is more difficult to conceive that motion may arise from impulse than that it may arise from volition?" (E. 73). And like Hume, he appears to have answered by speculating on the possibility of an active matter.[69]

In general, we can conclude that Cullen provided a solution—within the context of a Cartesian metaphysic—to the function dualism which we found so clearly expressed in Boerhaave. Like Boerhaave, Cullen

[67] It is tempting to think of Cullen's account as providing an explanation for a crude form of what today we would call "biofeedback". But for Cullen, like Boerhaave, we never have anything but a general sensation of the motions of the heart and other internal organs. Modern biofeedback phenomena appear to require continuous information about very specific changes in the condition of the body (G. Jones, *Visceral learning* (New York 1973)). Moreover, it is difficult to see how such phenomena could be explained on Cullen's Cartesian model of the will, which is based on the notion of an original correlation between the willed idea and the body motions.

[68] In stating the point in this way I have in mind Cullen's discussion in his lectures on the history of chemistry: "Aether and Inert matter are hence supposed to be the only matters in nature" (RCPE, MS. Cullen 10(1), fol. 87).

[69] On Hume's comments on the aether hypothesis see my *Sceptical realism of David Hume* (note 30 above), pp. 145, 161ff.; also Christie, in *Conceptions of ether* (note 58 above). In his 1772–73 physiology lectures Cullen became very defensive about his claims regarding animal electricity (NLM, III, fols. 15–19), probably in response to the attack on his student G. R. Brown's dissertation in the article on *Aether* in the first edition of the *Encyclopaedia Britannica*. See R. K. French, 'Aether and physiology', in *Conceptions of ether*, at p. 118.

maintained that the basic life functions are carried out independently of the mind. He argued that in one sense the visceral organs are constantly influenced by the mind, though their activity is not voluntarily willed; this influence is clearest in the case of the passions. But Cullen also argued that to a limited degree our corporeal functions can be voluntarily controlled by the mind—that is, by imagining certain objects which are naturally and habitually conjoined with our passions. Thus, while Cullen held that there is a basic dualism between mental functions on the one hand and vital and natural ones on the other, he also showed the nature of the causal relation between them. This causal interaction cannot, according to Cullen, be described in mechanical terms, since descriptions of mental processes are not in practice reducible to physical ones.[70] Thus, in Cullen's physiology, unlike that of Boerhaave, it was essential to discuss the conditions of mind conducive to life and health.[71]

Department of Philosophy
University of Windsor

[70] But such a reduction appears to be possible in principle. In his 1770 lectures, Cullen wrote against the Stahlians that "the force of impression is every where absolute; & it is according to the force of impression, and other mechanical conditions of the System, that the motions excited prove either salutary or pernicious" (NLS Cullen, fols. 159–60).

[71] This paper was written in 1986–87 while I was a visiting member of the Institute for Advanced Study (Princeton) and received a Grant-in-Aid from the Institute. I am grateful to my colleagues in the School of Historical Studies—especially to Professor Morton White—for their support. I am indebted to Roger Emerson, Ed Reed, M. A. Stewart, Paul Wood, and John Yolton for comments on an earlier draft, to Teresa Saunders for her help with translations from Latin, and to the owners of manuscripts quoted for permission to cite from the materials in their possession.

REVIEWS

Scepticism and reasonable doubt: the British naturalist tradition in Wilkins, Hume, Reid, and Newman
By M. JAMIE FERREIRA
Oxford: Clarendon Press, 1986. xii + 255 pp.

Reviewed by JOHN W. YOLTON

The subtitle of Professor Ferreira's book is explained in the opening sentence of the Preface: "Historically one of the ways in which people have attempted to counter scepticism has been by appeal to 'the make and temper of human nature', 'the laws of the mind', or 'the common voice of mankind'. These are all appeals to 'the natural'—to how we are constituted, to what we, as human beings, are and do in the arena of believing." In her 'Concluding applications', Professor Ferreira explains that she has worked with a distinction between "three main types of naturalism": sceptical, reasonable doubt, and justifying naturalism. The first type, usually "attributed to Hume, offers merely the counter-description of unavoidability of natural beliefs with no challenge to the sceptic's requirements, and so remains distinctively sceptical" (p. 234). The other two types of naturalism are anti-sceptical because they offer a challenge to the sceptic's requirements for justification. Reasonable doubt naturalism draws a distinction between reasonable and unreasonable doubt; it argues that "there is no reasonable ground for doubting fundamental beliefs of human nature". The third type seeks to justify beliefs, using a different model of justification from the stringent one demanded by the sceptic (p. 235).

Professor Ferreira's book is about scepticism and belief. It is informed by some recent discussions (e.g. articles by Unger and Lehrer in the Pappas and Swain collection), but essentially it is historically oriented. There is some question as to whether contemporary formulations of scepticism and justification have not influenced unduly her reading of historical texts, but on the whole, I find her analyses of the four writers mentioned in her subtitle accurate. Reid is the centre-piece of this study, receiving three chapters of attention. Newman is given about the same amount of space, but the influence of Reid on him highlights again the importance historically of Reid's account. Bishop Wilkins figures in

Professor Ferreira's analyses in part because he represents an earlier attitude toward knowledge and belief, an attitude which Professor Ferreira thinks was interrupted by Locke: the reliance upon the concept of moral certainty, where reasonable doubt is eliminated. Professor Ferreira picks up Hume's charge (in the *Treatise* and the first *Enquiry*) that Locke only recognized knowledge and probability, allowing for no third alternative. In between knowledge and probability, Professor Ferreira argues, Hume inserted *proof*, "such arguments from experience as leave no room for doubt or opposition" (E. 56n.). Hume's "proofs" were akin to the earlier "moral certainty", Professor Ferreira suggests.

Hume's use of the word 'proof' for what we learn from experience is curious, since it was a term usually applied to mathematical demonstrations, although there was another use of the term in law. The fact that Locke also used the same word in a quite different sense—"Those intervening *Ideas*, which serve to shew the Agreement of any two others" (*Essay*, IV. ii. 3)—leaves Hume's use of that term even more curious. A quick check of Chambers' *Cyclopaedia* (1728) and Johnson's *Dictionary* (1755) does not shed any light on Hume's sense of 'proof', meaning experience-based certainty. Nor does there seem to be any entry in the *Oxford English Dictionary* that quite matches Hume's use. The first edition of the *Encyclopaedia Britannica* (1768) gives only 'proof in law', i.e. the mechanism or argument used to evince the truth of anything. It would be interesting to know more about the background for Hume's use of this word.[1]

Arguments or proofs from experience are, of course, those based on cause and effect, on regular uniformities. Not all such experiences constitute *proof* for Hume: only those such as "fire burns", "water suffocates", "motion is produced by impulse and gravity", instances where "the past has been entirely regular and uniform" (E. 57–8). In such instances, Hume says, "we expect the event with the greatest assurance, and leave no room for any contrary supposition" (p. 58). Other regularities have had exceptions in the past; reasoning from experience in those cases does not constitute proof, but only yields probabilities. (See also T. 124.) Chapter 3 of Professor Ferreira's book, 'Hume's naturalism: proof and practice' (pp. 41–61), presents a detailed and convincing case for the conclusion that Hume finds *certainty* in proofs from experience, where the uniformities have been constant and regular. Professor Ferreira challenges the reading of Hume (e.g. as advanced by Popkin, Stove, or Norton) which treats *all* matters of fact as probable only. All matters of fact lack warranted certainty because, the standard reading goes, since matters of fact cannot be demonstrated,

---

[1] D. Wootton above, p. 199, n. 23, notes the likely influence of the Chevalier Ramsay.

their contrary is always possible. What this reading of Hume assumes is, Professor Ferreira remarks, that Hume accepted and shared with the sceptics an "'argument'-based paradigm" of certainty and truth (pp. 47, 51, 60). On her reading, some (but not all) matters of fact can be as certain as demonstrations.

Professor Ferreira does not claim that Hume formulated "a consistent epistemological distinction between proof and probability", but she makes a good case for saying that the development in later writers (e.g. Reid and Newman) builds on Hume's rejection of Locke's twofold classification (demonstration and probability). Hume did not, she insists, answer the sceptic simply by appealing to "nature" or "instinct", to the fact that our nature is such that we cannot sustain a disbelief in an external world or in the uniformity of nature.

While Reid did not "explicitly adopt the terminological distinction between demonstration, proof, and probability", Professor Ferreira argues that he did "effectively use a category equivalent to proof in his discussion of non-demonstrative reasoning" (p. 63). Probable evidence can yield certainty. Thus, such certainty for probable evidence introduces a distinction between certainty and probability *within* probable reasoning (p. 70). Professor Ferreira then proceeds, through the next three chapters, to an illuminating exposition and discussion of Reid's account of the certainty produced by *some* probable reasoning, differentiating that sort of certainty from the demonstrative entailment sort (p. 94), tracing the way in which practice and common sense fit into this category of proof or experiential certainty, and showing how such certainty is linked with the intuitive judgements of common sense so much stressed by Reid. (See esp. ch. 5.) Professor Ferreira also has a fascinating account of Reid's "reliance on the embeddedness of beliefs, implicit or explicit, in socio-linguistic practice" (p. 122), as well as "the way in which our beliefs are interconnected and presupposed by all our activities" (p. 140).

There are important textual and conceptual analyses in almost every chapter of Professor Ferreira's study. The presence of Newman in her account is useful if for no other reason than reminding us that we can often find significant material in authors not normally included in the "philosophers'" canon. Where I could have welcomed more explication is with certain central terms, e.g. 'argument', 'demonstration', or 'philosophical'. Professor Ferreira uses the term 'demonstration' in the logical sense of deduction or entailment, but of course there was a different sense of that term often at work in some writers of the period she covers, the sense of 'showing'. She could have made more of Locke's attack on formal logic and his defence of an informal logic of use. It may even be the case that some of that third type of certainty is at work in

Locke's attack against formalism. Some more explication of the *faculty* of reason in each of the four authors could also have been useful. The most pervasive unanalysed term in Professor Ferreira's book is 'philosophical'. She speaks of an "argument against the philosophical relevance of Hume's distinction between proof and probability" (p. 58), of "the philosophical relevance" of Reid's "appeal to the constitution of human nature" (p. 126), of the "philosophical relevance" of Reid's "mitigation of Pyrrhonism" (p. 138), of "a philosophical challenge to the status of the sceptic's charge" (p. 139), and of Reid's "philosophical account" (p. 143). There is a suggestion on p. 141 that 'philosophical' is paired with 'epistemological', and an even fainter hint that the latter is linked with 'justification'. Especially when writing about authors who frequently attack and reject views they credit to "philosophers", and champion the views of "the vulgar", it would seem necessary to clarify the differences between the learned and the vulgar, as well as to indicate how these authors viewed their own enterprise: was it science (psychology), description of ordinary beliefs, or, as Hume suggested, a metaphysic methodized and clarified by common sense?

These are very minor blemishes on an otherwise stimulating, careful exposition and critical analysis of the theme of scepticism and reasonable doubt in the seventeenth and eighteenth centuries.

Department of Philosophy
Rutgers University

The mind of God and the works of man
By EDWARD CRAIG
Oxford: Clarendon Press, 1987. x + 353 pp.

Reviewed by JOHN W. YOLTON

There are a number of themes running throughout Craig's book. He tells us that the initial impetus for the talks which preceded the book came from his interest in the gap between professional philosophy (the philosophy taught in university) and what he calls "Philosophies", those "sweeping maps of reality which the traditional philosopher figure of the popular intellectual image used to provide for our guidance in thought and behaviour" (p. 1). Another theme is the relation between history of philosophy and philosophy (p. 5). The main concern is with what Craig sees as "the more general formative influences on modern European philosophy, its goals and inspirations" (p. 3). His claim is that "modern philosophy consists of just two philosophies in various realisations".

These two are the "Image of God" doctrine (found from Descartes to Hegel) and the "Practice Ideal" or "Agency Theory" (found in post-Hegelian and pragmatist writings). In this review, I shall restrict myself to the first, focusing mainly on Craig's reading of Hume.

Craig is aware of the dangers of speaking of a dominant philosophy or doctrine, but he is convinced that the image of God doctrine (that man is made in God's image) "can clearly be seen as a central concern of nearly all the major philosophers of that period, even though they concerned themselves with it for different purposes and reacted to it in widely varying ways" (p. 13). He finds this doctrine reflected in accounts of knowledge as well as in views about reality. One could easily suggest other candidates for a "dominant" philosophy or doctrine, e.g. the substance-quality metaphysic, the two-substance doctrine, the principle of no cognition at a distance; but the important question is what do we accomplish by trying to interpret the whole of a philosopher's work by reference to one of these doctrines? Can the details of a philosophical system, or of a text, be explicated by reference to such general doctrines? The answer, I suppose, is simply that some aspects, even detailed features, may be explained or illuminated by reference to dominant themes: the test will be in the application. But more often than not, the yield is either some obvious feature of the writings being discussed or some considerable stretching of the claim. The "dominant theme" approach is no substitute for the painstaking explication of the details of some concept, term or claim by a close reading of a text, a reading always against the background of historical context. It is to the latter—the historical context—that Craig's study directs our attention. In some instances, his analysis does call attention to some feature of the philosophy which is highlighted by reference to his dominant theme. In other instances, the tilt towards his dominant theme tends to over-shadow other relevant historical and textual facts.

No question can be raised about Craig's claim that the image of God notion is reflected in much of what Malebranche wrote, in parts of Descartes's and Berkeley's texts. In fact, most of the philosophers in the modern period accepted the notion of man being made in God's image. What is in doubt is to what extent did that notion affect and influence those philosophers' accounts of knowledge, perception, and the nature of matter, or their methods of analysis and discovery? Before examining some aspects of Craig's interpretation of Hume, let me list briefly a few examples of his readings of earlier philosophers, readings which I find dubious or in need of more careful explication.

The famous passage in Clarke's second reply to Leibniz where he asserts the principle that "Nothing can any more act, or be acted upon, where it is not present than it can be where it is not", spoke of images being present in the mind as a necessary condition for perceptual awareness. Clarke had compared that presence with God's omnipresence, the latter being the way God knows all things. From this and a few similar passages in Newton's *Opticks*, Craig concludes that Newton believed that such knowledge from the presence of things to the mind was "complete and incorrigible" (p. 31). I find little evidence in either text for such a claim, but a more important and equally dubious claim is that Newton and Clarke are comparing human with divine knowledge. That there is some similarity, caught by the terms 'presence' and, in God's case, 'omnipresence', is correct; but what are the similarities between *omnipresence* and the *sensory* presence of images to the brains of men? Leibniz and Clarke (and others, too) debated the nature of God's omnipresence: was it spatial or only cognitive? However that property is analysed, great differences remain between God's presence to all things and the presence of images to a mind.

In the same vein, Craig says that Berkeley tried to argue that we know the real world in the same say that God knows it (p. 32). The fact that human knowledge is sensory, and God has no sense organs, needs to be addressed before such a claim as Craig makes can be properly assessed. A related issue in need of more analysis is Craig's easy assertion that Berkeley made "physical objects a species of perception" (p.34), or that "reality simply *is* a certain infinitely complex constellation of ideas" (p. 35). Before we can say what Berkeley's concept of reality was, we surely must explain his explicit denial that he had turned things into ideas. It was, Berkeley insisted many times, just the reverse: ideas *are* the things themselves, *and* ideas are *not* modes of mind.

A third example. Craig has some useful comments on Spinoza, especially on the way Spinoza does seem to have been motivated by the image of God doctrine. What is lacking from Craig's account is an explanation of what it means to talk of God within Spinoza's naturalism: the notion that God and nature are the same. Craig, and frequently Spinoza, move from one to the other. Sometimes Craig writes of God *or* nature (p. 45); other times it is God *and* nature (p. 48). What is it that is being imaged in Spinoza? Much debate has occurred over this question, but without some attempt to argue that the God of Spinoza is the same as the God of Newton or Descartes, it is difficult to see a common doctrine that can be named 'the Image of God'.

The title of Craig's chapter on Hume is modest: 'One way to read Hume'. His contention is that "knowledge of the 'dominant philosophy' can sometimes serve as a clue leading to revisions of interpretation", even that "it reaches down, as it were, to make itself felt in matters of fine textual detail" (p. 69). The claim is of course not that Hume uses the image of God doctrine, but that he reacts against it: "a philosopher's antagonism to the dominant philosophy of his time can be just as formative as support of it" (p. 69). Craig's bold claim is that Hume's philosophy aimed at no less than "the destruction of the doctrine of the image of God, and substituted for it an anthropology which looked not to the divine but to the natural world for its comparisons, and to the sciences for its methods" (p. 70). However, Craig makes very little use of the image of God doctrine in his extended discussion of Hume (pp. 69–130). Instead, he concentrates on the anthropology, especially on the account of belief in the *Enquiry* and *Treatise*, using the former text more than the latter.

This chapter reveals that Craig does not need the dominant doctrine as a tool for explication of a text. There is much good, detailed analysis here of Hume on causality and personal identity, viewed from the perspective of belief-formation. Craig suggests that too much stress has been placed by commentators on the theory of ideas and impressions, that in fact it was just a terminology taken over from Locke and employed to get the *Treatise* started. Running throughout this chapter, *its* dominant theme, is an attack on the logical positivist reading of Hume, a reading which seized on the theory of ideas and impressions, taking it as a theory of meaning and thinking. I had thought logical positivism had long ago died, but I guess it survives still, e.g. in excessive analytic interpretations of Hume (I think of Bricke's book). The reading that Craig opposes is typified by those who see in Hume's chapter on personal identity an ontological thesis: that the self is nothing but a string of perceptions. He points out nicely how Hume is motivated by a search for the bases of our beliefs about self and objects. Craig does not give an analysis of the entire chapter on personal identity, but what he does may help to correct the tendency (aided, it must be said, by some of what Hume says in that section) to say that, for Hume, the self is only a bundle of perceptions. There is, of course, ample material in that section of the *Treatise*, and especially in Book II, for a quite different view of the self. Hume there announces that there are two concepts of self or personal identity, the second referring to "our passions or the concern we take in ourselves", i.e. the view used in Book II.

Craig also shows the misleading reading of Hume which sees in his talk of ideas and impressions "a complete account of our thought-processes" (p. 123), reminding us that some of the most important contents of thought are fictions and also calling attention to the many mental operations of supposing, feigning, conceiving. We can even find support for this important point in the very first use of the term 'idea' in the *Treatise*, where it is explained that ideas are "all the perceptions excited by the present discourse", excepting those "which arise from the sight and touch and . . . the immediate pleasure or uneasiness it may occasion". Throughout Books I and II, there is a rich and subtle description of thinking, believing, and caring. The radical footnote at T. 96–7, where Hume indicates his definition of belief, linking it with conception, also takes issue with the standard notion of the faculties of the mind. Instead of the usual three or four operations or acts of the mind (sensing, judging, reasoning, imagining), Hume boldly asserts that "they all resolve themselves into" conception. Can Hume's many appeals to the imagination be shown to be modes of conceiving? Perhaps, but we need to recognize that the imagination is for Hume dynamic and creative, going beyond what we can discover about the world or ourselves through observation and attention.

Craig could have strengthened his case for saying Hume's view of thinking is not restricted to ideas and impressions had he given more attention to Hume's appeal to the imagination. Craig seems to suggest that there is a naturalizing of reason in Hume's writing, as opposed to the deductive reason of philosophers (pp. 81–3). He has in mind those passages where Hume speaks of inferences from experience when we form judgements about causality. He quite properly takes exception to those who say Hume confused logic (reason) with psychology (the imagination). Hume's "quasi-Newtonian theory of the workings of the mind" with its "associative mechanism" (p. 87) is linked with the imagination (p. 101).

It is the rejection of these efforts to use reason as a source for non-experiential knowledge of the world which Craig offers as evidence of Hume's aim being "the destruction of the doctrine of the image of God". Does Craig mean that Hume knew the object of his attack under that description, or even that he knew that those who gave pride of place to reason (or that those like Locke who, while denying it was possible for human reason, presented the details of an a priori science of nature) were talking about the image of God in man? Even if all that Craig claims is that the account of reason rejected by Hume fits the image of God doctrine, I think it doubtful (at least, unclear) that the uses of reason attacked by Hume do fit that doctrine. Craig's account of the doctrine emphasizes the qualities of *infallibility* and *incorrigibility*, qualities of knowledge and understanding which, he claims, led philosophers such as Descartes on a quest for certainty. Hence, mathematics became a model for all knowledge, along with the intuition needed to grasp the relations. That many philosophers did take mathematics as the ideal for all knowledge is not in doubt. What I question is (1) did those who took mathematics and deduction as the paradigm for human knowledge do so because they took God's knowledge as their model, (2) is that the way in which God is supposed to know what he knows, and (3) does the image of God doctrine really help us understand the modern philosophers that Craig discusses?

Department of Philosophy
Rutgers University

INDEX